Price Expectations in Goods and Financial Markets

Published with the support of the University of Paris-X Nanterre, France

Price Expectations in Goods and Financial Markets

New Developments in Theory and Empirical Research

Edited by
François Gardes

Professor of Economics at the University of Paris I-Panthéon-Sorbonne, member of the research group TEAM, France

Georges Prat

Director of Research at the National Center of Scientific Research (CNRS), member of the research group MODEM, University of Paris-X Nanterre, France

Preface by
M. Hashem Pesaran

Edward Elgar
Cheltenham, UK • Northampton, MA, USA

Published by
Edward Elgar Publishing Limited
Glensanda House
Montpellier Parade
Cheltenham
Glos GL50 1UA
UK

Edward Elgar Publishing, Inc.
136 West Street
Suite 202
Northampton
Massachusetts 01060
USA

HB
221
.P69
2000

A catalogue record for this book
is available from the British Library

Library of Congress Cataloguing in Publication Data

Price expectations in goods and financial markets : new developments in theory and empirical research / edited by François Gardes, Georges Prat.
    Includes bibliographical references and index.
    1. Prices—Econometric models. 2. Rational expectations (Economic theory)
    I. Gardes, François, 1950– II. Prat, Georges, docteur d'Etat en sciences économiques.

HB221 .P69 2000
338.5'2—dc21   99–087208

ISBN 1 84064 322 6

Printed and bound in Great Britain by MPG Books Ltd, Bodmin, Cornwall

Contents

Figures

Tables

Contributors

Alain Abou is Senior Researcher at the National Center of Scientific Research (CNRS) and member of the research group MODEM at the University of Paris-X Nanterre, France (abou@u-paris10.fr).

Roy Batchelor is the HSBC Professor of Banking and Finance at the City University Business School, London, United Kingdom (R.A.Batchelor@city.ac.uk).

Agnès Bénassy-Quéré is Deputy Director of the CEPII, Paris, and member of the research group THEMA, Nanterre and Cergy-Pontoise, France (a.benassy@cepii.fr).

Damien Besancenot is Associate Professor of Economics at the University of Paris II Panthéon-Assas, and member of the research group CEFIB, Paris, France (besancenot@u-paris2.fr).

Gabriel Desgranges is Associate Professor of Economics at the University of Cergy-Pontoise, and member of the research groups THEMA and DELTA, France (desgranges@delta.ens.fr).

François Gardes is Professor of Economics at the University of Paris I-Panthéon-Sorbonne, France, and member of the research group TEAM, Paris, France (gardes@univ-paris1.fr).

Salah Ghabri is associate researcher at the research group TEAM, University of Paris I, Paris, France, and at the Crefa, University of Laval, Quebec, Canada (ghabri@univ-paris1.fr).

Roger Guesnerie is Director of Research at the National Center of Scientific Research (CNRS), Director of Studies at the School of High Studies in Social Science (EHESS), and director of the research group DELTA at the Ecole Normale Supérieure (ENS), Paris, France (guesnerie@delta.ens.fr).

Ronald MacDonald is Professor of Economics at the University of Strathclyde, Glasgow, United Kingdom (r.r.macdonald@strath.ac.uk).

Jean-Loup Madre is Director of Research at the INRETS, director of the research group 'Economie de l'Espace et de la Mobilité', Paris, France (jean-loup.madre@inrets.fr).

André Orléan is Director of Research at the National Center of Scientific Research (CNRS), Associate Professor at the Ecole Polytechnique and member of the research group CEPREMAP, Paris, France (andre.orlean@cepremap.cmrs.fr).

M. Hashem Pesaran is Professor of Economics at Cambridge University and Professorial Fellow of Trinity College, Cambridge, United Kingdom (hashem.pesaran@econ.cam.ac.uk).

Marie-Claude Pichery is Professor of Economics at the University of Bourgogne, and member of the research group LATEC, Dijon, France (pichmc@u-bourgogne.fr).

Georges Prat is Director of Research at the National Center of Scientific Research (CNRS), and member of the research group MODEM at the University of Paris-X Nanterre, France (prat@u-paris 10.fr).

Hélène Raymond is Professor of Economics at the University of Metz, and member of the research group TEAM, Paris, France (raymond@phoenix.droit.univ-metz.fr).

Aimé Scannavino is Professor of Economics at the University of Paris II-Panthéon-Assas and director of the research group CEME, Paris, France (Aime.Scannavino@wanadoo.fr).

Christian Schmidt is Professor of Economics at the University of Paris IX-Dauphine, and director of the research group LESOD, Paris, France (schmidt@dauphine.fr).

Yamina Tadjeddine is Research Assistant at the University of Paris-X Nanterre, and member of the research group CREA at the Ecole Polytechnique, Paris, France (tadjeddy@poly.polytechnique.fr).

Remzi Uctum is Senior Researcher at the National Center of Scientific Research (CNRS), and member of the research group MODEM at the University of Paris-X Nanterre, France (uctum@u-paris10.fr).

Bernard Walliser is Professor of Economics at the Ecole Nationale des Ponts et Chaussées de Paris (ENPC) and member of the research groups CERAS and CREA, Paris, France (walliser@descartes.enpc.fr).

Firoozeh Zarkesh is econometrician at the Investment Property Databank of London, specializing in the commercial property market.

Acknowledgements

This book is a product of several scientific meetings (seminars, symposia) organized by the federal research team of the National Center of Scientific Research on 'Monetary and Financial Economy' (GDR N° 0098 'Economie Monétaire et Financière' of the CNRS, France). These meetings allowed the two editors to make fruitful contacts with researchers in the field of price expectations, especially within the workshop of the GDR which they organized, which was devoted to the formation of economic expectations. Some of the papers presented during these meetings and also papers especially written for this book are contained in this volume. The two editors acknowledge with thanks the participation of the twenty-one authors and are grateful to the GDR and also to the University of Paris-X for grants towards the editing of this book.

We have been greatly assisted by the helpful comments of an anonymous referee of the manuscript who was provided by the publisher, and extend our thanks to him. Finally, we wish to acknowledge Professor Hashem Pesaran, who honours the book with his preface.

Foreword

How expectations are formed and adapted to changing circumstances is of utmost importance for decision making at all levels: individuals, households, firms and government agencies. But despite its pervasive nature, the problem of expectations formation has not received as much attention in economic research as it deserves. In the aftermath of the rational expectations revolution, from the mid-1970s onwards, the expectations formation problem was in effect subsumed in the solution process of the intertemporal optimization problem facing the agent, under the assumption that the agent's decision environment was correctly specified. This adherence to the rational expectations hypothesis (REH) seemingly obviated the need for further analysis of the expectations formation process. The issue was not whether the REH is valid, but how it could come about through learning; and the literature on learning, often starting from a known model with a finite number of unknown parameters, provided a deeper theoretical justification for the REH, at least from a longer-term perspective.

Initially, serious attempts were made also to test the REH using survey data on expectations (the direct method) and indirectly by testing the cross-equation parameter restrictions implied by the solution to the decision problem under the REH. But this empirical literature came up against two major difficulties: survey data on expectations were often subject to measurement errors; and rejection of the cross-equation parametric restrictions could not be directly linked to the REH alone. Therefore, in the absence of a theoretically coherent and empirically more satisfactory expectations formation hypothesis the dominant role of the REH has continued.

The present book is a timely reminder that all is not well! The REH, at least in the sense advocated by Muth, may not be satisfactory in many circumstances. Following Muth, and under the influence of important econometric contributions by Sargent and Hansen, the empirical literature on the REH almost exclusively focused on the first moments of the underlying probability distribution functions. This is valid in the context of optimization problems with linear constraints and quadratic loss functions (the so-called LQ problems), and in general will not be sufficient. Expectations of higher-order moments will often be relevant to agents' behaviour. In modelling asset prices where, due to the fat-tailed nature of the underlying probability distributions, it could be that certain conditional moments may not even exist, it appears more appropriate to consider the expected forms of the whole probability distribution functions of the forcing variables. It is also unlikely that expectations are the same across agents, or that the expectations formation function is time-invariant. These and many other issues of critical importance to the analysis of dynamic economic processes have been addressed in this collection.

The book brings together important contributions over a wide area; ranging from conceptual and theoretical topics to the empirical analysis of inflation, unemployment, exchange rates and stock price expectations. The theoretical papers (in Part I) address the fundamental issues involved in the analysis of expectations and clearly demonstrate the need for a more general conceptualization of rationality. The Muthian concept of rational expectations is of limited value in the presence of asymmetric loss. Also, modelling expectations in the context of strategic games requires a more general concept of rationality where learning from opponents' actions is an integral part of the expectations formation process. The theoretical contributions also emphasize the importance of allowing for heterogeneity of expectations across agents, information revelation, common knowledge, the role of imitative expectations in financial markets, and the effect of rare events on expectations.

The empirical papers (Part II) bring together a wealth of information on survey data on expectations and provide rigorous analysis of a number of important issues. This is a welcome addition to the literature and should be of general interest to both academics and market practitioners. Using survey data from a number of markets and countries, the authors provide us with a number of interesting and novel results. For example, we learn that expectations formation models may have time-varying parameters, consistent with the pervasive evidence of model instability in empirical economics. We are reminded of the importance of considering expectations of higher-order moments. New evidence on time-varying risk premia in asset prices is provided which could, at least in part, be due to the fact that the REH may not always hold in asset markets. Very few believe that expectations are homogeneous across individuals, particularly across traders in financial markets, and this is corroborated. It is also shown that foreign exchange expectations across different forecast horizons tend to follow different models, thus presenting some doubt on the consistency of short- and long-term expectations.

This collection is timely and full of theoretical insights and interesting new empirical results. It is hoped that it will also help rekindle the interest of scholars and practitioners in this important, but relatively neglected, area of economics.

M. HASHEM PESARAN

General introduction

François Gardes and Georges Prat

WHY IS IT IMPORTANT TO ANALYSE PRICE EXPECTATIONS IN GOODS AND FINANCIAL MARKETS?

Papers focusing on price expectations are very uncommon and scattered in the literature, while most academic papers in economics need a hypothesis about the representation of these expectational variables. It seems then relevant to combine in one book different papers reflecting recent developments in price expectations. Although the confrontation between theoretical developments and empirical research is particularly important for expectation analysis, recent literature focuses exclusively on one or the other of these two aspects, so that the links between theoretical hypotheses and their empirical validation are largely neglected. The book aims to make a contribution to this subject. Moreover, the question of analysing price expectations is even more difficult since prices are highly volatile in most markets and expectational behaviour is heterogeneous and unstable. In order to appreciate the degree of generality of expectational behaviour, it seems appealing to analyse price expectations in a variety of markets, periods and countries. This volume presents such a variety, the main focus of the book being original work.

Modelling price expectations is essential, specially when goods and financial markets are analysed. Concerning the *goods market*, many models regard inflation expectations as direct determinants of agents' behaviour (Phillips curve in the labour market, Lucas supply curve, households' saving, extensions of the purchasing power parity (PPP) for the foreign exchange market, theories of asset valuation and so on). Market equilibrium is obtained for all these models by price changes which are themselves governed by expectations. Concerning the *financial market*, because asset price expectations govern actual market prices (this phenomenon is put forth by the traditional theory), knowledge of the process which generates asset price expectations is fundamental to understanding how market prices themselves are formed. A limit case is the efficient market hypothesis (EMH)

1

which supposes that expectations are formed rationally, including debates on the existence of rational bubbles. If expectations are not fully rational in financial markets, the EMH must be rejected and then rational bubbles cannot exist.

At the macro-level, the main problem is that price expectations are often modelled as 'hidden variables': either they are introduced in structural models with additional arbitrary hypotheses describing their determination (the system being then estimated as a reduced-form equation), or they are supposed to be embedded in external variables from which proxies for the expectational variables are derived. The first approach may be illustrated by the introduction of distributed lags of inflation rates in a model of money demand, these lags representing a proxy for inflationary expectations. An example for the second approach is given by supposing *a priori* true Fisher's model of interest rate determination, which permits the derivation of the value of the expected rate of inflation from the observed nominal interest rate, provided for example that the real interest rate is a constant. In both cases, strong hypotheses must underlie any empirical test of the model. Hence, to answer the question of how price expectations are formed contributes to overcoming an important indetermination in the economic theory, especially for goods prices, foreign exchange rates and stock prices. Concerning the micro-level of expectations, the inter-dependence between agents is an important phenomenon to be taken into account in order to understand expectations formation (theory of price revealing equilibrium; mimetic behaviour), and the multiple equilibria resulting from this phenomenon may be viewed as an important factor in the dynamics of financial markets.

Neither reference books on expectations (Sheffrin, 1983; Holden *et al.* 1986; Pesaran, 1987) nor more specific books on the subject (Lahiri, 1981; Visco, 1984; Walliser, 1985; Prat, 1988; Broze *et al.* 1990) are very recent. Therefore, these books are not concerned by many new developments and empirical tests which have widened expectation analysis. Moreover, these earlier books do not take sufficiently into account the financial markets which have represented the main field of analysis of expectations over the last ten years (foreign exchange rates, stock prices, interest rates and so on).

EXPECTATIONS: DEFINITION AND MEASUREMENT

First, what do economists consider that an expectation of an economic variable is? Expectations can be defined as probabilistic opinions on future states of nature on which agents cannot have any significant influence. This impossibility for any agent to change the future makes the difference between expectations and projects (a concept much studied in philosophy), although the distinction may not be clear to the *external* observer. One may consider that many agents have qualitative opinions of the future, even when they observe quantitative variables such as inflation, asset prices or economic growth, but almost all economic theories consider expectations as quantitative variables. In this book, this distinction is explicitly taken into account and the results obtained under both conceptions compared (see Chapter 7, by F. Gardes, S. Ghabri, J.-L. Madre and M.-C. Pichery).

Generally, the value expected by some agent at any time *t* is assumed to be the mathematical expectation of the variable (that is, its mean value) based on all possible states of the future. But it seems important to consider also the variance of this variable as an indicator of uncertainty (or degree of confidence) associated by the agent to her/his expectation (a fact early discussed by Shackle, in the 1950s). Indeed, uncertainty as well as the mean value determine economic decisions. Let us consider, for instance, two investors in the stock market who expect a price increase of 10 per cent for the following period (this value is therefore the mathematical expectation of each agent). However, if the standard error of the first agent is 5 per cent, this means, if the stock returns are normally distributed, that the first agent considers a probability of 0.95 that the future return will be between 0 per cent and 20 per cent. If, for the second agent, the standard error is 1 per cent, this means that the agent considers that the future price will be ranged between 8 per cent and 12 per cent with the same probability. Thus, even if the two investors have the same aversion toward risk, they will probably not adopt the same decision concerning their portfolio management. This very simple example shows that both *the mean* and *the dispersion* must be considered in price expectation analysis. From a theoretical point of view, the concept of sharpness of information refers to the precision of the information held by the economic agent on fundamentals, and plays an important role in the dynamics of financial markets (see Chapter 3 by G. Desgranges and R. Guesnerie and Chapter 5 by A. Orléan and Y. Tadjeddine). This phenomenon is empirically examined by R. Batchelor and F. Zarkesh (Chapter 8) who introduce the new concept of *variance-rationality* which differs from the usual *mean-rationality one* and which they test on inflationary expectation survey data. Also, the volatility of economic variables (a factor of uncertainty) is a time-varying phenomenon which is shown to influence the expectations processes in the empirical analysis of households' expectations (Chapter 7 by F. Gardes *et al.*).

The *heterogeneity* of expectations among the population should not be confused with the *dispersion* of an individual's opinion. Indeed, while the dispersion of an individual expectation is measured by the variance of the distribution associated with the different states of nature considered by the agent, heterogeneity corresponds to the variance of the mathematical expectations *across* agents. However, it seems intuitive that, other things being equal, the more individual opinions are dispersed, the larger will be the heterogeneity, to the extent that both phenomena depend on the volatility of the market price.

Another point concerns the distinction between traditional *economic theory* and *game theory*. As indicated by B. Walliser in Chapter 1, in *economic theory*, current variables (such as market prices) are concerned with agents' expectations. If in *game theory* the players' expectations concern first the opponents' strategies (C. Schmidt examines in Chapter 2 especially these kinds of expectations), it is nevertheless important to observe that these strategies are themselves often based on agents' expectations in the sense of economic theory (such as earnings), besides some structural factors which may also influence these strategies. Hence, these two types of behaviour are not conflicting but complementary. Moreover, game theory appears to be a powerful tool in implementing the analysis of interdependence of agents in expectational behaviour, as shown in Chapter 3 by G. Desgranges and R. Guesnerie and Chapter 4 by D. Besancenot.

In fact, three methods can be used to obtain an empirical measurement of expectations: the indirect method, the implicit method and the direct method. The *indirect method* simply uses proxies to represent expectations, such as a linear function of previous observations of the variable which is forecasted. The *implicit method* consists in inferring expectations from estimates of macroeconomic models, specially using consumption or saving functions, investment functions, models of interest rates or models of foreign exchange rates. For instance, the effect of unanticipated inflation on saving (as supposed by Deaton) allows one to compute price expectations in the framework of this model. The obvious weakness of the indirect and implicit methods is to assume that the underlying structural macroeconomic model is true. It is not the case for the *direct method* which uses directly survey data of individual opinions. These opinions concern the future change of microeconomic variables (such as level of being, durable purchase, income and so on) or macroeconomic variables (such as unemployment or economic growth, inflation, foreign exchange rates, stock market indexes, interest rates). Numerous survey data exist now which contain qualitative- or quantitative-form disaggregated opinions, and recent American literature makes substantial use of direct survey data on expectations. For many reasons, it seems unlikely that expectations provided by surveys would be identically equal to the 'true' values of expectations. However, empirical analyses are conducted under the less restrictive hypothesis that the 'true' value of an expectation is defined as a linear function of the survey data plus a random measurement error. Part II of the book is concerned with applications using the direct method.

RATIONALITY, FORMATION AND HETEROGENEITY OF EXPECTATIONS: GENERAL SCOPE

The General Equilibrium Theory and the Rational Expectation Hypothesis

In a world characterized by a complete system of forward commodity markets, a strict version of the general equilibrium theory involves all contracts being determined at the starting period, so there exists no theoretical justification for markets to open in the future. In this sense, this approach, followed by Arrow and Debreu, is essentially atemporal. However, if agents are supposed to anticipate prices and interest rates rationally at each point in time in the future (the debt market being assumed to be complete), commodity markets can be opened and are effectively operated, the final result being identical to the one described by the general equilibrium. But this theoretical importance of the rational expectations hypothesis (REH) must be compared with its limitations. Indeed, the hypothesis is not really specified, since several interpretations must be adopted: to what extent does the forecaster use prior information and know the true model? According to Muth (1961), agents know the true model and use optimally all the available information on fundamentals, while Radner in the 1960s and Lucas in the 1970s supposed that the market price reveals progressively the true information about the future values of the fundamentals. Another question is whether the processes of 'auto-validation' of expectations should be viewed as an endogenous phenomenon (self-fulfilling expectations) or as an implication of faith in exogenous determinants known as sunspots introduced by Azariadis (1981) ('confirmed expectations').

The Temporary Equilibrium Theory and the Existence of an Expectation Function

According to this theory (from Hicks in the 1930s), the economic system follows a sequence of temporary equilibria: *at any time*, the flexibility of prices ensures the equality between demand and supply (it is here necessary to prove the existence of a system of prices compatible with this equality, especially on the asset markets, and we need some theorems to do so). The main feature of the temporary equilibrium theory is that, because agents ignore the future state of the economy, they take their decisions on the basis of their imperfect expectations. As shown by Grandmont (1976), the knowledge of the *anticipation function*, which describes how expectations depend on the information held, becomes essential to the understanding of their behaviour and the determination of the path followed by the economy. The present book focuses especially on this function. When the set of information used is limited (for instance, reduced to the past and actual values of the variable which is expected), expectations are affected by systematic errors so that projects of agents are not co-ordinated and will be generally incompatible, contrary to what is involved in the REH.

The Hypothesis of a Representative Agent and the Existence of Heterogeneity in Expectations

The assumption of a representative agent leads to the consideration of a joint hypothesis which may involve aggregation biases: an hypothesis on collective preferences (such as a given utility function capturing the risk aversion), an hypothesis on choice conditions (such as the degree of volatility in the world), and an hypothesis on agents' behaviour (for example, each agent maximizes his/her utility). The empirical evidence presented in this book confirms the presence of such aggregation biases: F. Gardes *et al.* (Chapter 7) and A. Abou and G. Prat (Chapter 12) show that the estimation of expectational models differs following some specific criteria (socio-economic or professional) characterizing individuals. For instance, if one considers the traditional adaptive model, the previous expectation error consists of a common error made by all individuals plus an individual component, which are not corrected by the same amount. This gives rise to an overestimation of the 'coefficient of expectation' when estimation is run over aggregated data. In fact, neither the marginal cost of using information nor its marginal utility can be considered as identical across agents, and market characteristics reinforce this phenomenon: recent literature on the dynamics of financial markets shows that the interdependence of agents' behaviour on the market implies that the market may be, in certain circumstances, unable to produce symmetrical information and is then unable to base the non-informed agents' choices on those of the informed agents (see Chapter 5 by A. Orléan and Y. Tadjeddine).

These theoretical and empirical results show the importance of analysing expectation-generating processes on a microeconomic level. In fact, the central assumption of the financial market microstructure literature is that expectations are heterogeneous either because idiosyncratic agents face a common information set or because information sets differ across agents. Empirical evidence confirms that financial market participants indeed generate a diversity of individual expectations and that this heterogeneity is a time-varying phenomenon. This result contradicts the rational expectations hypothesis which implies no time variability in the heterogeneity (some authors even claim that the REH implies no heterogeneity). It is noteworthy that these heterogeneous expectations are an important phenomenon for the market dynamics, mainly because they generate mimetic behaviour leading possibly to multiple equilibrium prices (see Chapter 3 by G. Desgranges and R. Guesnerie, and Chapter 5 by A. Orléan and Y. Tadjeddine).

However, this does not alter the relevance of considering the dynamics of the consensus of expectations (that is, the mean opinion measured by the average of the answers). First, for instance, let a weak weight attributed to information X by some individuals (a limit case is given by a zero weight) be compensated by an important weight attributed to the same information X by some other agents (each individual uses a specific reference model in which X acts). In this context, expectation errors may cancel out one another, and therefore an expectational process (among them, the REH) may appear to be relevant at the aggregate level, agents using collectively the information set assumed by the model maker. Second, this concept of *collective expectations* is a central phenomenon in the theoretical analyses of interdependences between operators in the financial markets (see Chapter 3 by G. Desgranges and R. Guesnerie, and Chapter 5 by A. Orléan and Y. Tadjeddine). These theoretical developments show the opportunity for empirical analyses of expectations at an aggregated level. All papers presented in Part II of the book to some extent deal with this point.

NEW DEVELOPMENTS ON PRICE EXPECTATIONS PRESENTED IN THE BOOK: AN OVERVIEW

On the Concept of Rationality in Expectation Analysis

A first question is concerned with the collective or individual level of rationality. As an example, F. Gardes *et al.* (Chapter 7) show that the hypothesis of rationality of expectations is not rejected by qualitative data in the case of limited groups of households. Although this outcome does not prove that expectations are rational for these groups (because tests on qualitative data are not powerful enough to be conclusive), it shows the existence of groups of agents which do not use the same set of information. This is in accordance with the view of some authors who consider that mimetic behaviour is based on a transfer of informations from rational to irrational agents (see especially Chapter 4 by D. Besancenot and Chapter 5 by A. Orléan and Y. Tadjeddine). Moreover, there is a threshold beyond which uncertainty associated with his/her own expectations leads an individual to imitate other agents, and this corresponds to rational behaviour (see Chapter 5). Also concerned with this phenomenon, R. Batchelor and F. Zarkesh (Chapter 8) show that the dispersions of individual distributions of the expected state of the nature (here, inflation) are not only time varying, but also not rationally expected. The dispersion of expectations measuring an individual's degree of uncertainty about her/his opinion and the propensity to imitate being a decreasing function of the degree of uncertainty, the mimetic behaviour hypothesis may be justified in that manner by observed data. Moreover, this result puts into evidence a new important factor of instability of market prices, because it suggests that the propensity to imitate is itself a time-varying and unpredictable phenomenon. Finally, these results vindicate the view that risk premia should be introduced in financial asset price models, as is underlined in Chapter 9 by R. MacDonald.

Another main point examined in Part I of the book is that rationality may have several meanings. B. Walliser gives in Chapter 1 a typology of different concepts of rationality of expectations (among them, the 'self-correcting' model represents a kind of rational behaviour). A. Scannavino, in Chapter 6, examines the time structure of stock prices and starts from the observation that the dynamics of prices embed 'rare events' such as runs, extreme shocks, upward or downward trends: the author discusses to what extent these events are compatible with the efficient market hypothesis which is itself based on the REH. Chapter 4 by D. Besancenot shows that private information which is not common knowledge must be rationally neglected by speculators, and this leads to a conception of rationality different from the Muthian one. Part II of the book shows that these *theoretical* results are supported by the *empirical* studies, which state that expectation processes validated by surveys, embed implicitly 'rare events' and contain no distinguishable private information. Moreover, empirical studies show that the adaptive (that is 'self-correcting') process is the most representative model of expectational behaviour. Hence, these empirical results do not mean that limited information included in expectational processes is not compatible with any form of rationality. More generally, the possibility that expectational processes used by agents – which do not take into account all available information – are in accordance with the *economically* rational expectations hypothesis remains entire (Feige and Pearce,

1976). This last hypothesis takes into account additional availability and treatment costs with respect to the marginal utility that agents may expect to obtain. These features reinforce the interest to depict the expectational processes effectively used by agents and this point is all the more important since rationality in the Muthian sense (REH) is strongly rejected by econometric studies (see Chapters 7, 9, 10, 11 and 12). This last result, which does not mean that there is no other form of rationality in the formation of expectations, strongly suggests that rational bubbles are a mythical concept.

On the Question of How Expectations Are Formed: What Set of Information Is Used by Agents and How Is It Treated?

On this question this book offers a large set of original conclusions. Chapters by R. Macdonald, A. Bénassy-Quéré and H. Raymond, G. Prat and R. Uctum and A. Abou and G. Prat focus on the question of how expectations are formed in financial markets: these papers deal with the question of the degree to which expectations are described by limited information models. The two last papers show that the hypothesis of a mixed process leads to a valuable representation of expectations both in the foreign exchange market and in the stock market. Because regressive and adaptive components systematically appear to dominate the extrapolative process, expectations appear to be stabilizing in financial markets, at least for three- and six-month horizons. However, for shorter-term horizon (one month or less), some results of the literature conclude that the destabilizing *bandwagon* effect seems dominant (see Chapter 9). A. Bénassy-Quéré and H. Raymond in Chapter 10 confirm these outcomes for exchange rates: the long-term forecasts appear to be rather regressive while short-term forecasts are mainly determined by an extrapolative process. The authors examine whether forecasts at various horizons are consistent, that is, whether the series of short-run forecasts lead to the same long-run expectation as the long-run forecast itself. They test the consistency of expectations conditionally to limited information models and show that the forecasting model used by agents differs according to the horizon: the iteration of short-term extrapolative expectations does not converge to the long-term expectation of the exchange rate. Another original point is brought up by F. Gardes *et al.* (Chapter 7), who show that expectational processes may change over time (moreover, parameters depend upon temporal characteristics of the phenomenon which is expected, such as its volatility or level).

On the Heterogeneity, Uncertainty and Interdependence of Expectations

The empirical evidence of heterogeneity and uncertainty

As noted above, the disparity across agents (degree of heterogeneity measured by the cross-section change in mathematical expectations) has to be distinguished from the variance of expectations (degree of uncertainty of the future state of the variable for a given agent).

Concerning heterogeneity, this book offers several original findings. In Chapter 7 F. Gardes *et al.* show that all groups of households are not characterized by the same expectational process, and that parameters characterizing processes depend on individuals or groups of agents. Similarly, A. Abou and G. Prat (Chapter 12) and R. Macdonald (Chapter 9) compare estimations of processes using aggregated and disaggregated data, and show that aggregated data mask the existence of distinguishable groups of agents. The former finds that professional affiliation and the degree of pessimism are relevant criteria to observe differences in expectational behaviour in the stock market. The latter shows that there are idiosyncratic effects reflecting private information and thus explaining the heterogeneity of expectations. These results support the market microstructure hypothesis.

Concerning the uncertainty of expectations, R. Batchelor and F. Zarkesh (Chapter 8) use data on probability distributions of future inflation rates provided by the ASA-NBER surveys based on a sample of US economic forecasters. These data show that, at an individual level, both the *mean* and the *dispersion* are relevant phenomena to be considered in price expectation analysis. Moreover, Gardes *et al.* (Chapter 7) show that the parameter of the adaptive process depends on the volatility of the variable which is anticipated (here, inflation): the higher the volatility, the shorter the memory of the phenomenon.

Mimetic Behaviour and the Theory of Price Revealing Equilibria

Agents' behaviour is determined by two factors: the proportion of fully informed agents, and agents' degree of confidence in the information they have received on fundamentals. If agents are fully confident of this information, they may decide according to it. If they are not, they may try to obtain information by observing other agents' behaviour. If this mimetic behaviour exceeds some threshold, prices can be disconnected from the fundamentals. The same consequence may also result from information costs if the direct information on fundamentals is more costly than the information revealed by other agents' choices. This theory of price revealing equilibria has attracted most authors' attention in the literature after the mid-1970s (Grossman and Stiglitz, 1976, Radner, 1979). G. Desgranges and R. Guesnerie, D. Besancenot and A. Orléan and Y. Tadjeddine (Chapters 3–5) develop this research field. Assuming that both asset valuation model and rationality are common knowledge, the first contributors show that the 'sharpness' of information is a key hypothesis to show that information embedded in expectations (through a learning process) is fully revealed by market equilibrium prices. If that is so, these prices are also common knowledge. This kind of 'eductive' learning may be regarded as an original approach and shows the importance of considering the degree of confidence of informations at an individual level. D. Besancenot is concerned with the public or private character of information used to form expectations. His model with overlapping generations of speculators and rational expectations show that, when equilibrium is reached, the informational content of prices may be limited to public information: the price does not carry any private information (that is, that which is not common knowledge). This result may be linked with the empirical work in this book, in which expectational processes are based only on public information. A. Orléan and Y. Tadjeddine present the concept of 'propensity' to imitate as the main phenomenon which determines the (un)efficiency of the market. According to this approach, bubbles appear when this propensity exceeds a certain threshold.

THE CONTENTS OF THE TWELVE PAPERS

Part I is concerned with *conceptual and theoretical developments* on rationality, heterogeneity and formation of price expectations. Part II is concerned with *empirical developments* on rationality, heterogeneity and the formation of price expectations in goods markets, foreign exchange markets, stock and bond markets.

Conceptual and Theoretical Developments (Part I)

In Chapter 1, Bernard Walliser draws a parallel between the concept of expectations in economic theory and in game theory. Four concepts characterize agents' expectations and their underlying beliefs. *Self-fulfilling expectations* describe the impact of given expectations on the functioning of the system and examine the possibility of their *ex post* validation. *Rational expectations* are concerned with omniscient agents endowed with beliefs similar to the modeller's own, hence forming expectations automatically realized under certain conditions (those are Muthian expectations). *Confirmed expectations* are formed by agents who hold partial prior beliefs about their environment, but nevertheless make expectations which will be *ex post* self-fulfilled. *Self-correcting expectations* are generated by agents who are again endowed with imperfect beliefs which lead now to incorrect expectations, but who revise their forecasts on the basis of new observations until these forecasts eventually converge.

Christian Schmidt (Chapter 2) aims to examine the nature and the role of expectations, rationality and risk (or 'chance') in a game theory framework. The paper shows that works which have largely preceded the publication of *Theory of Games and Economic Behavior* by von Neumann and Morgenstern in 1944 are useful to understanding fully the nature of players' expectations, their endogenization and their importance in the question of discrimination between the multiplicity of the equilibria.

In Chapter 3, Gabriel Desgranges and Roger Guesnerie investigate a simple model in which private information is fully revealed through prices at equilibrium. It is shown that equilibrium price may not be common knowledge, even if one assumes, in the spirit of the 'rationalizability' theory, that the model and individual rationality are common knowledge. The analysis suggests that a key factor in the success of the guessing or learning process under consideration is the 'sharpness' of information held at the individual level (information is considered to be sharp when the agent takes a decision on the basis of this information with a sufficiently high level of confidence). Finally, the authors conjecture that their results have some robust features.

Damien Besancenot (Chapter 4) analyses the informational content of equilibrium prices in financial markets. The speculators are supposed to have short-run expectations and they have to take into account the behaviour of future traders on the market. Based on a model with overlapping generations of agents, it is shown that private information which does not become common knowledge must be rationally neglected by agents. As a consequence, in the rational expectations equilibrium, the informational content of prices may be limited to the public information set already known by everyone. The paper also covers the restrictive conditions under which private information may be worthwhile.

André Orléan and Yamina Tadjeddine analyse in Chapter 5 the role played by imitative expectations in financial markets. The authors build an original model which shows that imitation leads to a large spectrum of dynamics: it can improve market efficiency if imitation remains below a certain threshold, but will generate inefficiency if the degree of imitation exceeds this threshold. This multiplicity of dynamics seems to be in accordance with the functioning of financial markets. According to this result, financial bubbles are explained by an endogenous learning process (which can be rational) and not by some unknown and sudden irrational market behaviour.

In Chapter 6, Aimé Scannavino starts from the idea that stock prices seem to move in ways hard to explain by the efficient markets model, the latter being based on the traditional rational expectations hypothesis. Indeed, because observed stock market prices are characterized by the existence of 'rare events' (runs, extreme shocks, upward and downward trends), rational investors, who are risk-averse, must take into account such events both to form their expectations and to appreciate the degree of risk. Hence, events occurring with a small probability may have a significant influence on the decisions of rational agents. The author investigates the plausibility of long rare segments in random walks, martingales and diffusion processes, all models which are coherent with the efficient market hypothesis, that is with a kind of rationality in expectations. The probabilistic properties of these usual representations – on which the econometric works on stock market prices are grounded – are examined in a methodological and original perspective throughout the 'large deviation theory' which answers the question of what is meant by 'rare'.

Empirical Evidence (Part II)

In Chapter 7, François Gardes, Salah Ghabri, Jean-Loup Madre and Marie-Claude Pichery consider the question of how price expectations are formed in the goods market (and in the labour market). This study is based on *qualitative* answers provided by the surveys conducted over the period from 1972 to 1994 by the National Institute of Statistics and Economic Studies (INSEE). These surveys are based on approximately 2500 households responding over two consecutive years. With respect to *numerical* answers, the main advantage of this kind of answer is to embed rather weak measurement errors. Contrary to the results obtained for the whole population after a quantification of these data, the rationality properties are not rejected for the part of the population which expected a high level of inflation during the 1970s although the expectational model used by households is the more likely to be the adaptive process. This model is found to be characterized by time-varying parameters which depend on the level and the volatility of the phenomena.

Roy Batchelor and Firoozeh Zarkesh (Chapter 8) introduce the new concept of *variance* rationality. In fact, conventional tests of rationality focus on whether errors in mean forecasts are unsystematic. This paper tests whether errors in estimates of the variance surrounding their mean forecasts (an indicator of uncertainty) are also unsystematic. Data on probability distributions for future inflation rates provided by contributors to the ASA-NBER surveys of US economic forecasters suggest that, even when inflation expectations appear to be 'mean-rational', they are never 'variance-rational'.

In Chapter 9, Ronald MacDonald aims to provide a survey of the literature using survey data on asset prices, and to draw out what we have learnt about the behaviour of asset markets from using such data. Survey data are especially appropriate to measure the importance of risk premia in financial markets and to identify the different kinds of expectational mechanisms prevailing in the financial markets. First, the author concludes that, for the foreign exchange market, the bond market and the stock market, on the one hand, and for different levels of aggregation, on the other, expectations are not rational and that time-varying risk premia exist. Second, survey data suggest that expectations are excessively volatile and exhibit bandwagon effects, while longer-term expectations appear to be regressive and therefore stabilizing. Third, he shows that there are idiosyncratic effects supporting the market microstructure hypothesis based on the importance of heterogeneous expectations.

Agnès Bénassy-Quéré and Hélène Raymond examine in Chapter 10 the consistency of foreign exchange rate expectations. Consistency means that iterating the short-run forecasting model leads to the same expectation as the direct use of the long-run model. In the literature, the analysis of the consistency of expectations is viewed as a direct empirical test of the '*law of iterative predictions*' implied by the REH. This law is fundamental for proving the possibility of rational bubbles in asset prices when maturity is infinite. In this paper, the consistency of the forecast term structure of exchange rates does not imply rationality: using three different surveys, the consistency of expectations is tested conditionally to limited information models. The authors show that the type of forecasting model is horizon-dependent: the iteration of short-term forecasting models does not produce the same forecast as the long-run forecasting models.

Georges Prat and Remzi Uctum (Chapter 11) are also concerned with the foreign exchange market. Using expectations of six main exchange rates provided by Consensus Forecast survey (November 1989–June 1997), the authors show that none of the traditional extrapolative, regressive or adaptive processes is by itself sufficient to account for expectations. However, a weighted average of these three basic processes appears to be successful in explaining the exchange rate expectations for each of the six currencies considered. Moreover, the authors show by using a pooled data sample that the same set of parameters holds for all currencies, and this suggests that agents generate their expectations using the same mixed process irrespective of the currency; but the coefficients of the mixed model are characterized by time instability. Alternative hypotheses are suggested to explain this past result.

In the final chapter, Alain Abou and Georges Prat deal with stock price expectations. They use biannual microdata (1952–89) provided by Joseph

Livingston's survey on stock price expectations at the New York Stock Exchange (Standard and Poor's Industrial Index). The authors show that experts generate their forecasts neither rationally nor according to a naive model, but using a weighted average of the three traditional expectational processes. These results are similar to those found by Prat and Uctum for the foreign exchange market (see Chapter 11). This result prevails irrespective of the aggregation level. The widest aggregation level is obtained by pooling all individual responses; a second level consists in pooling answers given by groups of experts defined according to their professional affiliation or degree of pessimism; and the 'zero-aggregation' level is given by individual expectations time series. Because regressive and adaptive components systematically appear to be the dominant ones (as found by Gardes *et al.* for inflationary expectations and Prat and Uctum for exchange rate expectations), the authors conclude that expectations are stabilizing in the stock market. Moreover, the parameters of the mixed model are more time-varying and group-dependent than they are related to specific individual characteristics.

THE LESSONS OF THE BOOK IN A NUTSHELL

We can summarize the work presented in this volume in four lessons:

1. The rational expectation hypothesis should be enlarged to more general concepts. If the REH in a Muthian sense seems now rather invalidated, this result does not mean that there is no rationality at all in price expectations: expectations may be *economically* rational. But because the utility function is unknown, it seems difficult to prove that a process which is irrational in the Muthian sense is economically rational. Moreover, the theoretical approaches underline the importance of market behaviour in learning some rationality (revealing price equilibria hypothesis), and this learning process is different from the strict Muthian rationality.
2. It appears important to respect the individual nature of expectations both at the theoretical and empirical levels: generally, heterogeneity is not neutral either in reaching an economic equilibrium or in estimating expectational processes. An important field of research is to identify the relevant level of aggregation, that is, the criteria which allow the identification of groups of agents which are economically relevant.
3. Expectational behaviour changes over time: both the processes and

the parameters which intervene in these processes are time-varying. These phenomena are very rarely examined in the literature concerned with expectations. It is shown that a single basic process hypothesis with constant parameters over the sample period may lead to serious misspecification problems, although these biases appear to be largely weakened when basic processes are mixed. This field of research remains very promising because it asks the question of what this instability represents.

4. Expectational processes are rather extrapolative (that is, destabilizing) when the horizon is short (less or equal to one month) but are rather regressive (that is, stabilizing) when the horizon is large (more than one month). In further work, it should be interesting to analyse the dynamics of market prices throughout these two opposite cybernetic strengths.

As will be evident, these lessons are both results and directions to explore in further research on price expectations.

REFERENCES

Azariadis, C. (1981), 'Self-fulfilling prophecies', *Journal of Economic Theory*, 25(3), 380–96.

Broze, L., C. Gourieuroux and A. Szafarz (1990), *Reduced Forms of Rational Expectations Models*, Fundamentals of Pure and Applied Economics, vol. 42, Harwood Academic.

Feige, E.L. and D. K. Pearce (1976), 'Economically rational expectations: are innovations in the rate of inflation independent of innovations in measures of monetary and fiscal policy?', *Journal of Political Economy*, June, 499–522.

Grandmont, J.M. (1976), 'Théorie de l'équilibre temporaire général', *Revue Economique*, 805–43.

Grossman, S. and J. Stiglitz (1976), 'Information and competitive price systems', *American Economic Review*, May, 66(2), 246–53.

Holden, K., D.A. Peel and J.L. Thompson (1986), *Expectations: Theory and Evidence*, London: Macmillan.

Lahiri, K. (1981), *The Econometrics of Inflationary Expectations*, Amsterdam: North-Holland.

Muth, J.F. (1961), 'Rational expectations and the theory of price movements', *Econometrica*, July, 315–35.

Pesaran, M.H. (1987), *The Limits to Rational Expectations*, Oxford: Basil Blackwell.

Prat, G. (1988), *Analyse des anticipations d'inflation des ménages*, Paris: Economica.

Radner, R. (1979), 'Rational expectations equilibrium: generic existence and the information revealed prices', *Econometrica*, May, 47(3), 655–78.

Sheffrin, S.M. (1983), *Rational Expectations*, Cambridge: Cambridge University Press.

Visco, I. (1984), *Price Expectations in Rising Inflation*, Amsterdam: North-Holland.
Walliser, B. (1985), *Anticipations, Equilibres et Rationalité Economique*, Paris: Calmann-Levy.

PART I

Rationality, Heterogeneity and Formation of Expectations: Concepts and Theoretical Analyses

1. From self-fulfilling to self-correcting expectations

Bernard Walliser*

Two augurs cannot look at each other without laughing.
Cicero

INTRODUCTION

Expectations of a decision-maker about some variable of his environment have been studied according to three fundamental problems which are more or less involved in any precise expectation concept. The genesis problem considers expectations as exogenously given or rooted in a private model of the decision-maker about his surrounding system, itself already given or revised through time. The impact problem analyses how expectations influence the decision-maker's choice and, by combination of all choices, the whole system state and especially the variable under consideration. The truth problem studies under what sufficient conditions expectations can be collectively and at least asymptotically realized, the underlying beliefs being themselves globally or only locally validated.

Expectations are moreover separately examined in the two social configurations which are classically formalized, without being completely related in the literature. In economic theory, agents' expectations concern essentially common institutional variables such as market prices, and eventually some environmental variables acting upon the prices. In game theory, players' expectations concern mainly the opponents' strategies since players interact in a direct way, and eventually some structural factors which influence the strategies. In both configurations, the expectation concepts are closely related to equilibrium notions, and an always more precise correspondence between the respective equilibrium notions is established in other respects.

The paper is illustrated by a very simple static or dynamic model, bringing together two actors i and j (with action variables u^i and u^j), an

* I thank J.L. Rullière for helpful comments.

institution (with interface variable x) and a passive environment (with exogenous variable z). An institution rule, which summarizes the institution functioning, relates mechanically the interface variable to the action variables and to the exogenous (certain or random) variable: $x = f(u^i, u^j, z)$. A behaviour rule, which summarizes the agent's instrumental rationality (often embedded in an optimization programme), relates the individual action variable to the expected interface variable (denoted $^i\tilde{x}$): $u^i = g^i\,(^i\tilde{x})$. An expectation rule, which summarizes the agent's cognitive rationality, relates the interface variable expectation to the exogenous variable expectation (denoted $^i\tilde{z}$) and to some observations (denoted $^i\tilde{y}$): $^i\tilde{x} = h^i\,(^i\tilde{z},\,^i\tilde{y})$.

The paper presents successively the four basic expectation concepts, each illustrated both in economic theory and in game theory. Section 1.1 deals with self-fulfilling expectations which are exogenously given to the agents, influence their behaviour and the global system, and may coincide with the corresponding realizations. Section 1.2 deals with rational expectations which are derived by omniscient agents from beliefs similar to the modeller's model and are then automatically realized. Section 1.3 deals with confirmed expectations which are obtained by limited agents through partial beliefs, but are nevertheless true since the beliefs are now self-fulfilling. Section 1.4 deals with self-correcting expectations which are incorrect because they stem from imperfect beliefs, but may converge to true ones since beliefs are revised through time.

1.1 SELF-FULFILLING EXPECTATIONS

1.1.1 Economic Theory

Merton (1936) introduces the concept of self-fulfilling expectation in an historical example showing that the collective belief in banks' insolvency induces the simultaneous money withdrawals from all customers and leads effectively to the bankrupcy of the bank system. Keynes (1936) suggests, at the same time, that a common expectation of all economic investors in some future interest rate induces an adjustment of their choices and leads to an interest rate which happens to coincide with the expected one, at least in some domain of rates. Cagan (1956) later explains the German hyperinflation phenomenon by making explicit the mechanism by which an expected inflation by a representative agent brings about a real inflation of the same fixed size, or even of the same increasing rate.

A self-fulfilling expectation considers the process by which any expectation of an interface variable influences the agent's behaviour, their mutual interactions and the realization of the interface variable. More precisely, by considering together the institution rule and the behaviour rule, the illustrative model reduces to a single relation linking the real interface variable to its expectations: $x = F(^i\tilde{x}, ^j\tilde{x}, z)$. Under the auxiliary assumption that all agents hold the same expectation $\tilde{x}$ of the interface variable (attributed to a representative agent), the reduced relation is written even more simply: $x = F(\tilde{x}, z)$. Such a relation is (locally) characterized as well by its sign, an expectation favouring or hindering its realization, as by its intensity, a realization being more or less sensitive to its expectation.

A self-fulfilling expectation stems from the possibility of coincidence between the interface variable expectation and realization, seen from the modeller's point of view without exhibiting how it may be achieved. More precisely, it appears as a fixed point $\bar{x}$ (existing or not) of the loop between expectation and realization, for instance in a Walrasian equilibrium where prices are involved: $x = \tilde{x} = \bar{x} = F(\bar{x}, z)$. In the case of a unique fixed point, the modeller points it out since it appears as a stationary state, inasmuch as the representative agent is not induced to call it into question if it is publicly forecasted. In the case of several fixed points, the modeller is aware of several virtual stationary states and the selection of one expectation announced to the agent and accepted by him gives it a true self-fulfilling status.

Regarding the environment, known only to the omniscient modeller, the exogenous variable just parametrizes the self-fulfilling expectation inasmuch as the agents' behaviour is not directly influenced by it. When the behaviour rule is extended to the exogenous variable: $u^i = g^i (^i\tilde{x}, ^i\tilde{z})$, the reduced relation obtained with the institution rule is written as $x = F(^i\tilde{x}, ^j\tilde{x}, ^i\tilde{z}, ^j\tilde{z}, z)$ and is simplified when accepting the representative agent assumption: $x = F(\tilde{x}, \tilde{z}, z)$. A self-fulfilling expectation still concerns the only endogenous variable, but becomes conditional on the expectation of the exogenous variable, the last being true or false: $x = \tilde{x} = \bar{x} = F(\bar{x}, \tilde{z}, z)$. Hence if the interface variable is fixed to some specific value $\bar{x}$, it happens to be a fixed point for some (common or not) values of the realized and expected exogenous variable.

1.1.2 Game Theory

Merton (1936) illustrates the concept of self-fulfilling expectation by another historical example showing that whether the Whites consider the Blacks as reliable or not for syndical action in the US, they entrust them or not with responsibility and observe that their expectations are always satisfied. Cournot (1838) prepared the ground far earlier by considering a duopoly situation wherein each firm maximizes its profit conditionally to its expectation of the other's production, both expectations happening to be true at an equilibrium state. Simon (1957) later demonstrated that polls about voting intentions, according to the fact that the voters react to them in a conformist or anti-conformist way, influence the actual votes and may finally appear as self-fulfilling or self-defeating.

A self-fulfilling expectation emphasizes how a players's expectation about the opponent's action influences his own behaviour and the whole strategic interaction situation along two interpretations. In a first view, each player expects the interface variable by perfectly knowing the institution rule ($^i\hat{f} = f$) and his own action ($^i\hat{x}^i = x^i$): $^i\hat{x} = f\,(u^i, {}^i\tilde{u}^j, {}^i\tilde{z})$, hence a reduced behaviour rule obtains: $u^i = G^i({}^i\tilde{u}^j, {}^i\tilde{z})$. In a second view, which is the traditional one in game theory, no institution exists and the interface variable is nothing else than the couple of action variables for both players: $x \equiv (u^i, u^j)$. Hence the primitive behaviour rule relates the player's action to his expectation of the other's action (his own action being known to him), but also to the expected exogenous variable: $u^i = G^i({}^i\tilde{u}^j, {}^i\tilde{z},)$.

A self-fulfilling expectation results from the possibility of coincidence, for each player, of the expectation and realization of the other's action, an adequacy again seen from the sole modeller's point of view. More precisely, it appears as a fixed point $(\bar{u}^i, \bar{u}^j)$ of the loop linking both players' actions, and is achieved in a Nash equilibrium when players have maximizing behaviours: $\bar{u}^i = G^i\,(\bar{u}^j, {}^i\tilde{z})$ and $\bar{u}^j = G^j\,(\bar{u}^i, {}^j\tilde{z})$. If a unique Nash equilibrium exists, the modeller naturally favours such a stationary state, from which no player has an interest to deviate unilaterally, if he is initially placed in it. If several Nash equilibria exist, the modeller can select one of them and suggest the corresponding expectations of actions to the players, such a state having then a real self-fulfilling status if accepted.

As concerns the environment, considered previously as a natural state of nature conditioning the equilibrium, it may also be considered as an artificial signal favouring an equilibrium. More precisely, a 'correlating device' chooses, according to a given probability distribution, a signal z (generally an issue of the game) and gives to each player a more precise signal z^i (generally the corresponding action). A 'correlated equilibrium' is obtained when each (optimizing) player has an incentive to obey the signal (knowing the other is doing the same), a condition which is warranted by an adequate probability distribution. A correlated equilibrium is a weaker notion than a Nash equilibrium in mixed strategies, wherein the private signals correspond to independent probability distributions for the two players.

1.2   RATIONAL EXPECTATIONS

1.2.1   Economic Theory

Muth (1961) introduced the concept of rational expectation through the pork market example, in which consumers observe the present price, whereas producers forecast correctly the future price by simulating (in a stochasting framework) the supply and demand equilibrium. Hicks (1939) earlier suggested the concept of perfect expectations when stating that the agents forecast rightly the prices on future spot markets (in the absence of forward markets), but without making explicit how they modelled the price formation mechanism. Akerlof (1970) considers further the concept of revealing expectation illustrated by the car market, on which the buyer knows less about the quality of the car than the seller, but tries to reveal the exogenous quality through the price if the latter is sufficiently discriminating.

A rational expectation relies on the mental process which generates the agent's expectation itself, based on an individual representation of the surrounding system which is similar to the modeller's model. First, the agent is aware of a correct specification of the system, and knows the behaviour, institution and environment rules, or at least the reduced relation combining them (transparency): $^i\tilde{F} = F$. Second, the agent observes perfectly all past exogenous variables, hence expects perfectly the present exogenous variables, for instance through an autoregressive process (omniscience): $^i\tilde{z} = z$. Third, the agent is an optimal statistician who at best turns his structural and factual information about the system into a non-biased expectation of the interface variable (efficiency): $^i\tilde{x} = F(^i\tilde{x}, z)$.

A rational expectation ensures then its truth automatically, in the sense that the expectation coincides with its realization, a property now due to the rightness of the agent's representation. In fact, an expectation can be true only if all agents have the same: $^i\tilde{x} = ^j\tilde{x} = \tilde{x}$, and needs moreover some co-ordination between them if several common and true expectations are possible. In a deterministic framework, a common expectation will be true: $\tilde{x} = x$, when the expectation is a self-fulfilling one: $\tilde{x} = F(\tilde{x}, z)$, thus defining an even more reduced system relation: $\tilde{x} = x = \mathbf{F}(z)$. In a stochastic framework (generally due to a stochastic exogenous variable), a common expectation is only true on average: $\tilde{x} = E(x)$ and appears as a solution of a deterministic associated relation: $E(x) = EF(x, z)$.

Regarding the environment, if agents have asymmetric information (or expectations) about it, the less informed may reveal the information held by the most informed and thereby incorporated in the interface variable. Formally, since agents are directly concerned with the exogenous variable, the reduced relation is written again: $x = F\ (^{i}\tilde{x}, ^{j}\tilde{x}, ^{i}\tilde{z}, ^{j}\tilde{z}, z)$ and one possible fixed point is given by: $^{i}\tilde{x} = ^{j}\tilde{x} = x = F\ (^{i}\tilde{z}, ^{j}\tilde{z}, z)$. If agent i perfectly expects the exogenous variable: $^{i}\tilde{z} = z$, while agent j does not, the last may reveal it as $^{j}\tilde{z}$ by observing the interface variable and inversing the (known) relation F: $x = F\ (^{j}\tilde{z}, ^{j}\tilde{z}, ^{j}\tilde{z})$. However, one faces a harsh synchronization problem since agent i cannot observe the interface variable at the same time as he influences it through his action variable.

1.2.2 Game Theory

Keynes (1936) raises the crossed expectations concept in his famous photo contest where each player has to find the photo (among a set of them) considered the nicest by a majority of competitors, hence has to guess what the others guess to be the prefered one. Lewis (1969) conceptualizes the concept of crossed knowledge at successive levels between agents, culminating in the notion of common knowledge, where each player believes that the other believes that the other believes . . . some proposition, to infinity. Aumann (1976) gives an account of the notion of common knowledge in terms of possible worlds semantics and applies it to the implicit exchange of information between two agents who simultaneously assess the probabilistic value of some event.

Rational expectations consider the mental process by which players form crossed expectations about their respective actions, by assuming that the game structure is common knowledge. More precisely, each player is assumed to know perfectly the other's behaviour rule (for instance, his preferences and opportunities if optimizing) at all expectation levels: $G^{j} = ^{i}\tilde{G}^{j} = ^{ji}\tilde{G}^{j} = ^{iji}\tilde{G}^{j} = \ldots$. At the first level, if the exogenous variable is also known: $^{i}\tilde{z} = z$, he uses this rule to expect the other's action: $^{i}\tilde{u}^{j} = G^{j}\ (^{ij}\tilde{u}^{i}, z)$, which leads to a more complex rule for himself: $u^{i} = \overline{G}^{i}\ (^{ij}\tilde{u}^{i}, z)$. At all successive levels, the reasoning continues by introducing ever higher expectations about the opponent's action and more complex behaviour rules: $u^{i} = \overline{G}^{i}\ (^{ij}\tilde{u}^{i}, z)\ \overline{\overline{G}}^{i}\ (^{iji}\tilde{u}^{j}, z) = \ldots$.

Rational expectations deal with the possibility of convergence of the infinite hierarchy of crossed expectations towards an equilibrium, achieved exclusively through the mental reasoning of the players. More precisely, if crossed expectations converge, it must be towards a state $(\bar{u}^{i}, \bar{u}^{j})$ where an action of a player responds to its own expectation at some even level: $\bar{u}^{i} = \overline{\overline{G}}^{i}\ (\bar{u}^{i}, z)$, $\bar{u}^{j} = \overline{\overline{G}}^{j}\ (\bar{u}^{j}, z)$. Especially when the players optimize, a rationalizable equilibrium is any combination of rationalizable actions, that is, a best response to a best response to . . . until the loop is closed at some finite level. A rationalizable equilibrium is a weaker notion than a Nash equilibrium (where the loop is closed as early as level 2) and leads to many equilibrium states, requiring a convention among players in order to select one.

As concerns the environment, it is difficult for an uninformed player to find out some information from an informed one since the opponent's action is submitted to an ambiguous interpretation. If one introduces the players' expectations of exogenous variables, the behaviour functions become enriched at all successive levels: $u^i = \overline{G}^i (^{ij}\tilde{u}^i, {}^{ij}\tilde{z}, {}^i\tilde{z}) = \overline{\overline{G}}^i (^{iji}\tilde{u}^j, {}^{iji}\tilde{z}, {}^{ij}\tilde{z}, {}^i\tilde{z}, z) = \ldots$. At some fixed point $\bar{u}^i$ of player i, it is written: $\bar{u}^i = \overline{G}^i (^{ij}\tilde{z}, {}^i\tilde{z}) = \ldots$, hence player j, even if he observes the other's action $\bar{u}^i$, is not able to discriminate between all his expectations at successive levels. However, if player i is assumed to know the exogenous variable perfectly, all these expectations become similar: ${}^i\tilde{z} = {}^{ij}\tilde{z} = {}^{iji}\tilde{z}$ and player j may reveal z as ${}^j\tilde{z}$: $\bar{u}^i = \overline{G}^i (^j\tilde{z}, {}^j\tilde{z}, \ldots)$.

1.3 CONFIRMED EXPECTATIONS

1.3.1 Economic Theory

Azariadis (1981) introduced the concept of confirmed expectations with an example where common beliefs of all agents in a correlation of prices with sunspots (following a stochastic process) influence their behaviour and induce further the occurrence of the assumed correlation. Azariadis and Guesnerie (1982) generalize this model by considering two groups of agents: those who believe in sunspots and those who believe in moonspots, and by showing that the prices are such that the two groups find their theories corroborated, at least approximately. Radner (1979) exhibited earlier a market model where, if non-informed agents consider that the price of wine is correlated with its unknown quality, such a postulated relation will be validated thanks to informed agents ready to pay for a good bottle.

A confirmed equilibrium starts with a prior representation of the agent about his surrounding system, which influences his own behaviour and through the institution the whole system. More precisely, the agent believes in a prior relation between the interface variable and the exogenous variable: $x = h^i (z)$ and he uses it to expect the first from the second: ${}^i\tilde{x} = h^i ({}^i\tilde{z})$. By combination with the reduced institutional rule F, and when the representative agent assumption is made, a new relation links the interface variable to the exogenous variable: $x = F (h (\tilde{z}), z) = \mathbf{F} (\tilde{z}, z)$. Moreover, if the agent perfectly expects the exogenous variable, directly if certain: $\tilde{z} = z$, or by an auxilary relation if stochastic: $\tilde{z} = 1 (z)$, the final relation depends on it even if $\mathbf{F}$ (or F) does not: $x = \mathbf{F}^* (z)$.

A confirmed expectation obtains when the agent's representation is self-fulfilling, that is, it coincides at equilibrium with the modeller's model, itself conditional on the agent's model. More precisely, a self-fulfilling model assumes that the agent's representation and the modeller's model lead to the same interface variable whatever the exogenous variable: h $(z) = \mathbf{F}^* (z) = \mathbf{F} (z, z) = \mathbf{F} (h (z), z)$. When the exogenous variable is certain, the associated interface variable just results from the selection of one self-fulfilling expectation since any solution $\tilde{x} = h (z)$ of $\tilde{x} = \mathbf{F} (\tilde{x}, z)$ satisfies h $(z) = \mathbf{F} (h (z), z)$. When the exogenous variable is random, the one to one correspondence between self-fulfilling model and self-fulfilling expectation no longer holds and original self-fulfilling models become available.

When agents have heterogenous beliefs about the system, the interface variable is written as: $x = \mathbf{F} (h^i (^i\tilde{z}), h^j (^j\tilde{z}), z) = \mathbf{F} (^i\tilde{z}, ^j\tilde{z}, z)$, and even more precisely when the exogenous variable is known: $x = \mathbf{F}^* (h^i (z), h^j (z), z) = \mathbf{F}^*$ (z). When the exogenous variable is certain, the private models are simultaneously fulfilled if they coincide everywhere: $h^i (z) = h^j (z)$, but a weakened form of self-fulfilling models happen when it is random. In other respects, if agents have heterogeneous expectations about the exogenous variable, the less informed may try again to reveal the information held by the most informed at equilibrium. If the first is able to observe the interface variable (always with a problem of synchronicity), he can inverse his private model if the correspondence between interface and exogenous variables is one-to-one.

1.3.2 Game Theory

Schelling (1978) developed numerous examples where similar agents involved in interactive social situations have some prior beliefs about the others' aggregate behaviour, adjust their own action to those beliefs and generate social regularities which confirm the beliefs. Spence (1973) formalized a more precise model wherein an employer postulates a relation between the (unobservable) productivity and the (observable) education of an employee, adapts the wage to the expected productivity and sees the assumed relation self-fulfilled thanks to the employee's reaction. Rothschild and Stiglitz (1976) initiated models of the insurance market with adverse selection, where the insurer is uncertain about the exogenous risk faced by the insured and tries to reveal it through the demand the latter manifests against adequate prices.

A confirmed expectation considers that each player has some model of the other's behaviour which takes the form of a strategy, that is, an action which is conditional on the assumed environment. More precisely, each player i models player j by a direct relation between his action variable and the expected exogenous one: $u^i = k^i (^j\tilde{z})$ and uses it to expect the first when expecting the second: $^i\tilde{u}^j = k^j\,(^{ij}\tilde{z})$. By combination with his behaviour rule, a new relation directly links, for each player, his action variable to his expectation of the exogenous variable: $u^i = G^i\,(k^i\,(^{ij}\tilde{z}),\ ^i\tilde{z}) = G^i\,(^{ij}\tilde{z},\ ^i\tilde{z})$. Moreover, if each agent expects the other's expectation as his own: $^{ij}\tilde{z} = {}^i\tilde{z}$, or relates it to his own by an auxilary relation: $^{ij}\tilde{z} = l^i\,(^i\tilde{z})$, the synthetic behaviour rule is written: $u^i = G^i\,(k^i\,(^i\tilde{z}),\ ^i\tilde{z}) = G^{i*}\,(^i\tilde{z})$.

A confirmed expectation results from the possibility that the player's representation is self-fulfilling, that is the player's model coincides locally with that of the modeller, which is itself conditional on the player's model. More precisely, with optimizing players, a (Nash) Bayesian equilibrium is obtained when the player's model appears as a functional fixed point of the modeller's model: $k^i\,(^i\tilde{z}) = G^{j*}\,(^j\tilde{z}) = G^j\,(k^i\,(^i\tilde{z}),\ ^j\tilde{z})$. The exogenous variable may be a true state of nature, able in some respect to co-ordinate the agents as in the correlated equilibrium, even if it has its own law and is not determined voluntarily. The exogenous variable is more often the type of each player, which summarizes his opportunities and preferences in a single variable and is known by the player, contrary to his opponents.

When players have asymmetric information about the exogenous variable, an uninformed player may again reveal information from an informed player's action at some equilibrium where his belief is fulfilled. Consider for instance that player j has two possible types z_1 and z_2 and two possible actions u_1^j and u_2^j, then two polar equilibria are conceivable, a whole spectrum of hybrid ones lying between them. A separating equilibrium obtains when each player reveals his own type through his action (and has an interest in doing so if he is an optimizing player): $u_1^j = G^{j*}\,(z_1)$ and $u_2^j = G^{j*}\,(z_2)$. A pooling equilibrium obtains when each player hides his own type, since his reduced behaviour rule is no longer a one-to-one function: $G^{j*}\,(z_1) = G^{j*}\,(z_2) = u_1^j = u_2^j$.

1.4 SELF-CORRECTING EXPECTATIONS

1.4.1 Economic Theory

Nerlove (1958) introduces, using the price in the pork cycle model, the notion of adaptive expectation, where the present expectation is adjusted to the past one in accordance with the observed discrepancy between past expectation and past observation. Cyert and Degroot (1970) and Arrow and Green (1973) suggest in a duopoly model the notion of self-correcting expectation by which a firm tries to learn from past observations the reaction function of its competitor or the demand function of its customers. Allen (1981) considers a more sophisticated market model, where uniformed agents try progressively to reveal the quality of some good already tested by other agents from sequential observation of prices in different contexts.

A self-correcting expectation rests on the process by which the agent revises his belief about the system and the resulting expectation about the interface variable when receiving new information through time. More precisely, the representative agent forms an expectation based on a simplified model: $\hat{x}_t = \hat{h}(z_t, a_t)$, where a_t is a parameter adjusted in an extrapolative way from past observations $\hat{x}_{t-1}$ and $\hat{z}_{t-1}$: $a_t = q(a_{t-1}, \hat{x}_{t-1}, \hat{z}_{t-1})$. The extrapolative expectation assumes a purely parametric process: $\tilde{x}_t = \tilde{h}(a_t)$ with parameter depending only on the endogenous variable: $a_t = q(a_{t-1}, \hat{x}_{t-1})$, hence $\tilde{x}_t = \tilde{h}(\hat{x}_{t-1})$. A more complex expectation assumes a generalized process: $\tilde{x}_t = \tilde{h}(z_t, a_t)$ with its parameter adjusted period after period according to the Bayesian rule or globally estimated by a statistical method, hence: $\tilde{x}_t = \tilde{h}(\hat{x}_{t-1}, \hat{z}_{t-1})$.

A self-correcting expectation further considers the possible convergence along time of the postulated agent's model towards a locally true one, and of the expected interface variable towards the realized one. Formally, the combination of the true model of the system with the former expectation rule leads to the relation: $x_t = F(z_t, a_t)$ where the parameter a_t always adapts to past observations: $a_t = q(a_{t-1}, \hat{x}_{t-1}, \hat{z}_{t-1})$. Since the expectation scheme depends on past values (especially of the exogenous variable), the induced model of the system will depend on past values too, even if the prior model does not. The convergence of the process is restricted to analytical conditions, being possible only when the speed of learning of the agent is higher than the speed of evolution of the system (which depends on it).

If the agent has a correct specification of the system model: $\tilde{x}_t = F(z_t, a)$, where a is an actual parameter (especially when z_t is not relevant), the problem reduces to the convergence of the adjusted parameter to the actual one. If the agent has an incorrect specification, one may only hope that the adjusted parameter converges towards some value which renders the belief locally valid and the expectation precisely true. In other respects, if the exogenous variable is stationary and is not observed by some agent, it may be revealed from the interface variable provided that some other agent is informed. But in a dynamic setting, there is no longer a problem of synchronism since the interface variable is observed at one period and the information revealed from it is used at the next period.

1.4.2   Game Theory

Cournot (1838) builds in his duopoly model a dynamic process where each firm expects that the other will play in the ongoing period the action it played during the last period and chooses as its own action the best response to the other's. Fudenberg and Kreps (1988) study the 'fictitious play' process where each player expects the other's future (static) strategy to be a mixed strategy, the probability given to each possible pure strategy being equal to the frequency with which it was played in the past. Kalai and Lehrer (1993) consider a more sophisticated model where the opponent's possible (dynamic) strategies are progressively eliminated if they become incompatible with the observations, a kind of Bayesian learning of other's behaviour.

A self-correcting expectation focuses on the process by which each player modifies his belief about his opponent by observing his past actions and adapts his expectation about the opponent's future action. More precisely, player i has a belief about the behaviour rule of player j: ${}^i\tilde{u}_t^j = \tilde{h}^i\,({}^{ij}z_t,\,a_t^j)$, and the included parameter a_t^j is adapted to past observations of actions $\hat{u}_{t-1}^j$: $a_t^j = q\,(a_{t-1}^j,\,\hat{u}_{t-1}^j,\,\hat{z}_{t-1}^j)$. The 'fictitious play' rule assumes a purely parametric process: ${}^i\tilde{u}_t^j = \tilde{h}^i\,(a_t^j)$ with parameter defined by the past frequency of all strategies of the opponent: $a_t^j = k\,(\hat{u}_{t-1}^j)$, hence ${}^i\tilde{u}_t^j = \tilde{h}^i\,(\hat{u}_{t-1}^j)$. A more sophisticated expectation rule is obtained when a probability distribution is defined over a set of expectation schemes $\tilde{h}^j$ and when this distribution is revised according to observations.

A self-confirming expectation considers the possible convergence of the system state towards some one-shot or repeated game equilibrium, where the opponent's expected action becomes asymptotically realized. Formally, the combination of the true behaviour rule of player i (generally an optimizing one) with his expectation rule leads to the relation: $u_t^i = \mathbf{G}^i\,({}^{ij}z_t,\,a_t^j)$, where the parameter a_t^j always adapts to past observations. Since the expected action variable depends on its past values, the resulting behaviour rule will depend on other's past variables too, and hence appears as a dynamic rather than a static strategy: $u_t^i = \mathbf{G}^i\,(\hat{u}_{t-1}^j)$. The whole process may cycle and only converges under rather drastic conditions, since the players follow simultaneous and interactive learning processes, possibly at different speeds.

For several revision rules, convergence is towards a self-confirming equilibrium, a weaker notion than Nash equilibrium, where no observation induces any player to revise his beliefs. A more precise equilibrium obtains when a player's experimentation is not only passive (observations as byproducts of usual actions), but active (observations obtained by voluntary deviations from usual actions). In other respects, if some player is uncertain about the other's type (assumed to be invariant), he may reveal this type by observing his successive actions in various circumstances. Here again, the player may not only play his short-term optimizing action, but try original actions in order to test the opponent's reactions, and use the revealed information in the long term.

1.5 CONCLUSION

The four expectation concepts differ profoundly in their basic principles, since they are grounded on more or less realistic conceptions of time and become involved with more or less exogenously given factors. Self-fulfilling expectations are stated in the fictitious time of an external entity which simulates from outside under what conditions exogenous expectations allocated to the agents can be simultaneously realized. Rational or confirmed expectations are stated in the real but flattened time of the agents who deliberately form their expectations from their beliefs, even if these beliefs remain exogenous and if their fulfilment is examined from outside. Self-correcting expectations are stated in the real spread-out time of the agents who again derive expectations from prior beliefs, but these beliefs are revised through time according to past observations.

The four expectation concepts receive accordingly different justifications, inherited from the justifications of the associated equilibrium notions, since the expectations become realized at some equilibrium state. Self-fulfilling expectations define an equilibrium formally justified as a stationary state, in the sense that no agent has a tendency to deviate unilaterally from it if he is already in such a state. Rational or confirmed expectations define an equilibrium cognitively justified as a belief-consistent state, in the sense that all agents hold beliefs which are not refuted in such a state. Self-correcting expectations define an equilibrium dynamically justified as an asymptotic state, in the sense that the agents follow a cognitive learning process which converges towards such a state.

Finally, the four expectation concepts reflect different epistemological views, adopted more or less explicitly by the modeller when constructing his model, which serves as a reference for validating the players' beliefs. Self-fulfilling expectations express an instrumental view, where agents are endowed with pregiven and unconstrained expectations, which induce their realization in an unexplained and unconscious way. Rational and confirmed expectations express a hybrid view, where agents' beliefs are still given although strongly demanding, but influence concretely the individual behaviours and the social interactions. Self-correcting expectations express a realistic view, where agents have limited information and computation capacities, compensated by the unfolding of time in explicit learning processes.

REFERENCES

Akerlof, G. (1970), 'The market for lemons: quality uncertainty and the market mechanism', *Quarterly Journal of Economics*, 84 (3), 488–500.

Allen, B. (1981), 'Generic existence of completely revealing equilibria for economies with uncertainty when prices convey information', *Econometrica*, 49 (5), 1173–99.

Arrow, K. and J. Green (1973), 'Notes on expectations equilibria in Bayesian settings', Stanford University Paper.

Aumann, R. (1976), 'Agreeing to disagree', *Annals of Statistics*, 4, 1236–9.

Azariadis, C. (1981), 'Self-fulfilling prophecies', *Journal of Economic Theory*, 25 (3), 380–96.

Azariadis, C. and R. Guesnerie (1982), 'Prophéties créatrices et persistance des théories', *Revue Economique*, 33 (5), 787–806

Cagan, P. (1956), 'The monetary dynamics of hyperinflation', in M. Friedman (ed.), *Studies in the Quantity Theory of Money*, Chicago: University of Chicago Press.

Cournot, A. (1838), *Recherches sur les principes mathématiques de la théorie des richesses*, Paris: Librairie des Sciences Politiques et Sociales.

Cyert, R. and M.H. Degroot (1970), 'Bayesian analysis and duopoly theory', *Journal of Political Economy*, 78 (5), 35.

Fudenberg, D. and D. Kreps (1988), 'A theory of learning, experimentation and equilibrium in games', MIT and Stanford University, mimeo.

Hicks, J.R. (1939), *Value and Capital*, Oxford: Clarendon Press.

Kalai, E. and E. Lehrer (1993), 'Rational learning leads to Nash equilibrium', *Econometrica*, 61 (3), 547–73.

Keynes, J.M. (1936), *The General Theory of Employment, Interest and Money*, London: Macmillan.

Lewis, D.K. (1969), *Convention: A Philosophical Study*, Cambridge, MA: Harvard University Press.

Merton, M. (1936), 'The unanticipated consequences of purposive social action', *American Sociological Review*, 65, 22.

Muth, J. (1961), 'Rational expectations and the theory of price movements', *Econometrica*, 19, 315–35.

Nerlove, M. (1958), 'Adaptive expectations and cobweb phenomena', *Quarterly Journal of Economics*, 73, 35.

Radner, R. (1979), 'Rational expectations equilibrium: generic existence and the information revealed by price', *Econometrica*, 47, 655–78.

Rothschild, M. and J. Stiglitz (1976), 'Equilibrium in competitive insurance markets: an essay on the economics of imperfect information', *Quarterly Journal of Economics*, 90 (4), 629–49.

Schelling, T.C. (1978), *Micromotives and Macrobehavior*, New York: W.W. Norton.

Simon, H.A. (1957), 'Bandwagon and underdog effects and the possibility of predictions', *Public Opinion Quarterly*, 18 (3), 245–53.

Spence, M. (1973), 'Job market signalling', *Quarterly Journal of Economics*, 87 (3), 33.

2. About the origins of the player's expectations in game theory

Christian Schmidt

INTRODUCTION

Is our knowledge of price expectations improved by revisiting the early beginnings of game theory? A positive answer requires some justification. There is no doubt that strategic thinking refers to expectations about competitors' behaviour. Furthermore, the way in which players' expectations are mutually implicated in their interactive processes is really a cornerstone of the original game theory research programme. But as game theory developed, the very specific angle to approach players' expectations tended to disappear. Bayesian rationality, subjective interpretation of probabilities and finally the expected utility calculations used by game theory progressively reduced the gap between the formulation of players' expectations in a game situation and the expectations of an individual person under uncertainty. In spite of a few reactions from game theorists such as Binmore (1996, 1993), on one side, and from theoreticians of decisions, such as Hammond (1993, 1996), on the other, a majority of economists today consider expectations in game theory as a simple extension of the Savagian framework to many persons interacting. We do not share this common view and propose to come back to the origin of game theory to specify the content of the difference.

We shall first show that it is impossible to reconstruct the problematic of expectation within game theory from the point of departure of our current understanding of uncertainty in the theory of individual choice. This interesting action next leads to the formulation of a hypothesis regarding the origin of this impossibility and why it has been hidden. A return to the mathematical sources of game theory sheds light on two different approaches to the question, related to two conceptions of the study of games. The first, which we shall call 'strategic', considers the game exclusively from the point of view of the players' choices. The second is concerned primarily with mapping out the game situation in terms of

34

equilibrium, by placing oneself at the vantage point of the modeller (or of the theoretician). Thus a re-examination of various texts by Borel, Ville, de Possel and von Neumann, which all preceded by nearly a quarter of a century the publication of *Theory of Games and Economic Behavior*, can serve to place many contemporary debates about expectations in a new light. Finally, a connection will be sketched between those historical roots and the recently questioned concepts as basic to game theory such as strategies and mixed strategies (Rubinstein, 1991, Osborne and Rubinstein, 1994).

2.1 BOREL AND THE MIXED STRATEGIES

Borel is rightly credited with being the first to introduce the concept of the mixed strategy into game theory (Borel, 1921). The mixed strategies obtained by problematizing the pure strategies available to players refer to each player's definition of his expected payments. The notion of the expected payment is, for a contemporary theoretician, inseparable from the concept of the expected utility, which leads one to interpret mixed strategies as the result of a simple extension to games of the theory of expected utility (Aumann, 1987, 3 and 15–16).[1] This interpretation is corroborated by the fact that the theory of expected utility satisfies the axioms of the theory of utility presented in an appendix of *Theory of Games and Economic Behavior* by von Neumann and Morgenstern (1944).

Several historical arguments run counter to this reconstruction. In the first place, chronology. Borel uses mixed strategies in publications that date to well before the formulation of the theory of expected utility (Borel, 1921, 1924, 1927). Furthermore, the appendix on the axiomatization of utilities does not appear until the second edition of *Theory of Games and Economic Behavior* (1946), which suggests that our understanding of this work, and thus of the concepts contained in it, does not depend on this axiomatization. Finally, a parallelism between the Minimax theory and the theory of the two-person games was pointed out by Savage only in the early 1950s (Savage, 1954).

The analytical arguments are drawn from the content of Borel's publications (Borel, 1921, 1924, 1927) and lend themselves to more interesting elaborations. It is important for our purposes to note that it was Borel who, in the framework of games without pure strategy solution, introduced mixed strategies. The most famous example is that of the 'Stone, Paper, Scissors' game, which was also treated by von Neumann (1928) and thoroughly discussed in *Theory of Games and Economic Behavior*. Mixed strategies made their appearance there as a direct consequence of the general method formulated by Borel to permit players to eliminate what he calls 'bad ways of playing'. Borel wrote on this subject:

> When this best way [of playing] does not exist, one may ask oneself whether it is not possible, in the absence of a code chosen once and for all, to play in an advantageous manner by varying one's play. If one wanted to formulate a precise rule for varying one's play, a rule which would only take into account facts observed in the game, and not observations made about one's opponent, this rule would really be equivalent to the following statement: the probability for which, in a given moment of the game, A adopts, in order to decide his conduct at this moment, the code Ck is Pk.   (Borel, [1921] 1924, p. 200)

In concluding his treatment of this example, he does not neglect to underline the limits of his method, while at the same time he also traces the limits of the range of interpretations to be given to mixed strategies:

> Whatever the variety introduced by A in his play, from the moment that this variety is definitive, B has only to know it in order for him to gain an advantage over A; the opposite is equally true; we must conclude from this that the calcula-tion of probabilities can only serve to permit the elimination of bad ways of playing, and for the calculation of choices.   (Ibid., p. 201)

For Borel, consequently, mixed strategies impose themselves on the players just as naturally as pure strategies. And whether mixed or pure, the choice of a strategy is the player's response to the general problem of elim-inating 'bad ways of playing' while at the same time not allowing the other player to get the upper hand. The fact that he has recourse to probability values in order to so does not change the nature of the problem. As for interpreting these probability values, there is no particular difficulty since the games Borel considers are played over several rounds. Therefore, the reasoning that leads Borel to introduce mixed strategies in games where chance and the ability of the players intervene remains irrelevant to the operation of maximizing the expected utility.

An analysis that digs deeper into Borel's thought on the nature of prob-abilities allows one to isolate certain implications of this statement. Even though he is attached to a classical conception of objective probabilities, Borel offers no principled opposition to the idea of attributing a probabil-ity value to a subjective judgment.[2] He admits, in particular, the interpreta-tion by which these subjective probabilities may be revealed by a wager, even a virtual one, made by the person concerning the event in question. Borel observes, however, in the last two volumes of his *Traité des probabil-ités* that the analogy between these probability values and those that result from a wager disappear when, as in a poker game, a person finds himself led to wager on his own game (Borel, 1938, p. 97; 1939, pp. 74 and 144-5).[3]

In this case, the revelation of a player's subjective probabilities necessarily takes on a strategic meaning *vis-à-vis* his adversaries which complicates his interpretation. Now, what is very clear in the example of the poker game manifests itself more or less in all strategic games.[4] In developing Borel's reasoning, one arrives at the conclusion that the very rules 'of games where chance and the ability of the players intervene' invalidate the interpretation of subjective probabilities implied by the theory of the expected utility.

2.2 VON NEUMANN AND THE MINIMAX THEOREM

No one denies von Neumann credit for having been the first to demonstrate the Minimax theorem in the context of a two-player zero-sum game (von Neumann, 1928). According to this well-known theorem, where the game is represented by an arbitrary real Matrix A, there exists a real number v and probability vectors x and y, in such a way that: Max/Min xAy = Min/Max xAy. This demonstration is often linked to the individual maximization of the expected utility of each player. Nothing, however, is more incorrect. From the point of view of historical reality, first of all, the notion of utility is absent from this first demonstration, where the strategies of the players are defined in terms of expected gains, as in the games studied by Borel.[5] One must await the demonstration of the fundamental theorem in *Theory of Games and Economic Behavior* (von Neumann and Morgenstern, 1944) before the concept of the expected utility appears. This is not without analytical importance, for it proves that the reference to utility is not essential for the resolution of this class of game.

Whether the maximization bears on the expected gain or on the expected utility, the strategic calculations of the players are not assimilable to a maximization of subjective probabilities by an isolated individual. The reasons for this appear clearly in von Neumann's article of 1928. At first glance, however, the definition of 'a strategic game' proposed by von Neumann lends itself to this assimilation. Each of the two players makes his calculation based solely on the value of his expected gain, since he is supposed to chose his strategy in a state of ignorance about the other player's choice (von Neumann, 1928, 1959, p. 21). But the manner in which chance is grasped has nothing to do with the processing of that information by the individual decision-maker faced with an uncertain future.

The definition of the values Maximin and Minimax, which serve as the base for von Neumann's demonstration, raises a difficulty. Essentially, their calculation implies knowledge on the part of each player of the strategy chosen by the other. Thus an incompatibility arises between the players' definition of the values Maximin and Minimax which in von Neumann's language supposes that the strategy of each person has been 'discovered' by the other (von Neumann, 1928, 1959, pp. 23–34), and the initial hypothesis of the game according to which each player chooses his strategy in a state of ignorance about the choice of the others (Schmidt, 1995). Its consequences and the means proposed in order to avoid such a contradiction are then analysed at length by von Neumann and Morgenstern in *Theory of Games and Economic Behavior* (1944, pp. 90 165). In certain cases, as in the 'Stone, Paper, Scissors' game, this knowledge of the other's strategy even leads to an impasse, because in such cases the Maximin and the Minimax must take on different values (respectively -1 and 1).

The route chosen by von Neumann in 1928 in order to resolve this problem shows how the question of the equality of the values of Maximin and Minimax is linked to the information about the other's strategy which each player has at his disposal. It is the possibility offered to the players to anticipate with certainty the strategy chosen by their adversary which prevents the equality of Maximin and of Minimax and thus blocks the solution of the game. The artifice imagined by von Neumann to escape this difficulty consists in introducing chance into the game in the form of an initial aleatory drawing. In thus appealing to probabilities, each player finds himself protected from the risk of being 'discovered' by the other and neither of the two players retains any information advantage over the other. Chance re-establishes each player's ignorance about the strategy chosen by the other. This strategic use of chance in a class of game where it had been eliminated (so-called games of strategy) leads von Neumann to formulate the following general remark:

> Although in Section 1 chance was eliminated from the games of strategy under consideration (by introducing expected values and eliminating 'draws'), it has now made a spontaneous reappearance. Even if the rules of the game do not contain any elements of 'hazard' (i.e., no draws from urns) – as e.g., the two examples in 2 – in specifying the rules of behavior for the players it becomes imperative to reconsider the element of 'hazard'. The dependence on chance (the 'statistical' element) is such an intrinsic part of the game itself (if not of the world) that there is no need to introduce it artificially by way of the rules of the game: even if the formal rules contain no trace of it, it still will assert itself. (von Neumann, 1928, 1959, p. 26)

In a game situation, chance and the ignorance it engenders are inseparable from the strategic rationality of the players. The examples of the 'Stone, Paper, Scissors' game is significant in this regard. Chance manifests itself in the game at the level of the players' strategies, whether in the form of payment probabilities associated with mixed strategies (Borel), or by the intermediary of an initial drawing of lots which associates the probability values with pure strategies (von Neumann). Von Neumann's reasoning here joins Borel's argument and ends up in this example with the same result.[6] In both cases it is a question of a particular distribution of probabilities which is completely integrated with the strategic choices of the players. But this is not the meaning of chance for the individual decision-maker. If he knows nothing of the occurrence of the states, all the distributions of subjective probabilities he may define based on them are equally acceptable and rational. Chance is then completely independent from his strategic rationality (Hammond, 1996). The point goes far beyond the Minimax and the special case of two-persons zero-sum games. More than twenty years after von Neumann, Nash is much more explicit in his PhD dissertation devoted to equilibrium as a solution of non-cooperative games. He points out in a game played but once, that the basic question to be solved by the players can formulated as follows: What would be a 'rational' prediction of the behaviour to be expected of rational playing? He then concludes the necessity 'to assume the players know the full structure of the game in order to be able to deduce the prediction for themselves' (Nash, 1950, p. 23).

Anyway the endogenization of the player's anticipations appears clearly from the origin of game theory. Not only does the demonstration of the Minimax theorem owe nothing to expected utility, but its treatment of risk contradicts one of the foundations of subjective probabilities.[7]

2.3 BOREL'S PLAYERS AND VON NEUMANN'S PLAYERS

The works of Borel and of von Neumann evoked above show that the elaboration of the concept of the mixed strategy and the demonstration of the Minimax theorem are foreign to subjective probabilities. Their source is to be found in their shared idea that the risk, in the sense of the classic theory of probabilities, constitutes the common characteristic of every game situation; hence the historical links between probabilities and games. But the two authors do not extend this idea in the same direction and do not draw the same consequences from it. For Borel, the essential question is to know if the players can imitate hazard. For von Neumann, it is a matter of understanding how, in extending the properties brought into view by the Minimax theorem, the risk generated by hazard can contribute to the theoretical solution of games.

Borel considers games from the exclusive point of view of the players who concretely put into play, in the course of their decisions, the strategies they have decided to follow. Here he encounters two contradictory constraints that weigh on the player. On the one hand, the player must proceed in a rational manner in order to eliminate dominated strategies ('bad methods' in Borel's terminology). But on the other hand, he must make his attacks vary, as the rounds go on, in a random manner, in order not to reveal to his adversary his way of playing and thus give him the upper hand. We have already seen that, for Borel, this contradiction limits the scope of mixed strategies. He concludes his essay of 1921 by noting that the player must 'show a total incoherence of mind' and at the same time 'the intelligence necessary to eliminate bad methods' (Borel, 1921, 1924, p. 203).

In his last works, Borel deepened the analysis of this contradiction by examining whether it could be dispelled by the strategy of a player who deliberately, and thus rationally, forced himself to imitate chance so as to survive against his adversary. For Borel, this imitation of chance would consist for the player in utilizing the lessons of the calculation of probabilities, understood in the frequentist sense, in order to choose his attacks in the course of the different rounds of the game. That would concretely signify that the player was integrating the results of previous rounds into his game. Now, what characterizes chance in a game resides exactly in the fact that the probability of the player's choice in a given round is independent of his previous choices. Borel concludes from this that the imitation of hazard by players is impossible and that the contradiction he exposes is irreducible (Borel, 1938, pp. 119–20).

The point of view developed by Borel sheds light on the controversy started long ago by Frechet regarding Borel's and von Neumann's respective contributions to the birth of game theory (Frechet, 1953). It may seem surprising that Borel, after having discovered the solution to two games which do not have a pure strategy equilibrium ('Heads or Tails' and 'Stone, Paper, Scissors') by following a reasoning close to that of von Neumann, expressed reservations about its generalization (Dimand and Dimand, 1996). The commentary in which he has followed Ville's simplified demonstration of the Minimax theorem (Ville, 1938a) allows us to clear up this mystery. After qualifying von Neumann's theorem as 'important', Borel stresses, however, 'in order to avoid any misunderstanding', that the practical applications of this theorem for game of chance players seemed to him to be limited (Borel, 1938, p. 11). This commentary is immediately followed in the volume of the *Traité des probabilités* by Borel's note on the imitation of hazard. From there, things are very clear. Players cannot imitate hazard; hazard alone, however, prevents one player from gaining the upper hand through an asymmetry in information. From this results the impossibility of a player adopting a way of playing, that is, a strategy, which is best *in every case*. Finally, von Neumann and Morgenstern (1944, p. 164) say nothing different when, in posing the question of the existence of strategies that would *always* be optimal, they recognize that the response in general is negative. It is salient to note that the same games of 'Heads or Tails' ('Matching Pennies' is the American version) and 'Stone, Paper, Scissors' were used to support their assertion. In these two cases, the optimal strategies from the point of view of theory were valuable only as long as the players were in a defensive position.

Both are popular parlour games. In 'Stone, Paper, Scissors', each player can choose between one of those three elements. By definition, 'Stone' defeats 'Scissors', 'Scissors' defeats 'Paper' and 'Paper' defeats 'Stone'.[8] The normal form of the two-person game is the matrix in Figure 2.1, where Stone, Paper and Scissors are pure strategies and M the mixed strategy which corresponds to the solution.

Player 2

		Stone	Paper	Scissors	M
	Stone	0,0	−1,+1	+1,−1	0,0
	Paper	+1,−1	0,0	−1,+1	0,0
Player 1	Scissors	−1,+1	+1,−1	0,0	0,0
	M	0,0	0,0	0,0	0,0

Figure 2.1: 'Stone, Paper, Scissors' matrix

The demonstration of the Minimax theorem, which for von Neumann and Morgenstern is the foundation of determination of two-player zero-sum games, implies the adoption of a defensive posture on the part of the players, to the extent that it only allows the protection of each one of the players from the danger that a discovery of his strategy by the other would have entailed. It does not furnish, however, any information on what would happen if each player sought to exploit the errors of his adversary. Therefore, von Neumann and Morgenstern logically concluded that a strategy which would be permanently optimal does not exist in their theory (von Neumann and Morgenstern, 1944, p. 144).

Von Neumann and Morgenstern's observations on the scope and the limits of the Minimax theorem in game theory appear extremely fruitful for our purpose. First, beyond the mathematical similarities, the Minimax principle does not mean exactly the same thing for a player in a two-person zero-sum game and for an individual decision-maker in an uncertain world. Indeed, in games such as 'Stone, Paper, Scissors' or 'Matching Pennies', the Minimax principle is to be understood as the best strategy to avoid being 'found out' by the opponent. The reference to the idea 'to be found out' is a major component of players' expectations. For von Neumann and Morgenstern, a satisfactory theory necessarily harmonizes the two extreme cases where both player 1 and player 2 are 'found out', each on his own side; thus the purpose of the Minimax principle is to provide a way to implement such a harmonization. If the Minimax is a convincing principle for the two players, then it guides their mutual expectations for choosing the 'good' strategies. As rightly pointed out by Savage (1954, pp. 180–3), such a justification is meaningless when the Minimax is understood as a criterion for individual decision-making under uncertainty.

Second, the Minimax principle is not sufficient to be convincing for the players, even in a two-person zero-sum game. It would be convincing if it led the players to determine their best strategies in all situations consistent with the game. This is not the case in 'Stone, Paper, Scissors'. Therefore, additional assumptions are necessary, such as the rule of the defensive posture. An interesting feature of this defensive point of view is the kind of dependence *vis-à-vis* the other players. Let us recall the game 'Stone, Paper, Scissors'. If the opponent has chosen the strategy corresponding to the Minimax solution of the game, then the player's mistake would not matter (see Figure 2.1). It shows that the key point for the player's decision is the expected strategies of the others. Anyway, von Neumann and Morgenstern were perfectly aware of the limitation of their theory to the defensive domain. They sketched out some guidelines for an offensive theory in their model of bluffing in parlour games (von Neumann and Morgenstern, 1944, pp. 206–19). Borel also proposed a Model of Poker.[9]

Third, the assumption that a complete theory exists as a heuristic procedure to find a solution has been extensively followed by Nash to attempt the actual meaning of the equilibrium as a solution. If Nash's theory is common knowledge between the players and if it leads to a solution, such a belief is exactly what von Neumann and Morgenstern designated as an 'indirect proof' which remains questionable from von Neumann's viewpoint (von Neumann and Morgenstern, 1944, pp. 147–9). Players in game theory neither assume complete ignorance *vis-à-vis* the other players nor a total knowledge of their behaviour, but rather a common expectation to be derived from the theory. It must be emphasized that von Neumann and Morgenstern's solution with the Minimax does not refer to the same acceptance of rationality as Nash with the equilibrium concept which is closer to the Minimax-regret criterion. But this is not the point. Both theories are built on a common belief among the players about a convincing concept of solution, which shapes their mutual expectations.

To sum up, von Neumann analyses the games by placing himself at the point of view of the theoretical solution which could be given to them by the modeller. Certainly, some pieces of information for the players could be drawn from the theory. The analysis of *Theory of Games and Economic Behavior* thus extends the approach adopted by von Neumann in his article of 1928. If a complete theory of two-person zero-sum games exists, it permits the resolution of the contradiction concerning the information held by each player on the strategy of the other, which von Neumann had already brought to light in 1928. On this point, it ends up with the same result as in introducing hazard into the game (see p. 38). Each player knowing this theory will also know what the strategy chosen by the other will be, but this information will not give him the upper hand against his adversary since the adversary knows the same thing about him (von Neumann and Morgenstern, 1944, p. 148). However, this piece of information given to the players by the theory is expressly dependent on the completeness of the theory. One thinks again of Nash's equilibrium theory, whose scope for players is severely reduced because of the plurality of the equilibria combined with the absence of a criterion for discriminating between them.

Moreover, what may be learned from a complete theory only concerns the players at the moment when they make their choice of strategies. Now, what Borel has in mind when he thinks of a game theory is more a collection of rules that are of practical value to the players, as is found in popular strategy manuals.[10] Keeping this in mind, it is easier to understand his scepticism with regard to von Neumann's approach. He summarized it in the argument which closes his essay of 1924:

> It is for this reason that all the manuals will never be able to teach us to play these games in a superior manner. There is no doubt that if a player strictly followed all the rules of an excellent manual, and if his opponent knew it, this opponent could win by modifying his way of playing as a consequence. (Borel, 1924, p. 221)

The contributions of Borel and of von Neumann which confront each other here reflect back on a particular game situation. The parlour games which support the reasoning of these two authors are zero-sum games, but they are played over several rounds like repeated games. The influence of this characteristic on the intuitive interpretation of mixed strategies has already been noted. It explains equally why Borel and von Neumann do not understand one another. Considered from the point of view at which Borel places himself, the information drawn by the players from preceding moves cannot be of a statistical order since, it being a zero-sum game, each move constitutes a new event with regard to chance. Players are left only with the resources of psychology in treating this information in a pertinent manner (Borel, 1939, pp. 100–1). An inductive theory of the tactics of players, as Borel could have understood it, thus clearly finds itself doomed to failure. From von Neumann's point of view, however, this property is a bearer of hope. In all two-player zero-sum games it is possible to replace all the effects of chance by a combination of players' pure strategies in such a way that the strategic properties of the game remain identical (von Neumann and Morgenstern, 1944, p. 183). In other words, the ensemble of rounds in a game of chance such as those studied by our two authors is reducible to a single and unique game, a complete theory of which it is the theoretician's task to establish.

If the approach privileged by von Neumann reveals itself to be much richer for two-person zero-sum games, it still does not dispel the questions raised by Borel, which exist at a different level. It is necessary merely to leave the narrow framework of zero-sum games in order to see them reappear from the point at which, for example, the games are truly repeated and the players' processing of the available information on previous games can be posed in analytical terms. This is why recent developments in game theory have begun to show that the viewpoints on games developed by Borel and by von Neumann respectively are more complementary than antagonistic. In any case, anticipation does not mean exactly the same thing for Borel's player and for von Neumann's player. An examination of the way in which these two authors understood game situations will clarify the origin of this difference.

2.4   TYPES OF GAMES AND THE NATURE OF THE PLAYERS' EXPECTATIONS

The classification of the different sorts of games was one of the first projects for these pioneers of game theory. In these classifications are found none of the main categories familiar to contemporary theoreticians (zero-sum games/non-zero-sum games; cooperative games/non-cooperative games and so on). This should not be surprising. These classifications correspond to a preliminary stage in the recognition of a mathematical object starting either with games of chance (Borel) or with a larger definition of parlour games (von Neumann). The preliminary question that inspires this procedure is clearly posed by Borel in his *Traité des probabilités*, when he considers card games in these terms:

> One might ask oneself whether a card game could be the object of purely mathematical considerations. Henri Poincaré maintained that a game of checkers was not truly a mathematical object, because it could only be played on a 64-square board and thus its generalization . . . was impossible . . . If this criterion of possible generalization is considered to be the criterion that will allow us to decide if an object is or is not a mathematical object, then a card game is within the domain of mathematical entities; it is played essentially with $4n$ cards, n ordinarily being 8 or 13, but it is quite easy to conceive of a game played with $4n$ cards, n being any integer, and even of a game played with kn cards, the number of colors no longer being 4 but rather any integer.   (Borel, 1938, pp. 39–40)

However archaic it may seem to us today, this attempt at classification must be re-examined if we are to comprehend where exactly lies the specificity of these game situations which condition a grasping of, and particular a processing of, the players' expectations. Two questions are often confused here: that of identifying the different components of a game, and that of mapping out the different types of games based on the manner in which, in a given game, all or part of its components are combined. The first of these questions is the more important, since the definition of the game which will be retained as the object of the theory depends on it. It will be distinguished from the second question by speaking of it as a game situation.

The comparison of the components of a game in Borel's *Traité des probabilités* and in von Neumann's article of 1928 sheds an interesting light on the similarities and the differences in their approaches. Borel identifies a game situation via three components which have been later systematized by de Possel (1936): hazard (or chance), reason (or calculation), and the ability of the players (or 'ruse'). Von Neumann only sets up two components: chance and the free decision of the players (von Neumann, 1928, 1959, p. 14).

Both men share the idea, as we have seen, that chance and the rational choice of the players constitute two indispensable and irreducible ingredients characterizing all game situations. This shared view leads them to distinguish two main types of game, according to whether it is the first component that predominates, or the other components that occupy the central place: games of 'pure chance' and 'games where chance and the ability of the players intervene', according to Borel; 'games of chance' and 'games of strategy', for von Neumann. Both authors privilege the study of the second category, which has become the object of game theory. This decision was historically determinant because it meant a break with the previous mathematical approach to games, such as is found in particular in Bachelier's work on speculation and on what he called the mathematical theory of *the* game (Bachelier, 1900, 1901). The conclusion of Bachelier's second essay provides the best summary:

> One can conclude from the foregoing that the theory of the game is not only an exercise in analysis, but also presents an especial interest in and of itself, for it makes known to us one of the most curious laws that science has revealed: the law of chance. (Bachelier, 1901, p. 206)[11]

The path followed by Borel and by von Neumann also had as a consequence the focusing of their research on the analysis of the relations between players' strategic choices and the manifestations of chance particular to the game itself, a central question which theoreticians have recently rediscovered after it had been forgotten for nearly a half century.[12]

These similarities must not mask the difference between Borel's classification and that of von Neumann. In order to understand better Borel's presentation, it is useful to go back to the typology that de Possel derived from Borel's three components. De Possel distinguished three types of 'pure games', each of which corresponded to a single one of these components: 'games of pure reflection', 'games of pure chance', and 'games of pure ruse' (de Possel, 1936, pp. 86–8).

This way of proceeding reveals several difficulties when one seeks to apply Borel's categories directly to concrete games. Thus, the game 'Heads or Tails' only belongs to the category of 'games of pure chance' if the number of moves is both finite and known in advance to the players. The game 'Stone, Paper, Scissors' is presented as an example of the category 'games of pure ruse'. But one need only modify it slightly and it no longer belongs to this category. This is so when the hope of gain is no longer identical to the mathematical expectation, which is precisely the result obtained by Borel through the introduction into the game of mixed strategies. These examples show that few parlour games correspond, unequivocally, to the types of 'pure games' constructed according to Borel's categories. One may certainly see in this result a justification of Borel (and also of von Neumann), who proposed as the object of game theory the study of mixed categories rather than of pure categories. But it can also be understood as indicative of the distance separating this theoretical object from concrete parlour games; a fact which Borel and von Neumann would each interpret differently.

It is the existence or the absence of deception (ruse) as a component of game situations which most neatly separates the definitions that Borel and von Neumann associate respectively with the games they study. One's first reaction, faced with this difference, is to think, along with de Possel, that the question of ruse had been definitively solved by von Neumann in favour of his definition of the game of strategy, with the demonstration of the Minimax theorem (de Possel, 1936, p. 119). By taking from the players the possibility of gaining the advantage through discovering the other's strategy, or of taking a risk through revealing oneself, it is irrefutable that von Neumann at the same time eliminated the category of 'games of pure ruse' in the class of two-player zero-sum games. But that does not mean, however, that the players have no possibility to manoeuvre, and consequently it does not mean the complete elimination of deception in games. The results of many games, even zero-sum games, are not independent of the order in which the players have their turns, when this order is not fixed by the rules of the game.[13] The information advantage conferred on the player by the order in which his turn comes amounts to a sort of deception in the larger sense once it results in a deliberate scheme by the player.

The difficulty with the ruse is that it is hard to dissociate it from the other components of the game if its domain is not reduced to the psychological interpretation given to it by Borel. The example of the bluff in a poker game is revealing on this point. It is why one can, *mutatis mutandis*, apply von Neumann's observations on chance to deception. Even taken out of the game by powerful instruments such as the Minimax theorem, deception reappears in other forms, for the very reason that game theory is incomplete. Borel was therefore not entirely wrong to insist on its importance. The later exploration of games of incomplete information, and the role that deception can play in them in the expectations of the players, has retrospectively shown that he was right.

2.5 TOWARDS A REVISION OF THE CONCEPT OF STRATEGY IN THE LIGHT OF THE PLAYERS' MUTUAL EXPECTATIONS

Borel defined a strategy as a code that determines for every possible circumstance exactly what the player should do (pure strategy) or as a precise rule for varying the play (mixed strategy). Von Neumann's definition was almost the same. In addition, von Neumann specified that 'all the information about the notions of participants and the outcome of "draws" is incorporated in the strategy' and then deduced that 'each player must choose his strategy in complete ignorance of the choices of the rest of the players and the results of the "draws"' (von Neumann, [1928] 1959, p. 19). According to the result, the player, at least in a game of perfect information, chooses his strategy with a complete knowledge of the relevant information about

the other players and, at the same time, a complete ignorance of the strategies actually chosen by the others. Borel remained sceptical about the
validity of such an implication, because playing a game consists for players
in varying the rules of the play, which precisely contradicts the notion of
strategy itself based on fixed rules. Von Neumann's interpretation of a
strategy has been accepted by game theorists without discussion. Recently,
however, Borel's objections have reappeared for other considerations.

Reformulated in modern terms, a strategy is a complete contingency plan
which determines for each player every move from the beginning to the end
of the game. Thus, a strategy is in part the result of the player's decision but
in part also, the consequence of his belief about the other player's moves.
The relationship between these two components is dramatically illuminated
in the case of several sequences in a finite game in extensive form. The
example of the well-known centipede game in Figure 2.2 illustrates the
point.

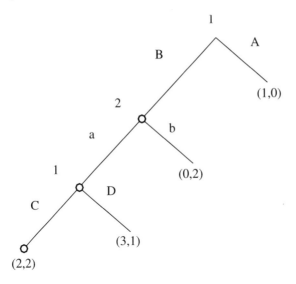

Figure 2.2: The centipede game

Choosing strategy A for player 1 implies that player 2 takes into account
that player 1 could choose B as his strategy. Furthermore, player 1 must
also plan his move if he has to choose at stage 2 between C and D, which
assumes that he has not chosen his best strategy at the beginning of the
game. In other words, the definition of the right strategy logically implies
taking into account mistakes at different levels of expectations. Rubinstein
(1991) pointed out on this basis an inconsistency between the classical

definition of a strategy in game theory inherited from Borel and von Neumann and the process necessarily followed by the players for choosing their strategy. Briefly speaking, the rational expectations incorporated in the definition of players' strategies, whatever its precise content, are intricately linked to the treatment of mistakes by the other players. Unfortunately, game theory, in spite of a few tentatives (Aumann, 1992)[14] has not up to now provided a clear analysis of what exactly is an expected mistake. Does it mean a lack of information or of rationality; and, on the second hypothesis, does irrationality concern each sub-game (or move) or the game as a whole?

Such basic questions lead back to the beginning of game theory. Borel in his colourful style even evoked the necessary combination of incoherence of mind and intelligence of reasoning (Borel, 1921). Von Neumann, for his part, bound players' rationality to the defensive posture. Anyway, rationality, even common knowledge, is not by itself a sufficient condition for harmonizing mutual expectations.

NOTES

1. Having maintained that, for the most part, Savage's doctrine is equally applicable to the situations of interaction which characterize games, Aumann takes care to specify that Savage's analysis is only valuable within what Savage calls the 'small world'. Several categories of games, like stochastic games and repeated games, are clearly not assimilated to a small world in Savage's sense of the term. What is in question here relates in a more fundamental way to the relevance of the basic concepts defined in Savage's small world (states of the world, actions and consequences) to the representation of a game situation.
2. Borel devotes a somewhat sympathetic analysis to Keynes's *Treatise on Probability* (1921) in a long article published in the *Revue philosophique* in 1924. This article is taken up again in note 11 of the last volume of Borel's *Traité de probabilité*, entitled *Valeur pratique et philosophie des probabilités*, 1939, pp. 134–46.
3. Incidentally, Keynes does not take into account any such situation in *A Treatise on Probability* (1921), which was surprising to Borel.
4. On this point, see Sorin (1995).
5. It is not specified that the payments distributed to the players at the end of the game are monetary. Von Neumann clearly distinguishes in his definition of strategic games between the results of the game (outcomes) and the payments to the players (payments). While the former are determined by chance and/or by the free decision of the players, the second may be calculated based on a determined rule (von Neumann, 1928, 1959, p. 14). Such a distinction is especially relevant to the parlour games extensively studied by the founder of game theory.
6. The similarity of this result makes clear the strategic equivalence between the distribution of probabilities introduced by chance in a game under intensive form and that associated with mixed strategies.
7. The origin of this difficulty must be sought in the idea of a conditional rationality which would take the form of *hypothetical* probabilities attached by each player to the strategies of the other players (Hammond, 1996, pp. 36–7).
8. No order can be defined between 'Stone', 'Paper' and 'Scissors'. This property has

been used when the game has been studied in a dynamic perspective (Maynard Smith, 1982).
9. Borel (1938, pp. 89–103).
10. Borel himself wrote, in collaboration with Chéron, the *Théorie mathématique du bridge à la portée de tous* [Mathematical Theory of Bridge for Non-specialists] (1940). The game of bridge is a main reference for Borel. The point must be stressed for understanding some of the difficulties pointed out by Borel to formalize the player's expectations in a game situation.
11. Let us notice that game is then used in the singular.
12. The introduction of perturbations into the framework of repeated games constitutes an active domain of recent research. Cf. Sorin (1995).
13. Ville has, in an indirect way, already shown this relation between the probabilities of gain and the conventions defined on the order in which the players play (Borel, 1938, pp. 34–7). The advantage procured by the player who goes last, from the fact that he knows the strategy effectively chosen by the other, is at the origin of the *minorant* and *majorant* games introduced by von Neumann and Morgenstern in *Theory of Games and Economic Behavior* (1944, pp. 100–5) in order to facilitate the interpretation of the Minimax theorem. This idea was generalized by Howard (1971) by means of the metagame concept. On this question generally, cf. Schmidt (1995).
14. In order to take into account 'irrationality' in game theory framework, Aumann uses the tool of the metagames, directly derived from a von Neumann idea (see *majorant* and *minorant*), (Aumann, 1992; Dasgupta *et al.* pp. 214–27).

REFERENCES

Aumann, R.J. (1987), 'Game theory', in J. Eatwell, M. Milgate and P. Newmann (eds), *The New Palgrave: A Dictionary of Economics*, London: Macmillan.
Aumann, R.J. (1992), 'Irrationality in game theory', in P. Dasgupta, D. Gale, O. Hart and E. Maskin (eds), *Economic Analysis, Markets and Games*, Cambridge, MA: MIT Press.
Bachelier, L. (1900), 'Théorie de la spéculation', *Annales scientifiques de l'Ecole Normale Supérieure*, 3ème série, 17, 21–86.
Bachelier, L. (1901), 'Théorie mathématique du jeu', *Annales scientifiques de l'Ecole Normale Supérieure* 3ème série, 18, 143–210.
Binmore, K. (1993), 'De-Bayesing game theory', in K. Binmore, A. Kirman and P. Tani (eds), *Frontiers of game theory*, Cambridge: The MIT Press, pp. 320–39.
Binmore, K. (1996), Rationality and backward induction, Center for Economic Learning and Social Evolution, University College London, mimeo.
Borel, E. (1921), 'La théorie du jeu et les équations, intégrales à noyau symétrique gauche', reproduced as Note III in *Eléments de la théorie des probabilités*, Paris: Librairie Scientifique, Hermann.
Borel, E. ([1921] 1924), 'Sur les jeux où interviennent le hasard et l'habilité des joueurs', reproduced as Note IV in *Eléments de la théorie des probabilités*, Paris: Librairie Scientifique, Hermann.
Borel, E. (1927), 'Sur les systèmes de formes linéaires à déterminant symétrique gauche et la théorie générale du jeu', *Comptes rendus de l'Académie des Sciences*, 184, 52–3.
Borel, E. (1938), *Applications de la théorie des probabilités aux jeux de hasard*, Paris: Gauthier-Villars.

Borel, E. (1939), *Valeur pratique et philosophie des probabilités*, Paris: Gauthier-Villars.

Borel, E. and A. Cheron (1940), *Théorie mathématique du bridge à la portée de tous*, Paris: Gauthier-Villars.

Dasgupta, P., D. Gale and O. Hart (1992), *Economic Analysis of Markets and Games*, Cambridge, MA: MIT Press.

de Possel, R. (1936), 'Sur la théorie mathématique des jeux de hasard et de réflexion', in H. Moulin (ed.) *Fondation de la théorie des jeux*, Paris: Hermann.

Dimand, R.W. and M.A. Dimand (1996), *A History of Game Theory*, vol. 1, London: Routledge.

Frechet, M. (1953), 'Emile Borel, initiator of the theory of psychological games and its applications', *Econometrica*, 2, 95–127.

Hammond, P.J. (1993), 'Aspects of rationalizable behavior', in K. Binmore, A. Kirman and P. Tani (eds), *Frontiers of game theory*, Cambridge: The MIT Press, pp. 227–305.

Hammond, P.J. (1996), 'Consequentialism, structural rationality, and game theory', in K. Arrow, E. Colombatto, M. Perlman and C. Schmidt (eds), *The Foundation of Rational Behaviour in Economics*, London: Macmillan.

Howard, N. (1971), *Paradoxes of Rationality: Theory of metagames and political behavior*, Cambridge, MA: MIT Press

Keynes, J.M. (1921), *A Treatise on Probabilities*, London: Macmillan; reprinted in *The Collected Writings of John Maynard Keynes*, vol. VIII, London: Macmillan, 1973.

Maynard Smith, J. (1982), *Evolution and the theory of games*, Cambridge: Cambridge University Press.

Nash, J. (1950), 'Non-cooperative game theory', unpublished PhD thesis, Princeton: Princeton University.

Osborne, M.J. and A. Rubinstein, (1994), *A Course in Game Theory*, Cambridge, MA: MIT Press.

Rubinstein, A. (1991), 'Comments on the interpretation of game theory', *Econometrica*, 59, 909–924.

Savage, L.S. (1954), *The Foundations of Statistics*, New York: John Wiley.

Schmidt, C. (1995), 'Les Héritiers hétérodoxes de von Neumann et Morgenstern', *Revue d'economie politique*, 4, 560–582.

Sorin, S. (1995), 'Bluff et réputation', *Revue d'economie politique*, 4, 583–600.

Ville, J. (1938a), 'Sur la théorie générale des jeux où intervient l'habilité des joueurs', in *Applications aux jeux de hasard*, Paris: Gauthier-Villars, pp. 105–13.

Ville, J. (1938b), 'Etude d'un jeu dissymétrique où l'avantage est donné à chaque coup, au perdant du coup précédent', in *Applications aux jeux de hasard*, Paris: Gauthier-Villars, pp. 34–7.

von Neumann, J. (1928), 'Zur Theorie der Gesellschafsspiele', *Mathematische Annalen*, 100; English translation, 'On the theory of games of strategy', in vol. IV, A.W. Tucker and R.D. Luce (eds), *Contributions to the Theory of Games*, Princeton, NJ: Princeton University Press, pp. 13–42.

von Neumann, J. and O. Morgenstern, (1944), *Theory of Games and Economic Behavior*, Princeton, NJ: Princeton University Press.

3. Common knowledge and the information revealed through prices: some conjectures

Gabriel Desgranges and Roger Guesnerie

INTRODUCTION

Information-revealing equilibria[1] are here examined in a specific perspective: can the knowledge of these equilibria be derived from common knowledge of the underlying model? We consider the question within a simplified setting:

- Uncertainty bears upon the value of some random variable θ.
- There is a continuum of agents (each agent is infinitesimal) but they are divided into several groups. Each group may receive one piece of information on θ,[2] the same for everybody in the group.[3]
- Agents consider buying an asset. Their notional demand for the asset, when its price is p, is $E(\theta) - p$, where $E(.)$ denotes the expected value of a random variable.
- The market works as follows: agents simultaneously submit a demand curve (that is, a function of p) to an auctioneer. The auctioneer then computes the equilibrium price and allocates the asset, the net supply of which is taken as being equal to zero (without loss of generality).

The problem is extremely simple: we assume that the model is common knowledge and we wonder whether it implies, when the agents' rationality is also common knowledge, that an information-revealing equilibrium is also common knowledge.[4]

We proceed to the analysis of this model by successively considering three cases, whose characteristics will be defined later:

- 'sharp' information with many informed agents;
- 'sharp' information with few informed agents;
- 'diffuse' information.

3.1 'SHARP' INFORMATION WITH MANY INFORMED AGENTS

Information is to be said 'sharp' (see later for more precise discussion) when knowledge of it gives 'sufficient' confidence to the agents to base their actions on it. An extreme and clear case of when information is 'sharp' is when there is only one informed group that exactly knows θ.[5]

Take first the case when θ can only take two values, let us say R (good news, that stimulates demand) and V (bad news). Assume that α per cent of the agents observe θ, when $(1 - \alpha)$ per cent observe nothing.

It is easy to describe a *mental process* (which only relies on common knowledge assumptions) that will *trigger co-ordination* on the price-revealing equilibrium.

Step 1

- If θ, it is a dominant strategy for the informed agents to announce the demand curve $\theta - p$.
- Uninformed agents' supply is any function $\varphi(p)$ such that:

$$V - p \leq \varphi(p) \leq R - p \qquad (3.1)$$

It follows rather straightforwardly that when $\theta = R$ (or, respectively, V) the equilibrium price cannot be smaller than $p' = \alpha R + (1 - \alpha)V$, (respectively, higher than $p'' = \alpha V + (1 - \alpha)R$) (see Figure 3.1).

Step 2

- Given an understanding of step 1, the uninformed agents know that an equilibrium price in the interval $[p_v, p'']$, (resp. $[p', p_R]$), signals for certain the occurrence of V (resp. R). Their best response is a demand curve that coincides with $V - p$ (resp. $R - p$) on the first (resp. second) interval. Note that with $\alpha > 1/2$, then $p'' < p'$.
- This fact is sufficient to have an excess demand curve as in Figure 3.2(a) (in the case of V) or as in Figure 3.2(b) (in the case of R) and to induce the price-revealing equilibrium: p_v if V, p_R if R.

Then, as argued by Desgranges (1994), and with the terminology of Guesnerie (1992), the following is true:

1. The full information price equilibrium is strongly rational whenever $\alpha > 1/2$.
2. The argument extends to the case where θ can take M values when α is large enough.[6]

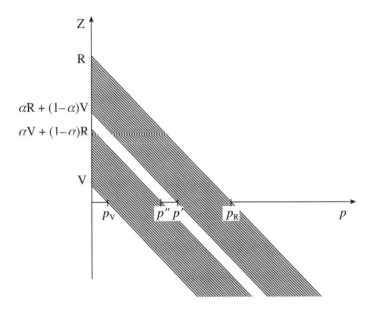

Figure 3.1: Possible aggregate demands in states V and R after step 1

With the neat case we are considering here, it is reassuring that with many informed agents the equilibrium can be guessed. It is, however, not clear that with few informed agents the result still holds: this is discussed next.

3.2 'SHARP' INFORMATION WITH FEW INFORMED AGENTS

We come back to the case where θ can take two values: V and R, but now with $\alpha \leq 1/2$. A first difficulty, which was overlooked before, is that the price-revealing equilibrium may not be uniquely defined. For example, in the case under consideration, the above p' becomes smaller than p'' so that if, for example, a significant part of the uninformed agents mimic the R-informed agents for $p \geq p'$ (Figure 3.3), a fact that cannot be ruled out from our mental process, then, if V obtains, the aggregate demand will exhibit two equilibria, p_v and one between p' and p'' (Figure 3.4 with the second equilibrium price exactly equal to p'').

The difficulty here is not only a difficulty with the mental process; it is a difficulty with the equilibrium itself. It occurs because, in order to clarify the strategic aspects of the situation, we have asked the agents to submit explicit demand curves.[7]

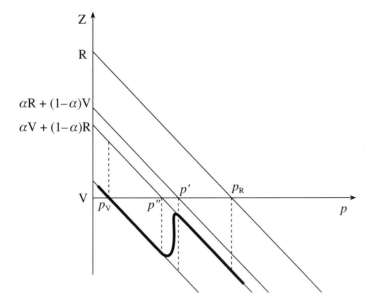

Figure 3.2(a): An example of aggregate demand in state V after step 2

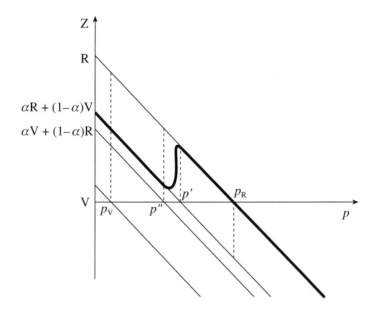

Figure 3.2(b): An example of aggregate demand in state R after step 2

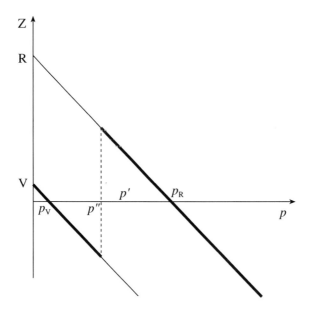

Figure 3.3: An example of individual demand

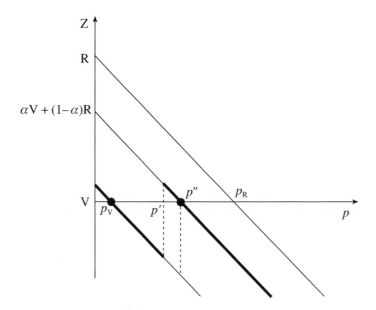

Figure 3.4: An example of multiple equilibrium prices in state V

The reader may convince him- or herself that there is no way to resolve the difficulty (for the viewpoint of the unambiguous existence of the revealing equilibrium as well as for the co-ordination problem) without stating a clear selection rule, credibly announced by the auctioneer.

We then assume:

(A) *When there are several equilibria, the auctioneer always chooses the 'left' one.*

This is not enough, however: in this simple non-noisy setting we need to avoid a certain number of problems associated with the fact that the best response of agents may not be single-valued (implicitly, we have not allowed them to creep in previously, but they have to be faced now). We then assume:[8]

(B) *The auctioneer only accepts demand curves belonging to the following class*:

- they are continuous except at a finite number of points where there are 'upward' jumps;
- at each point where they are continuous, they have slope -1.

The 'eductive' argument starts as follows:

Step 1

Informed agents 'play' R or V.

Non-informed agents keep in their strategy set any function φ meeting (B) such that $V - p \leq \varphi(p) \leq R - p$.

The equilibrium prices p' and p'' can be defined as above, but, as already argued, we have now $p' \leq p''$.

Step 2

As above, eliminating weakly dominated strategies, the non-informed agents keep demand functions φ such that:

$$\varphi(p) = V - p \text{ for } p < p',$$
$$\varphi(p) = R - p \text{ for } p > p'',$$

and φ satisfies (B) in between (when, at this stage, the equilibrium price can 'signal' either R or V).

Step 3

Given the remaining strategies, and given the selection rule (A), it is necessarily the case that p_v obtains, if V occurs. Then, given (B), the uninformed agents eliminate responses that do not coincide with $R - p$ over $[p',p'']$.

This terminates the argument.

Proposition 1 The fully revealing equilibrium is strongly rational, whatever the proportion of uninformed agents.

We conjecture that the proposition holds true:

- with a finite number of θ: the argument is along the same lines, but requires more iterations;
- with noise with a single peaked density: the argument has, however, to be significantly modified; prices, instead of being impossible, are implausible and the upper bounds of their probability of occurrence have to be computed at each iteration.

It is remarkable, and satisfactory on intuitive grounds, that the difficulty of guessing the equilibrium increases with the proportion of non-informed agents and with the number of signals that can be received by the informed agents.

3.3 'DIFFUSE' INFORMATION

Take the case where there are three groups of equal size; each group either receives R or V, but the signal may differ across groups. Hence, there are four states of aggregate information: RRR, RRV, RVV, VVV. Associated with these states are four numbers that are supposed to decrease from RRR to VVV, the expected value of θ in each of the aggregate state.

The eductive argument proceeds as follows:

1. For each state of aggregate uncertainty, consider the best response strategies of each group: if R is observed (resp. V), then the non-dominated strategies satisfy:

   VVR (resp. VVV) $- p \leq \varphi(p) \leq$ RRR (resp. VRR) $- p$

   Then it follows, as previously, that in any such state there is a subset of prices that cannot be equilibrium prices, and then that prices in this subset cannot signal such a state. For example, with the notation of Figure 3.5, the reader can easily check that after the first iteration it is common knowledge that:

AD is impossible if RRR,
AC   "   "   " VRR,
AB   "   "   " VVR,
EH   "   "   " VVV,
EG   "   "   " VVR,
EF   "   "   " VRR.

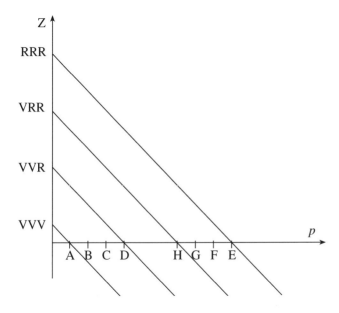

Figure 3.5: Intervals of prices after step 1

2. The argument then goes on by exploiting the elimination that is triggered by the informational consequences of the first step. The process will stop once the equilibria generated from the strategy restrictions of step t do not trigger new restrictions.
3. Consider now any subset of strategies φ that have the following properties:

$$\text{for } p \in [DH], \quad VVR - p \leq \varphi(p) \leq VRR - p$$

and this independently of whether R or V has been observed (as suggested in Figure 3.6).

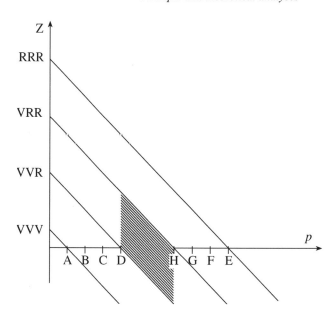

Figure 3.6: Demands sustaining equilibrium prices in (DH)

4. We claim that if the strategy of step t, for each agent, has this property, then it keeps this property for any later $t' \geq t$. The reason is the following: first, given this strategy set, the fact that a price belongs to DH is uninformative on whether VVR or VRR has obtained; second, if VRR, no agent (group) can guess (and know that the others are in the same position) whether VVR or VRR has occurred (when the fact RRR or VVV has not occurred is known by some participants). It follows that any price in DH is a possible equilibrium price, if VVR or if VRR, and hence that the next step strategy set still satisfies . . .

It follows from the argument that the eductive argument leads only to partial revelation of information: A (resp. E) reveals VVV (resp. RRR).

Information, which is here shared by three groups, may be called diffuse.[9]

3.4 CONCLUSION

The above analysis of a simple problem shows that it is possible to guess price-revealing equilibria, along the lines of the procedures that refer to common knowledge arguments. However, it suggests that successes of eductive learning are unlikely, unless information is sharp in a sense, a first assessment of which has been attempted here.

NOTES

1. The theory of price revealing equilibria has attracted much attention in the literature, particularly from the mid-1970s: Grossmann (1976, 1981); Grossmann and Stiglitz (1980); Radner (1979) are the starting points of a large literature. Only a small segment of the literature has been concerned with learning, but not, to the best of our knowledge, with the kind of 'eductive' learning under consideration here. This concern, however, intersects with the concerns of Dutta and Morris (1997).
2. Information may have been obtained at random, so that agents who hold it are not known from the others. However, their size has to be known.
   It might even be assumed that individual demand responds to unobservable shocks, as soon as these shocks are idiosyncratic: what matters for the analysis is the fact that the aggregate demand of the set of informed agents is known.
3. The purpose of this modelling option is to reconcile price-taking behaviour and absence of informational monopoly power with the fact that individual information is not infinitesimal.
4. Here, we deliberately ignore some technical difficulties, due to the face in particular that agents are infinitesimal (so that, often, no strategy is strongly dominated). We conjecture that they are artefacts of a stylization (adding a small noise in the model would alleviate the conceptual difficulties, at the price of increasing technicalities) which gives easy access to the intuition.
5. For our purpose, and in the present setting where only the expectation of θ matters, knowing θ or observing a signal that gives information on its mean does not make any difference to the analysis.
6. In the case where the values are equidistant, then the condition is $\alpha > 1 - 1/M$.
7. Traditional theory on price-revealing equilibria was initially very silent on the strategic framework it was using and some of the most important results (for example, the 'generic' existence of fully revealing equilibria; Radner, 1979) seem difficult to interpret in a fully specified strategic setting. The option taken here (agents announce demand curves) is the most natural, particularly in view of generalizations of the argument.
8. Assumption (B) allows us to properly define demand curves in any context. However, given Assumption (A), it is no longer necessary to obtain the results stated here.
9. The situation is different with two groups, a case that is outside the scope of our analysis.

REFERENCES

Desgranges, G. (1994), 'Stabilité divinatoire d'un équilibre à anticipations rationelles en asymétrie d'information', unpublished.
Dutta, J. and S. Morris (1997), 'The revelation of information and self-fulfilling beliefs', *Journal of Economic Theory*, 73, 231–44.
Grossman, S. (1976), 'On the efficiency of competitive stock markets where traders have diverse information', *Journal of Finance*, 31, 573–85.
Grossman, S. (1981), 'Rational expectations under asymmetric information', *Review of Economic Studies*, 48, 541–89.
Grosmann, S. and J. Stiglitz (1980), 'On the impossibility of informationally efficient markets', *American Economic Review*, 70, 393–408.

Guesnerie, R. (1992), 'An exploration of the eductive justifications of the rational expectations hypothesis', *American Economic Review*, 82, 1254–78.

Radner, R. (1979), 'Rational expectations equilibrium: generic existence and the information revealed by prices', *Econometrica*, 47, 655–78.

4. Private information, public information, expectations and prices in financial markets

Damien Besancenot

INTRODUCTION

Since the seminal work proposed by Grossman (1976), equilibrium prices in financial markets are generally assumed to reflect some information. Because agents use their information to choose their portfolio, the resulting equilibrium price captures the available information and becomes a new information source. In turn rational agents must take into account the informational content of these prices.

When speculation is driven by the short run, one may, however, question whether all information is effectively revealed by prices. As Keynes (1936) showed through his famous example of the beauty contest, since future prices rely on the behaviour of future operators, a speculator trying to forecast a price must guess the behaviour of his followers instead of computing the intrinsic value of the asset. In this case, prices may be independent of fundamental values.

Hence, in models with speculative bubbles (Harrisson and Kreps, 1978; Tirole, 1982) or in sunspot equilibria (Azariadis, 1981; Cass and Shell, 1983), prices move away from the fundamental value because market operators believe that the expectation scheme to be used by their followers will not only refer to the asset's intrinsic value. By adopting the generally accepted model, they allow the self-realization of this model. As a result, the price may systematically diverge from the intrinsic value.

When traders explicitly base their price expectations on the fundamental value of the asset, the relation between the equilibrium prices and the asset's intrinsic value holds. However, nothing ensures that all the available information will be used by traders. As speculators influence one another, information may be lost and the price may move away from the value that an auctioneer, using all the information, would naturally set (Orléan, 1995; Devenow and Welch, 1996).

In fact, as future price relies on future expectations, speculators must forecast the content of these expectations. They have to guess today which information will be used tomorrow. Forecasting a price thus requires a reliable estimation of the information that will be used by future generations of speculators (Brennan, 1990; Froot *et al.*, 1992; Hirshleifer *et al.*, 1994).

Information is worthwhile if its future influence on the market is certain. But, when information is private, nothing ensures that a piece of private information will be made public. Therefore, it may be rational to neglect some information about the value of an asset: if the future price is not supposed to take the information into account, this information does not bring any element on this price and must therefore be neglected today. Finally, taking the behaviours of future operators into account leads to a new paradox about information: the rational use by a speculator of private information may consist in ignoring it partially or totally.

As an illustration, consider a speculative market with overlapping generations of speculators. Each generation is divided into two groups of identical size with asymmetric information. As the generations of the first group (group A) have private information which leads them to estimate the value of a risky asset at 120 CU, the generations of the second group (group B) have only a part of group A's information and estimate this value at 100 CU. At each period, the members of the old generation sell their assets to the new generation at the newcomers' average expectations of the future price. Which price should then prevail if speculators make rational expectations?

If expectations rely on the asset's intrinsic value, the equilibrium price resulting from the two evaluations should logically be 110 CU. However, the rationality of group A's operators prevents the price being set at this level. Since the information allocation remains the same from period to period, the members of group A who know both the public and the private information are able to expect that the future price will also be 110 CU. With this new expectation of group A's agents, the price should be set at 105 CU. In this case, however, the self-reference principle leads the rational speculator to consider that future generations of group A will also update their price expectation to 110 CU. As the future price should therefore be 105 CU, this induces speculators to update their expectations again, and so on.

The fixed point of this updating process is achieved when agents of group A act as if they completely neglect their private information. Then, the equilibrium price, which is therefore 100 CU, only reflects the common information held by everybody in the market. No additional information is captured in this price. *In this rational expectations equilibrium, the price does not carry any private information.*

This paper suggests a formal generalization of this example. It reveals the existence of a rational expectations equilibrium in which private information is completely neglected.

We consider a speculative market of an asset which pays no dividend. In a linear model (Hirshleifer *et al.*, 1994), it is shown that the holders of private information concerning the intrinsic value of the asset must rationally forecast a gap between their personal estimation of the asset and the expectation of the future price. Since someone must neglect a part of their private information to make a correct forecast, we verify that equilibria with partial use of information may exist. Moreover, even when speculators take into account the informational content of price, the equilibrium price driven by rational expectations will only reflect the public information set.

This result leads to a discussion about the conditions wherein the use of private information makes sense. It will be checked that all information about the content of the future public information set is useful, but that only this information can be used. In the case of insider trading, the possession of a piece of information before its public announcement gives an advantage. Likewise, an information provider who tries to sell private information has to convince the buyers that this information will become common knowledge in the near future. In these two cases, private information may be useful today only because it will be public tomorrow.

This paper is organized as follows: section 4.1 presents the general assumptions of the model; section 4.2 characterizes the rational expectations equilibrium; section 4.3 studies the particular situation when information is useful to its holder; and the last section concludes the paper.

4.1 GENERAL ASSUMPTIONS

Let us consider a perfect competitive market. On this market a perfectly divisible asset is traded which involves a property right on the capital of a firm. By assumption, the firm pays no dividend.

4.1.1 Traders on the Market

Two kinds of traders operate on the market: investors and speculators. Both are price takers.

Investors are the global owners of the capital of the firm. They buy or sell the assets according to the evolution of their cash management. At each period, their financial operations lead to a net excess supply or demand which will have to be balanced by the speculators.

Speculators' activity is mono-periodic: at date t, a new generation of speculators enters the market; according to the market price and their information, they buy or sell the asset. At date $t+1$, they close their position and leave the market while a new generation of speculators enters the market.

Each generation of speculator is composed of identical risk-averse agents. The risk-aversion coefficient is assumed to be constant and equal to 1. At date t, the demand function of a speculator i is: $x_t^i(P(t), R^i(t+1))$. This demand function increases with the spread between $R^i(t+1)$, the estimation of the future return of the asset (the price of the asset at date $t+1$) and the current price $P(t)$. Demand decreases with $\sigma_i^2(t)$ measuring at date t the variance of the random expectation error:[1]

$$x_t^i(P(t), R^i(t+1)) = \{R^i(t+1) - P(t)\}/\sigma_i^2(t) \tag{4.1}$$

4.1.2 Information and Expectations

The fundamental value of the asset, F_t, follows a random walk:

$$F_t = F_{t-1} + e_t \text{ with } e \text{ iid and } e \rightsquigarrow \mathcal{N}(0, \sigma_e^2) \tag{4.2}$$

In order to estimate this fundamental value, speculators use public information (that is, *common knowledge*) and private information.

At date t, the public information set is Ω_t^p. It includes the complete collection of past and present prices, the initial fundamental value of the asset F_0 and partial estimations $\{\bar{e}_j\}_{j=1}^t$ of past realizations of $\{e_j\}_{j=1}^t$. The relation between $\bar{e}_j$ and e_j is given by the following equation:

$$e_j = \bar{e}_j + \epsilon_j, \text{ for all } j = 1, \ldots, t \text{ with: } \begin{cases} \bar{e} \rightsquigarrow \mathcal{N}(0, \sigma_{\bar{e}}^2) \\ \epsilon \rightsquigarrow \mathcal{N}(0, \sigma_\epsilon^2) \end{cases} \tag{4.3}$$

where $\bar{e}$ and ϵ are two independent random variables, normally distributed with zero mean and respective variance $\sigma_{\bar{e}}^2$ and σ_ϵ^2. Given the public information $\bar{e}_j$, for $j = 1, \ldots, t$, e_j may be considered as a realization of a random variable, normally distributed, with mean $\bar{e}_j$ and variance σ_ϵ^2.

The public information set at date t is:[2]

$$\Omega_t^p = \{F_0, \{P(j)\}_{j=1}^t, \{\bar{e}_j\}_{j=1}^t\} \tag{4.4}$$

Speculators may obtain some more information about the intrinsic value of the firm from an information provider. This provider – whose characteristics will be denoted with a superscript a – computes the estimation of some realizations of $\{e_j\}_{j=1}^t$ and sells this private information on the market. Private information is costly and a fixed share of the speculators buy the information.[3] The costly information, μ_j^a, is a noisy signal of the realization of e_j with:

$$\mu_j^a = e_j + \theta_j^a, \text{ for all } j = 1, \ldots, t; \text{ with: } \theta^a \rightsquigarrow \mathcal{N}(0, \sigma_\theta^2) \qquad (4.5)$$

θ^a is a random variable, independent of e, normally distributed, with zero mean and finite variance σ_θ^2. We assume that everybody knows the characteristics of the distribution of $\bar{e}$, θ^a and ϵ.

In order to simplify the general problem we assume that the information provider computes a single piece of information at date $t = 1$. At date t, a buyer of the private information – called hereafter an *informed trader* – has the information set Ω_t^a.

$$\Omega_t^a = \{\Omega_t^p, \mu_1^a\}, \forall t \geq 1 \qquad (4.6)$$

According to their own information set, each speculator is able to compute a conditional expected fundamental value of the firm. It is now possible to define the expected returns. Let $R_\alpha^a(t+1)$ denote the return expected by an informed trader and $R^p(t+1)$ the expectation of a speculator using the public information. We assume that $R^i(t+1)$ has the following general shape:

$$\begin{cases} R_\alpha^a(t+1) = \alpha E[F_{t+1}|\Omega_t^a] + (1-\alpha)E[F_{t+1}|\Omega_t^p] \\ R^p(t+1) = E[F_{t+1}|\Omega_t^p] \end{cases} \qquad (4.7)$$

When agents compute their expected return, they refer explicitly to the fundamental value. However, the expected return takes different values according to the importance given to private information. For an informed trader, α measures the extent to which private information is used. This parameter allows the adjustment of the relative weights of private and public information in the estimation of the expected return. Of course, as far as possible, speculators will tend to choose $\alpha = 1$ and will use all the available information.

4.1.3 The Equilibrium Price

At each period, the demand expressed by investors corresponds to the total value of the assets on the market increased by a random excess of demand.

Let D_t denote the value of this excess of demand at date t, D_t is the realization of a random variable normally distributed with zero mean. This excess demand is balanced by speculators. The market is composed of N speculators and the equilibrium condition $\sum_{i=1}^{N} n_t^i(P(t), R^i(t+1)) = -D_t$ leads to the price:

$$P(t) = \sum_{i=1}^{N} c_i(t) R^i(t+1) + \phi_t \text{ with} \begin{cases} c_i(t) = \dfrac{1}{\sigma_i^2(t)} \left[\sum_{j=1}^{N} \dfrac{1}{\sigma_j^2(t)} \right]^{-1} \\[4mm] \phi_t = D_t \left[\sum_{j=1}^{N} \dfrac{1}{\sigma_j^2(t)} \right]^{-1} \end{cases} \quad (4.8)$$

The equilibrium price is thus a linear combination – with $\sum_{i=1}^{N} c_i(t) = 1$ – of the expected returns of speculators. The excess of demand by investors induces an independent random perturbation ϕ, normally distributed with zero mean and variance $\sigma_\phi^2(t)$. Finally, let $c_a(t)$ denote the weight on the market of these informed traders, $(1 - c_a(t))$ is the weight of operators who use only public information; these weights are assumed to be computable by everyone. The equilibrium price may be written as:

$$P_\alpha(t) = c_a(t) R_\alpha^a(t+1) + (1 - c_a(t)) R^p(t+1) + \phi_t, \text{ with:} \begin{cases} c_a(t) \in]0, 1[\\ \phi \leadsto \mathcal{N}(0, \sigma_\phi^2(t)) \end{cases} \quad (4.9)$$

4.2   PRICE SYSTEM AND RATIONAL EXPECTATIONS

In order to avoid the analysis of any informational content of past prices, the argument will start from the first day of pricing, that is, at date $t = 1$. By induction, the results of this section may be easily generalized.

4.2.1   First period

Let us assume that, at date $t = 1$, the informed speculators choose $\alpha = 1$. Their expected return is thus: $R_{\alpha=1}^a(2) = E[F_2|\Omega_1^a] = E[F_1|\Omega_1^a]$. Following the work of Hirshleifer *et al.* (1994), we shall assume that speculators compute the expected fundamental value of the asset from a linear combination of the available information: $\Omega_1^a = \{F_0, \bar{e}_1, \mu_1^a, P_{\alpha=1}(1)\}$, and $\Omega_1^p = \{F_0, \bar{e}_1, P_{\alpha=1}(1)\}$ with:

$$\begin{aligned} E[F_1|\Omega_1^a] &= F_0 + B_0 + B_1\bar{e}_1 + B_2\mu_1^a + B_3 P_{\alpha=1}(1) \\ E[F_1|\Omega_1^p] &= F_0 + A_0 + A_1\bar{e}_1 + A_2 P_{\alpha=1}(1) \end{aligned} \quad (4.10)$$

The resulting equilibrium is then linear and the conjecture is self-fulfilling.

Proposition 1: At date $t=1$, the random variables in the sets $\{\bar{e}_1, P_{\alpha=1}(1)\}$ and $\{\bar{e}_1, \mu_1^a, P_{\alpha=1}(1)\}$ are jointly normal. The conditional expected fundamental values are linear combinations of the available signals.

Proof: Given equation (4.10), we have:

$$\begin{cases} E[e_1|\Omega_1^p] = E[e_1|\bar{e}_1, P_{\alpha=1}(1)] = A_0 + A_1\bar{e}_1 + A_2 P_{\alpha=1}(1) \\ E[e_1|\Omega_1^q] = E[e_1|\bar{e}_1, \mu_1^a, P_{\alpha=1}(1)] = B_0 + B_1\bar{e}_1 + B_2\mu_1^a + B_3 P_{\alpha=1}(1) \end{cases} \quad (4.11)$$

The equilibrium price $P_{\alpha=1}(1)$ may then be written as:

$$\begin{aligned} P_{\alpha=1}(1) &= c_a(1)R_{\alpha=1}^a(2) + (1-c_a(1))R^p(2) + \phi_1 \\ &= c_a(1)\{F_0 + B_0 + B_1\bar{e}_1 + B_2\mu_1^a + B_3 P_{\alpha=1}(1)\} \quad (4.12) \\ &\quad + (1-c_a(1))\{F_0 + A_0 + A_1\bar{e}_1 + A_2 P_{\alpha=1}(1)\} + \phi_1 \end{aligned}$$

It follows that:

$$\begin{aligned} P_{\alpha=1}(1) &= \frac{F_0 + c_a(1)[B_0 + B_1\bar{e}_1 + B_2(\bar{e}_1 + \epsilon_1 + \theta_1^a)]}{1 - (1-c_a(1))A_2 - c_a(1)B_3} \\ &\quad + \frac{(1-c_a(1))(A_0 + A_1\bar{e}_1) + \phi_1}{1 - (1-c_a(1))A_2 - c_a(1)B_3} \end{aligned} \quad (4.13)$$

The price $P_{\alpha=1}(1)$ can be obtained by a linear combination of the basic random variables $\{\bar{e}_1, \epsilon_1, \theta_1^a, \phi_1\}$. The vector $\{e_1, \bar{e}_1, \mu_1^a, P_{\alpha=1}(1)\}$ has a joint normal distribution. The conditional expectation of e_1 – and by extension of F_1 – is then defined as a linear combination of the available information.■

If Ω denotes a set of normally distributed signals and x an additional signal of the same nature, the law of iterated projections implies (Sargent, 1979):

$$E[e_1|\Omega, x] = E[e_1|\Omega] + \eta(x - E[x|\Omega]) \quad (4.14)$$

with:

$$\eta = \frac{E[(x - E[x|\Omega])(e_1 - E[e_1|\Omega])]}{E[(x - E[x|\Omega])^2]} \quad (4.15)$$

For informed traders, the application of this law leads to:

$$\begin{cases} B_0 = 0 \\ B_1 = \sigma_\theta^2/(\sigma_\epsilon^2 + \sigma_\theta^2) \\ B_2 = 1 - B_1 \\ B_3 = 0 \end{cases} \quad \text{i.e.: } E[F_1|\Omega_1^a] = F_0 + B_1\bar{e}_1 + (1 - B_1)\mu_1^a \tag{4.16}$$

For informed traders, the equilibrium price does not reveal any additional information on the value of e_1. Their estimation of the fundamental value relies only on the public signals F_0 and $\bar{e}_1$ and on the private information μ_1^a. For speculators who do not have the private signal, the price reveals an additional piece of information about the fundamental value of the asset. Equation (4.13) shows that the price $P_{\alpha=1}(1)$ – correlated with the private information $\mu_1^q = \bar{e}_1 + \epsilon_1 + \theta_1^q$ – presents an informational content. Then:

$$E[e_1|\Omega_1^p] = E[e_1|\bar{e}_1, P_{\alpha=1}(1)]$$

$$= E[e_1|\bar{e}_1] + \eta(P_{\alpha=1}(1) - E[P_{\alpha=1}(1)|\bar{e}_1])$$

$$= \bar{e}_1 + \eta\left[P_{\alpha=1}(1) - \frac{F_0 + c_a(1)\bar{e}_1 + (1 - c_a(1))(A_0 + A_1\bar{e}_1)}{1 - (1 - c_a(1))A_2}\right] \tag{4.17}$$

From (4.15), we find:

$$\eta = \frac{c_a(1)B_2\sigma_\epsilon^2[1 - A_2(1 - c_a(1))]}{(c_a(1)B_2)^2(\sigma_\epsilon^2 + \sigma_\theta^2) + \sigma_\phi^2(1)} \tag{4.18}$$

By assumption, the general shape of expectations is given by equation (4.10). An examination of equation (4.17) shows that when speculators use all the available information, this assumption is true. Identification of the parameters affecting $P_{\alpha=1}(1)$ in equations (4.17) and (4.10) leads to the equality of η and A_2; by reordering the terms of (4.17) and (4.18), we finally obtain:

$$\begin{cases} A_0 = -A_2F_0 \\ A_1 = 1 - A_2 \\ A_2 = \dfrac{c_a(1)B_2\sigma_\epsilon^2}{(c_a(1)B_2)^2(\sigma_\epsilon^2 + \sigma_\theta^2) + c_a(1)B_2\sigma_\epsilon^2(1 - c_a(1)) + \sigma_\phi^2} \end{cases} \tag{4.19}$$

that is:

$$E[F_1|\Omega_1^p] = A_1(F_0 + \bar{e}_1) + (1 - A_1)P_{\alpha=1}(1) \tag{4.20}$$

4.2.2 Second period

At date $t = 2$, the set of public information is increased by the additional signal $\bar{e}_2$. The public information set becomes $\Omega_2^p = \{F_0, \bar{e}_1, \bar{e}_2, P_{\alpha=1}(1), P_{\alpha=1}(2)\}$ and $\Omega_2^q = \{F_0, \bar{e}_1, \bar{e}_2, \mu_1^a, P_{\alpha=1}(1), P_{\alpha=1}(2)\}$ is the information set of informed traders. This modification leads to the following equilibrium price:

$$P_{\alpha=1}(2) = c_a(2)R_{\alpha=1}^a(3) + (1 - c_a(2))R^p(3) + \phi_2 \qquad (4.21)$$

with:

$$\begin{cases} R_{\alpha=1}^a(3) = E[F_3|\Omega_2^q] = E[F_1|\Omega_2^q] + E[e_2|\Omega_2^q] \\ R^p(3) = E[F_3|\Omega_2^p] = E[F_1|\Omega_2^p] + E[e_2|\Omega_2^p] \end{cases} \qquad (4.22)$$

Since at date $t = 2$, $\bar{e}_2$ is the only information concerning e_2, we have: $E[e_2|\Omega_2^q] = E[e_2|\Omega_2^p] = \bar{e}_2$. The price is therefore:

$$P_{\alpha=1}(2) = F_0 + \{c_a(2)E[e_1|\Omega_2^q] + (1 - c_a(2))E[e_1|\Omega_2^p]\} + \bar{e}_2 + \phi_2$$

For informed traders, the expectation of e_1 is not altered. Since the set of public information Ω_2^p, is included in Ω_2^q the conditional expected fundamental value for an informed trader is:

$$E[F_2|\Omega_2^q] = F_0 + B_1\bar{e}_1 + B_2\mu_1^a + \bar{e}_2 \qquad (4.23)$$

For the users of the public information set, the price $P_{\alpha=1}(2)$ presents an additional signal on the realization of e_1. Let us assume that the variables in the set $\{e_1, \bar{e}_1, \mu_1^a, P_{\alpha=1}(1), P_{\alpha=1}(2)\}$ have a joint normal distribution. The conditional expectation of e_1 is thus defined as linear combination of the available information. According to the law of iterated projections (4.14), the conditional expectation of the flow e_1 may then be written as:

$$\begin{aligned} E[e_1|\Omega_2^p] &= E[e_1|\bar{e}_1, P_{\alpha=1}(1), P_{\alpha=1}(2)] \\ &= E[e_1|\Omega_1^p] + A_3(P_{\alpha=1}(2) - E[P_{\alpha=1}(2)|\Omega_1^p]) \end{aligned} \qquad (4.24)$$

with $0 < A_3 < 1$ and $\Omega_1^p = \{F_0, \bar{e}_1, P_{\alpha=1}(1)\}$. Since $E[e_2|\Omega_1^p] = 0$ and $E[\phi_2|\Omega_1^p] = 0$, and because $E[E[e_1|\Omega_2^i]|\Omega_1^p] = E[e_1|\Omega_1^p]$ whatever i in the set $\{a, p\}$, we verify $E[P_{\alpha=1}(2)|\Omega_1^p] = F_0 + E[e_1|\Omega_1^p]$. It follows:

$$E[e_1|\Omega_2^p] = (1 - A_3)E[e_1|\Omega_1^p] + A_3(P_{\alpha=1}(2) - F_0) \qquad (4.25)$$

and:

$$E[F_2|\Omega_2^p] = F_0 + (1 - A_3)E[e_1|\bar{e}_1, P_{\alpha=1}(1)] + A_3(P_{\alpha=1}(2) - F_0) + \bar{e}_2 \quad (4.26)$$

The equilibrium price $P_{\alpha=1}(2)$ which results from an exhaustive use of information is finally:

$$P_{\alpha=1}(2) = F_0 + \frac{(c_a(2)E[e_1|\Omega_1^q] + (1 - c_a(2))(1 - A_3)E[e_1|\Omega_1^p]) + \bar{e}_2 + \phi_2}{1 - A_3(1 - c_a(2))}$$

(4.27)

It is easy to check that the random variables in $\{e_1, \bar{e}_1, \mu_1^a, P_{\alpha=1}(1), P_{\alpha=1}(2)\}$ have a joint normal distribution. Our previous assumption is self-fulfilling.

4.2.3   Inefficiency of an Exhaustive Use of Information

Equation (4.27) describes the equilibrium price resulting from individual demands when information is used exhaustively. By definition, this price leads to a rational expectations equilibrium if, whatever $i \in \{a, p\}$, the estimated return $R_{\alpha=1}^i(2) = E[F_2|\Omega_1^i]$ is identical to the expected future price $E[P_{\alpha=1}(2)|\Omega_1^i]$. This is not true in our context.

Proposition 2: The use of private information by informed speculators is not consistent with a rational formation of expectations.

Proof: Equation (4.27) may be rewritten as:

$$P_{\alpha=1}(2) = E[F_2|\Omega_2^q] + \frac{(1 - c_a(2))(1 - A_3)}{1 - A_3(1 - c_a(2))}(E[e_1|\Omega_1^p] - E[e_1|\Omega_1^q]) + \xi_2 \quad (4.28)$$

with:

$$\xi_2 = \frac{1}{1 - A_3(1 - c_a(2))}[\phi_2 + A_3(1 - c_a(2))\bar{e}_2] \text{ and } E[\xi_2|\Omega_1^i] = 0, \forall i \in \{a, p\}$$

(4.29)

At date $t = 1$, the expected price $E[P_{\alpha=1}(2)|\Omega_1^i]$ is then equal to the estimated fundamental value $E[F_2|\Omega_1^i]$ if and only if:

$$\frac{(1 - c_a(2))(1 - A_3)}{1 - A_3(1 - c_a(2))}E[E[e_1|\Omega_1^p] - E[e_1|\Omega_1^q]|\Omega_1^i] = 0, \forall i \in \{a, p\} \quad (4.30)$$

Since $c_a(2) < 1$, the fraction is strictly positive.[4] According to the law of iterated projections, the value $E[E[e_1|\Omega_1^p] - E[e_1|\Omega_1^q]|\Omega_1^p]$ is nil. The users of the public information make an unbiased forecast. On the contrary, this result does not hold true for informed traders:

$$E[E[e_1|\Omega_1^p] - E[e_1|\Omega_1^q]|\Omega_1^q] = E[e_1|\Omega_1^p] - E[e_1|\Omega_1^q] \neq 0 \qquad (4.31)$$

For these agents, there is a bias between the estimated fundamental value and the expected future price. This bias prevents rational informed agents making an exhaustive use of their information.■

Since the use of private information does not allow speculators to make an unbiased forecast, a rational expectations equilibrium consistent with an exhaustive use of available information does not exist.

4.2.4 Expectations Updating and Equilibrium

The bias explained in the last section comes from the ability of an informed speculator to forecast a gap between his own expectations and the expectations of future uninformed traders. Let A denote the value $(1 - c_a(2))(1 - A_3)/[1 - A_3(1 - c_a(2))]$. From equation (4.28), and pointing out that the gap between $E[e_1|\Omega_1^p]$ and $E[e_1|\Omega_1^q]$ is equivalent to the gap between $E[F_2|\Omega_1^p]$ and $E[F_2|\Omega_1^q]$, it can be shown that the price may be written as:

$$P_{\alpha=1}(2) = (1 - A)E[F_2|\Omega_2^q] + AE[F_2|\Omega_2^p] + \xi_2 \qquad (4.32)$$

thus:

$$E[P_{\alpha=1}(2)|\Omega_1^q] = (1 - A)E[E[F_2|\Omega_2^q]|\Omega_1^q] + AE[E[F_2|\Omega_2^p]|\Omega_1^q]$$
$$= (1 - A)E[F_2|\Omega_1^q] + AE[F_2|\Omega_1^p] \qquad (4.33)$$

For informed traders the mathematical expectation of the fundamental value gives too important a weight to the private information. Since only a part of the future speculators of the second period will be in possession of the private information, this information must not be exhaustively used at date $t = 1$. Informed speculators thus have to trim down the weight of their information. From equation (4.7) we have:

$$R_\alpha^q(2) = \alpha E[F_2|\Omega_1^q] + (1 - \alpha)E[F_2|\Omega_1^p] \qquad (4.34)$$

By comparing equations (4.34) and (4.32), one can see that the informed traders just have to set $\alpha = (1 - A)$ to make an unbiased forecast of the future price.

At this point, the self-reference principle implies that an informed speculator must admit that this updating of the forecast process may also be run by all future speculators. The generalization, for a given α, of the updating estimation process, induces the formation of a price $P_\alpha(2)$, such that:[5]

$$P_\alpha(2) = c_a'(2) \left(\alpha E[F_2|\Omega_2^q] + (1-\alpha)E[F_2|\Omega_2^p]\right) + (1 - c_a'(2))E[F_2|\Omega_2^p] + \phi_2$$
$$= \alpha c_a'(2)E[F_2|\Omega_2^q] + (1 - c_a'(2)\alpha)E[F_2|\Omega_2^p] + \phi_2 \qquad (4.35)$$

Speculators must find a forecast process such that the return expectations for a given α lead to an equilibrium price consistent with this expectation scheme. A rational expectations equilibrium is then achieved for each value of α such that the conditional expectation of the future price – equation (4.35) – is equal to the expectation given by (4.34), that is:

$$R_\alpha^a(2) = E[P_\alpha(2)|\Omega_1^q] \qquad (4.36)$$

Proposition 3:   The rational expectations equilibrium is achieved for $\alpha = 0$ when informed agents neglect their private information.

Proof: From (4.34) and from the conditional expectation of (4.35), the bias of the forecast method may be written as an increasing function of α:

$$R_\alpha^a(2) - E[P_\alpha(2)|\Omega_1^q] = \alpha(1 - c_a'(2)) \left[E[F_2|\Omega_1^q] - E[F_2|\Omega_1^p]\right] \qquad (4.37)$$

Since $(1 - c_a'(2))$ is always different from 0, and because $[E[F_2|\Omega_1^q] - E[F_2|\Omega_1^p]]$ is never nul,[6] the existence of an equilibrium without bias implies $\alpha = 0$.∎

For $\alpha = 0$, the expectations scheme leads to a rational equilibrium. However, it must be noticed that, for this equilibrium, the private information of each agent is ignored. Agents focus on the collective appreciation $R_{\alpha=0}^a(2) = R^p(2) = E[F_2|\Omega_1^p]$ of the fundamental value rather than on their personal estimation $E[F_2|\Omega_1^q]$.

In this equilibrium, the price captures only the public information which is common knowledge from the outset. This result challenges in an essential way the widespread belief according to which prices are always a source of information on speculative markets. In our context, from period to period, the informational content of prices is limited to public information; it does not capture any private information and cannot be used as a source of information.

It is important to note that this equilibrium is achieved if, and only if, $c_a'(t) < 1$ for $t = 2 \ldots \infty$. Even if in the future 99 per cent of the speculators of each generation buy the private information, this information has to be neglected at date $t = 1$. At this time, the use of all information implies the restrictive necessary condition that $c_a'(2) = 1$.[7]

4.3 WHAT KIND OF INFORMATION IS USEFUL ON THE MARKET?

The foregoing analysis implies a discussion of the nature of information carried by prices on speculative markets. It leads to the conclusion that all information not deemed to be *common knowledge* must be neglected and cannot be captured by the price. By contrast, all information that will become public is useful today as it allows the forecasting of the behaviour of future speculators.

In order to focus on the economic consequences of these results, we shall study two kinds of information management on the market. We begin with an analysis of the nature of insider trading; second, we shall consider the strategy of free publication by the information provider.

4.3.1 Insider Trading

Let us assume that private information held by the informed agent on date $t = 1$ coincides with future public information $\bar{e}_2$.[8] In this case, private information actually brings information about the future price. After publication of $\bar{e}_2$, the equilibrium price will take the value:

$$P_{\alpha=0}(2) = E[F_3|\Omega_2^p] - \phi_2 = E[F_3|\Omega_1^p] + \bar{e}_2 + \phi_2$$

$$= E[F_3|\Omega_1^p, \bar{e}_2] + \phi_2 \tag{4.38}$$

In this very special case, the use of information at date $t = 1$ does not induce any bias and reduces the error of prevision. Because the insider benefits from information on the future content of public information, he can forecast the price modification and rationally use his private information.

By extension, information is valuable if it is to become public. All information about the future public information set is therefore worthwhile.

4.3.2 Free Delayed Diffusion by the Information Provider

In the equilibrium in section 4.3, it is impossible to make a profit from the use of private information. This leads to an important result: because information is useless, the information provider will fail to find a purchaser for his costly information. He will have to stop his activity. However, according to the previous analysis, an information provider may exist if he adopts a strategy of delayed free communication. If he can convince speculators that the information he sells now will be public in future, he will find buyers for his information.

Formally, let us assume that the information provider officially publishes, at the beginning of date $t = 2$, the private information sold at the beginning of period $t = 1$. As this information becomes *common knowledge*, it will be taken into account by all agents. The market price $P_{\alpha=0}(2)$ which captures all the public information may be written as:

$$P_{\alpha=0}(2) = E[F_3|\Omega_2^p] + \phi_2$$
$$= E[F_2|\bar{e}, \mu_1^a, \bar{e}_2] \tag{4.39}$$

At date $t = 1$, an informed trader may then make profitable use of his private information:

$$P_{\alpha=0}(2) = E[F_2|\Omega_1^q] + \bar{e}_2 + \phi_2$$
$$= E[F_2|\Omega_1^p] + (1 - B_1)(\mu_1^a - \bar{e}_1) + \bar{e}_2 + \phi_2 \tag{4.40}$$

with $\Omega_1^q = \{F_0, \bar{e}_1, \mu_1^a\}$ and $\Omega_1^p = \{F_0, \bar{e}_1, P_{\alpha=0}(1)\}$.

Because the sum of random variables $(\bar{e}_2 + \phi_2)$ presents a zero mean for any operator at date $t = 1$, informed speculators who use all their information make unbiased forecasts: $E[P_{\alpha=0}(2)|\Omega_1^q] = E[F_2|\Omega_1^q]$. Furthermore, the variance of the forecast error is weaker for an agent using the set of private information Ω_1^q than for an agent who uses only the public information Ω_1^p.[9] According to the price of information and to the market share of the information provider, it may be profitable for risk-averse agents to buy private information.

In the case of perfect – but delayed – dissemination of information by the information provider, private information is useful and valuable. Speculators will thus buy and use the private information. Free direct diffusion of information allows the information provider to find a market for his private information. As expectations reflect public and private information, prices capture all the relevant information and are again a new information source.

4.4 CONCLUDING REMARKS

Traditional analysis justifies the informative efficiency of financial markets by the traders' learning process about the informational content of prices. Our model proposes a different interpretation of the informational content of prices. Because information is worthless today if it is not reflected in tomorrow's price, speculators may rationally decide not to take a signal into account. In this case, the signal does not influence the equilibrium price and this price may only reveal the public information, which is known by everybody and is free.

Hence, we claim that all information concerning the content of the future public information set – but only this information – is worthwhile. If current private information is not to become common knowledge, operators are naturally led to neglect this private information (first equilibrium). Knowing today that the future generation will use all the available information – including what is currently private – is a sufficient condition to induce each speculator to use his own private information (equilibrium with publication by the information provider, or insider trading).

In traditional analysis, private information is always to be published after a more or less long period. In turn, private information is always usable. On the contrary, our approach emphasizes that the use of any information relies on the necessary condition that the available private information will become common knowledge. This condition seems to be strong – at least for a very simple argument: as collecting information is time-consuming, information is costly. On the other hand, when everyone has a piece of information, this information has no private value in a speculative activity. It is thus difficult to assume that everyone will agree to pay for useless information. Costly private information is therefore unlikely to become common knowledge.

If prices do not systematically reflect information, it will, however, be observed that the market prompts information providers to transmit information directly. A constructive conclusion of this paper is thus that informative efficiency may be reached with free dissemination of information on the market.

NOTES

1. Such a demand function may result from the maximization of a utility function (CARA) with a constant absolute risk aversion. As speculation is carried out in the very short run, the actualization rate will be omitted.
2. As F_0 is a constant, it will be omitted hereafter in the information set leading to conditional expectations.

3. The consequences of the information cost on the speculative behaviour will not be considered here as, in our model and whatever this cost could be, each speculator will refuse to buy the private signals. For a study of the influence of such a cost in an economy where information will become common knowledge in the future, see Grosmann and Stiglitz (1980).

4. When $c_a(2) = 1$, condition (4.30) is verified whatever the information set used by speculators at date $t = 1$. The use of the complete information set is then rational. However, this means that private information will become *common knowledge* at date $t = 2$. This point will be discussed in the next section.

5. During the updating process, the variances of expectation errors are modified. The weights $(c_a(2), 1 - c_a(2))$ of each information set in the equilibrium price are also altered. The notation $c'_a(2)$ and $(1 - c'_a(2))$ will be used to denote the new values of the weights.

6. Actually, when α decreases, the informative content of prices diminishes and the signal transmitted to uninformed agents is weaker. $E[e_1|\Omega_2^p]$ moves away from $E[e_1|\Omega_2^q]$ and converges toward $\bar{e}_1$ when α tends toward 0. During the expectations updating process the gap $[E[F_2|\Omega_1^q] - E[F_2|\Omega_1^p]]$ increases.

7. Assume that $c'_a(3) = 1$, the private information may be used at date $t = 2$. At this date, however, the price will capture the private information according to the weight $c'_a(2)$. If this value is less than one, informed speculators of date $t = 1$ will have a set $\alpha = c'_a(2) < 1$. Private information will only be partially used.

8. This case occurs, for example, when a member of a firm knows the content of the annual balance sheet of his firm before its official publication.

9. If all information is used by informed agents, the price defined in $t = 1$ for $\alpha = 1$ again carries information. The prevision error made by the user of public information is written: $P_{\alpha=0}(2) - E[F_2|F_0, \bar{e}_1, P_{\alpha=1}(1)]$ and takes the value:

$$= \bar{e}_1 A_1 \left[\frac{B_1}{1 - (1 - c_a)(1 - A_1)} - 1 \right] + \mu_1^a \left[\frac{(1 - B_1)(1 - c_a(1 - A_1))}{1 - (1 - c_a)(1 - A_1)} \right] + \bar{e}_2 + \phi_2$$

The variance of this term is higher than the variance of the prevision error of an informed agent.

REFERENCES

Azariadis, C. (1981), 'Self-fulfilling prophecies', *Journal of Economic Theory*, 25, 380–96.

Brennan, M. (1990), 'Latent assets', *Journal of Finance*, 45 (3), 709–30.

Cass, D. and K. Shell (1983), 'Do sunspots matter?', *Journal of Political Economy*, 91, 193–227.

Devenow, A. and I. Welch (1996), 'Rational herding in financial economics', *European Economic Review*, 40, 603–15.

Froot, K., D. Scharfstein and J. Stein (1992), 'Herd on the street: informational inefficiencies in a market with short term speculation', *Journal of Finance*, 47 (4), 1461–84.

Grossman, S. (1976), 'On the efficiency of competitive stock markets where traders have diverse information', *Journal of Finance*, 31, 573–85.

Grossman, S. and J. Stiglitz (1980), 'On the possibility of informationally efficient markets', *American Economic Review*, 73, 393–408.

Harrisson, M. and D. Kreps (1978), 'Speculative investor behaviour in a stock market with heterogeneous expectations', *Quarterly Journal of Economics*, 92, 323–36.

Hirshleifer, D., A. Subrahmanyam and S. Titman (1994), 'Security analysis and trading patterns when some investors receive information before others', *Journal of Finance*, 49 (5), 1665–98.

Keynes, J.M. (1936), *The General Theory of Employment, Interest and Money*, London: Macmillan.

Orléan, A. (1995), 'Bayesian interactions and collective dynamics of opinion: herd behavior and mimetic contagion', *Journal of Economic Behavior and Organization*, 28, 257–74.

Sargent, T. (1979), *Macroeconomic Theory*, New York: Academic Press.

Tirole, J. (1982), 'On the possibility of speculation under rational expectations', *Econometrica*, 50, 1163–81.

5. Imitative expectations and informational paradox

André Orléan and Yamina Tadjeddine

INTRODUCTION

Since Hayek's (1945) and Fama's (1970) seminal papers, much work has been devoted to informational efficiency. The issue is a fundamental one: processes of information aggregation are at the core of the market's functioning. Grossman and Stiglitz's contribution to this debate is, in this light, central. They have established the impossibility of informationally efficient markets, to quote the title of one of their articles (1980). They have shown that informationally efficient prices lead to a paradox. As they put it: 'if the market aggregated their information perfectly, individuals' demands would not be based on their own information, but then, would it be possible for markets to aggregate information perfectly' (Grossman and Stiglitz, 1976). The present paper is devoted to this question.

Similar paradoxes can be observed in numerous examples involving equilibrium reasoning. Imagine a series of spatially dispersed shops offering the same good. If an agent believes that equilibrium prevails, he will go to the nearest shop to get his good, because he knows that equilibrium entails a unique price. This behaviour is one that takes the best advantage of the existence of equilibrium by limiting search costs. But if every agent follows this maximizing behaviour, there will be no incentive for shops to offer the equilibrium price. This paradox follows the same logic as the Grossman and Stiglitz paradox (GSP): behaviours which take advantage of equilibrium do not enforce it. Such an equilibrium is self-contradictory.

Most authors have tried to bypass the difficulties put forward by Grossman and Stiglitz by introducing some additional source of uncertainty. Consistent with this additional hypothesis, the price is efficient no more: it does not reveal all of the information and the paradox disappears (Grossman and Stiglitz, 1980; Hellwig, 1980; Gennotte and Leland, 1990). However, the question remains of how information is aggregated when this additional hypothesis does not hold. Our conjecture is that an under-standing of this process requires a dynamic framework.

This idea is in fact quite natural. Recall that REE (rational expectations equilibrium) analysis, such as that proposed by Grossman and Stiglitz, is implicitly grounded on a dynamic process. Grossman (1976) tries to sketch out such a process. The central idea is that traders make some conjectural hypotheses about how price P is linked to a set of private information $y = (y_1, \ldots, y_n)$ possessed by n agents. Let us call f this conjecture. It significates that the expected price P^e is such that: $P^e = f(y)$. The equilib-rium market price is thus a function of the conjecture f formed by the agents on the basis of their private information. If we denote this function Tf, then $P = Tf(y)$. The REE is a situation such that $Tf^* = f^*$, that is, indi-vidual expectations are fulfilled. But how is such an equilibrium obtained? Grossman (1976) briefly describes a process which is supposed to converge towards a REE. The idea is that traders learn the joint distribution (f, Tf) and they will then modify their conjecture until the fixed point f^* is reached.

To build a more precise dynamic framework, we will refer to Orléan (1995, 1997a, 1997b). We propose a simplified model where the issue of convergence can be handled. The fundamental feature of this model relies on the fact that rational interpretation of price as revealing private information leads to imitative expectations.

Keynes (1937) clearly emphasized the important influence of market opinion on individual decision-making, stressing the role of imitation in financial markets; but such an approach was later abandoned. It has only been since the beginning of the 1980s, and above all after the October 1987 crash, that this issue has attracted the interest of scholars. The analysis of survey data has highlighted the importance of imitative expectations on markets. For instance, Case and Shiller (1989) notice that home buyers in cities where house prices have increased rapidly in the past anticipate greater future price appreciation than in cities where prices have been stable or have decreased. Shiller (1989) surveys traders' expectations in the wake of the 1987 market crash and finds that most sellers sold because they had anticipated further decline. It seems that they decided to sell only by refer-ring to market opinion instead of their own private signal. Frankel and Froot (1988) show the same pattern for the dollar exchange rate in the 1980s: traders continued to buy even though they estimated that the dollar was overpriced relative to its fundamental value. Here again there is a contradiction between traders' private signals ('the dollar is overpriced') and market opinion (bull market). Traders decided to follow the majority and not their own information.

Such imitative expectations are not always irrational. Indeed, it has been shown (Banerjee, 1992; Bikhchandani *et al.*, 1992) that informational influences can lead to rational imitation. For instance, if an agent A observes an agent B buying a stock X, he will revise his own expectation about the future prospects of X in order to take into account this new fact. This taking into account depends on his evaluation of the relevance of agent B's action. If agent A believes that agent B is very well informed, this could lead him to imitate agent B and to buy the stock X even if his own private information was not in favour of such a choice. On the contrary, if agent A does not trust agent B's expertise, he will not give much importance to agent B's action. Applying Bayes's rule, it can be shown that the propensity to imitate depends on agent A's estimation of the accuracy of agent B's hidden information. Thus, in such a framework, imitation is a consequence of a Bayesian calculus which weighs the two sources of information, private signals and others' behaviours, according to their relative accuracy. In market situations, the behaviour of others can only be known through the observation of prices. Assuming imitative behaviour through which agents are trying to infer the hidden information conveyed by the price, it is then possible to model the dynamic process through which agents revise their opinions in the light of the observed price, and then to evaluate the informational efficiency of the price.

A series of recent work has analysed informational influences within a sequential framework: rational individuals enter the market one by one, observe their predecessors and take a unique and irreversible decision. These studies have shown that pure informational influences can lead to imitative decision processes such as 'herd behaviour' (Banerjee, 1992; Scharfstein and Stein, 1990), 'informational cascade' (Bikhchandani *et al.*, 1992), or contagion (Lux, 1995; Kirman, 1993). Hence, optimizing agents can rationally decide to follow what previous agents have chosen rather than to use their private information, and such behaviour generates price dynamics akin to a speculative bubble.

The sequential assumption, which is crucial in the herd behaviour and informational cascade models, does not seem appropriate for understanding the functioning of a market. In financial markets, in particular, agents are simultaneously present and they revise their opinions in a continuous mode, and not once and for all. That is why we propose in section 5.2 a dynamic non-sequential model in order to study informational influences and their consequences on price. The results obtained are quite different from those obtained in the previous literature. Here, imitation does not lead necessarily to an informational cascade: the role of imitation is ambivalent. This result is quite intuitive: it is efficient for me to imitate the others as long as they are better informed than I am, but it becomes inefficient if they are also imitators. When the propensity to imitate is smaller than a certain threshold, imitative behaviour is efficient. It improves individual (and collective) performances because it allows access to global information whose accuracy is any greater than an individual's private information. But beyond a certain threshold, a self-validating process appears in which the price is disconnected from fundamental information. Such a process can give rise to a speculative bubble.

In section 5.2, the propensity to imitate, namely μ, is taken to be an exogenous parameter. In section 5.3, we consider a game situation where each agent is able to choose the value of μ that seems to him the most appropriate. We then show that if the average propensity to imitate of the group is weak, then to be a pure imitator is the best strategy. But if the average propensity of the group to imitate is too high, then agents should rely only on their own information. In such a situation where the optimizing behaviour consists in doing the opposite of what the crowd does, no equilibrium exists. This result can be understood as a new formulation of the GSP. Expressed in dynamic terms, it leads to cyclical dynamics. In the first place, agents rely on their private information. This leads to a situation where the price is more informationally efficient than private information. Agents slowly discover this fact. Then their propensity to imitate grows. As a result, both the price and private expectations become more efficient. It follows that imitation increases. But, once the threshold μ^* is attained, price is no longer efficient. A bubble appears. After a while, this inefficiency is discovered. At this point, agents will no longer use price as a relevant source of information and the bubble bursts. We are brought back to the point of departure. Hence, our model shows a cyclical dynamic, where normal and pathological episodes alternate.

It should be emphasized that this alternation is not grounded on a qualitative modification of individual behaviour. Bubbles appear and burst because of endogenous modifications in the value of μ. This is the consequence of a bifurcation in the dynamic system. This is coherent with what we know about markets. There is no sudden emergence of irrationality within the market. As Kindleberger (1978) observed, agents' behaviours are 'rational – or would be, were it not for the fact that others are behaving in the same way'. This analysis places the emphasis on the role played by long swings within markets. This hypothesis should be tested precisely, but seems to express some important features of financial markets which show recurrent episodes such as 1929, 1987 or 1997.

This paper is organized as follows. Section 5.1 describes the Grossman–Stiglitz paradox by emphasizing its dynamic nature. Section 5.2 presents a dynamic non-sequential model with imitative expectations. Section 5.3 proposes a game framework in which the propensity to imitate becomes a strategic variable. Section 5.4 concludes.

5.1   THE GROSSMAN-STIGLITZ PARADOX

Grossman (1976) considers a situation where n agents have the choice between two assets: a riskless asset whose return is equal to r, and a risky asset with stochastic return. At the time $(t=0)$, according to the usual hypotheses,[1] it is possible to write the individual demand of the risky asset:

$$z_i(I_i, P_0) = \frac{E(\tilde{P}_1 | I_i) - (1 + r)P_0}{a_i \text{Var}(\tilde{P}_1 | I_i)} \quad (5.1)$$

where P_0 is the price in 0, $\tilde{P}_1$ the stochastic price in $(t=1)$, a_i the level of risk aversion and I_i the individual information, with $I_i = (y_i, P_0)$. We suppose that agent i receives the information y_i defined by:

$$\tilde{y}_i = \tilde{P}_1 + \tilde{\epsilon}_i \quad (5.2)$$

We assume that the vector $(\tilde{P}_1, \tilde{\epsilon}_i, \ldots \tilde{\epsilon}_n)$ is a multinormal variable, with mean $(\overline{P}_1, 0, \ldots 0)$ and the variance–covariance matrice's diagonal written $(\sigma^2, s^2, \ldots, s^2)$. The equilibrium condition is:

$$Z = \sum_{i=1}^{n} z_i(I_i, P_0) \quad (5.3)$$

with Z the exogeneous quantity of risky assets.

The rational expectations equilibrium (REE) is determined as a price P_0 defined as a function f of $y = (y_1, \ldots, y_n)$ which is a solution of equation (5.3) whereas the agents use this function to calculate their expectations, that is:

$$E(\tilde{P}_1 | I_i) = E(\tilde{P}_1 | y_i, P_0; f)$$

Hellwig (1980) remarks that the determination of REE is a fixed point problem in the space of functions $f(y)$. If we denote this solution $P_0^*(y)$, it appears that: '$P_0^*(y)$ is a self fulfilling expectations equilibrium: when all traders think that prices are generated by $P_0^*(y)$, they will act in such a way that the market clears at $P_0^*(y)$' (Grossman, p. 577).

Grossman demonstrates that this problem has one linear solution:

$$P_0^*(y) = \alpha_0 + \alpha_1 \bar{y}, \qquad \bar{y} = \sum_{i=1}^{n} y_i / n \quad (5.4)$$

where α_0, α_1 are some constants depending on the parameters of the problem. By observing the clearing price $P_0^*(y)$, every agent can deduce the value of $\bar{y}$ which is a better estimation of the future price P_1 than their private information, y_i. More precisely, it can be shown that P_0 is a sufficient statistic. This means that an agent's expectation will only depend on the price P_0^* because:

$$E(\tilde{P}_1 | P_0^*, y_i) = E(\tilde{P}_1 | P_0^*) \qquad (5.5)$$

Thus, in equilibrium, the current price summarizes all the information in the market. This apparently very positive result leads to a paradox: if all the relevant information appears in the market price, then the private information will become superfluous. If information is costly, each agent will stop collecting information because the information in P_0^* is superior to y_i and free. Hence, with the positive information costs, equilibrium does not exist.

A very first preliminary effort to build a dynamic analysis of the GSP goes as follows. Under the same assumptions as before, we assume that agents, in order to form their expectations, calculate a weighted sum of the two types of information, that is:

$$l_i = E(\tilde{P}_1 | P_0, y_i) = a_i y_i + (1 - a_i)P_0 \qquad (5.6)$$

This expectation is not necessarily a rational expectation. It is based on a certain belief of the individual i concerning the relative precision of y_i and P_0. On the basis of this belief, given that the two variables are Gaussian, one obtains equation (5.6). The more the individual believes in the superiority of the price over the information y_i as a source of information, the closer the parameter a_i is to 1. The dynamic problem, then, is the manner in which individual agents revise the value of a_i as a function of their observations of the correlation between P_0 and P_1.

Let us assume that all the agents choose the same value of a_i, named a, and that the market price is equal to the arithmetic mean of the private estimates l_i:

$$P_0 = \frac{1}{n} \sum_{i=1}^{i=n} l_i \qquad (5.7)$$

It follows from (5.7) that:

$$P_0 = \frac{1}{n} \sum y_i = \bar{y} \qquad (5.8)$$

This result is independent of the parameter a. We assume that traders in order to revise the value of the precision a calculate the variance of their estimator:

$$\text{Var}(l_i) = [(n-1)a^2 + 1]\frac{s^2}{n} + \sigma^2 \qquad (5.9)$$

We notice that the private estimation is more precise when *a* is smaller. This is easy to understand because, as in GSP, equation (5.8) means that P_0 is a sufficient statistic. Then traders are motivated to take a smaller and smaller value of *a*. In doing this, agents take advantage of the informational efficiency of the price. But, when *a* is equal to 0, we are in the situation described by Grossman and Stiglitz in the REE. Agents' behaviour is completely rational but, at the same time, price loses its informational quality. When $a = 0$, then $l_i = p$ (see equation (5.6)) and traders no longer use their private information, the price cannot be an efficient aggregate of the private information: every value of *p* could be an equilibrium.

This first preliminary modelization could benefit from greater precision. Nevertheless, it shows that the problem lies in the fact that the accuracy of price, its ability to convey information, is not an exogeneous parameter. It depends on the way agents use it to form their expectations. But here is a contradiction: when prices become more precise, agents are motivated to rely more on the price, but doing this can lead to a diminution of the price quality. For this reason, no fixed point can exist. This is the kind of dynamics that will be described in the next section.

5.2   GROSSMAN–STIGLITZ PARADOX AND IMITATION: A DYNAMIC APPROACH

Let us consider an economy composed of N agents denoted *i*, $i \in \{1,2,\ldots N\}$. The state of the world, named θ, is either {H} or {L} with equal prior probability. The agents cannot observe θ directly. In order to discover it, each individual independently observes a signal σ defined as follows: σ can be either {+} or {−} according to the following conditional probabilities:

$$\begin{cases} P(\sigma = +|H) = P(\sigma = -|L) = p > 0.5 \\ P(\sigma = -|H) = P(\sigma = +|L) = 1 - p < 0.5 \end{cases} \quad (5.10)$$

σ_i, the value of the independent observation of σ made by agent *i*, is called his private information.

Let us assume that each agent is risk neutral and has to choose between two assets, a riskless asset whose return is equal to *r* and a risky asset X whose return R depends on the state θ:

$$R = \begin{cases} r + M & \text{if } \{\theta = H\} \\ r - M & \text{if } \{\theta = L\} \end{cases} \quad (5.11)$$

According to the conditional probabilities (5.10), each agent is able to calculate:

$$\begin{cases} E(R|\sigma = +) = r + (2p - 1)M \\ E(R|\sigma = -) = r - (2p - 1)M \end{cases}$$

Because $\{p > 0.5\}$, the agents will choose the risky asset when they observe $\{+\}$, and buy the riskless asset when they observe $\{-\}$. We call n the number of agents who choose the risky asset and $f = n/N$ the proportion of such agents. It is the equivalent of buying X and thinking that $\{\theta = H\}$ is more probable than $\{\theta = L\}$. This choice will be right if indeed $\{\theta = H\}$. We shall assume that the market price of X is a bijective function of f, that is, it is equivalent to observe the market price or to observe f.

If agents make their choice on the sole basis of their private information, the average proportion of agents who make the right choice will be equal to p. For example, if $\{\theta = H\}$, the probability of observing $\{+\}$ and then buying the risky asset will be equal to p according to equation (5.10). If $\{\theta = L\}$, the probability of choosing the riskless asset will be equal to p. In either case, the probability of making the wrong choice is equal to $(1 - p)$. The more precise the signal, the closer is p to 1, and the better are the individual and collective performances of the group. This is a natural result. The efficiency of the market price depends on the accuracy of the information.

The preceding decision rule relies only on private information. Will it be possible to improve the accuracy of individual decision-making by taking into account not only the private information σ_i but also the price, that is, f? In other terms, is the price an informationally efficient variable? To answer this question, we have to consider a general decision rule. It will be defined by a couple of functions $q_\mu(f, \sigma_i)$ determined as the probability of buying the risky asset when agent i's private information is equal to σ_i and when he observes f. In this new framework, the preceding rule will be named q_0. It is equal to:

$$\begin{cases} q_0(f, +) = 1 \\ q_0(f, -) = 0 \end{cases} \tag{5.12}$$

This rule does not depend on f. It says that when an agent's information is $\{f, +\}$, the probability of choosing the risky asset is always equal to 1 and does not depend on the collective opinion f. When an agent's information is $\{f, -\}$, it is equal to 0, that is, the agent always chooses the riskless asset.

Let us consider the general case. When $\{\sigma_i = +\}$ and $\{f > 0.5\}$, the two pieces of information are convergent. They lead to the same decision: to buy the risky asset. It follows that q_μ is equal to 1 in such a situation. When $\{\sigma_i = +\}$ and $(f < 0.5)$, the two signals are contradictory. The trader must decide to follow one or the other. We note μ, the probability of choosing according to f, ($\mu \in [0.1]$), that is, to follow the market opinion. Thus μ measures the propensity of an agent to imitate the crowd. The value of this parameter can be deduced from a Bayesian calculus that compares the relative accuracy of the two signals, σ and the price f. When μ is close to 1, this means that the agent believes that the price is a much better signal than the private information. When μ is close to 0, this is a consequence of a certain *a priori* belief of the agent who does not believe in the efficiency of the price. It is then possible to write the general decision rule q_μ, the probability to buy X, as:

$$\begin{cases} f \geq 0.5 \Rightarrow q_\mu(f,+) = 1 & \text{and} \quad \begin{cases} f > 0.5 \Rightarrow q_\mu(f,-) = \mu \\ f \leq 0.5 \Rightarrow q_\mu(f,-) = 0 \end{cases} \end{cases} \quad (5.13)$$

Then we have the relation:

$$q_\mu(f,-) = 1 - q_\mu(1-f,+)$$

that expresses the symmetry between $\{-\}$ and $\{+\}$. $(1 - \mu)$ measures the agent's propensity to choose according to his own private information.

When $\mu = 0$, that is, when agents strictly follow their private information, the average error of the group is $(1 - p)$. For the opposite, with $\mu = 1$, the trader is totally imitative: he follows the market opinion whatever his private signal. Our central question is: What happens when every agent follows the rule q_μ with $\mu > 0$? In such a situation, the choices of individual agents are no longer independent: the decision of agent i depends on previous agents' choices. It follows that, in order to understand how f is determined, we have to be more precise about the definition of the dynamic interaction process. Before studying this point, it should be emphasized that we model a process in which incentives are such that every agent, at each period, tries to 'choose' the true value of θ. We do not integrate within this schematic framework the role played by the variation of the price in the determination of the profitability of the various strategies. It means that what is important is the position of each agent when the true state of the world is publicly revealed. But, as they do not know when this will occur, they try at each period to be coherent with their information.

In $t = 0$, the state of the economy is drawn according to the probabilities $P(H) = P(L) = 0.5$ and will remain constant until date T. The sequence $[0,T]$

can be understood as a specific round amid a global process which began before time 0 and will continue after time T. $f(0)$ will be considered as an arbitrary parameter depending on what has happened before $t = 0$. At time t, $t > 0$, one individual i is drawn at random. He observes $f(t-1)$ and the signal σ_i. Then he changes his previous choice according to the rule q_μ (f, σ_i). We suppose that all the traders have the same propensity to imitate and that this propensity is constant over the time. In section 5.3, we shall change this hypothesis.

Notice that agent i does not take into account in t the information that he could have observed before t. This simplifying hypothesis can be justified because of the short memory of the agents, or by the traders' overreacting to the news. It can also be justified by the fact that agents do not know when θ is changing and, consequently, do not know if their past information is still relevant. Besides, we have assumed that only one agent is drawn at each instant. The qualitative results are unchanged by taking L agents.

This set of hypotheses define a Markovian stochastic process. The variable we are interested in is the law of probability P $(f;t)$ followed by $f(t)$. To what does it converge? To answer this, we have to know the probability $J(f,\mu,\theta)$ of buying X at $(t+1)$ when $f(t) = f$ and the state of the world is θ. We obtain:

$$\begin{cases} J(f,\mu,H) = pq_\mu(f,+) + (1-p)q_\mu(f,-) \\ J(f,\mu,L) = (1-p)q_\mu(f,+) + pq_\mu(f,-) \end{cases} \qquad (5.14)$$

Knowing the probability J, we can calculate:

$$\begin{cases} P[f(t+1) = f(t) + 1/N] = P(f \rightarrow f + 1/N) = (1-f)J(f,\mu,\theta) = W_+(f,\mu,\theta) \\ P[f(t+1) = f(t) - 1/N] = P(f \rightarrow f - 1/N) = f[1 - J(f,\mu,\theta)] = W_-(f,\mu,\theta) \end{cases}$$
$$(5.15)$$

These hypotheses determine completely the stochastic process followed by $f(t)$, that is, the way P (f,t) varies through time. The exact description of this process in terms of discrete numbers n is called the master equation (Weidlich and Haag, 1983, ch. 2). To simplify the notation, it is more convenient to use an approximate description in terms of continuous variables. Because the exact form of the stationary distribution can be calculated in both cases, we have been able to verify that the continuous description constitutes a reliable approximation when N is large. The continuous stochastic process is a diffusion process defined by the standard form of a Fokker–Planck equation in one dimension (Weidlich and Haag, 1983):

$$\frac{\partial P(f;t)}{\partial t} = -\frac{\partial}{\partial f}[K(f)P(f;t)] + \frac{1}{2N}\frac{\partial^2}{\partial f^2}[Q(f)P(f;t)]$$

with:

$$\begin{cases} K(f) = W_+(f) - W_-(f) \\ Q(f) = W_+(f) + W_-(f) \end{cases}$$

For $0 \leq \mu < 1$, it can be shown that the process is ergodic; whatever $P(f, 0)$, $P(f, t)$ converges to an unique stationary distribution $P_{st}(f, \mu, \theta)$, for a given state θ.

To present the results, we only consider the case where the state θ is $\{H\}$. It is then easy to evaluate the collective efficiency of the price: the closer f is to 1, the more efficient is the market. $\{f = 1\}$ means that every agent has made the right choice.

We demonstrate the existence of a μ value, noted μ^* such that for $\mu \leq \mu^*$, $P_{st}(f,\mu, \theta)$ is a unimodal distribution (see Figure 5.1). Its sole peak, denoted $f_1(\mu, H)$, is defined by:

$$f_1(\mu,H) = p + (1-p)\mu \qquad (5.16)$$

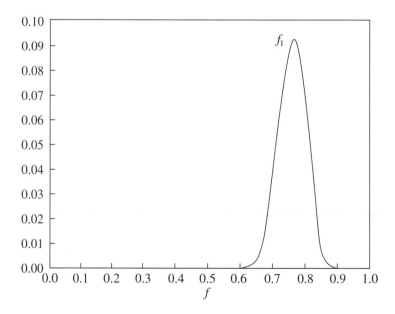

Figure 5.1: Stationary distribution $P_{st}(f)$ with $\mu = 0.2$

For $\mu = 0$, we find $f_I(0,H) = p$. We recognize the situation without imitation: traders' decisions are only based on their private information (σ_i). When μ increases but stays inferior or equal to μ^*, the value of $f_I(\mu, H)$ increases (see equation (5.16)). The performance of the group is better: more traders make the right choice. This interpretation is justified by the fact that the stationary distribution is very concentrated near the peak f_I. The imitation improves the market efficiency: it enables some unlucky agents who have received the bad signal ($\{-\}$ when $\{\theta = H\}$) to correct their error by observing the market opinion. The probability of choosing the right strategy when the information set is $\{f, -\}$ with $f > 0.5$, becomes μ (see equation (5.13)). The average proportion of individuals making the wrong choice is $(1 - \mu)(1 - p)$, which is inferior to $(1 - p)$. The greater μ is, the better the performance of the group. Being imitative is efficient: it leads to better performance than following the independent rule q_0.

So imitation appears to be a rational behaviour: traders understand that the market price contains some relevant information. Imitation can be viewed as the specific manner through which global information is scattered within decentralized information structures. The market becomes more efficient because of imitation.

When μ becomes superior to μ^* but inferior to 1, the shape of the stationary distribution is qualitatively affected. The stationary distribution becomes bimodal (see Figure 5.2). A new peak (M) appears, $f_M (\mu, H) = (1 - \mu)p$. At this peak, the percentage of traders making the good choice falls below 0.5. It is possible to calculate the error in the state f_M: $[1 - p(1 - \mu)]$. It is always greater than the average error $(1 - p)$ that would prevail if there were no imitation at all. The state $f_M(\mu, H)$ is the result of a self-validating process: because the propensity to imitate is large, the power of conformism dominates the role of information, that is a large proportion of agents who have received the good signal $\{+\}$ will choose $\{L\}$ when $\{f(t) < 0.5\}$. This propensity to conform to the majority can lead the collective opinion towards a configuration where almost everybody has chosen the wrong opinion. For μ close to 1 and $\{\theta = H\}$, we can observe a quasi-unanimity on $\{L\}$!

This pathological situation appears during a speculative bubble: traders follow the market opinion without focusing on their private information about fundamental values. For example, suppose that the true state is $\{H\}$ but the majority of traders sell. So a trader who has received a positive signal will prefer to follow the others and buy the riskless asset.

For example, Soros (1995) reports that in October 1987 he had taken a short position in Japan and a long position in the US. He was persuaded of the existence of a speculative bubble in Japan. But, even if it were true and this bubble had exploded, in 1987 a majority of traders had trust in the

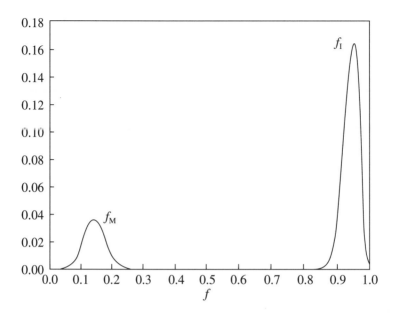

Figure 5.2: Stationary distribution $P_{st}(f)$ with $\mu = 0.8$

Japanese economy and had no confidence in the American economy. So the crash did not take place in Japan as Soros had expected, but in the US. Soros lost a lot, as he said. Thus, it can be risky to trade against the market opinion. We do not want to discuss here the 'contrarian' strategy: this strategy consists in playing against the majority. We encourage you to read articles on contrarian strategies, such as Chan (1988) and Lo and MacKinlay (1990).

To have an accurate understanding of the way our system behaves when μ is greater than μ^*, it should be emphasized that the probability of transition from one peak to the other is very small when N is great. The transition time is proportional to e^N. It follows that the process is 'quasi' non-ergodic for large N: $f(t)$ remains either in the vicinity of $f_I(\mu, \theta)$ or in the vicinity $f_M(\mu, \theta)$. For a plausible time of observation T, we shall not observe a transition from one peak to the other.

Figures 5.3 and 5.4 show simulations of our process where $p = 0.7$ and N = 100; 5000 periods are calculated. In $t = 0, f(0)$ is supposed to be equal to 0.5, and the state $\{\theta = H\}$ is drawn. Every 1000 periods, the state θ changes. In Figure 5.3, we assume that μ is equal to 0.2 which is inferior to $\mu^* = 0.28$. In that case, the stationary distribution is unimodal: $f_I(\mu, \theta) = 0.76$. When θ changes from $\{H\}$ to $\{L\}$ the proportion of choices $\{H\}$ moves from the

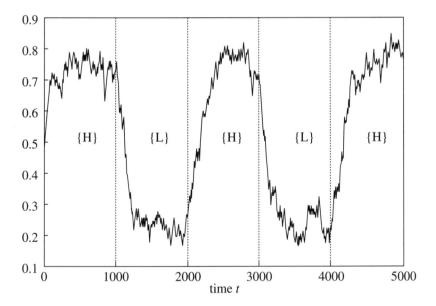

Figure 5.3: $f_I(0.2,H) = 0.76$ and $f_I(0.2,L) = 0.24$

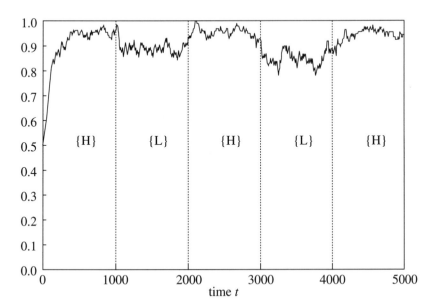

Figure 5.4: $f_I(0.8,H) = 0.94$ and $f_M(0.8,L) = 0.86$

neighbourhood of the mode $f_I(\mu, H)$ to the neighbourhood of the mode $f_I(\mu, L)$.

In Figure 5.4, μ is assumed to be equal to 0.8. The stationary distribution becomes bimodal and the dynamic is very different. In the first round $(t < 1000)$, $f(t)$ converges to the neighbourhood of the right mode $f_I(\mu, H)$. Its value is equal to 0.94. Almost every agent has found the right value of the state θ. The average error is inferior to the one prevailing in the previous case. But when θ changes from $\{H\}$ to $\{L\}$, $f(t)$ no longer converges to $f_I(\mu, L)$ but to the wrong mode $f_M(\mu, L) = 0.86$. In that case only 14 per cent of the population makes the right choice $\{L\}$. The average error is equal to $0.46 = (0.06 + 0.86)/2$ which is worse than $0.3 = (1 - p)$. It would have been better to use the decision rule q_0. This is a general result when $\mu > \bar{\mu}$. Then the global average error is $(1 - p) - \mu(2p - 1) > (1 - p)$.

When the propensity to imitate is large, changes in the state of the world have only a small impact on the collective choice because agents give insufficient weight to their private information relative to f. Speculators base their anticipations mainly on the market opinion. When $\mu = 1$, the process is strictly non-ergodic: $\{f = 0\}$ and $\{f = 1\}$ are absorbing states.

To conclude, imitation is ambivalent: to imitate is efficient only if the average propensity to imitate is small; it becomes counterproductive otherwise. This result conforms to intuition. To imitate is efficient if the individual I imitate is well-informed; it is not if the individual I imitate is himself an imitator.

5.3   THE PROPENSITY TO IMITATE AS A STRATEGIC VARIABLE

From now on, we are interested in the trader's choice of μ. We abandon the hypothesis of a constant and given μ. Every trader independently chooses his own propensity μ_i to be imitative. We admit that this choice depends only on the market price's informative quality. To describe such a situation, we have to consider the non-cooperative game defined as follows:

1. the N agents are the N players;
2. each agent i has to choose a strategy μ_i with μ_i belonging to $[0,1]$;
3. the payoff from playing the strategy μ_i is given by the probability of making the right choice when the stationary distribution is obtained;
4. the agents are 'price-takers': they make the assumption that their choice does not affect the price.[2]

Let us examine whether there exists an equilibrium for this game. Before addressing this question, it should be noted first that if every agent chooses a propensity μ_i to imitate, the global process that will be obtained is the one defined by $J(f, \bar{\mu}, \theta)$ (equation (5.14), with $\bar{\mu}$ being the average value of the distribution $\{\mu_i\}_{i=1,..N}$. It is not difficult to prove this result as soon as one has noticed that:

$$\sum_{i=1}^{N} \frac{1}{N} q_{\mu_i}(f,\sigma_i) = q_{\bar{\mu}}(f,\sigma_i) \qquad \text{with} \qquad \bar{\mu} = \frac{1}{N} \sum_{i=1}^{N} \mu_i \qquad (5.17)$$

We consider agent N's choice. He is facing the set of strategies $\{\mu_i\}_{i=1,..N-1}$. Because he believes that his action has no impact on the price, he takes the value of $\bar{\mu}$ as given and equal to:

$$\bar{\mu} = \frac{1}{N-1} \sum_{i=1}^{i=N-1} \mu_i \qquad (5.18)$$

Agent N's optimal choice depends on the value of $\bar{\mu}$. If $\bar{\mu} \leq \mu^*$, it follows from the preceding results that on average the market is always on the right side. So it is optimal for the agent N to be a complete imitator: $\mu_N = 1$. If $\bar{\mu} > \mu^*$, the market is less efficient than the private information σ. Therefore it is optimal for agent N to rely only on his own information: $\mu_N = 0$.

First, these results confirm our intuition: it is better to be imitative when the others are not, and not to be imitative when the others are. There exists no pure equilibrium. Second, our analysis gives more precision about the nature of the dynamics of the individual strategies. We have not yet built a model of this process, but we can provide a qualitative analysis. Let us assume that the initial situation starts with $\bar{\mu} < \mu^*$. In such a case, traders gradually learn the correlations between the state of the nature (θ) and the market price, as described by Grossman (1976). They realize that the price is a good estimator. They will give a larger weight to f in their decision and $\bar{\mu}$ will then increase. The agents who have chosen a large μ obtain better performance than others. This situation generates a strong incentive to become imitative. In a first step, this process is collectively positive because it improves the collective efficiency. But when μ goes beyond the threshold μ^*, the collective signal suddenly decreases. As long as the economic state has not changed $\{\theta = H\}$, there is no problem. But if the state changes, this new situation will not be perceived at once by the agents. Ultimately they will understand that the collective signal becomes a 'bubble': it does not reveal fundamental information any more. It follows that traders reduce the weight of market opinion in their decision and μ decreases. Then the price contains a greater variety of private information, and it becomes efficient again. So the cycle recommences. This kind of cyclical process can explain certain features of financial dynamics where a succession of normal and pathological periods can be observed.

5.4 CONCLUDING REMARKS

Our model has tried to show the important role played by imitation within financial markets. Taking imitation into account leads to a large spectrum of dynamics: it can improve market efficiency or give rise to self-validating processes. It seems to us that such a multiplicity of dynamics is observed in financial markets. The power of the imitation hypothesis lies then in its ability to explain such a multiplicity on the ground of only quantitative modifications of individual behaviours. Bubbles are not the result of some sudden irrational collective behaviour. They are generated by an endogenous learning process which could be rational if it were not followed by everyone.

NOTE

1. 'Agent i maximizes the expected utility of consumption. The utility function exhibits constant absolute risk aversion. Under this assumption agent i's demand for the risky asset is independent of his initial wealth' (Hellwig, 1980, p. 479).
2. If this fourth condition is not verified then it is easy to recognise the 'minority game'.

REFERENCES

Banerjee, A.V. (1992), 'A simple model of herd behavior', *Quarterly Journal of Economics*, 107, 797–817.

Bikhchandani, S., D. Hirshleifer and I. Welch (1992), 'A theory of fads, fashion, custom, and cultural change as information cascades', *Journal of Political Economy*, 100 (5), 797–817.

Case, K.E. and R.J. Shiller (1989), 'The efficiency of the market for single family home', *American Economic Review*, 79 (2), 125–37.

Chan, K.C. (1988), 'On the contrarian investment strategy', *Journal of Business*, 61, 147–63.

Fama, E.F. (1970), 'Efficient capital markets: a review of theory and empirical work', *Journal of Finance*, 25, 383–417.

Frankel, J. and K. Froot (1988), 'Explaining the demand for dollars: international rates of return and the expectations of chartists and fundamentalists', in R. Chambers and P. Paarlberg (eds), *Agriculture, Macroeconomics and the Exchange Rate*, Boulder, CO: Westfield Press.

Genotte, G. and H. Leland (1990), 'Market liquidity, hedging and crashes', *American Economic Review*, 80 (5), 999–1021.

Grossman, S.J. (1976), 'On the efficiency of competitive stock markets where traders have diverse information', *Journal of Finance*, 31, 573–85.

Grossman, S.J. and J.E. Stiglitz (1976), 'Information and competitive price systems', *American Economic Review*, 66 (2), 246–53.

Grossman, S.J. and J.E. Stiglitz (1980), 'On the impossibility of informationally efficient markets', *American Economic Review*, 70 (3), 393–408.

Hayek, F.A. (1945), 'The use of knowledge in society', *American Economic Review*, 35 (4), 519–30.

Hellwig, M.F. (1980), 'On the aggregation of information in competitive markets', *Journal of Economic Theory*, 22, 477–98.

Keynes, J.M. (1937), 'The general theory of employment', *Quarterly Journal of Economics*, 51, 209–23.

Kindleberger, C.P. (1978), *Manias, Panics, and Crashes: A history of financial crisis*, London: Macmillan.

Kirman, A. (1993), 'Ants, rationality, and recruitment', *Quarterly Journal of Economics*, 108, 137–56.

Lo, A.W. and C.A. MacKinlay (1990), 'When are contrarian profits due to stock market overreaction?', *Review of Financial Studies*, 3, 175–205.

Lux, T. (1995), 'Herd behaviour, bubbles and crashes', *Economic Journal*, 105, 881–96.

Orléan, A. (1995), 'Bayesian interactions and collective dynamics of opinion: herd behavior and mimetic contagion', *Journal of Economic Behavior and Organizations*, 28, 257–74.

Orléan, A. (1997a), 'The ambivalent role of imitation in decentralized collective learning', in N. Lazaric and E. Lorenz (eds), *The Economics of Trust and Learning*, Aldershot, Hants: Edward Elgar.

Orléan, A. (1997b), 'Informational influences and the ambivalence of imitation', in J. Lesourne and A. Orléan, Advances in Self-organization and Evolutionary Economics, Paris: Economica.

Scharfstein, D.S. and J.C. Stein (1990), 'Herd behavior and investment', *American Economic Review*, 80, 465–79.

Shiller, R.J. (1989), *Market Volatility*, Cambridge, MA: MIT Press.

Soros, G. (1995), *Soros on Soros*, New York: John Wiley.

Weidlich, W. and G. Haag (1983), *Concepts and Models of a Quantitative Sociology*, Berlin, Heildelberg, New York: Springer-Verlag.

6. Rare events and stock price expectations

Aimé Scannavino

Stocks are bought on expectations – not on facts.
Burton G. Malkiel

INTRODUCTION

The subject of this study is essentially methodological. We are going to reason from the point of view of *efficient stock markets*, a complex context since it includes considerations on the distribution of informations between agents and the modes of their diffusion on a stock exchange, the formation of expectations, their interdependences and their self-fulfilling character, the effects of conjugated decisions. This hypothesis covers a logic of determination of stock prices modelling their evolutions with various stochastic processes such as random walks, martingales and diffusion processes. Here, our purpose is to examine the probabilistic properties of these usual representations laying foundations for the statistical and econometrical works devoted to the movements of asset prices; nevertheless, the preoccupations underlying this research will be original, to focus on rare events.

It is well known that rational expectations induce a multiplicity of equilibrium price trajectories (Taylor, 1977; Blanchard, 1979; McCallum, 1983), a really difficult question, truly important (related to *speculative bubble analysis* and *sunspot theory*). Actually, to expect a market evolution means to attribute probabilities to the conceivable equilibrium trajectories. Forming his anticipations, an agent responsible for an assets portfolio, for example, often will have to focus particularly on the possible price evolutions exposing to the highest risks; the development of *value at risk* analysis in financial management attests to this requirement. The confidence that he could grant to his forecasts, a very important theme in J.M. Keynes's work, will depend greatly on his aptitude to take into account the emergence of events definable as 'rare' and, especially, to estimate their probability of occurrence.

Also, everybody knows that in finance studies the tests of the 'efficient market/rational expectations hypothesis' present 'runs' as antithetic to this hypothesis (Taylor, 1986; Mills, 1993; Cuthbertson, 1996). Our intention is to deepen traditional analyses of 'runs' or fluctuations of the stock index, to evaluate the probabilities of the occurrence of such uncommon events; and, here, we shall deny the usual assertions supporting the tests.

More generally, our intention is to identify scientifically, that is, in terms of probability, various atypical evolutions of a stock index, using *large deviations theories*, a field which is among the most active today in probability theory and whose developments are likely soon to invest economic analysis. To our knowledge, this approach is used here for the first time in economics.

By setting up the notion of *rarity*, such a thought process permits the grasping of structures within the set of expectations conceived by an agent, but also the refinement of his rules of choice, as we shall demonstrate. Nevertheless, the foreseeable applications are really extensive: decision theory or the methodology of intertemporal optimization analyses, in particular, to explore the permanent income hypothesis (where it is shown that consumption can move according to a random walk or a martingale, Hall, 1978), the elaboration of optimal seigneuriage rules and so on, could be appreciably influenced by these new techniques.

In section 6.1 of this study we present the 'large deviations principle', a technical and rather complex concept, linked to *weak convergences* of probability measures. Section 6.2 evokes briefly the usual stochastic representations of stock prices. The last two sections propose taking advantage of various 'large deviations' theorems that we apply to financial models conceived in terms of random walks and martingales. Models of financial efficiency hypothesis dealing with diffusion processes, so important in 'continuous finance' (the Black–Scholes model for option pricing and interest rates structure, for instance) will not be presented in this study, although they are relevant to this analysis (through the theory of Freidlin and Wentsell – see Freidlin and Wentsell, 1984; Stroock, 1993).

6.1 THE CONCEPT OF 'LARGE DEVIATIONS'

To reason about the probability of *rare events* it is necessary to enter the stochastic inequalities field, current research about which never stops expanding. In order to clarify the notion of a *large deviation*, we must focus our attention on measures of events converging exponentially fast. An introductory approach will be given in terms of Chernoff and Hoeffding bounds. Then we shall be able to state a first theorem of large deviations, suggested by Chernoff, that will familiarize us with the notion of 'rate function'. Afterwards, the 'large deviation principle', a rather deep notion, will be stated. Throughout this section, our concerns are mainly didactic.

6.1.1 Chernoff and Hoeffding Bounds

Some elementary inequalities

Various usual inequalities in probability theory come from Markov's inequality (Nelson, 1995); notably, Chernoff's bound is a direct consequence of this statement. We individualize the following inequalities according to the informations that they require. They are greatly involved in large deviation analysis, and are also illustrative of exponentially fast convergence.

Markov's inequality   Let X be a random variable (r.v.) with density function $f_x(t)$ and let h be a non-negative and non-decreasing function; as $P[X \geq t] = \int_t^\infty f_x(z)dz$ and according to the definition of the mathematical expectation $E(h(X)) = \int_{-\infty}^\infty h(z)f_x(z)dz$ (this integral is assumed well-defined and finite), it readily follows that:

$$P[X \geq t] \leq \frac{E(h(X))}{h(t)} \qquad (6.1)$$

a statement called *Markov's inequality*. Since the knowledge of $E(X)$ is only required, it is termed a 'first order' inequality.

Chebyshev's inequality   Now, we assume that the variance of the r.v. X is known and finite. Writing $h(x) = x$ in (6.1) and considering $Y \equiv (X - E(X))^2$, so $E(Y) = var(X) \equiv \sigma_X^2$, we can state $\forall t > 0$ $P[Y \geq t^2] \leq E(Y)/t^2$; from $P[Y \geq t^2] = P[(X - E(X))^2 \geq t^2] = P[|X - E(X)| \geq t]$ we derive:

$$\forall t > 0 \ P[|X - E(X)| \geq t] \leq \frac{\sigma_X^2}{t^2}, \qquad (6.2)$$

the *Chebyshev's inequality*. Since it requires informations about the first two moments of the r.v. X, it is viewed as a 'second order' inequality. It asserts that wide divergences from the mean are unlikely as soon as the variance is small.

Chernoff's bound   The next statement requires the knowledge of all the 'moments' of a r.v. Let us consider the Markov's inequality, writing $h(x) = e^{\theta x}$ (for $\theta \geq 0$), and assume known the 'moment generating function' of a r.v. X (Feller, 1957) with probability density $f_x(x)$, defined by:

$$M_X(\theta) \equiv \int_{-\infty}^{\infty} e^{\theta x} f_x(x) dx \equiv E(e^{\theta x}) \tag{6.3}$$

(for $\theta > 0$ and if this integral exists). Expanding the exponential as a power series, we get:

$$M_X(\theta) = 1 + \theta E(X) + \frac{\theta^2 E(X^2)}{2!} + \frac{\theta^3 E(X^3)}{3!} + \dots$$

So it is clear that $M_X(0) = 1$ and the *n*th moment is given by $E(X^n) = M_X^{(n)}(0)$ (the knowledge of this function gives informations about all the moments, so its name is explained). With Markov's inequality (6.1) it is possible to assert that $\forall \theta \geq 0$ we have $P[X \geq t] \leq e^{-\theta t} M_X(\theta)$, hence:

$$P[X \geq t] \leq \inf_{\theta \geq 0} \{ e^{-\theta t} M_X(\theta) \} \tag{6.4}$$

a relation termed *Chernoff's bound* (according to the informations required, this inequality will be tighter than the preceding ones); we emphasize that it is typical of an exponentially fast convergence.

Hoeffding's bound   Now, we state another inequality[1] with an exponential rate of convergence, representative of a sequence of r.v. almost surely bounded (having a moment generating function), not necessarily identically distributed. Let $X_1, X_2, \dots, X_k, \dots$ be independent r.v. such that $\forall k \geq 1$, $P[X_k \in [0,1]] = 1$. Let $\mu_k = E(X_k)$ be the expectation of the r.v. X_k ($\forall k \geq 1$) and $\bar{\mu}_n$ be the mean of the expectations of the n first terms ($\bar{\mu}_n = \frac{1}{n}\sum_{k=1}^{n} \mu_k$ for $n \geq 1$). Let $\hat{S}_n = \frac{1}{n}\sum_{k=1}^{n} X_k$ be the mean of the realizations of the n first r.v. X_k (for $n \geq 1$). Then, we have:

$$P[|\hat{S}_n - \bar{\mu}_n| > \epsilon] \leq [\rho(\epsilon, \bar{\mu}_n)]^n + [\rho(\epsilon, 1 - \bar{\mu}_n)]^n \tag{6.5}$$

with $\rho(\epsilon, \beta) = \inf_{t>0}\{e^{-(\beta+\epsilon)t}[1 + \beta(e^t - 1)]\}$ for $\beta \in]0,1[$ and $\beta + \epsilon \in]0,1[$. Hence, it can be said that $(\hat{S}_n - \bar{\mu}_n) \to 0$ 'in probability', with an exponential rate of convergence.

Use of these inequalities for stock price modelling
With an heuristic concern, we are going to consider simple applications of these inequalities, what follows being only illustrative of our purpose.

Example 1:   Stock market trend
Consider a stock price moving upward or downward on several periods, such as for example the day, and let us identify simply each of its evolutions by a Bernoulli random variable X_i: 1 will designate a 'rise' with probability

p and 0 a 'decrease' (or an unvarying price) with probability $(1-p)$. Let us suppose that these evolutions are independent and that rises and declines are equiprobable (this hypothesis $p=\frac{1}{2}$ could be linked to our limited information; but, of course, it can be easily surrendered in deeper modelling). Therefore, taking into account the partial sum $S_n = X_1 + X_2 + \ldots + X_n$ of the independent and identically distributed (i.i.d.) Bernoulli r.v. X_i, we shall be able to evaluate the number of rises throughout the period $[0,n]$. It is clear that $E(S_n) = \frac{n}{2}$, $\sigma^2_{S_n} = \frac{n}{4}$ and that the moment generating function of S_n verifies:

$$M_{S_n}(\theta) = [M_X(\theta)]^n = [\sum_{x=0}^{\infty} P[X=x]e^{\theta x}]^n = \left[\frac{1+e^\theta}{2}\right]^n$$

Our purpose will be to estimate the probability of a number of rises larger than αn during a period of n days, with $\alpha > \frac{1}{2}$ (for example, such a perspective underlies the binomial tree model of the evaluation of options developed by Cox–Ross–Rubinstein).

Hence, according to Markov's inequality, we see that $P[S_n \geq \alpha n] \leq \frac{1}{2\alpha}$ (this bound, which does not depend on n delivers rather poor information).

With Chebyshev's inequality we get $P[S_n - \frac{n}{2} \geq (\alpha - \frac{1}{2})n] \leq \frac{1}{4n(\alpha - \frac{1}{2})^2}$ and, since $P[S_n - \frac{n}{2} \geq (\alpha - \frac{1}{2})n] \equiv P[S_n \geq \alpha n]$, we derive the statement:

$$P[S_n \geq \alpha n] \leq \frac{1}{4n(\alpha - \frac{1}{2})^2}$$

Finally, with Chernoff's bound it is possible to state $P[S_n \geq \alpha n] \leq \inf_{\theta \geq 0} \{e^{-\theta\alpha n}[\frac{1+e^\theta}{2}]^n\}$ and, using elementary calculus, we get the value of the infimum, $\theta^* = \log\frac{\alpha}{1-\alpha}$; as we are interested in the case $\alpha > \frac{1}{2}$, it follows that $\theta^* > 0$. By substitution, we end with:

$$P[S_n \geq \alpha n] \leq \left[\left(\frac{1}{2(1-\alpha)}\right)^n \Big/ \left(\frac{\alpha}{1-\alpha}\right)^{\alpha n}\right] = \left[\frac{(1-\alpha)^{(\alpha-1)}}{2\alpha^\alpha}\right]^n$$

and, setting $\beta \equiv \log\frac{1}{1-\alpha} + \alpha \log\frac{\alpha}{1-\alpha}$, we can state $P[S_n \geq \alpha n] \leq e^{-n\beta}$. Hence, with a fixed value for α, it is clear that $P[S_n \geq \alpha n]$ is decreasing exponentially fast according to n. Such speeds of convergence constitute the preoccupation of large deviation analyses. In a similar context, by relaxing the hypothesis of independence, we could easily take advantage of Hoeffding's bound.

6.1.2 Towards the 'Large Deviations' Theorem of Chernoff

To clarify the 'large deviations principle', it is useful to refer to the *weak law* and the *strong law of large numbers* as well as to the *central limit theorem*.

It is convenient to observe that these laws of large numbers make use respectively of 'convergence in probability' and 'convergence almost sure', whereas the central limit theorem is related to 'weak convergence', a point of view constitutive of large deviations analysis.

The laws of large numbers and the central limit theorem

The weak law of large numbers   Consider several identical reiterations of an experiment, through conditions ensuring the independence of the issues: let us refer therefore to a sequence of r.v. X_i i.i.d. according to the law of a r.v. X; moreover, suppose that the mean and the variance of X are finite. Then, the weak law of large numbers asserts the legitimacy of estimating the probability of an event from its frequency of occurrence. Indeed, if one focuses one's attention on the random variable $S_n = \sum_{i=1}^{n} X_i$ representative of the sum of the issues X_i of the n first experiments, one can 'naturally' consider that the value of the observed frequency (the statistical average) $\frac{S_n}{n}$ $\equiv \hat{S}_n$ is close to $E(X)$: this conviction must be rationalized. Since $E(\hat{S}_n) = E(X)$ and var $(\hat{S}_n) \equiv \sigma_{\hat{S}_n}^2 = \frac{1}{n}\sigma_X^2$, by applying Chebyshev's inequality we get $P[|\hat{S}_n - E(X)| \geq t] \leq \frac{\sigma_X^2}{nt^2}$ and a passage to the limit is enough to prove that:

$$\forall t > 0 \qquad \lim P[|\hat{S}_n - E(X)| \geq t] = 0, \tag{6.6}$$

a well-known expression entitled the *weak law of large numbers*. It is stated in terms of 'convergence in probability' $\hat{S}_n \to E(X)$ when $n \to \infty$.

The strong law of large numbers   Furthermore, one can show, with more difficulty but in various manners, that:

$$P[\lim_{n \to \infty} |\hat{S}_n - E(X)| \geq t] = 0, \tag{6.7}$$

an assertion called the *strong law of large numbers*. It is stated in terms of 'convergence almost surely' $\hat{S}_n \to E(X)$ a.s. Of course, the strong law of large numbers implies the weak law. Remember that one can give various other statements of these laws[2] by modifying the hypotheses stated here.

The central limit theorem   A very well-known assertion, for n r.v. X_i i.i.d. according to a r.v. X with mean $E(X)$ and standard deviation σ, the central limit theorem states that:

$$\lim_{n \to \infty} P\left[\frac{S_n - n(E(X))}{\sqrt{n}} \leq t\right] = \Phi(t; \mu = 0, \sigma^2) \tag{6.8}$$

with:

$$\Phi(t; \mu,\sigma^2) \equiv \frac{1}{\sigma\sqrt{2\pi}} \int_{-\infty}^{t} \exp\left\{ -\frac{(z-\mu)^2}{2\sigma^2} \right\} dz,$$

the (cumulative) distribution function of the normal law $\mathcal{N}(\mu, \sigma^2)$. Therefore, it means that $\sqrt{n}[\frac{S_n}{n} - E(X)]$ 'converge in law'[3] to $\mathcal{N}(0, \sigma_X^2)$. One can also formulate central limit theorems for r.v. not identically distributed (Sen and Singer, 1993; Port, 1994). The laws of iterated logarithm and several theorems proposed by Berry–Esseen, by Mann–Wald and so on (Shorack–Wellner, 1986) specify the convergence asserted by the central limit theorem (this field of inequalities is particularly wide). Large deviation analysis deepens such studies.

A large deviation theorem stated by Chernoff
We introduce now some major concepts of large deviation theories. By taking the logarithm of Chernoff's bound (6.4) it is possible to state:

$$\log P[X \geq t] \leq \inf_{\theta \geq 0} [\log M_X(\theta) - \theta t] \equiv -I(t) \qquad (6.9)$$

by writing:

$$I(t) = \sup_{\theta \geq 0}[\theta t - \log M_X(\theta)] \qquad (6.10)$$

We call $I(t)$ the *large deviation rate function*; very soon the reason for this terminology will become clear: this function occurs in the following exponential equation (6.11), representing a rate of decrease. One can show easily that this function $I(t)$ is convex and $\min_t\{I(t)\} = I(E(X)) = 0$.

The significance of this statement is clear: the strong law of large numbers says that the average $\hat{S}_n \equiv (X_1 + \ldots + X_n/n)$ of a sequence of r.v. X_i i.i.d. converges almost surely to $E(X)$ when $n \to \infty$, but without giving information on the speed of this convergence, in other words on the probability that $\hat{S}_n$ remains greater than a value $t \geq E(X)$. A 'large deviations' analysis readily allows us to state, with more precision, that:

$$\forall t \geq E(X) \qquad P[\hat{S}_n \geq t] = e^{-nI(t)+o(n)}, \qquad (6.11)$$

a *Chernoff's bound* (Nelson, 1995) asserting that divergences to the average exponentially decrease at a rate $-I(t)$ when $n \to \infty$. Now, we apply this analysis to the stock price modelling developed in Example 1.

Example 2: Probability of upward trends of a stock index
For a discrete r.v. X we have $M_X(\theta) = \sum_{x=0}^{\infty} P[X = x]e^{\theta x}$, hence for the Bernoulli's law considered here (with $p = \frac{1}{2}$) we can write $M_X(\theta) = \frac{1}{2}(1 + e^{\theta})$

and verify that $E(X) = \frac{1}{2} = M_X^{(1)}(0)$, $E(X^2) = \frac{1}{2} = M_X^{(2)}(0)$, and so on, with $M_X(0) = 1$. As a result, the large deviations rate function will be stated:

$$I(t) = \sup_{\theta \geq 0}[\theta t - \log M_X(\theta)] = \sup_{\theta \geq 0}[\theta t - \log(\frac{1}{2}(1 + e^\theta))]$$

Furthermore, the value of θ which maximizes $I(t)$ is $\theta^* = \log\frac{t}{1-t}$, and it can be proved readily that $I(t = \theta^*) = t\log t + (1 - t)\log(1 - t) + \log 2$. Thus, we end with:

$$P[\hat{S}_n \geq t] = \left[\frac{(1 - t)^{t-1}}{2t^t}\right]^n e^{o(n)}$$

Taking into account the case $t = \alpha$ with $\alpha > \frac{1}{2}$, examined previously, we can assert:

$$P[\hat{S}_n \geq \alpha] = \left[\frac{(1 - \alpha)^{\alpha-1}}{2\alpha^\alpha}\right]^n e^{o(n)}$$

so it would be possible (by giving values to α) to complete the informations already supplied by the inequalities of Markov, Chebyshev and Chernoff.

We now formulate explicitly the 'large deviations principle'.

6.1.3 The Large Deviations Principle

Today, large deviations analyses constitute one of the major axes in probability theory research – Azencott et al, 1978; Dacunha–Castelle and Duflo, 1982; Freidlin and Wentsell, 1984; Deuschel and Stroock, 1989; Stroock, 1993; Duflo, 1996; Dembo and Zeitouni, 1997 – and the *large deviations principle* is there unifying; we are going to present plainly this rather abstract notion.

An illustration

Consider a sequence of r.v. $X_1, \ldots, X_n$ i.i.d. according to a standard Gaussian law $\mathcal{N}(0, 1)$. The empirical average $\hat{S}_n = \frac{1}{n}\sum_{i=1}^n X_i$ is, obviously, a Gaussian variable with mean 0 and variance $1/n$. By the weak law of large numbers and the central limit theorem, we can assert:

$$\forall \delta > 0 \qquad \lim_{n \to \infty} P[|\hat{S}_n| \geq \delta] = 0 \qquad (6.12)$$

$$\forall A \subset \mathcal{R} \qquad \lim_{n \to \infty} P[\sqrt{n}\hat{S}_n \in A] = \frac{1}{\sqrt{2\pi}}\int_A \exp\left\{-\frac{x^2}{2}\right\}dx \qquad (6.13)$$

Moreover, since $\hat{S}_n \sim \mathcal{N}(0, \frac{1}{n})$, we get (with a simple change of variable):

$$\forall \delta > 0 \qquad P[|\hat{S}_n| \geq \delta] = 1 - \frac{1}{\sqrt{2\pi}} \int_{-\delta\sqrt{n}}^{\delta\sqrt{n}} \exp\left\{-\frac{x^2}{2}\right\} dx$$

As a result:

$$\lim_{n\to\infty} \frac{1}{n} \log P[|\hat{S}_n| \geq \delta] = -\frac{\delta^2}{2}. \qquad (6.14)$$

The steady value of $\hat{S}_n$ is from (6.13) of the order of $\frac{1}{\sqrt{n}}$, but assertion (6.14)

underlines that with a small probability, of the order of $e^{\frac{-n\delta^2}{2}}$, $|\hat{S}_n|$ can have large values (Dembo and Zeitouni, 1993).

Relations (6.12) and (6.13) are always true when the r.v. (X_i) are only identically distributed, with mean 0 and variance 1; this remark makes one wonder whether assertion (6.14) is still admissible for the not Gaussian r.v. X_i: is it possible to get rid of a reference to a precise probability distribution? We shall state, with Cramer's theorem, that $\lim_{n\to\infty} \frac{1}{n} \log P[|\hat{S}_n| \geq \delta]$ always exists (taking values dependent on the probability distribution of the r.v. X_i).

Definition of a 'rate function'
Let (μ_ϵ) be a family of probability measures on the probability space $(X, \mathcal{B})$ where X is a topological space and $\mathcal{B}$ its complete Borel σ-field; let $\epsilon \downarrow 0$. First, we recall that a function $I : X \to [0, +\infty]$ is said to be *lower semi-continuous* if $\forall \alpha \in [0, +\infty]$ the subset $\Psi_I(\alpha) \equiv \{x \in X / I(x) \leq \alpha\}$ is closed in X. The following terminology is admitted by most of the authors.

Definition 1: Rate function
A rate function is a function $I : X \to [0, +\infty]$ lower semi-continuous. The 'effective domain' of the function I is the subset of X where I takes finite values; it will be denoted D_I. A rate function I is a 'good' rate function if $\forall \alpha$ the subset $\Psi_I(\alpha)$ is compact.

Simply, it is convenient to observe that a 'good' rate function[4] is reaching its infimum on every closed subset. At present, we can state the 'large deviations principle'.

The 'large deviations' principle
The statement of the large deviations principle is rather abstract: it gets its meaning only through applications in different probabilistic contexts (such as random walks, martingales, diffusion processes, and so on) and it needs illustrations. We shall reason in terms of 'weak convergence'. Let X be a complete separable metric space (Polish space) equipped with its Borel σ-field; let (P_ϵ) be a family of probability measures.

Definition 2: Varadhan, large deviations principle
A sequence of probability measures (P_ϵ) satisfies the 'large deviations' principle with respect to a rate function I there exists a function $I : X \to [0, \infty]$ such that:

1. I is lower semi-continuous;
2. $\forall a < \infty$ the subset $\Psi_I(a) \equiv \{x \in X / I(x) \le a\}$ is compact in X;
3. for every closed subset C in X

$$\lim_{\epsilon \to 0} \sup \epsilon \log \{P_\epsilon(C)\} \le - \inf_{x \in C} I(x);$$

4. for every open subset G in X

$$\lim_{\epsilon \to 0} \inf \epsilon \log \{P_\epsilon(G)\} \ge - \inf_{x \in G} I(x).$$

Now, we can formulate Cramer's theorem which asserts that a sequence of r.v. i.i.d. verifies this principle.

Theorem 1: Cramer
Let ξ_i be a sequence of independent r.v. with a same law μ, defined on $\mathcal{R}$; consider the sequence of probability distributions P_n linked to $\hat{S}_n \equiv \frac{\xi_1 + \dots + \xi_n}{n}$. We assume that the moment generating function

$$M(\theta) = E\{e^{\theta \xi_i}\} = \int e^{\theta \xi_i} d\mu(x)$$

is finite $\forall \theta$. We admit also that the smallest closed interval of $\mathcal{R}$ to which μ attributes a probability 1 is $\mathcal{R}$. We define a function $I(x) = \sup_\theta \{\theta x - \log M(\theta)\}$. Under these conditions, the sequence (P_n) satisfies the 'large deviations' principle with respect to a rate function $I(x)$.

The function $x \mapsto \sup_\theta \{\theta x - \log M(\theta)\}$ is called 'Cramer's transform' or 'Fenchel–Legendre's transform' of $\theta \mapsto \log M(\theta)$.

Similar analyses can be deepened by considering random vectors and, especially, by relaxing the hypothesis of independence (this is the purpose of the Gartner–Ellis theorem, used here in subsection 6.3.1). Let us take an example.

Example 3: Sequence of r.v. i.i.d. according to a normal density N(0, 1)
Consider a sequence of independent r.v. ξ_i defined on $\mathcal{R}$ and having a same law N(0, 1); let P_n be a family of probability distributions linked to $\hat{S}_n \equiv \frac{\xi_1 + \dots + \xi_n}{n}$. We can easily calculate the moment generating function

$M(\theta) = E\{e^{\theta\xi}\} = \exp\frac{\theta^2}{2}$. According to Cramer's theorem, the sequence (P_n) satisfies the large deviation principle with the rate function $I(x) = \sup_\theta \{\theta x - \log M(\theta)\} = \frac{x^2}{2}$.

6.2 USUAL REPRESENTATIONS OF STOCK PRICES

Next we consider models representative of stock index evolutions, assuming that prices integrate, rapidly and correctly, the information possessed by the traders (LeRoy, 1989; Guimaraes *et al.*, 1989; Malkiel, 1991; Shiryaev, 1999), stock markets being said to be 'informationally efficient'. Indeed, this efficiency hypothesis is very complex to specify since it covers considerations about the distribution of informations between agents and the modes of their diffusion on financial markets, the elaboration of expectations, their interdependences and so on.

6.2.1 The Hypothesis of Informational Efficiency

Until the 1930s, financial analysis gave its attention exclusively to the notion of the 'fundamental value' of a financial asset, defined for an action, to set an example, by the actualized value of future dividends anticipated, assuming that its price usually fluctuates around its fundamental value. The analysis of investment opportunities needed, therefore, essentially the collection and the processing of all the available information about the perspectives of stock dividends. Then, the trading rule for investors was to acquire assets whose price was estimated lower than the fundamental value. Nevertheless, now it appears that recourse to such a strategy was not so profitable as expected (Cowles, 1933; Morgenstern, 1959).

In 1934, Working observed that successive variations of stock prices presented weak correlations and he suggested the idea that movements of the price p_t of a financial asset could be rendered in terms of the statistical concept of the 'random walk'. Later, Samuelson showed that such a randomized price modelling could be explained by reference to 'idealized' capital markets: if all the available information is integrated into prices and if those react without delay to the arrival of new information, then the price movements will appear erratic. Since the 1950s, several statistical studies of the stock index, conducted by M.G. Kendall, C.W.J. Granger, O. Morgenstern and so on were received as validations of such a concept.

6.2.2 Stock Price Modelling in Terms of 'Random Walks'

The first representation of the financial efficiency hypothesis, the random walk model of stock prices (see Holden *et al.*, 1990; Mills, 1993; Enders, 1995; Cuthbertson, 1996; Shiryaev, 1999) is formulated simply as $p_t = p_{t-1} + e_t$ with e_t a *white noise*: at any time, all the information is encompassed within the market price of a stock, so the future movements of the price will be due to the arrival of radically new information, which is in consequence unforeseeable today. It is so hard to predict, because the available information as a whole is already processed on the market. Therefore, this stochastic process (also stated $\Delta p_t = \epsilon_t$) is a particular case of the process AR(1) $p_t = a + \alpha p_{t-1} + e_t$ (the r.v. e_t being i.i.d.) characterized by $a = 0$ and $\alpha = 1$. So, with an initial condition p_0, this model will be formulated $p_t = p_0 + \Sigma_{i=1}^t e_i$. As $E(p_t) = E(p_{t-s}) = p_0 \; \forall s$, we can see that the mean of p_t is a constant; but the variance of a random walk var $(p_t) = $ var $(e_t + e_{t-1} + \ldots + e_1) = t\sigma^2$ (denoting var $(e_t) = \sigma^2$) will not be invariable (depending on t) and therefore a random walk is not a *stationary* stochastic process (Guikhman and Skorokhod, 1980; Karlin and Taylor, 1975 and 1981; Merton, 1990). Actually, each random shock e_t will have a persistent influence (without progressive attenuation) on the sequence $\{p_t\}$, their cumulation being constitutive of a 'stochastic trend'. Let us consider an example of stock price econometric modelling with reference to such a random process.

Example 4: Stock price random processes with drift
Sometimes, to test the efficiency ('weak efficiency', according to Fama) of a market asset, econometric studies use models of the kind

$$p_t = a + \alpha p_{t-1} + e_t, \tag{6.15}$$

where $\{p_t\}$ is a time series of observations about an asset price, a is a drift and e_t a random term. If we cannot reject the null hypothesis [$H_0 : \alpha = 1$] assuming the existence of a unit root, we will be encouraged to consider that price variations are random and, therefore, that the market is efficient. The statistical estimation (Chan and Lai, 1993) gives, for example, for the period 1988–90 in France (Agefi's index of weekly data), $\hat{\alpha} \cong 1$, moreover the chronological series p_t appears integrated of order 1, favouring weak efficiency consideration.

6.2.3 Stock Price Modelling in Terms of a 'Martingale'

The random walk models imply, nevertheless, too restrictive sets of hypotheses concerning the independence of asset price successive variations; actually, the statistical stock market studies suggested that this consideration was excessive. So the use of models stated in terms of *martingales* appeared interesting.

We must be more explicit in statements concerning the modelling of information arrival (Guikhman and Skorokhod, 1980; Karlin and Taylor, 1975 and 1981; Merton, 1990; Prokhorov and Shiryaev, 1998). This consideration is supposed to refer to the mathematical concept of *filtration*: let $(\Omega, \mathcal{F}, P)$ be a probability space and $\mathbf{F} = \{\mathcal{F}_0, \mathcal{F}_1, \ldots\}$ be a sequence of σ-fields contained in $\mathcal{F}$; if $\forall n\ \mathcal{F}_n \subset \mathcal{F}_{n+1}$ then $\mathbf{F}$ will be called a *filtration*. Economically, each $\mathcal{F}_n$ will be the set of information available at the date n and we envisage a temporal accumulation of news without any surrender of information (increasing families of subsets). A process $Y = \{Y_n, n \geq 0\}$ will be *adapted* to this filtration if $\forall n$ the r.v. Y_n is $\mathcal{F}_n$-measurable.

Definition 3: Martingale adapted to a filtration
Let $\mathbf{F}$ be a filtration of the probability space $(\Omega, \mathcal{F}, P)$ and Y be a sequence of r.v. which is adapted to this filtration. We call the pair $(Y, \mathbf{F}) = \{(Y_n, \mathcal{F}_n)/n \geq 0\}$ a martingale if

$$\forall n \geq 0 \quad \begin{cases} E(|Y_n|) < \infty, \\ E(Y_{n+1}/\mathcal{F}_n) = Y_n. \end{cases}$$

A finite sequence $\{(Y_n, \mathcal{F}_n)/0 \leq n \leq N\}$ which satisfies the preceding definition will be also termed a martingale.

Thus, we don't rely upon the hypothesis of independence of stock price evolutions which underlies the random walk modelling. In the general case, a representation in terms of a martingale is less restrictive than a reference to the random walk model. It imposes for a price sequence that $E(p_{t+1} - p_t/\mathcal{F}_t) = 0$, but does not dictate special requirements for the conditional variances and correlations. Thereby, a very important observation, the martingale model can deal with persistent upward or downward trends on stock exchanges, evolutions assuming often an autocorrelation of conditional variances. We just mention that several inequalities and central limit theorems for martingales have been elaborated; later we consider martingales from the point of view of 'large deviations'.

6.3   RANDOM WALKS AND 'LARGE DEVIATIONS'

Now, we consider the representations of stock price evolutions stated in terms of random walks, the expression of the 'efficient market hypothesis', and so of rational expectations. With such perspectives, the organizational logic of research studies is canonical.[5] Once stated as an hypothesis, with specification of the underlying stochastic process, all the econometric tests relevant to its validation or confirmation must be conducted: autocorrelation tests, spectral tests, the famous Shiller's volatility tests, and the well-known search for 'runs' (Taylor, 1986). Actually, the purpose of our study is to investigate the real significance of the usual analysis: even if markets present a form of efficiency connected to such processes, nothing would exclude, for example, the possibility of realizations (sample paths) of these processes presenting persistent upward[6] or downward trends. Our goal will be to consider rigorously, that is to say in terms of probability, the occurrence of such uncommon events. Here, we intend to deny somewhat that 'runs' are necessarily an antithesis to the 'efficient market/rational expectations hypothesis'. After characterizing the usual stock index movements, we examine the probabilities of infrequent, persistent evolutions and then we focus on 'runs' and long-lasting upward or downward tendencies, called here 'long segments'. In fact, we are interested in various kinds of price *volatility*. We introduce an original approach to such questions, making use of large deviations techniques.

6.3.1 The Asymptotics of a 'Stochastic Trend'

Here we propose a further development of a well-known concept in econometrics and finance, the 'stochastic trend'. We come back to equation (6.15) of a stock price, $p_t = a + \alpha p_{t-1} + e_t$ (the r.v. e_t being i.i.d. for $t \geq 1$) and to the decisive hypothesis test, whether $\alpha = 1$ or $\alpha < 1$. To focus on the stochastic trend we simplify this relation, assuming $a = 0$, writing then $(1 - \alpha L)p_t = e_t$ (with $Lp_t = p_{t-1}$, the lag operator). Just for greater convenience we pose $p_0 = 0$. Is this price index, following a random walk $p_t = p_{t-1} + e_t$ (an AR(1) with a unit root, so a non-stationary process; actually this process is I(1) 'integrated of order one') or an AR(1) process $p_t = \alpha p_{t-1} + e_t$ without a unit root (since $(1 - \alpha L) = 0$ induces $L = \frac{1}{\alpha} > 1$, a requirement for stationarity)? In the first case $p_t = \sum_{i=1}^{t} e_i$ and the index exhibits a 'stochastic trend', that is, every perturbation e_t maintains its effect indefinitely (contributing to the formation of an erratic tendency), whereas this one is vanishing with time in the second case, since $p_t = \sum_{i=1}^{t} \alpha^{t-i} e_i$. We propose, by large deviation analysis, to distinguish two models of these kinds by their asymptotics. Let us reason about the asymptotic evolution (that is, $t \to \infty$) of the averaged variation of a stock price $(\sum_{i=1}^{t} \Delta p_i)/t$.

   If the econometrics – as in Example (4) – has shown that such an index follows a random walk model $p_t = p_{t-1} + e_t$, so $\Delta p_t = e_t$ and $p_t = \sum_{i=1}^{t} e_i = \sum_{i=1}^{t} \Delta p_t$ (supposing $p_0 = 0$ through a suitable adaptation of the basis of the price index), we just have a sum of i.i.d. r.v. e_i, and the application of Cramer's theorem leads to a simple relation representative of the probability for the mean

$$\frac{\Sigma_{i=1}^{t}\Delta p_i}{t} = \frac{\Sigma_{i=1}^{t}e_i}{t} = \frac{p_t}{t}$$

to exceed a threshold β, a guide for a trader conceiving of his expectations:

$$\liminf_{t\to\infty} \frac{1}{t} \log \{P\left[\frac{\Sigma_{i=1}^{t}\Delta p_i}{t} \in]\beta, \infty[\right]\} \geq -\inf_{x>\beta} I(x) = -\inf_{x>\beta}\{\sup_{\theta}$$

$$\{\theta x - \log M_{e_1}(\theta)\}\} \tag{6.16}$$

with $M_{e_1}(\theta)$ being the moment generating function of the r.v. e_1.

Now, we envisage that $\Delta p_t = \epsilon_t$ but $\epsilon_t = \alpha\epsilon_{t-1} + u_t$ with (u_t) an i.i.d. process: in this new model, the price variations (ϵ_t) form an AR(1) process without unit root. We have $\Sigma_{i=1}^{t}\Delta p_i = p_t - p_0 = \Sigma_{i=1}^{t}\epsilon_i$ (admitting freely $\epsilon_0 = 0$); again if $p_0 = 0$ we shall have

$$\frac{\Sigma_{i=1}^{t}\Delta p_i}{t} = \frac{\Sigma_{i=1}^{t}\epsilon_i}{t} = \frac{p_t}{t}.$$

We can assert with the Gartner-Ellis theorem (Bucklew, 1990; Dembo and Zeitouni, 1997):

$$\liminf_{t\to\infty} \frac{1}{t} \log \{P[\frac{\Sigma_{i=1}^{t}\Delta p_i}{t} \in]\beta,\infty[]\}$$

$$\geq -\inf_{x>\beta} I(x) = -\inf_{x>\beta} \{\sup_{\theta} \{\theta x - \lim_{t\to\infty}\frac{1}{t}\log Mp_t(\theta)\}\}$$

$$= -\inf_{x>\beta} \{\sup_{\theta} \{\theta x - \log M_{u_1}(\frac{\theta}{1-\alpha})\}\}$$

$$= -\inf_{x>\beta} \{\sup_{\theta} \{\theta x - \log M_{\frac{u_1}{1-\alpha}}(\theta)\}\} \tag{6.17}$$

(with a nice hypothesis on u_i such that E $(u_1) = 0$ and $P[u_1 \in [a, b]] = 1$). Equations (6.16) and (6.17) show that the asymptotic evolution of the sum $\Sigma_{i=1}^{t}\epsilon_i$ of a sequence of non-i.i.d. r.v. $\epsilon_i = \alpha\epsilon_{i-1} + u_i$, is the same as the one of the sum of a sequence of i.i.d. r.v. distributed as $u_1/(1-\alpha)$.

6.3.2   The Regularities of Stock Price Movements

To deal with this problem, we are going to take into account simple random walks, but more complex forms could be considered.

The swings of tendencies

We examine probabilities of the usual phases of stock price evolutions assumed to be in accordance with a symmetric random walk.

Example 5: Analysis of upward trends
Let us consider stock price models[7] where the sequence of rises and decreases may be represented in terms of the r.v. X_i i.i.d. characterized by $P[X_i=1]=P[X_i=-1]=\frac{1}{2}$ for instance (we focus on the direction of movements, not on their amplitude). The partial sum sequence $\{S_n=\Sigma_{i=1}^{n}X_i, n\geq 0\}$ (with $S_0=0$) constitutes then a symmetrical random walk. Let $\{Y_n, n\geq 1\}$ be a process defined by $Y_n=0$ if $S_n=0$, $Y_n=1$ if $S_n>0$ and $Y_n=-1$ if $S_n<0$: the case $Y_n=1$ being representative therefore of the fact that the number of 'rises' has been larger than that of 'decreases'.

We are going to study the probability that up to the date $2n$ there have been $2k$ positive price variations (rises) and to prove that this probability is given by an arcsinus law. Let us note $u_n=P[S_{2n}=0]=P[Y_{2n}=0]$; it is not difficult to see that $u_n=\binom{2n}{n}\frac{1}{2^{2n}}$ and thereafter $u_n=\frac{2n-1}{2n}u_{n-1}$. Then the probability that the symmetrical random walk reaches the level 0 for the first time on the fixed date $2n$ will be:

$$P[S_1\neq 0,\dots,S_{2n-1}\neq 0, S_{2n}=0]=\frac{\binom{2n}{n}\frac{1}{2^{2n}}}{2n-1}=\frac{u_n}{2n-1}$$

We can also assert that $P[S_1\neq 0,\dots,S_{2n-1}\neq 0, S_{2n}\neq 0]=u_n$ and with Stirling's formula ($n!\cong n^{n+\frac{1}{2}}e^{-n}\sqrt{2\pi}$) we derive:

$$u_n\cong\frac{(2n)^{2n+\frac{1}{2}}e^{-2n}\sqrt{2\pi}}{n^{2n+1}e^{-2n}\sqrt{2\pi}2^{2n}}=\frac{1}{\sqrt{n\pi}} \quad (6.18)$$

so it is clear that $\lim_{n\to\infty}u_n=0$. By making use of these assertions, we see that the symmetrical random walk will go back to the origin (with as many 'rises' as 'decreases') almost certainly.

Moreover, for $k=0,\dots,n$ we can prove simply that:

$$P[S_{2k}=0, S_{2k+1}\neq 0, S_{2k+2}\neq 0,\dots,S_{2n}\neq 0]=u_k u_{n-k} \quad (6.19)$$

Note $E_{k,n}$ the event 'up to the date $2n$, the symmetrical random walk has been positive $2k$ times', with $p_{k,n}$ pointing out the probability of this event; we can prove that $p_{k,n}=u_k u_{n-k}$. Precisely, the probability distribution of a r.v. X given by the formula:

$$P[X=2k]=u_k u_{n-k}=\binom{2k}{k}\frac{1}{2^{2k}}\binom{2(n-k)}{n-k}\frac{1}{2^{2(n-k)}} \quad (6.20)$$

is called a 'discrete probability distribution in arcsinus'.

Actually, we underline the not too obvious fact that the frequency of upward movements (stock price increases) does not converge therefore to a constant value (the probability distributions would converge to a point mass, not towards the arcsinus law). This observation leads us to focus on the possibility of 'large deviations'. Notably, the probability that the price index will not reach the level 0 between the instants $2nx$ and $2n$ (with $x \in]0, 1[$) is approximately equal to $\frac{2}{\pi} \arcsin(\sqrt{x})$, as can be proved.

The recurrent fluctuations

Now, let us examine the stock price oscillations.

Example 6: The property of 'reverting to the mean'

Consider again the former example: let $X_1, X_2, \ldots$ be i.i.d. r.v., each of them taking the value 1 (rise of the price) with a probability p, and -1 (decrease) with a probability $1 - p$, a process modelling the evolutions of a stock index, from date to date (again we are in line with the point of view of the binomial model for the evaluation of options developed by Cox *et al.*, 1979); by these convenient hypotheses the amplitudes of 'rises' and 'decreases' do not matter. The partial sum $S_t = \sum_{i=1}^{t} X_i$ will represent therefore the movement of the stock price evolutions. The discrete time random sequence $S = (S_t)$ is a simple random walk reproducing all the conceivable movements of the stock index. It starts at the origin if $S_0 = 0$: naturally, in such a context, the origin designates, simply, the date of the first observation. Obviously, we can put a lot of questions relative to this process[8] and, notably, we wonder when it will return to the starting point.[9]

We note $p_0(n) = P[S_n = 0]$ the probability of a comeback to the origin after n steps. Let $f_0(n)$ be the probability that the first return to the origin occurs at the nth step: so, $f_0(n) = P[S_1 \neq 0, \ldots, S_{n-1} \neq 0, S_n = 0]$. We note, respectively, the probability generating functions[10] linked to $p_0(n)$ and $f_0(n)$:

$$P_0(s) = \sum_{n=0}^{\infty} p_0(n)s^n \qquad F_0(s) = \sum_{n=0}^{\infty} f_0(n)s^n$$

Manifestly, by definition of a generating function, we can state $F_0(s) = E(s^{T_0})$, thus $F_0(s)$ is the generating function of the r.v. T_0 which designates the (random) period preceding the first return of the stock prices to the origin. Indeed, for this process, it is easy to prove that:

$$P_0(s) = 1 + P_0(s)F_0(s), \qquad P_0(s) = \frac{1}{\sqrt{1 - 4pqs^2}}, \; F_0(s) = 1 - \sqrt{1 - 4pqs^2}$$

The proofs of the following propositions are elementary:

1. For the considered process, we evaluate the probability that the stock price evolutions come back to the origin with the formula:

$$\sum_{n=1}^{\infty} f_0(n) = F_0(1) = 1 - |p - q|.$$

2. If a return to the origin is sure (that is, $p = q = \frac{1}{2}$ and $F_0(1) = 1$) then its average time (its expectation[11]) will have for its estimate:

$$\sum_{n=1}^{\infty} n f_0(n) = F_0'(1) = \infty.$$

It is said that a process is 'recurrent' (or persistent) if a return to the origin is 'almost sure'. It is clear that a process underlying such stock price evolutions will be recurrent if and only if $p = \frac{1}{2}$. But, even in this case, the time preceding a first return to the origin will have an infinite mean.

Crossing some threshold
Now, we are concerned with the possibility for a stock index to reach a fixed level r. As a financial illustration and to make easier the appreciation of the contribution of large deviations theorems, we propose simple models for crossing thresholds and reaching maxima.

Example 7: Crossing thresholds
We define, naturally, the probability that the stock index reaches for the first time the threshold r at the date n as $f_r(n) = P[S_1 \neq r, \ldots, S_{n-1} \neq r, S_n = r]$ and we consider the generating function $F_r(s) = \sum_{n=1}^{\infty} f_r(n)s^n$. The proof of the next assertion does not present any difficulty: for the process taken into account:

$$F_r(s) = F_1(s)^r \quad \text{if } r \geq 1, \quad F_1(s) = \frac{1 - \sqrt{1 - 4pqs^2}}{2qs}$$

As a result, the probability that the stock price evolutions could take values larger than the origin, will be estimated[12] according to:

$$F_1(1) = \frac{1 - |p - q|}{2q} = \min\left\{1, \frac{p}{q}\right\}$$

Numerically, if we had as the probability of a 'rise' $p = \frac{1}{4}$, for example, then the probability of having the index above its origin will not exceed $\frac{1}{3}$.

Example 8: Reaching maxima
From the same point of view, we say that a random walk $S_n = X_1 + \ldots + X_n$ (with X_i r.v. i.i.d. taking values in Z) is 'right continuous' if $P[X_i \leq 1] = 1$: so it is almost sure that the amplitude of a rise will be lower than 1. By convenience, we shall only take into account right continuous random walks with $P[X_i = 1] > 0$. In such a case, we can consider the probability distribution of random walk maxima. Spitzer's identity gives us rich information about this probability distribution of the maxima of the process (that is, the

stock price evolutions). It is stated: Let S be a right continuous random walk and consider the maximum reached by our process at time n, that is, $M_n = \max \{S_i, i \in [0,n]\}$; so we get[13] for $|s|, |t| < 1$ and $S_n^+ = \max\{0, S_n\}$:

$$\log \left\{ \sum_{n=0}^{\infty} t^n E(s^{M_n}) \right\} = \sum_{n=1}^{\infty} \frac{t^n}{n} E(s^{S_n^+}) \qquad (6.21)$$

6.3.3 Analysis of Rare Persistent Evolutions

Next, we make specific use of large deviations techniques.

Persistent evolutions
The laws of large numbers and the central limit theorem are already able to provide information about persistent evolutions of stock prices considered according to references to random walks.

Example 9: Persistent stock price evolutions
Let X_i be a sequence of r.v. i.i.d. with finite mean μ; we know from the law of large numbers that $\hat{S}_n \equiv \frac{S_n}{n}$ converges to μ when $n \to \infty$ and, hence, S_n converges to $n\mu$. What can be said about $S_n - n\mu$?

When the r.v. X_i have finite variance σ^2, the central limit theorem says that (for $n \to \infty$) $(S_n - n\mu)/\sqrt{n\sigma^2}$ converges in law to $\mathcal{N}(0, 1)$; this means, on the one hand, that $S_n - n\mu$ is of the order of $\sqrt{n}$ and, on the other hand, that the distribution of $(S_n - n\mu)/\sqrt{n}$ converges to the normal distribution when $n \to \infty$, whatever the distribution of X_i.

We saw that, for a simple random walk (that is, with increments i.i.d. getting values $\{-1, 1\}$ with respective probabilities p and $q = 1 - p$), the necessary and sufficient condition for 'persistency' (an almost certain return to the origin, that is, $\exists n \geq 1\ P[S_n = 0] = 1$) was 'symmetry': $p = q$ (in other words, we must have $E(X_i) = 0$). The law of large numbers informs about such 'persistence' of a random walk with increments X_i i.i.d. taking integer values, linked to the elementary following theorem:[14] a random walk will be 'persistent' if $E(X_i) = 0$ and 'non-persistent' if $E(X_i) \neq 0$. Therefore, a 'persistent' random walk has to return to its origin infinitely often.

A 'large deviations' theorem for the analysis of stock price trends
We know already that the deviations of $S_n = X_1 + \ldots + X_n$ with respect to $n\mu$ are of the order of $\sqrt{n}$, and now we shall be interested in $P[|S_n - n\mu| > n^\alpha]$ when $n \to \infty$ for $\alpha > \frac{1}{2}$, a problem of 'large deviations'. We shall take advantage of the following theorem.[15]

Theorem 2: Convergence at exponential speed
Let X_i be a sequence of r.v. i.i.d. with mean 0 and suppose that the moment generating function $M(t) = E(e^{tX_1})$ takes finite values in a neighbourhood of 0. If $a > 0$ and $P[X_1 > a] > 0$ then:

$$\lim_{n \to \infty} P[S_n > na]^{\frac{1}{n}} = e^{-\lambda(a)}$$

with $\lambda(a) \equiv -\log \{\inf_{t > 0} \{e^{-at} M(t)\}\} > 0$.

Hence, we know that $P(S_n > na]$ is decreasing to 0 with an exponential speed given by the term $e^{-n\lambda(a)}$.

Example 10: Analysis of stock market trends in terms of 'large deviations'
We come back to our fundamental example, relative to stock price evolutions with 'rises' and 'decreases' assumed *a priori* equiprobables and of unit amplitude. Note h_n the number of 'rises' and b_n the number of 'decreases' up to date n; we can prove easily, with the preceding theorem, that the gap $e_n \equiv h_n - b_n$ between the numbers[16] of 'rises' and 'decreases' will be determined according to the probability:

$$P[e_n > an]^{\frac{1}{n}} \to \frac{1}{\sqrt{(1+a)^{1+a}(1-a)^{1-a}}}$$

for $a \in]0, 1[$, when $n \to \infty$. It is clear that such information, readily quantifiable, is absolutely similar to the evaluation earlier given with reference to the theorems of Chernoff (equation (6.11)) and Cramer (Theorem 1).

6.3.4 Analysis of Runs and Long Segments

From the same point of view, we consider stock price evolutions satisfying the 'financial efficiency hypothesis' formulated in terms of a random walk, being mainly interested in 'runs', that is, increase without breaks in a stock index, then focusing attention on the possibility of long-lasting evolutions with given properties of a stock index, which we propose to call 'longs segments'. We contest the current idea that runs are ineluctably antinomic to 'efficient market/rational expectations hypothesis'.

We introduce the notion of 'long segments' for the following reason: the definition of a run is problematic, the identification of their bounds being always delicate: for example, is it necessary to take into account a 'brief' and 'minor' reversal of the tendency in an upward trend or is it rather convenient to ignore it? In practice, it is always difficult to take such a decision when dealing with those questions, especially in the framework of econometric tests of the efficiency hypothesis. From the point of view of our long segments, identified by stock prices remaining inside some measurable subsets (hence, we are interested in more complex sequences than series of rises), these difficulties are solvable.

The occurrence of runs

We identify a run with a sequence of increasing numbers:[17] for example, the series {1, 4, 6, 3, 7, 9, 5, 4} will be divided according to |1, 4, 6|3, 7, 9|5|4. Thus, a sequence of numbers $\{x_1, x_2, \ldots\}$ wil begin with a vertical bar and we shall put a bar between x_i and x_{i+1} as soon as $x_i > x_{i+1}$. It is possible to study runs by reference to various probability distributions. Here, as an example, we shall consider the uniform law: let $X_1, X_2, \ldots$ be a sequence of i.i.d. r.v. uniformly distributed on]0, 1[and our purpose is to evaluate the probability distribution of the length of runs.

Probability distribution of the first run   We note the first L_1 and we prove that:

$$P[L_1 \geq m] = \frac{1}{m!} \quad m = 1, 2, \ldots \tag{6.22}$$

(an estimation of the probability that the first m values are in increasing order).

It is clear that $P[L_1 \geq 1] = 1$. FWhat is more, we have:

$$P[L_1 \geq 2] = 1 - P[L_1 < 2] = 1 - P[x_1 > x_2] = P[x_2 \in]x_1, 1[]$$

$$P[x_2 \in]x_1, 1[] = \int_0^1 \left(\int_{x_1}^1 1_{]0,1[}(x_2)\, dx_2 \right) dx_1 = \int_0^1 (1 - x_1) dx_1 = 1 - \int_0^1 x\, dx = \frac{1}{2}$$

thus, $P[L_1 \geq 2] = P[x_2 \in]x_1, 1[] = \frac{1}{2}$. Similarly, we get:

$$P[L_1 \geq 3] = 1 - P[L_1 < 3] = 1 - \{P[x_1 \leq x_2] + P[x_3 \leq x_2/x_1 < x_2]\}$$

$$= 1 - \frac{1}{2} - P[x_3 \leq x_2/x_1 < x_2]$$

$$P[x_3 \leq x_2/x_1 < x_2] = \int_0^1 \left(\int_{x_1}^1 \left(\int_0^{x_2} 1_{]0,1[}(x_3)\, dx_3 \right) dx_2 \right) dx_1$$

$$= \int_0^1 \left(\int_{x_1}^1 x_2\, dx_2 \right) dx_1 = \frac{1}{3}$$

so, $P[L_1 \geq 3] = \frac{1}{6}$. By recurrence, the announced result is proved.

Probability distribution of a run length   First, we shall determine the probability distribution of the length of a run knowing the initial value x of the stock price: we shall have $P[L \geq m/x] = [(1-x)^{m-1}]/[(m-1)!]$: indeed, the length of a run will be larger than m if the $(m-1)$ values following x are superior to this initial value (the probability of such an event is $(1-x) \ldots (1-x)$) and if they are in an increasing order (event with probability $1/(m-1)!$).

It is necessary to state, then, the non-conditional probability distribution of the length of a run. Let us denote I_n the initial value of the nth run. The process $\{I_n, n \geq 1\}$ is clearly a Markov chain with continuous state space (the interval $]0, 1[$). We can evaluate the probability $p(y/x)$ that the next run begins with an initial value y knowing that a run is beginning with an initial value x:

$$p(y/x) = \begin{cases} e^{1-x} & \text{if } y < x \\ e^{1-x} - e^{y-x} & \text{if } y > x. \end{cases}$$

This probability $p(y/x)$ characterizes the transitions between states x and y of the Markov chain I_n.

In order to get the limit distribution $\pi(y)$ of I_n, we could prove first that $\pi(y) = 2(1-y)$ for $y \in]0, 1[$. On this basis, we could estimate $\lim_{n\to\infty} P[L_n \geq m]$ the non-conditional limit distribution of the length of a 'far' run:

$$\lim_{n\to\infty} P[L_n \geq m] = \int_0^1 \frac{(1-x)^{m-1}}{(m-1)!} 2(1-x)dx = \frac{2}{(m+1)(m-1)!}$$

Finally, we could estimate the average length of a run: $\lim_{n\to\infty} E(L_n) = 2$.

Presence of long segments in a random walk
The following analysis will appear more general and powerful. Let $S_k = \Sigma_{i=1}^k X_i$ be a random walk, the r.v. X_i being i.i.d. and taking values in $\mathcal{R}^d$ and let $S_0 = 0$. Note R_m the maximal length[18] $(l-k)$ of the segments (S_k, S_l) in the interval $[0, m]$ (with $k, l \in [0, m]$) whose empirical average belongs to a measurable subset $A \subset \mathcal{R}^d$. Formally:

$$R_m = \max \{l-k / k, l \in [0, m], \frac{S_l - S_k}{l-k} \in A\}$$

Example 11: Long segments in stock price evolutions
Let us consider stock price model (so $d = 1$) elaborated according to the former random walk; the term R_m will designate the maximal length of an observed daily sequence verifying some given property (the observed stock price being a 'realization' of the random walk process) along the period

$[0, m]$. For example, we can take into account segments of the stock index evolutions whose average exceeds a fixed magnitude. Notably, our purpose could be to evaluate the probability of occurrence of a lasting sequence of the daily stock index evolutions such that the increment of the index has been at least equal, on average, to a fixed level. In this sense, we have spoken of 'long segments'. To look for these long segments is equivalent to searching for stock price evolutions characterized by maximal length; in this way, we deal with 'trend reversal'.

We investigate minimal date,[19] denoted T_r, at which we could meet a segment with length superior or equal to r and average corresponding to A. So we consider *stopping times*. Formally:

$$T_r = \inf \; \{l / \frac{S_l - S_k}{l - k} \in A \text{ for } k \in [0, l-r]\}$$

Example 12: Continuation
Therefore, in our perspective of study, we have to deal with the problem of identifying the temporal horizon which will almost surely allow us to observe a first segment of (minimal) fixed length and verifying, for example, some typical property. Specifically, our purpose would be to know, in terms of probabilities, the date at which it is just possible to encounter 30 consecutive days throughout which, on average, the stock index rise would exceed a fixed level.

Actually, we shall have $R_m \geq r \Leftrightarrow T_r \leq m$. We can specifiy the limits of the sequence $\{R_m\}$ and $\{T_r\}$ when m and r take increasing values (converging to ∞), with the help of the following powerful theorem (Dembo and Zeitouni, 1993).

Theorem 3: Occurrence of long segments in a random walk
Let μ_n be the probability distribution of a random walk average $\hat{S}_n = \frac{1}{n} S_n$; if the event A is such that the limit $I_A = - \lim_{n \to \infty} \frac{1}{n} \log \mu_n(A)$ is well-defined (it exists) then, almost surely:

$$\lim_{m \to \infty} \frac{R_m}{\log m} = \lim_{r \to \infty} \frac{r}{\log T_r} = \frac{1}{I_A}$$

Here $I_A = - \lim_{n \to \infty} \frac{1}{n} \log \mu_n(A)$ is a large deviations rate function.

6.4   MARTINGALES AND 'LARGE DEVIATIONS'

Now, let us consider representations of stock prices in terms of martingales. We state *Hoeffding's inequality* and *Azuma's inequality* that inform about the 'large deviations' of martingales, more precisely on their propensity to fluctuate (Grimmett and Stirzaker, 1992). Another result, useful to the elaboration of decision filters, for example, will be also evoked.

6.4.1 Hoeffding's Theorem and its Applications

Let $\mathbf{F}$ be a filtration of the probability space $(\Omega, \mathcal{F}, P)$ and let $(Y, \mathbf{F}) = \{(Y_n, \mathcal{F}_n)/n \geq 0\}$ be a martingale. A *martingale differences* associated with Y is a stochastic process $D = \{D_n, n \geq 1\}$ defined by $D_n = Y_n - Y_{n-1}$. As a result, $Y_n = Y_0 + \sum_{i=1}^{n} D_i$. It is clear that the sequence of r.v. D_n verifies the following properties: D_n is $\mathcal{F}_n$-measurable, $E(|D_n|) < \infty$ and $\forall n \; E(D_{n+1}/\mathcal{F}_n) = 0$. The next theorem will indicate the probability of large deviations of $|Y_n - Y_0|$, under the hypothesis that the martingale differences $D_n = Y_n - Y_{n-1}$ is (almost surely) bounded.

Theorem 4: Hoeffding
Let $(Y, \mathbf{F}) = \{(Y_n, \mathcal{F}_n)/n \geq 0\}$ be a martingale. We assume that there exists a sequence of real numbers $\{K_1, K_2, \ldots\}$ such that $\forall n \; P[|Y_n - Y_{n-1}| \geq K_n] = 1$. Then $\forall x > 0$:

$$P[|Y_n - Y_0| \geq x] \leq 2 \exp\left\{ \frac{-\frac{1}{2}x^2}{\sum_{i=1}^{n} K_i^2} \right\}$$

Next, we consider an application of this theorem, coming back to the Example (1) studied earlier, relative to the number of rises of a stock price.

Example 13: The frequency of rises of a stock price
We consider, therefore, a sequence of r.v. X_i i.i.d. having the Bernoulli probability distribution with parameter p, and we interpret $X_i = 1$ as a 'rise' and $X_i = 0$ as a 'decrease' (or a constant level) of the stock index; thus, $S_n = X_1 + \ldots + X_n$ will record the number of rises during n days. We are interested in the process $Y_n = S_n - np$, which is a martingale. By Hoeffding's theorem, we can assert, with $\mu = \max \{p, 1-p\}$, that:

$$\forall x > 0 \qquad P[|S_n - np| \geq x\sqrt{n}] \leq 2 \exp\left\{ \frac{-x^2}{2\mu} \right\}$$

So we measure the probability of a gap between the number of rises and the 'normal' (most probable) value np.

6.4.2 Azuma's Theorem for Large Deviations and Martingale Convergence

We present a generalized Azuma inequality (Ross, 1996) valid for random variables that do not change 'too rapidly' and exhibiting a martingale structure.

Theorem 5: Generalized Azuma inequality

Let $\{X_n,\ n \geq 1\}$ be a martingale with mean $X_0 = 0$ such that $-\alpha \leq X_n - X_{n-1} \leq \beta$ $(\forall n \geq 1)$. Then $\forall c > 0$ and $\forall m \in \mathcal{N} \setminus \{0\}$ one will have for some $n \geq m$:

$$(1)\ \ P[X_n \geq nc] \leq e^{\frac{-2mc^2}{(\alpha+\beta)^2}}$$

$$(2)\ \ P[X_n \leq -nc] \leq e^{\frac{-2mc^2}{(\alpha+\beta)^2}}$$

A financial application may be deduced from this assertion.

Example 14: Average number of stock price rises

Let $S_n = \sum_{i=1}^{n} X_i$ be a process representative of evolutions of a stock price, with $\{P[X_i = 1] = p;\ P[X_i = 0] = q = 1-p\}$ (r.v. X_i being independent), recording the number of rises until date n. It is clear that $Y_n = S_n - np = \sum_{i=1}^{n} (X_i - p)$ is a martingale such that $E(Y_n) = 0$ and $Y_n - Y_{n-1} \in [-p,\ 1-p]$. According to the preceding theorem:

$$P[|\hat{S}_n - p| \geq \epsilon \quad \text{for } n \geq m] \leq 2e^{-2m\epsilon^2}$$

Notably, the probability that $\hat{S}_n$ differs from p by more than 5 per cent, after 1000 days, will be of the magnitude:

$$P[|\hat{S}_n - p| \geq 0.05 \quad \text{for } n \geq 1001] \leq 2e^{-2 \times 1001 \times 0.05^2} \cong 0.0135 = 1.35 \text{ per cent}$$

6.4.3 Backward-Martingale Convergence Theorem

Let **G** be a decreasing sequence of σ-fields; let Y be a process which is adapted to **G**. We designate (Y, **G**) a *backward martingale* or *reverse martingale* if:

$$\forall n \geq 0 \quad \begin{cases} E(|Y_n|) < \infty, \\ E(Y_{n+1}/G_{n+1}) \leq Y_{n+1}. \end{cases}$$

It can be seen that $\{(Y_n, G_n); n = 0, 1, 2, \ldots\}$ is a backward martingale if and only if the reversed sequence $\{(Y_n, G_n); n = \ldots, 2, 1, 0\}$ is a martingale.

Theorem 6: Convergence of backward martingale
Let (Y, G) be a backward martingale; the r.v. Y_n converges to a limit Y_∞ almost surely and in mean.

Briefly, we present a property (Grimmett and Stirzaker, 1992) which may be the principle of construction of a financial filter (the demonstration being easy).

Example 15: A financial filter
Let $X_1, X_2, \ldots$ be a sequence of r.v. i.i.d. taking their values in $\mathcal{N}$ (the daily variations of a stock index); we focus our attention on the process $S_n = X_1 + \ldots + X_n$ (the level of the stock index). Suppose that $P[S_N = b] > 0$; then one can prove that:

$$P[S_k \geq k/k \in [1, N], \quad S_N = b] = \min\left\{1, \frac{b}{N}\right\} \qquad (6.23)$$

We have just identified the probability that $S_k \geq k$ knowing that later, to the period N, the random walk will be in a state b. Therefore this reasoning is a backward one. Economically, the interpretation of this proposal would be the following: if it is thought that a stock index can reach a threshold b at a future period N, equation (6.23) allows a reply to the question: 'What is the probability that in a former period k the index $S_k = X_1 + \ldots + X_k$ exceeded the level k?'

6.5 CONCLUSION

As we stated in the introduction, the subject of this study is methodological, dealing mainly with the presentation of large deviations techniques and intending to attest their interest to finance and economic analysis. It was necessary to underline their aptitude to formalize the notion of the 'rare occurrence' of an event and to give a first idea of their usefulness in decision theory. Here, we have not tackled another application for this approach dealing with econometrics, estimation theory.

NOTES

1. Refer to Sen and Singer (1993). We could state several other inequalities of such a kind: notably, refer to Ross (1996); Shorak and Wellner (1986), van der Vaart and Wellner (1996); Csörgö-Horváth (1993).
2. See, for example, Port (1994); Shorak and Wellner (1986); Sen and Singer (1993).
3. Let (F_n) be a sequence of probability distributions on $\mathcal{R}$ and F a probability distribution on $\mathcal{R}$. We say that F_n 'converges weakly' to F if and only if we have $\lim_n F_n(B) = F(B)$ for every Borel subset $B \subset \mathcal{R}$ whose boundary is F-negligible (a null set, that is, $F(\partial B) = 0$). We note $F_n \Rightarrow F$. If a r.v. X_n has a probability distribution F_n, if a r.v. X has a probability distribution F and if F_n 'converge weakly' to F then we say that (X_n) converges in distribution (or in law) to X. The notion of weak convergence has been examined at length in the probabilistic works of P. Billingsley. See Billingsley (1968); Davidson (1994); Port (1994); Sen and Singer (1993); Shorack and Wellner (1986); Stroock (1984); Swartz (1994); van der Vaart and Wellner (1996); Wagschal (1995). It may be noted that such terminology is misleading: the notion of 'weak convergence' in probability theory corresponds to that of '*-weak convergence' in functional analysis.
4. We notice that some authors – notably Varadhan (1984) and Dupuis and Ellis (1997) – call a 'rate function' what we have just designated as a 'good' rate function (therefore, defining it by the compactness of $\Psi_1(\alpha)$); here, this distinction will be non-operative.
5. The same observation can be done for the *permanent income analysis*. In the general outline of the formalizations proposed by Hall (1978), the intertemporal optimization calculations, with rational expectations, lead to the consideration of trajectories linked to random walks or martingales and the right thing to do is to conduct econometric validations of these formal statements: such is the logical structure of the papers devoted to this model of trade-off between consumption and savings. Nevertheless, while conforming to a random walk, consumption could possibly present various persistent upward trends or downward trends and so on. Such events could be qualified as *rare* and it would be convenient to estimate their probability of occurrence. The analyses that we present in this study would be applicable.
6. As a result, the observation of such movements of prices (but, actually, a realization of a random walk process) could induce misleading judgements. Traders on a stock exchange could be victims of their perception of uncommon share price evolutions, such as persistent upward trends, inducing them to doubt the efficiency of markets on which they intervene: they could identify erroneously the working out of expectations, overestimate the market imperfections, exaggerate the influence of some agents, and so on, the context being able to induce the emergence of 'speculative bubbles'. Analyses of large deviations, by estimating the probability of these stock price movements, could deliver more objective appreciations of market functioning.

   Furthermore, these approaches would be interesting in examinations of the principles of various *chart analyses* used by operators to define their purchase and sale strategies on stock markets. For example, a reference to 'Bollinger's bands' assumes that market and behaviour structures would vary as soon as distance between stock prices and their tendency become larger than two standard deviations: this divergence could just be a 'large deviation' and not a modification of the underlying process.
7. Mathematical principles of the following developments can be found, notably, in books such as Ross (1996); and Port (1994).
8. Such a model is a very general one and we do not have to question its validity: the random walk hypothesis is its pre-eminent character.
9. Here, we deal with 'regenerative processes' whose mathematical developments can be found in Grimmett and Stirzaker (1992).
10. The *'generating function'* of a r.v. X is stated $G(s) = E(s^X)$. For a discrete r.v. X taking values in $\mathcal{N}$, we have $G(s) = \sum_{i=0}^{\infty} P[X=i]s^i$ therefore $G(0) = P[X=0]$ and $G(1) = 1 = P[X < \infty]$.
11. We remember that if a r.v. X has a generating function $G(s)$ hence $E(X) = G'(1)$. Here,

$F_0(s)$, being the generating function of $f_0(n)$, we get $F_0'(1) = E(f_0(n))$. With $p = q$ we have $F_0(s) = 1 - \sqrt{1 - s^2}$; so, by deriving with respect to s and making this variable converge to 1, we get the announced result.

12. Therefore, we are considering the generating function associated with the probability that stock prices reach the threshold 1.
13. The utility of this 'identity' is to provide complete information about the probability distribution of the maxima on the basis of the probability distribution of the random walk. We obtain this result, with $f_j(n) = P[T_j = n]$, by observing that:

$$\forall k \geq 0 \quad P[M_n = k] = \sum_{j=0}^{n} f_k(j)P[T_1 > n - j]$$

$$\sum_{n=0}^{\infty} t^n E(s^{M_n}) = \sum_{k=0}^{\infty} s^k \left(\sum_{n=0}^{\infty} t^n P[M_n = k] \right) = \sum_{k=0}^{\infty} s^k F_k(t) \left(\frac{1 - F_1(t)}{1 - t} \right)$$

14. Cf. Grimmett and Stirzaker (1992).
15. Ibid.
16. Specifically, if we associate with a rise the value 1 and with a decrease the value -1 then the sequence of issues: $\{1, 1, -1, -1, 1\}$ will be characterized by $h_n = 3$, $b_n = 2$, $e_n = h_n - b_n = 1$ and hence $e_n = S_n = 1 + 1 - 1 - 1 + 1 = 1$.
17. See Ross (1996). Other analyses of runs may be found in works such as those in Godbole and Papastavridis (1994).
18. The quantity R_m represents therefore the dimension of the longest segments (which we can observe between the instants 0 and m) whose average belongs to a measurable subset A (that is, in concrete terms it takes values in one or several specified intervals).
19. In others terms, it will be necessary to observe the stock index on the period $[0, T_r]$ to find the first segment of length r whose average agrees with event A.

REFERENCES

Azencott, R., Y. Guivarc'h and R.F. Gundy (1978), *Ecole d'été de probabilité de Saint-Flour VIII–1978*, Berlin: Springer-Verlag.
Billingsley, P. (1968), *Convergence of Probability Measures*, London: John Wiley.
Blanchard, O.J. (1979), 'Backward and forward solutions for economies with rational expectations', *American Economic Review* 69, 114–18.
Bucklew, J.A (1990), *Large Deviation Techniques in Decision, Simulation, and Estimation*, New York: John Wiley.
Chan, K.C. and P. Lai (1993), 'Unit root and cointegration tests of world stock prices', in S.R. Stansell (ed.), *International Financial Market Integration*, Oxford: Basil Blackwell.
Cox, D.R. and H.D. Miller (1987), *The Theory of Stochastic Processes*, London: Chapman and Hall.
Cox, J.C., S. Ross and M. Rubenstein (1979), 'Option pricing: a simplified approach', *Journal of Financial Economics*, 7, 229–64.
Cowles, A. (1933), 'Can stock market forecasters forecast?', *Econometrica*, 1 (4), 309–24.
Csörgö, M. and L. Horváth (1993), *Weighted Approximations in Probability and Statistics*, New York: John Wiley.
Cuthbertson, K. (1996), *Quantitative Financial Economics*, Chichester, Sussex: John Wiley.

Dacunha-Castelle, D. and M. Duflo (1982), *Probabilités and statistiques. Problèmes à temps fixe*, Paris: Masson.

Davidson, J.E.H. (1984), *Stochastic Limit Theory*, Oxford: Oxford University Press.

Dembo, A. and O. Zeitouni (1993), *Large Deviations Techniques and Applications*, London: Jones and Bartlett.

Dembo, A. and O. Zeitouni (1997), 'Moderate deviations for iterates of expanding maps', in Y.M. Kabanov, B.L. Rozovskii and A.N. Shiryaev, *Statistics and Control of Stochastic Processes*, London: World Scientific.

Deuschel, J.D. and D.W. Stroock (1989), *Large Deviations*, London: Academic Press.

Duflo, M. (1996), *Algorithmes stochastiques*, Berlin: Springer-Verlag.

Dupuis, P. and R.S. Ellis (1997), *A Weak Convergence Approach to the Theory of Large Deviations*, Chichester, Sussex: John Wiley.

Enders, W. (1995), *Applied Econometric Time Series*, Chichester, Sussex: John Wiley.

Feller, W. (1957), *An Introduction to Probability Theory and its Applications*, Chichester, Sussex: John Wiley.

Freidlin, M.I. and A.D. Wentsell (1984), *Random Perturbations of Dynamical Systems*, Berlin: Springer-Verlag.

Godbole, A.P. and S.G. Papastavridis (1994), Runs and patterns in probability, selected papers', Dordrecht: Kluwer Academic Publishers.

Grimmett, G.R. and D.R. Stirzaker (1992), *Probability and Random Processes*, Oxford: Clarendon Press.

Guikhman, I.I. and A.V. Skorokhod (1980), *Introduction à la théorie des processus aléatoires*, Moscow: Mir.

Guimaraes, R.M.C., B.G Kingsman and S.J. Taylor (1989), *A Reappraisal of the Efficiency of Financial Markets*, Berlin: Springer-Verlag.

Holden, K., D.A. Peel and J.L. Thompson (1990), *Economic Forecasting*, Cambridge: Cambridge University Press.

Hall, R.E. (1978), 'Stochastic implications of the life cycle-permanent income hypothesis: theory and evidence', *Journal of Political Economy*, 86, 971–88.

Karlin, S. and H.M. Taylor (1975), *A First Course in Stochastic Processes*, London: Academic Press.

Karlin, S. and H.M. Taylor (1981), *A Second Course in Stochastic Processes*, London: Academic Press.

LeRoy, S.F. (1989), 'Efficient capital markets and martingales', *Journal of Economic Literature*, 27, 1583–621.

Malkiel, B.G. (1991), *A Random Walk Down Wall Street*, New York: W.W. Norton.

McCallum, B.T. (1983), 'On non-uniqueness in rational expectations models', *Journal of Monetary Economics*, 11, 139–68.

Merton, R.C. (1990), *Continuous-time Finance*, Oxford: Basil Blackwell.

Mills, T.C. (1993), *The Econometric Modelling of Financial Time Series*, Cambridge: Cambridge University Press.

Morgenstern, O. (1959), *International Financial Transactions and Business Cycles*, Princeton, NJ: Princeton University Press.

Nelson, R. (1995), *Probability, Stochastic Processes and Queueing Theory*, Berlin: Springer-Verlag.

Port, S.C. (1994), *Theoretical Probability for Applications*, Chichester, Sussex: John Wiley.

Prokhorov, Y.V. and A.N. Shiryaev (1998), *Probability Theory III*, Berlin: Springer-Verlag.

Ross, S. (1996), *Stochastic Processes*, Chichester, Sussex: John Wiley.

Sen, P.K. and J.M. Singer (1993), *Large Sample Methods in Statistics*, London: Chapman and Hall.

Shiryaev, A.N. (1999), *Essentials of Stochastic Finance: Facts, models, theory*, London: World Scientific.

Shorack, G.R. and J.A. Wellner (1986), *Empirical Processes with Applications to Statistics*, Chichester, Sussex: John Wiley.

Stroock, D.W. (1984), *An Introduction to the Theory of Large Deviations*, Berlin: Springer-Verlag.

Stroock, D.W. (1993), *Probability Theory*, Cambridge: Cambridge University Press.

Swartz, C. (1994), *Measure Integration and Function Spaces*, London: World Scientific.

Taylor, J.B. (1977), 'Conditions for unique solutions in stochastic macroeconomic models with rational expectations', *Econometrica*, 45, 1377–85.

Taylor, S.J. (1986), *Modelling Financial Time Series*, Chichester, Sussex: John Wiley.

van der Vaart, A.W. and J.A. Wellner (1996), *Weak Convergence and Empirical Processes*, Berlin: Springer-Verlag.

Varadhan, S.R.S. (1984), *Large Deviations and Applications*, Philadelphia, Pennsylvania: Society for Industrial and Applied Mathematics.

Wagschal, C. (1995), *Topologie et analyse fonctionnelle*, Paris: Hermann.

PART II

Rationality, Heterogeneity and Formation of
Expectations: Lessons from Survey Data

7. Rationality of price and unemployment expectations: tests on French qualitative microdata

François Gardes, Salah Ghabri, Jean-Loup Madre and Marie-Claude Pichery*

INTRODUCTION

There are two ways to implement direct rationality tests on households' expectations. When these expectations are collected as qualitative items, a first approach consists in quantifying these answers. Quantification theory relies on two approaches: probabilistic (Carlson and Parkin, 1974; Batchelor, 1986; Pesaran, 1987) and regressive (Pesaran, 1990; Smith and McAleer, 1995). However, limitations of the probabilistic approach appear, because it is necessary to estimate the perception threshold of respondents and to make assumptions on the functional form of the distribution of responses. Implemented on aggregate data from UK surveys (Batchelor, 1986) and on individual data from the French INSEE conjunctural surveys (Gardes and Madre, 1991; Gardes and Ghabri, 1996), these tests tend to reject the conventional hypothesis of rationality (that is, no bias and efficiency). The second approach consists in implementing directly qualitative tests (Nerlove, 1983; Gouriéroux and Pradel, 1986; Ivaldi, 1992) without quantifying the responses. These tests require panel data containing at least two periods to test efficiency and three periods to test the absence of autocorrelation.

The work presented in this chapter follows this second approach, which is more qualitative. In the first section, the survey data and the results obtained with the quantitative approach are presented. The second section introduces the qualitative analysis by computing a synthetic index of perceptions and expectations based on contingency tables. The third section presents the methodology of the Gouriéroux–Pradel test (1986)

* We are grateful to the INSEE for providing the individual data of the *Enquête de conjoncture INSEE auprès des ménages*. This research was partially supported by the CREDOC.

and its implementation on the INSEE conjunctural surveys data. The fourth section defines the expectations processes corresponding to the structure of qualitative answers of each household. This allows us to count the distribution of expectation processes among the population in each period.

7.1   THE INSEE HOUSEHOLDS' CONJUNCTURE SURVEYS

Since the late 1950s to 1994, the French National Institute of Statistics and Economic Studies (INSEE) has conducted three times a year a conjuncture survey by interviewing 6000–8000 households (since 1994, this survey has been replaced by a European monthly phone survey). In these surveys, the same household was interviewed in two consecutive years during October–November. It allowed a comparison of its expectations at the first interview with its perception of the changes which had occurred between the two interviews. By matching this information for the period 1972–94, we have built 22 short panels (only two years long), containing around 2500 households each. Expectation and perception questions concern *the general standard of living, the situation of the labour market, inflation, and the household's financial situation and their saving intention.* Responses are qualitative and pre-coded. Except for inflation, it consists of five ranked items: 'much worse', 'worse', 'no changes', 'better' and 'much better'. The complete list of items is in Appendix A.

On average, non-response rates for expectations and perceptions are 15.4 per cent for inflation, 16.9 per cent for unemployment and 17.2 per cent for the general standard of living in France. The empirical study of the rationality of households' behaviour is generally conducted by comparing their expectations and perceptions of an economic variable at different points in time.

7.2   SUMMARY OF RESULTS BASED ON QUANTIFIED DATA

A first analysis concerned the permanent income hypothesis (Gardes and Madre, 1990). Answers to questions on two consecutive years allow us to compute permanent and transitory incomes by classifying households according to the sign of the transitory (not expected) income. It appears that car purchases are affected by the transitory incomes received by the household.

Before estimating the process of inflation and unemployment expectations, Gardes and Madre (1991), Gardes and Ghabri (1996) and Ghabri (1998) quantified individual perceptions and expectations of French households using probability models. Answers are supposed to be normally or logistically distributed. The principal results are:

1. *Strong rejection of the weak form of the rational expectations hypothesis (REH)* The weak form of the REH is strongly rejected at the individual and the aggregate level for the unemployment variable. It is only accepted for aggregate macro series of inflation. This is probably due to the correlation between the actual and the quantified series of inflation expectations and their perceptions.
2. *Aggregation bias in the estimation of the adaptive model* The adaptive model estimated in times series data overestimates the coefficient of adaptation (approximately equal to unity), while estimation at the micro-level gives estimates inferior to 0.5. This discrepancy results from a complete correction of the macro forecast error (common to all households) compared to a partial correction of the specific error made by each household (see different estimations of the adaptive model in Appendix A).
3. *The dependency of the expectation process on the volatility of inflation and unemployment* The coefficients of the simple adaptive model (obtained for all the estimations of paired surveys from 1972–3 to 1993–4) vary mainly according to the volatility of inflation (or unemployment) rather than according to their levels. This result confirms the relevance of the Turnovsky hypothesis rather than the Cagan hypothesis.

7.3 CONTINGENCY TABLE AND INDEXES

7.3.1 Contingency Table

The measurement of association between two quantitative variables can be obtained by the correlation coefficient. For qualitative information classified into k items, different indexes have been proposed by statisticians or have been widely used by sociologists and psychologists. Statisticians propose synthetic indexes such as the χ^2 of Pearson or the γ of Goodman and Kruskal (1963). Sociologists and psychologists use more disaggregated indexes in order to capture an agreement between two judgements; a synthesis is developed in Liebetrau (1983) and an extension is proposed in Pichery (1989).

$_{t-1}X^e_t$ Expectation

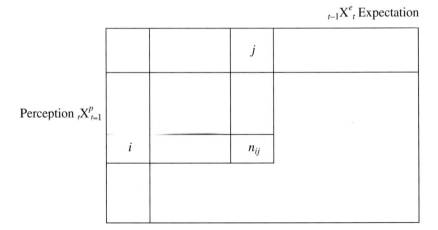

Perception $_tX^p_{t-1}$

Figure 7.1: Contingency table

These indexes need a preliminary calculation from a contingency table in the form shown in Figure 7.1. In this table, $_{t-1}X^e_t$ represents expectation made in $t-1$ for the period t and X_t is the corresponding perception made in t for the period $(t-1, t)$. For n individuals, observations for expectations and perceptions are given in k classified items. The term n_{ij} gives the number of households perceiving the item i in t when they had expected the item j in $t-1$. By dividing each cell by n, the total of households responding in two successive surveys, one is in a position to construct a new matrix, the elements of which are given in terms of probability ($p_{ij}=n_{ij}/n$). By completing that information with the marginal probabilities $p_{i.}$ and $p_{.j}$, one disposes of full information on *the probability distribution for the observed phenomenon*, for period t.

7.3.2 Indicators

In order to characterize the sample empirically, it may be helpful to define and use two synthetic indexes (the mean absolute error E_a, the coefficient γ of Goodman and Kruskal) and two disaggregated indexes (the agreement coefficients I_a and disagreement coefficients I_d). A presentation of these indicators is developed below.

Synthetic indexes
The *mean absolute error* E_a is calculated from the difference between the marginal probabilities $\epsilon_{i.}=p_{i.}-p_{.i}$. A null value means that the probabili-

ties to expect and to perceive a specific item i are identical although concerned households are not necessarily the same. However, the case of a positive difference (respectively negative) is particularly interesting because it reveals a disagreement between the responses: the probability of perceiving the item i is greater than the probability of expecting it (respectively smaller). Such a situation means the existence of a systematic expectation error and allows the pessimist or optimist nature of households to be picked up when expected and perceived modalities are not the same.

From these differences, the mean absolute error E_a is calculated for k modalities:

$$E_a = \frac{1}{k} \sum_{i=1}^{k} |p_{i.} - p_{.i}|$$

The existence of a relation between two judgements can be pointed out by means of *the γ coefficient of Goodman and Kruskal* calculated by using the number of pairs of concordant and discordant responses. It is used to determine whether or not there exists an association between identical responses. A positive coefficient (maximal for $\gamma = 1$) means a general agreement between two judgements.

Disaggregated indexes: agreement and disagreement coefficients
Disaggregated indexes are associated with each possible pair of responses (each cell of the contingency matrix) and are calculated by using conditional probabilities.

Given $\theta_i = \frac{p_{ii}}{p_{.i}}$ and $\theta_i^* = p_{i.}$, Light (1971) defines an agreement coefficient between two classifications by:

$$K_{ii} = \frac{\theta_i - \theta_i^*}{1 - \theta_i^*} = \frac{p_{ii} - p_{i.}p_{.i}}{p_{.i} - p_{i.}p_{.i}}$$

Pichery (1989) proposes an extension in order to calculate conditional disagreement coefficients, K_{ij}, corresponding to responses in items j for expectation and i for perception:

$$K_{ij} = \frac{T_{ij} - T_{ij}^*}{1 - T_{ij}^*} = \frac{p_{ij} - p_{i.}^* p_{.j}}{p_{.j} - p_{i.}^* p_{.j}} \qquad \text{with } T_{ij} = \frac{p_{ij}}{p_{.j}} \text{ and } T_{ij}^* = p_{i.}$$

Each coefficient varies between an inferior limit $K_{ij}\text{inf} = K_{ii}\text{inf} = -p_{i.}/(1 - p_{i.})$ which is always negative but not constant, and a superior limit which is equal to 1. A normalization is used to have new coefficients with values between 0 and 1, permitting direct comparisons:

$$K_{ij}^* = \frac{K_{ij} + |K_{ij}\text{inf}|}{1 + |K_{ij}\text{inf}|} = \frac{p_{ij}}{p_{.j}} = T_{ij}$$

This is a ratio between the probability p_{ij} and the marginal probability $p_{.j}$ giving a new interpretation for T_{ij}, the conditional probability.

Other synthetic coefficients can be obtained from the above individual coefficients such as:

- a global coefficient for agreement: $\quad I_a = \sum_i K_{ii}^*$

- two coefficients for disagreement, one of which is positive I_p if the realization is better than the expectation, and the other one I_n is negative in the opposite case. In this way, if the k items are classified according to a decreasing order (from a strong improvement to a strong decline), then the formulae for the last coefficients are in the following form:

$$I_p = \sum_{i=1}^{k} \sum_{j<i}^{k} K_{ij}^* \qquad I_n = \sum_{i=1}^{k} \sum_{j>i}^{k} K_{ij}^*$$

I_p is calculated by means of all elements above the main diagonal (realization i is better than expectation j in terms of satisfaction or utility); I_n corresponds to elements under the main diagonal.

The following convention and interpretation are then: *a positive disagreement* is associated with a case where perception is a better situation than the one which was expected (for example, less unemployment or less inflation perceived than expected); this can be interpreted in terms of a household's behaviour as *an* a priori *pessimistic attitude* towards the considered phenomenon. In the opposite case with a negative disagreement, the coefficient reveals an *a priori* optimistic attitude towards employment or prices. Such an interpretation opens up a new direction to apprehend the optimism and the pessimism of households.

Optimism, pessimism
For an individual, a behaviour is or has been optimistic when the perceived or realized situation corresponds to a decrease compared to the expected situation; thus, as regards prices, optimism is associated with the case where perceived inflation will be higher than what was expected, and indicates an underestimation of future inflation.

At an aggregate level, by using data from INSEE conjuncture surveys, only the number of households which expect and subsequently perceive a particular situation is known. The following understanding is adopted: a general or global behaviour of the full population will be optimistic when, for households expecting a specific situation, the proportion of those which perceive a worsening situation is greater than the proportion of those which perceive an improving one.

Three indicators (defined in percentages) are used to resume these positions, one related to a correct expectation (CC), the two others associated respectively with optimistic and pessimistic behaviours (IO and IP); the first one is calculated from the upper triangle of the contingency matrix, the second from the lower triangle, the modalities being ordered as increasing:

$$CC = \Sigma p_{ii} \qquad IO = \Sigma\Sigma p_{ij} \qquad IP = \Sigma\Sigma p_{ij}$$

Finally, the disagreement coefficients, respectively negative and positive, correspond to a difference of one item [$Id_n(1)$ and $Id_p(1)$] or of two items or more [Id_n and Id_p]. Their values are between 0 and 1:

$$I_a = \frac{1}{k}\sum_{i=1}^{k} K_{ii}^* \qquad I_{dp(1)} = \frac{1}{k-1}\sum_{i=2}^{k} K_{ii-1}^* \qquad I_{dn(1)} = \frac{1}{k-1}\sum_{i=1}^{k-1} K_{ii+1}^*$$

$$I_{dp} = \frac{1}{(k-2)(k-3)}\sum_{i=3}^{k}\sum_{j=1}^{i-2} K_{ij}^* \qquad I_{dn} = \frac{1}{(k-2)(k-3)}\sum_{i=1}^{k-2}\sum_{j=i+2}^{k} K_{ij}^*$$

$$I_d = \frac{1}{k(k-1)}\sum_{i=2}^{k}\sum_{j=1}^{i-1} K_{ij}^* + \frac{1}{k(k-1)}\sum_{i=1}^{k-1}\sum_{j=i+1}^{k} K_{ij}^* .$$

Empirical results

The empirical values of the different indexes are given in Tables 7.1–7.3.

Table 7.1 reveals the existence of a strong relationship between expectations and perceptions, and a high homogeneity of behaviours and judgements through time. This is pointed out by the weak value of the empirical standard error: the mean absolute error is of the same order for prices and employment and indicates the existence of a systematic error around 7 per cent between the proportions of households expecting and perceiving a same item. The coefficient γ is highly significant for prices and employment. The global conditional agreement coefficient I_a is very close for the two variables and indicates reasonable agreement, less volatile for employment than for prices. Finally, these results indicate that a positive relationship exists between expectations and perceptions.

Table 7.2 shows that perception is correct for a great proportion of households, but this proportion tends to decrease in the middle of the 1980s for prices, in favour of *a priori* optimistic position. Such an evolution is confirmed by the values of IO which show optimism more clearly for prices than for employment: households perceive an inflation more important than the one they had expected, and thus underestimate inflation. Concerning employment, the three indexes are very close; the less volatile corresponds to households which have coherent judgements; optimism and

Table 7.1:   *Mean values and standard errors for synthetic indexes,*
1972–94

	Prices		Employment	
E_a	6.8850	(2.2700)	6.4500	(3.2530)
γ	0.3545	(0.0402)	0.2622	(0.0495)
I_a	0.2730	(0.0300)	0.2641	(0.0262)

Table 7.2:   *Mean values and standard errors for optimistic and pessimistic*
indexes (%)

	Prices		Employment	
CC	41.06	(7.84)	38.37	(3.519)
IO	36.54	(6.97)	33.52	(10.797)
IP	22.43	(9.50)	28.12	(9.875)

Table 7.3:   *Mean values and standard errors for disagreement and*
agreement coefficients, 1972–94

	Prices		Employment	
$I_{dp(1)}$	0.149	(0.073)	0.159	(0.0450)
I_{dp}	0.044	(0.033)	0.052	(0.0250)
$I_{dn(1)}$	0.290	(0.023)	0.259	(0.0270)
I_{dn}	0.269	(0.102)	0.280	(0.0570)
I_d	0.182	(0.007)	0.183	(0.0037)
I_a	0.273	(0.030)	0.264	(0.0262)

pessimism are more variable from one year to another, with a break in 1994, revealing a general anxiety about the persistency and the intensification of unemployment.

Table 7.3 shows that a negative disagreement appears for prices as well as for unemployment. This worsening of inflation and unemployment associated with an *a priori* optimistic behaviour confirms the above results concerning IO. Disagreements related to one or more items are different, depending on whether households are pessimistic (I_{dp}) or optimistic (I_{dn}); in the case of a negative disagreement, it is higher for a difference on one item than for more items; this means that, if households are pessimistic, they make a small error, contrary to the opposite situation where an important disagreement appears when they are optimistic.

Finally, the coefficients are very close for prices and employment, implying that judgements, behaviours and attitudes are similar for these two variables.

7.4 RESULTS FOR QUALITATIVE TESTS

7.4.1 The Gouriéroux–Pradel Test

The literature offers a large number of tests for the rational expectation hypothesis (Pesaran, 1987; Gouriéroux and Pradel, 1986). According to the available information, they are direct or not, and concern quantitative or qualitative data. For classified qualitative data, for which one has the probability distribution noted in a contingency table, Gouriéroux and Pradel (1986) propose a direct test. We are in a similar position with survey data. In their proposition, they consider two modalities i and j, and with the above conventional writing, their proposition is the following: '*The rational expectation hypothesis is satisfied if and only if*: $p_{jj} > \text{Max } p_{ij}$.'

Therefore, given the contingency table defined above, it is sufficient to ensure that for each item j, the element of the main diagonal is greater than or equal to each element of the same column, associated with expectation of item j. It is easy to establish that such a condition is the same as the following: $K_{jj}^* > \text{Max } K_{ij}^*$. When information is available through time, a graphic verification is easy to do by ensuring that the graph for K_{jj}^* is above the other ones. In the case of a positive test, it is possible to accept the hypothesis of rational expectation: households have rational behaviour when they consider the variations of prices and employment, and when they use all the available information. Another interesting conclusion can be drawn from this information by considering all elements of a row i, that is, elements which correspond to the perception of a particular item, i; the inequality $K_{ii}^* > \text{Max } K_{ij}^*$ corresponds simultaneously to an *a posteriori* statement and to the necessary and sufficient condition for *a correct expectation*.

7.4.2 Empirical Results

Figures for visual information are given in Appendix B. They permit the following comments: for prices, the period is characterized by a high level of inflation until 1982, then a clear decreasing trend and finally, since 1986, a steady-state inflation with a rate between 2 per cent and 4 per cent. In such a situation, *the rational expectation hypothesis is highly verified for house-holds which respond with item 1 until 1985, then items 2 or 3 from 1986 until 1994.* Concerning employment, the period is characterized by a permanent situation of unemployment with an increasing trend. It is not surprising to observe that for households which expect a worsening of employment, *the hypothesis of rational expectation is valid and highly verified always for item 1, frequently for item 2, but never for modalities 4 and 5* (improvement of employment).

It seems that the REH is verified for those households which perceive correctly the actual phenomena. To develop such a test properly, we shall first match the perceived modalities and the real evolution of the variables in each sub-period. Such a procedure permits the determination of homogeneous sub-periods with regard to the formulation of questions and periods where a part of households have a behaviour in conformity with the rational expectations hypothesis.

Judgements in terms of prices
Given the formulation of questions for perceptions in terms of price variations, the evolution can be measured by the price index for consumption or by a deflator of GNP. The first is more appropriate because it is measured quarterly; the complete period has been separated in two sub-samples according to two different manners. The first one distinguishes years with a high level of inflation (items 1 and 2) and others; weak satisfactory results obtained under such a hypothesis and the ambiguity of questions in terms of acceleration rather than in terms of variation have encouraged the use of a second decomposition in terms of increasing, constant and decreasing inflation. The results are given in the Table 7.4 and the figures in Appendix B.

For the first decomposition of the period, the REH is well verified for item 1 in the first period (Figure A7.1), and for item 2 and 3 after 1984. The second decomposition is less relevant: households perceiving very weak or a decreasing inflation (items 4 and 5) do not generally expect rationally in

Table 7.4: Judgement of price evolution

Evolution of prices	Item no. of answer	Periods
Strong inflation	1	1973–83
Weak inflation	2 and 3	1984–94
Increasing inflation	1	1973–4 and 1979–82
Constant inflation	2	1977–8, 1987–90
Decreasing inflation	3	1975–6, 1983–6, 1991–4

the corresponding sub-periods 3, except for the last years 1991–94 and perception of item 4.

We can conclude that rationality is well verified for households which perceive increasing inflation correctly, and only partially for those which perceive a constant or decreasing inflation correctly. On the whole, the REH is verified when the situation is correctly perceived. This shows the importance of considering individual data in order to test rationality for specific households instead of making the test for the whole population. Indeed, subpopulations have different expectation behaviours and aggregation biases the result for the whole population towards a rejection of rationality.

Judgements in terms of employment
In order to characterize the periods, the rate of unemployment and the number of unemployed people have been used. The period is marked by increasing unemployment since 1975 at a relatively constant rate; it means a clear worsening of the labour market. The decomposition for the period is outlined in Table 7.5.

Table 7.5: Judgement of employment evolution

Evolution of employment	Item no. of answers	Periods
Worsening of employment	1	1975–85, 1992–4
Weak worsening	2	1986–8
Weak modification	3	1973–4, 1989–91

Given such an allocation, it appears that households generally expect and perceive unemployment in coherence with the rational expectation hypothesis, as the REH is verified for households perceiving an increase of unemployment (Figure 7.2). Thus, our results point to the existence of a category of households which expect rationally the evolution for some variables in their environment and thus who use optimally the information given through the media.

Correct expectations
Correct expectations are established by a comparison between K_{ii}^* and K_{jj}^*. The graphs give much less information than for rational expectation hypothesis. For prices, expectations are correct *a posteriori* only for the first item of answers; for the two following items, graphs do not show continuous and coherent results, except at the end of the period, since 1985–6 and the beginning of the decreasing inflation. Concerning employment, the

correct expectation hypothesis is generally verified only for short periods corresponding to different items, except for the fourth which is associated with the perception of a weak reduction of employment between 1979 and 1989, a perception in clear opposition to the objective reality.

7.5　CHANGES OF HOUSEHOLDS EXPECTATION PROCESS OVER PERIODS

7.5.1　The Method

We use the qualitative micro-informations of households' perceptions and expectations corresponding to the first and second interviews of the same household, to define the expectation process corresponding to the set of items chosen by each household in answer to the perception and expectation questions. Due to the lack of a third period, only simple processes of expectation are considered.

For instance, in the case of the adaptive model, the expectation of some households made at time t is composed by the previous expectation at time $(t-1)$ and a part of its recent error forecast at time t. Therefore, a household i which made an expectation error for period $(t-1, t)$ and does not correct its expectation at time t or a household j which has a null perception error but different expectations at time t and time $(t-1)$ will not be counted as adaptive. For instance, the following sequence characterizes a non-adaptive model:

$$\{_{t}x_{t+1}^{e}=1, \,_{t-1}x_{t}^{e}=2, \,_{t}x_{t-1}^{p}=2\}$$

where:

$_{t}x_{t-i}^{p}$ is the perception of the past evolution of variable x made at time t for the period $(t-1, t)$;

$_{t-1}x_{t}^{e}$ is the expectation of the variable x, made at time $(t-1)$ for the period $(t-1, t)$;

$_{t}x_{t+1}^{e}$ is the expectation of the variable x, made at time t for the period $(t, t+1)$.

Concerning the counting of extrapolative-regressive model, we consider the following relation:

$$_{t}x_{t+1}^{e}=\,_{t}x_{t-1}^{p}+m(_{t}x_{t-1}^{p}-\,_{t-1}x_{t-2}^{p}).$$

If $m>0$, then households extrapolate the observed trend and use the strict extrapolative model. If $m<0$, they inverse the past trend and their expectation behaviour corresponds to a strict regressive process.

7.5.2   Expectations Processes in Different Macroeconomic Periods

The results are given in Tables A7.2 and A7.3 and the corresponding figures in Appendix B. The adaptive model is clearly the main expectation process, as more than 50 per cent of households use the adaptive model for the two variables. After the adaptive model, the regressive process appears relatively more frequently than the extrapolative.

Some substitution appears between the regressive and the adaptive models: the number of individuals using the adaptive model increases in the periods when the economic evolution of variables (inflation and unemployment) is uniform and the other households using the extrapolative model diminishes. The inverse substitution occurs when the conjuncture is characterized by a high volatility of inflation (or unemployment). Therefore, households correct their forecast errors if the evolution of economic phenomena is regular, while any structural change of conjuncture affects the treatment of information and diminishes the possibilities of a fine adaptation of expectation according to the comparison of past expectations and perceptions.

However, the substitution between expectation processes is thus more clearly shown than by estimating the different processes on quantified data.

7.6   CONCLUSION

The analysis of French households' perceptions and expectations of price and unemployment based on qualitative information from the INSEE conjuncture survey shows that the Muth criterion of rationality is not systematically rejected for all households and for the whole period; the Gouriéroux–Pradel test indeed shows that the rational expectations hypothesis can be accepted for particular categories of households, especially those which expected a clear degradation of unemployment or a high level of inflation during the 1970s. This result partially contradicts the strong rejection of the weak rationality obtained with quantified individual data.

The counting of processes based on qualitative information, as well as the estimation of quantified data, indicates that the adaptive model is the main process of households' expectations but that households change their expectations according to the trend and the volatility of the phenomena.

However, some limitations of the qualitative tests exist:

* the Gouriéroux–Pradel test is essentially based on the optimization algorithm which maximizes the efficient use of information, but it

does not really explain how individuals use their information since it does not takes into account other variables contained in the information set. Moreover, it does not test for autocorrelation of the expectation error.

•   the procedure of counting the processes is compatible with a two-period panel, but could be made more precise if panels contained more than two periods. We intend to build a pseudo-panel containing three periods and to implement a more complete test of the REH by using a latent variable model on the pseudo-panel, based on the same INSEE conjuncture surveys.

APPENDIX A: PRESENTATION OF THE SURVEY AND SUMMARY OF RESULTS ON QUANTIFIED DATA

A1.1   The French INSEE Survey Enquêtes de conjoncture auprès des ménages

The French INSEE survey *Enquêtes de conjoncture auprès des ménages* (harmonized with European surveys) was conducted three times a year (October, January, May) with between 6000 and 8000 households until 1994; half of the October survey was conducted again each year, so that 2500 households were interviewed in two consecutive years. Beside questions on the socio-economic characteristics of the households, their durable equipment and various expenses (holidays, purchase of cars and so on) it contained questions on the perception and anticipation of macro conditions (unemployment, inflation) and of the past and the future economic situation of the household.

General questions

(1)   Do you think that, for the last year, the standard of living of French people has:
    1. been clearly improved   *2. been a little improved*
    3. remained stationary   *4. been a little decreased*
    5. clearly decreased   *6. do not know*

(2)   Do you think that, for the year to come, the standard of living of French people will:
    1. clearly improve   *2. improve a little*
    3. remain stationary   *4. decrease a little*
    5. clearly decrease   *6. do not know*

(3) According to what you see around you, do you think that the situation of the labour market has during recent months:
   1. *clearly improved*   2. *improved a little*
   3. *remained stationary*   4. *decreased a little*
   5. *clearly decreased*   6. *do not know*

(4) Do you think that, in the months to come, the number of unemployed will:
   1. *clearly improve*   2. *improve a little*
   3. *remain stationary*   4. *decrease a little*
   5. *clearly decrease*   6. *do not know*

(5) Do you feel that, over several months, prices have:
   1. *much increased*   2. *mainly increased*
   3. *decreased a little*   4. *hardly varied*
   5. *slightly decreased*   6. *do not know*

(6) Compared to the present situation, do you think that for the next few months:
   1. *there will be a greater price increase*   2. *a similar price increase*
   3. *a smaller price increase*   4. *prices will remain stationary*
   5. *prices will slightly decrease*   6. *do not know*

(13) Over six months, has your financial situation:
   1. *much improved*   2. *improved a little*
   3. *remained stationary*   4. *worsened a little*
   5. *much worsened*   6. *do not know*

(14) Over the next few months, do you think that your financial situation will:
   1. *much improve*   2. *improve a little*
   3. *remain stationary*   4. *worsen a little*
   5. *worsen a lot*   6. *do not know*

Questions 7–12 report the willingness to buy durable goods (especially cars); the willingness to save and the nature of expected savings. These questions are analysed in Gardes and Madre (1990) to test the consistency of households' expectations and the nullity of the transitory income elasticity of consumption and savings.

A1.2 Different Estimations of the Adaptive Model

Adaptive model in difference

Two-year panel

$$[x^a_{i,t/t+1} - x^a_{i,t-1/t}] = \beta[x^p_{i,t/t-1} - x^a_{i,t-1/t}] + \epsilon_{i,t}$$

Aggregate time series

$$[x^a_{t/t+1} - x^a_{t-1/t}] = \beta[x^p_{t/t-1} - x^a_{t-1/t}] + \mu_t$$

Pseudo-panel This takes account of fixed-period effects via dummies:

$$[x^a_{j,t/t+1} - x^a_{j,t-1/t}] = \beta[x^p_{j,t/t-1} - x^a_{j,t-1/t}] + \sum_{t=1}^{T} \gamma_t D_t + \nu_{i,t},$$

j being a cell grouping of households defined by three criteria (education, cohorts and geographic area) with $x^a_{i,t/t'} = {}_t x^e_{t'}$ for individual i, and the same for perceptions.

Table A7.1: Coefficients β of adaptation for different data

	Two-year panels	Pseudo panel	Time series
Price	0.30[a]	0.20	0.97
	(0.03)	*(0.02)*	*(0.06)*
Unemployment	0.33[a]	0.10	0.89
	(0.03)	*(0.03)*	*(0.01)*

Notes:
[a] Computed on the average of coefficients.
Figures in brackets are the estimated standard deviation.

APPENDIX B: GOURIÉROUX–PRADEL TEST

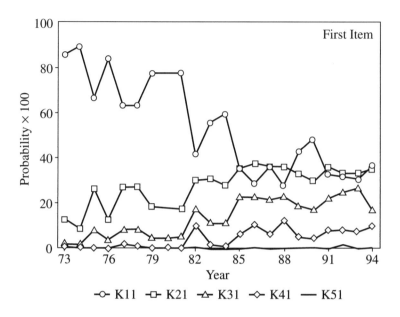

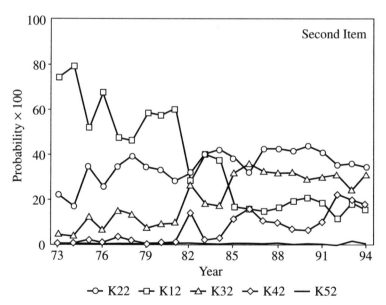

Figure A7.1: Price expectations

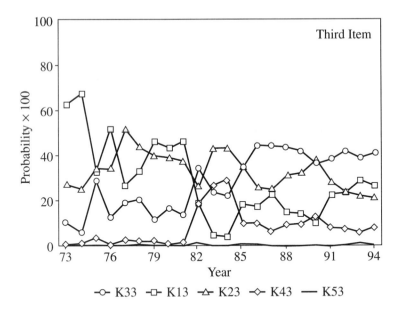

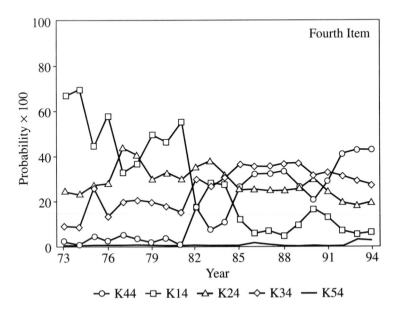

Figure A7.1: (cont.)

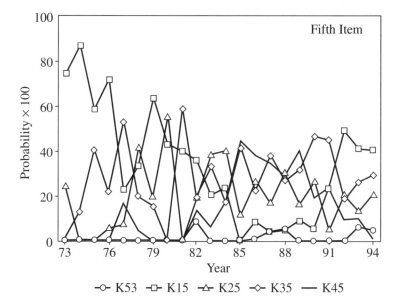

Figure A7.1: (cont.)

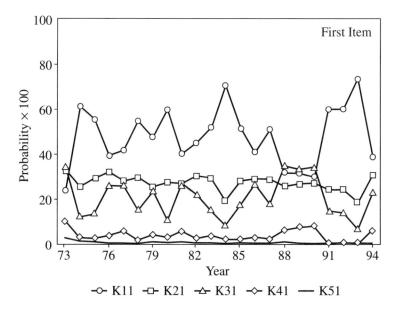

Figure A7.2: Employment expectations

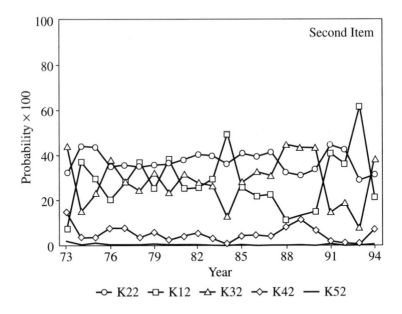

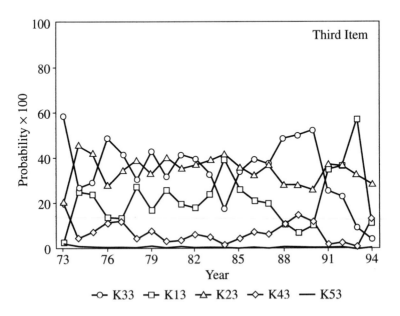

Figure A7.2: (cont.)

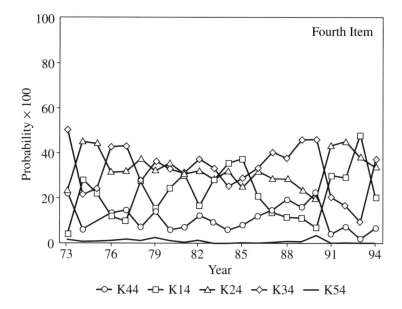

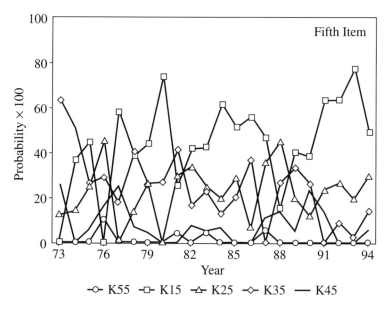

Figure A7.2: (cont.)

APPENDIX C: COUNTING PROCESSES

Table A7.2:   Inflation processes

Panels	% Adaptive	% Non-adaptive	% Extrapolative	% Regressive
1972–73	80	20	7	5
1973–74	76	24	5	9
1974–75	85	15	17	4
1975–76	72	18	8	14
1976–77	84	16	17	6
1977–78	87	13	9	7
1978–79	84	16	7	7
1979–80	84	16	6	5
1980–81	75	25	11	8
1981–82	66	34	14	25
1982–83	81	19	11	11
1983–84	86	14	12	7
1984–85	82	18	24	7
1985–86	80	20	23	10
1986–87	77	23	16	13
1987–88	79	21	15	12
1988–89	81	19	12	11
1989–90	75	25	16	13
1990–91	81	19	14	10
1991–92	82	18	21	10
1992–93	77	23	21	12
1993–94	79	21	21	15

Table A7.3:   Unemployment processes

Panels	% Adaptive	% Non-adaptive	% Extrapolative	% Regressive
1977–78	63	37	13	22
1978–79	60	40	11	22
1979–80	59	40	10	18
1980–81	56	44	10	29
1981–82	66	34	10	22
1982–83	63	37	11	21
1983–84	53	47	8	23
1984–85	62	38	8	18
1985–86	64	36	9	24
1986–87	67	33	10	17
1987–88	67	33	8	26
1988–89	71	29	13	24
1989–90	74	26	12	19
1990–91	61	38	11	24
1991–92	56	44	10	19
1992–93	48	52	8	22
1993–94	62	38	6	31

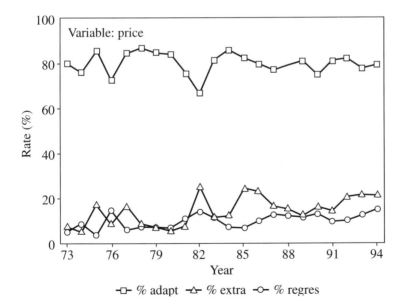

Figure A7.3:   Proportion of inflation process formation

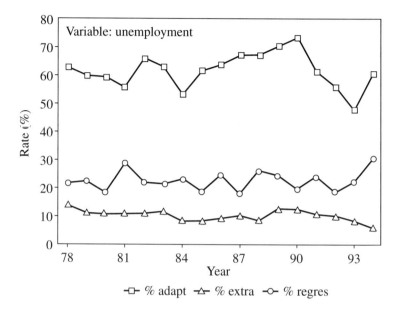

Figure A7.4: Proportion of unemployment process formation

REFERENCES

Batchelor, R. (1986), 'The psychophysics of inflation', *Journal of Economic Psychology*, 7, 269–90.

Carlson, J.A. and M. Parkin (1974), 'Inflation expectations', *Economica*, 42, 123–38.

Gardes, F. and S. Ghabri (1996), 'Analyse de la rationalité et des processus de formation des anticipation: apport des données de panel', Working Paper LAMiA, 1996–5.

Gardes, F. and J.L. Madre (1990), 'Consumption and transitory income: an estimation on a panel of French data', *Economics Letters*, 34, 197–202.

Gardes, F. and J.L. Madre (1991), 'Les anticipations des ménages dans les enquêtes de conjoncture de l'INSEE: comment se forment les anticipations d'inflation?', *Economie et Prévision*, No. 99.

Ghabri, S. (1998), 'Les processus de formation des anticipations des ménages: une analyse à partir des enquêtes de conjoncture de l'INSEE', *unpublished PhD*, Université de Paris (Panthéon-Sorbonne).

Goodman, L.A. and W.H. Kruskal (1963), 'Measures of association for cross clarifications III: approximate sampling theory', *Journal of American Statistical Association*, 58, 310–64.

Gouriéroux, C. and J. Pradel (1986), 'Direct test of the rational expectation hypothesis', *European Economic Review*, 30 (2), 265–84.

Ivaldi, M. (1992), 'Survey evidence on the rationality of expectations', *Journal of Applied Econometrics*, 7, 225–41.

Liebetrau, A.M. (1983), 'Measures of association', Sage Publications Paper series: Quantitatives Applications in the Social Sciences, London.

Light, R.J. (1971), 'Measures of responses agreements for qualitative data: some generalisations and alternatives', *Psychological Bulletin*, 76 (5), 365–77.

Nerlove, M. (1983), 'Expectations, plans, and realisations in theory and practice', *Econometrica*, 51, 1251–79.

Pesaran, H. (1990), *The Limits of Rational Expectations*, Oxford: Basil Blackwell.

Pichery, M.C. (1989), 'Agreement and disagreement between expectations and realizations', *Document de l'IME* No. 9001, September.

Smith, J. and M. McAleer (1995), 'Alternative procedures for converting qualitative response data to quantitative expectations: an application to Australian manufacturing', *Journal of Applied Econometrics*, 10, 165–85.

8. Variance rationality: evidence from inflation expectations

Roy Batchelor and Firoozeh Zarkesh

INTRODUCTION

In a much-cited paper, Muth (1961) defines expectations as rational if:

> expectations of firms (or more generally the subjective probability distribution of outcomes) tend to be distributed for the same information set, about the prediction of the theory (or the 'objective' probability distribution of outcomes).

More formally, suppose that at time t forecaster i has information consisting of variables x_{it}, and makes a forecast for the value p_{t+k} of some variable k periods in the future in the form of a probability distribution $p^e_{it,k}$ with mean $\mu_{it,k}$ and variance $\sigma^2_{it,k}$. Then the subjective probability distribution is rational in the sense of Muth if it is identical to the objective conditional probability distribution for p_{t+k}, with conditioning done on the information set x_{it}.

In this paper we further define $p^e_{it,k}$ as 'mean-rational' if $\mu_{it,k} = E\{p_{t+k} | x_{it}\}$, and as 'variance-rational' if $\sigma_{it,k} = E\{|p_{t+k} - \mu_{it,k}| | x_{it}\}$. Muth-rationality is sufficient for a forecast to be both mean and variance rational. Mean-rationality and variance-rationality are necessary but not sufficient for a forecast to be Muth-rational. Mean-rationality and variance-rationality respectively imply that in:

$$p_{t+k} - \mu_{it,k} = \epsilon_{it,k} \qquad (8.1)$$

$$|\epsilon_{it,k}| - \sigma_{it,k} = \eta_{it,k} \qquad (8.2)$$

the errors $\epsilon_{it,k}$ and $\eta_{it,k}$ in subjective assessments of the mean and standard deviation of the forecast variable must satisfy the unbiasedness and orthogonality conditions:

$$E(\epsilon_{it,k}) = 0, \ Cov(\epsilon_{it,k}, x_{it,k}) = 0 \qquad (8.3)$$

$$E(\eta_{it,k}) = 0, \; Cov(\eta_{it,k}, x_{it,k}) = 0 \qquad (8.4)$$

Many empirical tests of the mean-rationality conditions (8.3) have been conducted, using published forecasts as estimates of the means of individual forecasters' probability distributions for future values of economic variables, including McNees (1978); Figlewski and Wachtel (1981); Pearce (1984); Urich and Wachtel (1984); Zarnowitz (1985); and Swidler and Ketcher (1990). Most recently, Keane and Runkle (1990) have shown that errors in one-quarter of ahead price level forecasts made by the professional economists contributing to the ASA–NBER surveys pass stringent orthogonality tests.

In contrast, few tests of variance-rationality have been conducted. This is not because the question of whether individuals are variance-rational is unimportant. Economic theory suggests that, in general, consumers and firms will change their behaviour in response not only to changing mean expectations but also to changes in uncertainty, as measured by the variance surrounding these means (see, for example, the literature reviewed in Hey, 1979). Econometric practice is to maintain the rationality assumption in order to obtain empirical proxies for uncertainty. Cukierman and Wachtel (1982), for example, use (8.2) and (8.4) to argue that the variance of expected inflation can be proxied by the mean squared error in the inflation forecasts made by contributors to the Livingston survey of economic forecasters. Engle (1982, 1983) assumes a particular information set x_{it}, and argues that inflation uncertainty can be proxied by a time-varying conditional variance of a model relating inflation to these variables, the ARCH model. However, it has been difficult to obtain measures of subjective variances on which to test the validity of these procedures. Batchelor and Jonung (1988, 1989) do conduct tests for variance rationality, but their variance measure is simply a qualitative score, measuring the 'degree of confidence' of lay individuals about their inflation forecasts.

In this paper, we use quantitative estimates of the mean and variance of the inflation forecasts of professional forecasters to test the bias and orthogonality conditions (8.4) for variance-rationality, as well as the mean-rationality conditions (8.3). The variance estimates come from responses to the ASA–NBER surveys, and are described in section 8.1. Because the data consist of pooled cross-section and time series information on forecasts for various forecast horizons, and because they contain measurement error, care is necessary in making inferences about rationality. Section 8.2 describes the econometric techniques used. Section 8.3 analyses the test results. Mean rationality is rejected for long-horizon but not short-horizon forecasts. Variance rationality is strongly rejected at all horizons. There is no significant correlation between a forecaster's estimate of the subjective variance surrounding an inflation forecast and the accuracy of his/her mean forecast. Implications of this finding are discussed in the concluding section of the paper.

8.1   ESTIMATING THE VARIANCE OF INFLATION FORECASTS

Every quarter since 1968Q4, the American Statistical Association (ASA) and the National Bureau of Economic Research (NBER) have conducted a survey of the outlook for various US macroeconomic variables, by means of a mail questionnaire among a panel of economic forecasters. The survey is described in Zarnowitz (1969), and the accuracy and rationality of aggregate and individual price level forecasts are analysed in Zarnowitz (1985).

A unique feature of the ASA–NBER survey is that forecasters are invited not only to provide point predictions of price levels for the current and five following quarters, but also a summary probability distribution for future annual inflation rates. The precise question asked about the probability distribution of inflation has changed a little over time. Initially, forecasters were asked:

> Please indicate what probabilities you would attach to the following percentage changes from 1968 to 1969 in . . . the implicit price deflator (annual figures):
>
> 10 per cent or more/9 to 9.9 per cent/8 to 8.9 per cent/ . . . 0 to 0.9 per cent/−1 to −0.1 per cent/ . . . /below −3 per cent.

As mean expected inflation rose in the 1970s, these ranges were all raised by 2 per cent in 1973Q2 and again by 4 per cent in 1974Q4. In 1981Q3 the number of ranges was halved, their size doubled, and levels reduced by 2 per cent, so that possible responses became:

> 12 per cent or more/10 to 11.9 per cent/8 to 9.9 per cent/6 to 7.9 per cent/4 to 5.9 per cent/rise less than 4 per cent.

The ranges were further reduced by 2 per cent in 1985Q2.

To estimate the mean and variance of inflation forecasts from responses to the survey questions, assumptions must be made about the limits of the highest and lowest response ranges, and about the form of the subjective probability distributions. We follow Zarnowitz and Lambros (1987) in assuming that extreme ranges have a width of 2 per cent, and that probability is uniform within each range. Lahiri and Teigland (1987) compute means, variances and higher moments using slightly different assumptions, but note that their results are not sensitive to alternative assumptions about the little-used extreme ranges. We additionally apply Sheppard corrections to all variance estimates to compensate for the effect of the change in the width of the central ranges after 1981Q3.

Suppose that the upper and lower bounds of the *j*th range in the survey conducted in quarter *t* are written U_{jt} and L_{jt}; that the width of the central ranges is W_t; and that the probability provided by forecaster *i* at time (quarter) *t* for the inflation rate in the year ending quarter *t + k* lying in the *j*th range is $P_{ijt,k}$. Our estimates of the mean and variance of forecaster *i*'s subjective probability distribution for inflation are:

$$MEAN_{it,k} = \sum_{j=1}^{r} P_{ijt,k} \cdot \frac{(U_{jt} - L_{jt})}{2} \tag{8.5}$$

$$VAR_{it,k} = \sum_{j=1}^{r} P_{ijt,k} \cdot \frac{(U_{jt}^3 - L_{jt}^3)}{3(U_{jt} - L_{jt})} - MEAN_{it,k}^2 - W_t^2/12 \tag{8.6}$$

where $r = 12$ or 6, and $W_t = 2$ or 4, depending on whether data are from surveys before or after 1981Q3. The subjective standard deviation of inflation is estimated by the square root of $VAR_{it,k}$, and is denoted $SDEV_{it,k}$. $MEAN_{it,k}$ and $SDEV_{it,k}$ are estimates of the expected value and standard deviation $\mu_{it,k}$ and $\sigma_{it,k}$ of the subjective probability distribution for future inflation.

Because they depend on possibly incorrect assumptions about the form of the probability distribution, these estimates may contain measurement error. In addition, because incentives on forecasters to supply accurate figures to the ASA–NBER survey are weak, the estimates may not represent the best that forecasters can do. This is unlikely to be a problem for the mean forecasts, since respondents typically also publish their mean inflation forecasts in a commercial environment, so their accuracy can be easily monitored. On the other hand, the variance estimates are not subject to any similar market test, and so may contain more noise.

In the surveys conducted in the first three quarters of each year up to 1981, the surveys asked for forecasts of the average rate of inflation between the previous year and the current year. In the fourth quarter forecasts switched to inflation between the current year and the following year. This means that the maximum forecast horizon *k* shrinks from four quarters (forecast made in Q4 for the following year) to one quarter (forecast made in Q3 for the current year). From 1981Q3 onwards, forecasts are sought for both the current and the following year, so that the forecasting horizon shrinks from seven quarters to zero quarters. In this paper, we consider only one- to four-quarter horizons, for which data are available throughout the history of the survey.

The number of forecasters providing probability distribution information has fallen steadily: from over 60 in the early years of the survey to less than 20 in recent years. The ASA–NBER survey was discontinued in the first quarter of 1990 and responsibility for the survey passed to the Federal Reserve Bank of Philadelphia. Details of the survey are given at their website http:///www.phil.frb.org. Our data end with the 1989Q4 forecasts of inflation between 1988 and 1989. As a result, our data consist of 3361 mean and variance estimates, covering the 21 target years 1969–89. Of these, 815 are one-quarter ahead forecasts, 833 are two-quarter ahead, 790 three-quarter ahead and 923 four-quarter ahead. Because the composition of the panel changes over time and not all panellists provide probability distribution data, it is not possible to compile complete time series on individual forecasters.

Questionnaires are mailed out towards the end of the first month of each quarter, and are typically returned towards the end of the second month. This means that when they complete the survey in the first quarter of each year, respondents know the preliminary estimate of inflation in the previous year, released in mid-February. We assume that forecasters are judged on their ability to predict this first available estimate of inflation in the GNP deflator rather than any revised estimate. Inflation between year ending with quarter $t + k - 4$ and target year $t + k$ is denoted INFL_{t+k}.

8.2   ECONOMETRIC ISSUES IN RATIONALITY TESTING

Our rationality tests are based on the properties of errors in the mean and standard deviations of subjective probability distributions. We write the error in the mean forecast made by individual i at time t for horizon k as $\text{MERR}_{it,k} = \text{INFL}_{t+k} - \text{MEAN}_{it,k}$ and the error in the subjective standard deviation as $\text{SDERR}_{it,k} = |\text{MERR}_{it,k}| - \text{SDMEAN}_{it,k}$. Bias and orthogonality in these errors is tested by conducting three regressions with $\text{MERR}_{it,k}$ as dependent variable, and three parallel regressions with $\text{SDERR}_{it,k}$ as dependent variable. The regressions are:

Mean rationality:

$$\text{MERR}_{it,k} = a + e_{it,k} \tag{8.7}$$

$$\text{MERR}_{it,k} = a + b\text{MEAN}_{it,k} + c\text{SDEV}_{it,k} + e_{it,k} \tag{8.8}$$

$$\text{MERR}_{it,3} = a + b\text{MERR}_{it-2,1} + c\text{SDERR}_{it-2,1} + e_{it,k} \tag{8.9}$$

Variance rationality:

$$\text{SDERR}_{it,k} = a + h_{it,k} \tag{8.7'}$$

$$\text{SDERR}_{it,k} = a + b\text{MEAN}_{it,k} + c\text{SDEV}_{it,k} + h_{it,k} \tag{8.8'}$$

$$\text{SDERR}_{it,3} = a + b\,|\,\text{MERR}_{it-2,1}\,| + c\text{SDERR}_{it-2,1} + h_{it,k} \tag{8,9'}$$

Regressions (8.7) and (8.7') test the unbiasedness conditions $E(\epsilon_{it,k}) = 0$ and $E(\eta_{it,k}) = 0$. Under rationality, we expect $a = 0$ in (8.7) and (8.7'). Note that if expectations are rational, the regression residuals $e_{it,k}$ and $h_{it,k}$ are estimates of the forecast errors $\epsilon_{it,k}$ and $\eta_{it,k}$ in the subjective mean and standard deviation of expections.

Regressions (8.8) and (8.8') test the orthogonality of errors in subjective expectations of the mean and standard deviation of future inflation with respect to two variables which are certainly in forecaster i's information vector x_{it} at t – namely, the levels of the subjective mean and standard deviation themselves. Under the rationality conditions $\text{cov}\{\epsilon_{it}, (\mu_{it,k}, \sigma_{it,k})\} = 0$ and $\text{cov}\{\eta_{it,k}, (\mu_{it,k}, \sigma_{it,k})\} = 0$ we expect $a = b = c = 0$ in (8.8) and (8.8') respectively. Regression (8.8) can be regarded as a generalization of the conventional test for mean-rationality in which the actual level of inflation is regressed on the mean expectation, as:

$$\text{INFL}_{it,k} = a + (1 + b)\text{MEAN}_{it,k} + e_{it,k} \tag{8.10}$$

and the coeffients tested for $a = b = 0$. Although often termed an 'unbiasedness test' (for example, Brown and Maital, 1981), (8.10) actually tests for orthogonality between the forecast error in the mean and the level of the subjective mean, as can be seen if it is rearranged as:

$$\text{MERR}_{it,k} = a + b\text{MEAN}_{it,k} + e_{it,k} \tag{8.11}$$

Our regression (8.8) adds another known parameter of the subjective probability distribution, the subjective standard deviation, to the right-hand side of (8.11).

Regressions (8.9) and (8.9') test the orthogonality of errors in the subjective mean and standard deviation with respect to past expectations errors. Since past errors made in forecasting are first revealed when the preliminary inflation figures are published in the first quarter of each year, (8.9) and (8.9') regress errors in the mean and standard deviations of forecasts made in the first quarter of each year, $\text{MERR}_{it,3}$ and $\text{SDERR}_{it,3}$, on known errors in the most recent forecasts made for inflation in the previous

year, the one-quarter ahead forecasts made in the third quarter of the previous year, $MERR_{it-2,1}$ and $SDERR_{it-2,1}$. Since the subjective standard
deviation is likely to be influenced by the size of any past errors, irrespective
of their sign, the absolute value of $MERR_{it-2,1}$ is used as a regressor in
(8.9'). Since not all forecasters provide probability distribution information
in all quarters, (8.9) and (8.9') are estimated on a sub-sample of 437
observations of forecasters who provided such data in both the first quarter
of one year and the third quarter of the previous year. Under the rational-
ity conditions $cov\{\epsilon_{it,3}, (\epsilon_{it-2,1}|, \eta_{it-2,1})\} = 0$ and $cov\{\eta_{it,3}, (|\epsilon_{it-2,1}|, \eta_{it-2,1})\}$
$= 0$, we expect $a = b = c = 0$ in (8.9) and (8.9') respectively.

Inferences about the coefficients of regressions (8.7)–(8.9) and
(8.7')–(8.9') are complicated by two main factors: non-independence and
heteroscedasticity of the residuals, and measurement error in the regressors.

As we have seen, under rationality the regression residuals are forecast
errors in the mean and standard deviation of expectations. These forecast
errors are likely to be correlated across forecasts made for the same target
date but at different horizons, and across forecasts made by different forecasters for a given target date. Under these conditions, the conventional
OLS estimate of the variance–covariance matrix of the regression
coefficients is biased and inconsistent. Because some years may be easier to
forecst than others, forecast errors for different target dates may also be
heteroscedastic.

We have eliminated the problem of overlapping forecast horisons by estimating (8.7) and (8.8), (8.7') and (8.8') separately on data for different forecast horizons. In general, this is undesirable since it reduces the efficiency
of estimates of the regression coefficients. However, in our particular data
set, the hypothesis that coefficients are equal at all horizons is rejected, so
there is no justification for pooling.

We have dealt with the problem of correlations in errors across forecasters and with the possibility of heteroscedasticity by estimating the
coefficients of all regressions by OLS, but estimating the variance–covariance matrix of the coefficients by a special generalized method of moments
(GMM) estimator which Hansen (1982) has shown to be autocorrelation-
and heteroscedasticity-consistent. This approach has been used in several
earlier rationality tests, including Brown and Maital (1981) and Keane and
Runkle (1990). The estimator has the general form:

$$V = (X'X)^{-1}X'CX(X'X)^{-1} \tag{8.12}$$

where X is the matrix of observations on regressors. For our problem, C is
a block-diagonal weighting matrix of the form:

$$C = \begin{bmatrix} C_1 & 0 & \cdots & 0 \\ 0 & C_2 & \cdots & 0 \\ \vdots & & \ddots & \vdots \\ 0 & 0 & \cdots & C_m \end{bmatrix} \tag{8.13}$$

and the submatrices $C_1, C_2, \ldots, C_m$ contain estimates of the variances and covariances of forecast errors made by forecasters for the m ($=21$) target years covered by this study.

These variances and covariances are estimated using the OLS residuals $_{eit,k}$ from (8.7)–(8.9), or $_{hit,k}$ from (8.7′)–(8.9′), as follows. We assume that the error in an individual's k-quarter forecast made at t for the year ending in quarter $t+k$ consists of independent individual-specific and common components, as $e_{it,k} = f_{it,k} + g_{it,k}$, with $\text{var}(f_{it,k}) = \pi^2_{it,k}$, $\text{var}(g_{t,k}) = \tau^2_{t,k}$ and $\text{cov}(f_{it,k}, g_{t,k}) = 0$. That is, the error variances of individual k-horizon forecast errors made at t are all equal to $\pi^2_{t,k} + \tau^2_{t,k}$, but may vary with the forecast horizon and with the target year. Similarly, the covariances between all pairs of k-horizon forecasts made at t are all equal to $\tau^2_{t,k}$, but may vary with forecast horizon and target year. Estimates of the variances and covariances of errors in the forecasts based on the OLS residuals are then:

$$\hat{\pi}^2_{t,k} + \hat{\tau}^2_{t,k} = \sum_{i=1}^{n_{t,k}} (\hat{e}_{it,k})^2 / n_{t,k} \tag{8.14}$$

$$\hat{\tau}^2_{t,k} = \sum_{i=1}^{n_{t,k}} \sum_{j \neq i} (\hat{e}_{it,k})(\hat{e}_{jt,k}) / (n^2_{t,k} - n_{t,k}) \tag{8.15}$$

where $n_{t,k}$ is the number of forecasters producing probability distributions for inflation in the year ending $t+k$. Suppose the target year ending in quarter $t+k$ is indexed as T. Then the corresponding $(n_{t,k} \times n_{t,k})$ submatrix C_T of estimated forecast error variances and covariances in (8.13) is:

$$C_T = \begin{Bmatrix} \hat{\pi}^2_{t,k} + \hat{\tau}^2_{t,k} & \hat{\tau}^2_{t,k} & \cdots & \hat{\tau}^2_{t,k} \\ \hat{\tau}^2_{t,k} & \hat{\pi}^2_{t,k} + \hat{\tau}_{t,k} & \ddots & \hat{\tau}^2_{t,k} \\ \hat{\tau}^2_{t,k} & \hat{\tau}^2_{t,k} & \cdots & \hat{\pi}^2_{t,k} + \hat{\tau}^2_{t,k} \end{Bmatrix} \tag{8.16}$$

This generalizes the GMM covariance matrix estimator suggested by Keane and Runkle (1990) for pooled cross-section and time series observations, to the case where forecast errors are heteroscedastic.

If the coefficient vectors in (8.7)–(8.9), or (8.7′)–(8.9′), are written as a, then the rationality restrictions $a=0$ can be tested using the result that, under this null, the statistic $a'Va$ is distributed as χ^2_ℓ where ℓ is the number of coefficients.

As noted earlier, measurement error is liable to be present in our estimates of the mean and standard deviation of inflation forecasts, and hence of inflation forecast errors. OLS estimates of coefficients in regressions like (8.8), (8.9), (8.8') and (8.9') are therefore liable to be biased and inconsistent. Apart from the discussions in Lahiri (1981) and Pesaran (1987, ch 8.5), little account has been taken of the effects of measurement error in earlier tests of rationality. The general problem of obtaining consistent coefficient estimates in regressions such as (8.8) and (8.9), and (8.8') and (8.9'), where two regressors are measured with error, is, however, treated in Maddala (1988, ch. 11.3). If measurement errors are independent, serially uncorrelated, and uncorrelated with the true values of the regressors, consistent coefficient estimates b^* and c^* are related to their OLS estimates $\hat{b}$ and $\hat{c}$ as:

$$(1-\rho^2-\lambda_b)b^* + \rho\lambda_c c^* = (1-\rho^2)\hat{b} \qquad (8.17)$$

$$(1-\rho^2-\lambda_c)c^* + \rho\lambda_b b^* = (1-\rho^2)\hat{c} \qquad (8.18)$$

where λ_b and λ_c are the ratios of the variance of measurement error to total variance of the regressors to which the coefficients b and c are attached, and ρ is the correlation between the two regressors.

Fortunately, an estimate of the size of measurement errors in our probability-distribution-based estimates of the mean inflation forecast can be obtained by comparing them with the point inflation estimates implied by the price level forecasts which are also provided by the ASA–NBER respondents. As noted by Zarnowitz and Lambros (1987), differences between the point inflation forecasts and the means of subjective probability distributions are small. Assuming that the price level forecasts represent the true means of forecasters' subjective probability distributions, the standard errors in the means of the probability distributions in our data are 0.38, 0.47, 0.45 and 0.53 per cent for the one-, two-, three- and four-quarter horizons respectively. These compare with standard deviations of probability-distribution-based mean forecasts of 2.27, 2.10, 2.26 and 2.25 per cent, giving estimates of λ_b of 0.02, 0.05, 0.04 and 0.05. For simplicity, we take $\lambda_b = 0.05$. In view of our earlier argument that forecasters have fewer incentives to report their variance estimates accurately, we assume $\lambda_c = 4\lambda_b = 0.20$. The correlations ρ between regressors are $-0.05, 0.10, 0.24$ and -0.02 for the one-, two-, three- and four-quarter ahead versions of (8.8) and (8.8'), and -0.02 and 0.83 for (8.9) and (8.9').

Finally, it is worth noting that the regressors in all our test equations are sub-sets of the whole information set x_{it} of forecaster i at t. The omission of some possible determinants of forecast errors will therefore bias coefficient estimates and standard errors. However, Abel and Mishkin

(1983) show that the bias will be towards non-rejection of rationality. Hence if rationality is rejected for one of the sub-sets we consider, it will certainly be rejected for the whole information set.

8.3 RESULTS OF RATIONALITY TESTS

Table 8.1 contains the results of tests for mean rationality based on (8.7) and (8.8). The column headed 'Bias' sets out estimated values of the bias coefficient *a* in regression (8.7). Beneath each estimated coefficient is an estimated standard error based on the GMM covariance matrix V of (8.12) above. None of the estimated bias coefficients is significantly non-zero, so the hypothesis that mean forecasts are unbiased at all horizons cannot be rejected.

Table 8.1: Tests for mean rationality

Dependent variable	n	Bias	Constant	Coefficient on: $\text{MEAN}_{it,k}$	$\text{SDEV}_{it,k}$	χ^2_3
$\text{MERR}_{it,1}$	815	−0.0497	0.8164	−0.1212	−0.2047	5.87
				−0.1303	−0.2564	
		(0.17)	(0.48)	(0.08)	(0.13)	
$\text{MERR}_{it,2}$	833	−0.0165	0.6559	−0.0262	−0.5947*	15.12*
				−0.0117	−0.7452	
		(0.19)	(0.53)	(0.09)	(0.17)	
$\text{MERR}_{it,3}$	790	0.2038	1.6600*	−0.1400	−0.7502*	21.51*
				−0.0967	−0.9507	
		(0.31)	(0.50)	(0.10)	(0.22)	
$\text{MERR}_{it,4}$	923	0.1699	2.1763*	−0.2705*	−0.5988*	17.43*
				−0.2879	−0.7489	
		(0.33)	(0.58)	(0.09)	(0.17)	

Notes:
1 Results of tests for forecast bias, and for orthogonality of errors in mean forecasts with respect to subjective mean and standard deviation of forecast, based on text equations (8.7) and (8.8). Two sets of coefficient estimates are shown for (8.8), the first based on OLS, the second on OLS corrected for measurement error in the regressors, as in text equations (8.17) and (8.18).
2 Figures in parentheses beneath estimated coefficients are GMM estimates of coefficient standard errors.
3 The χ^2_3 statistic tests all coefficients in (8.8) against zero, and has a 5 per cent critical value of 7.81.
4 Statistics rejecting zero restrictions at the 5 per cent level are marked with an asterisk.

The rest of Table 8.1 sets out the estimated coefficients a, b and c in regression (8.7) of the mean forecast error on the mean and standard deviation of the subjective probability distribution. The first row shows OLS coefficient estimates. Beneath these are shown measurement-error-consistent coefficient estimates, based on (8.17) and (8.18) above. In parentheses beneath the coefficient estimates are estimated standard errors, based on the GMM covariance matrix.

The χ_3^2 statistics test the restriction that the OLS coefficients are jointly zero. They show that this restriction cannot be rejected for the one-quarter ahead horizon, but that it is rejected for longer forecast horizons. The main reason for rejection is that mean forecast errors are negatively correlated with forecaster's subjective standard deviations; that is, more confident forecasters tend to underestimate inflation, and vice versa. In addition, at the longest four-quarter horizon, there is negative correlation between mean forecast errors and the mean expected inflation rate. This constitutes 'bias' in the conventional sense of equation (8.10), with forecasters tending to underestimate inflation when inflation is expected to be high, and vice versa.

Because measurement error is small and collinearity between regressors low, our consistent estimates are close to the OLS estimates. More important, in all cases they suggest that measurement error has if anything biased the significant coefficient estimates towards zero. The presence of significant deviations of the OLS coefficients from the zero values expected under rationality cannot therefore be ascribed to measurement error.

These findings are less favourable to the mean rationality hypothesis than, but not inconsistent with, the results of previous work on the ASA–NBER forecasters. Keane and Runkle (1990) find that errors in short-term, one-quarter ahead, price level forecasts are unbiased, uncorrelated with the level of the mean forecast itself, and with known past errors and a range of published economic indicators. We also find short-term forecasts to be mean-rational. But at longer horizons, we find that errors in mean forecasts are not uncorrelated with an element of the forecasters' information set not considered by Keane and Runkle, namely the level of the standard deviation surrounding the mean forecast.

Table 8.2 contains results of the parallel regressions (8.7') and (8.8') testing for variance rationality. The first column shows the estimated bias in the subjective standard deviation of inflation forecasts, the difference between the mean absolute forecast error and the mean subjective standard deviation. For one- and two-quarter horizons, the bias is negative and very small, and not significantly non-zero. For the three-quarter horizon the bias is positive, but not significant. For the four-quarter horizon, the bias

Table 8.2:   Tests for variance rationality

Dependent variable	n	Bias	Coefficient on: Constant	$\text{MEAN}_{it,k}$	$\text{SDEV}_{it,k}$	χ_3^2
$\text{SDERR}_{it,1}$	815	−0.0842	0.6696*	−0.0317	−0.6835*	113.86*
				−0.0424	−0.8550	
		(0.07)	(0.18)	(0.03)	(0.08)	
$\text{SDERR}_{it,2}$	833	−0.0201	0.5944*	0.0206	−0.8348*	139.69*
				0.0440	−1.0464	
		(0.09)	(0.23)	(0.05)	(0.08)	
$\text{SDERR}_{it,3}$	790	0.2086	0.8024*	0.0535	−0.9980*	186.71*
				0.1247	−1.2689	
		(0.19)	(0.28)	(0.86)	(0.11)	
$\text{SDERR}_{it,4}$	923	0.3714*	1.0190*	0.0056	−0.7587*	69.45*
				0.0019	−0.9485	
		(0.18)	(0.30)	(0.10)	(0.10)	

Notes:
1 Results of tests for forecast bias, and for orthogonality of errors in standard deviation forecasts, with respect to subjective mean and standard deviation of forecast, based on text equations (8.7′) and (8.8′). Two sets of coefficient estimates are shown for (8.8), the first based on OLS, the second on OLS corrected for measurement error in the regressors, as in text equations (8.17) and (8.18).
2 Figures in parentheses beneath estimated coefficients are GMM estimates of coefficient standard errors.
3 The χ_3^2 statistic tests all coefficients in (8.8) against zero, and has a 5 per cent critical value of 7.81.
4 Statistics rejecting zero restrictions at the 5 per cent level are marked with an asterisk.

is more positive still, and significant. The unbiasedness condition for variance rationality is therefore rejected at the longest forecast horizon.

The bias estimates show that for four-quarter ahead forecasts, forecasters tend to be overconfident about the likely size of their errors. In fact, not only are forecasters too confident relative to the actual errors they make in their four-quarter ahead forecasts, they are also on average just as confident about their four-quarter ahead forecasts as about their shorter-term forecasts. The mean subjective standard deviations for four-, three-, two- and one-quarter horizons in our sample are 0.89, 0.90, 0.88 and 0.84 per cent. However, the mean absolute errors in the mean forecast decrease uniformly as the forecast horizon decreases from four- to one-quarter, from 1.28 to 1.10, 0.86 and 0.75 per cent.

The rest of Table 8.2 sets out estimates of the coefficients in regression (8.8′), and tests them against zero. The χ_3^2 statistics show that this condition

Lessons from survey data

for variance rationality is very strongly rejected at all horizons. The coefficients *b* are not significantly non-zero, so there is no suggestion that forecasters who expect a high inflation rate are over- or underconfident about the accuracy of their forecasts. However, the coefficients *c* are all significantly negative. That is, forecasters who make a high estimate of the standard deviation surrounding their mean forecast typically overestimate the size of the absolute error in their mean forecast, and vice versa. In the cases of two-, three- and four-quarter ahead forecasts the hypothesis $c = -1$ cannot be rejected, suggesting that there is no relation whatever between forecasters' subjective standard deviations and the size of the errors in their mean forecasts.

In all the regressions reported in Table 8.2, measurement error can again be seen to bias the significant OLS coefficients towards zero. Our finding of deviations from variance rationality cannot therefore be ascribed to measurement error.

Table 8.3 sets out the results of tests for the orthogonality of errors in both subjective mean and variance estimates with respect to known past errors, based on regressions (8.9) and (8.9′). Although the estimated coefficient *c* in (8.9) is significantly non-zero, the χ_3^2 statistic does not reject the hypothesis that all coefficients are jointly zero at the 5 per cent significance level. The mean rationality hypothesis cannot therefore be

Table 8.3: Tests for error orthogonality with respect to past errors

Dependent variable	n	Constant	$\text{MERR}_{it-2,1}$	$|\text{MERR}_{it-2,1}|$	$\text{SDERR}_{it-2,1}$	χ_3^2
$\text{MERR}_{it,3}$	437	0.1253	0.0875		0.2909*	7.43
			0.0936		0.3638	
		(0.34)	(0.18)		(0.15)	
$\text{SDERR}_{it,3}$	437	0.7128*		−0.5762*	0.7826*	35.74*
				−2.7275	3.2103	
		(0.29)		(0.16)	(0.18)	

Notes:
1 Results of tests for orthogonality of forecast errors with respect to known past forecast errors, based on text equations (8.9) and (8.9′). Two sets of coefficient estimates are shown, the first based on OLS, the second on OLS corrected for measurement error in the regressors, as in text equations (8.17) and (8.18).
2 Figures in parentheses beneath estimated coefficients are GMM estimates of coefficient standard errors.
3 The χ_3^2 statistic tests all coefficients in (8.8) against zero, and has a 5 per cent critical value of 7.81.
4 Statistics rejecting zero restrictions at the 5 per cent level are marked with an asterisk.

rejected. However, both coefficients in (8.9') are significant, and the χ_3^2 statistic strongly rejects variance rationality. Although the effects of measurement error on the regression (8.9') are large, they again imply that use of OLS biases the tests against rejecting rationality.

Our estimates of (8.9') show that forecasters are prey to two systematic errors in revising their subjective standard deviations for future inflation. The negative b coefficient means that a forecaster's estimate of the standard deviation surrounding the mean forecast for the current year is likely to be too high if the absolute error in the mean forecast made in the previous year was large. Forecaster confidence is excessively sensitive to recent forecast performance. The positive c coefficient means that the standard deviation for the current year is also likely to be too high if the forecaster's subjective standard deviation for the previous year was too high. Forecasters persist in being overly optimistic or pessimistic about the accuracy of their mean forecasts.

8.4 CONCLUSIONS

In this paper, we have introduced the concept of variance rationality, and tested the rationality of the mean and variance of the inflation forecasts made by a group of US forecasters. We have found that the forecasts are mean-rational at short forecast horizons, but not at long horizons. However, forecasts are not variance-rational. Forecasters are typically overconfident at long forecast horizons. Their subjective standard deviations bear little relation to the accuracy of their mean forecasts; and they fail to adjust their standard deviation estimates appropriately in the light of past performance, giving too much weight to the size of recent errors in mean forecasts, and too little to their long-term accuracy record.

Our findings imply that the practices of proxying inflation uncertainty by mean squared forecast errors (Cukierman and Wachtel, 1982) or by variances from regressions of inflation on some specific information set x_{it} (Engle, 1982, 1983) are questionable, since both rely on the maintained assumption of variance rationality. Similar techniques are in common use in finance, where the riskiness of investments is regularly proxied by the variance (and covariances) of returns around mean values predicted by some information set (for an ARCH implementation, see Bollerslev *et al.*, 1988). If our finding of irrationality in estimates of the variance of price inflation in goods markets is due to the innate difficulty of the problem, then it is also unlikely that variance rationality will characterize forecasts of asset market prices, since price fundamentals are much less clear. However, if our finding of irrationality in inflation forecasts simply reflects the lack of incentives to produce accurate risk measures for goods prices, then it is less likely to carry over into asset markets, where financial incentives to produce variance-rational forecasts are greater.

REFERENCES

Abel, Andrew B. and Frederic S. Mishkin (1983), 'An integrated view of tests of rationality, market efficiency and the short-run neutrality of monetary policy', *Journal of Monetary Economics*, 11, 3–24.

Batchelor, Roy and Lars Jonung (1988), 'Confidence about inflation forecasts: evidence from surveys of Swedish consumers', in K. H. Oppenlander and G. Poser (eds), *Contributions of Business Cycle Surveys to Empirical Economics*, Aldershot: Gower Press, 211–40.

Batchelor, Roy and Lars Jonung (1989), 'Cross-sectional evidence on the rationality of the mean and variance of inflation expectations', in K. Grunert and F. Olander (eds), *Frontiers in Economic Psychology*, Dordrecht: Reidel, 93–106.

Bollerslev, Tim, Robert F. Engle and Jeffrey M. Wooldridge (1988), 'A capital asset pricing model with time-varying covariances', *Journal of Political Economy*, 96, 116–31.

Brown, Bryan W. and Shlomo Maital (1981), 'What do economists know? An empirical study of experts' expectations', *Econometrica*, 49, 491–504.

Cukierman, Alex and Paul Wachtel (1982), 'Inflationary expectations and further thoughts on inflation uncertainty', *American Economic Review*, 72, 508–12.

Engle, Robert F. (1982), 'Autoregressive conditional heteroscedasticity with estimates of the variance of United Kingdom inflation', *Econometrica*, 50, 987–1007.

Engle, Robert F. (1983), 'Estimates of the variance of US inflation based upon the ARCH model', *Journal of Money, Credit and Banking*, 15, 286–301.

Figlewski, S. and P. Wachtel (1981), 'The formation of inflationary expectations', *Review of Economics and Statistics*, 63, 1–10.

Hansen, Lars-Peter (1982), 'Large sample properties of generalized method of moments estimators', *Econometrica*, 50, 1029–54.

Hey, John D. (1979), *Uncertainty in Microeconomics*, Oxford: Martin Robertson.

Keane, Michael P. and David E. Runkle (1990), 'Testing the rationality of price forecasts: new evidence from panel data', *American Economic Review*, 80, 714–35.

Lahiri, Kajal (1981), *The Econometrics of Inflationary Expectations*, Amsterdam: North-Holland.

Lahiri, Kajal and Christie Teigland (1987), 'On the normality of probability distributions of inflation and GNP forecasts', *International Journal of Forecasting*, 3, 269–79.

Maddala, G.S. (1988), *Introduction to Econometrics*, New York: Macmillan.

McNees, Stephen K. (1978), 'The rationality of economic forecasts', *American Economic Review*, 68, 301–5.

Muth, John F. (1961), 'Rational expectations and the theory of price movements', *Econometrica*, 29, 315–35.

Pearce, Douglas K. (1984), 'An empirical analysis of expected stock price movements', *Journal of Money, Credit and Banking*, 16, 317–27.

Pesaran, M. Hashem (1987), *The Limits to Rational Expectations*, Oxford: Basil Blackwell.

Swidler, Steve and David Ketcher (1990), 'Economic forecasts, rationality, and the processing of new information over time', *Journal of Money, Credit and Banking*, 22, 65–76.

Urich, Thomas and Paul Wachtel (1984), 'The structure of expectations of the weekly money supply announcements', *Journal of Monetary Economics*, 13, 183–94.

Zarnowitz, Victor (1969), 'The new ASA–NBER survey of forecasts by economic statisticians', *American Statistician*, 23, 12–16.

Zarnowitz, Victor (1979), 'An analysis of annual and multiperiod quarterly forecasts of aggregate income, output and the price level', *Journal of Business*, 52, 1–33.

Zarnowitz, Victor (1985), 'Rational expectations and macroeconomic forecasts', *Journal of Business and Economic Statistics*, 3, 293–311.

Zarnowitz, Victor and Louis A. Lambros (1987), 'Consensus and uncertainty in economic prediction', *Journal of Political Economy*, 95, 591–621.

9. Expectations formation and risk in three financial markets: surveying what surveys say

Ronald MacDonald*

INTRODUCTION

Using survey data to measure expectations of inflation has a fairly long pedigree in the economics literature and various aspects of inflationary expectations have been intensively scrutinized by the profession.[1] However, it is only comparatively recently that survey data have been used to measure and analyse the expectations of financial asset prices such as exchange rates, stock prices and bond prices. The differential speed with which researchers have examined financial market survey data, compared to commodity price data, runs counter to the adjustment speed in most macroeconomic models, where asset prices react earlier than commodity prices. The failure, until recently, of researchers to exploit financial survey data probably reflects two factors: first, compared to inflationary expectations, it is only comparatively recently that financial survey data have been collected on a consistent basis, and, second, there seems to have been a recognition lag before researchers started to exploit such data. There is now, however, a voluminous and growing literature which exploits survey data obtained from companies who specalize in the collection and collation of financial market survey data.

The purpose of this paper is to provide both a logical record of the extant literature which uses survey data on asset prices, and also to draw out what can be learnt about the behaviour of asset markets from using such data. In particular, and as we shall argue, survey data are especially valuable in trying to unravel the importance of risk premia in financial markets and also for determining the kinds of expectational mechanisms that best

* I am grateful to the editors for very useful comments on an earlier draft of this paper. The usual disclaimer applies.

characterize the evolution of expectations. The latter is seen as especially important since financial markets are often described as being irrational or 'will-of-the-wisp'. The markets which we overview in this paper are: the foreign exchange market; the bond market; and the stock market.[2] There is a natural complementarity between research into the former two markets, since the kinds of issues examined are very similar and relate to the formation of expectations and the time-variability of risk premia; research pertaining to the latter market concentrates almost exclusively on expectations formation.

The outline of the remainder of this paper is as follows. In section 9.1 we present some general relationships which have been utilized for research in all three financial markets. In section 9.2 we discuss some of the most widely used data sets and also address some econometric issues which are widely encountered in the financial markets literature. Our overview of research relating to the foreign exchange market is considered in section 9.3, and bond and stock market research is detailed in sections 9.4 and 9.5, respectively. The paper has a concluding section which summarizes the main findings and gives pointers to future research.

9.1   THE ADVANTAGES OF SURVEY DATA IN TESTING PROPOSITIONS USING DERIVATIVES

One way of motivating our discussion of survey data is to ask the question: how does a researcher test the properties of financial market data, such as the informational efficiency of market prices or the behaviour of forecast errors in the absence of survey data? This question may be answered in the following way. Consider the logarithm of the spot price of an asset, s_t, and the logarithm of the associated forward, or futures, price with maturity $t + k, f_t^{t+k}$.[3] We discuss below how these three variables are defined for each of the markets considered here. We define the forward premium[4] as $f_t - s_t$ and this consists of two components: the expected change in the spot rate, $\Delta s_{t+k}^e = s_{t+k}^e - s_t$, where s_{t+k}^e is the logarithm of the 'true' subjective expectation of the spot rate plus the expected excess return from taking a forward position, λ_t:

$$fp_t = \Delta s_{t+k}^e + \lambda_t. \tag{9.1}$$

The final term in (9.1) is interpreted as a risk premium in the foreign exchange market literature, a term premium in the term structure of interest rates literature and has no particular interpretation in the stock market literature. Henceforth in this section we refer to this term as the 'premium'.

In the absence of an independent measure of expectations, a common expression of the efficient markets hypothesis, especially as it relates to the foreign exchange market, is to adopt the joint hypothesis that subjective expectations are formed rationally and that the risk premium is zero or, less restrictively, equal to a constant, $\lambda_t = \alpha_0$. The former assumption may be expressed as:

$$\Delta s_{t+k} - \Delta s^e_{t+k} + \eta_{t+k}, \; \Delta s^e_{t+k} = E[\Delta s_{t+k} | I_t], \tag{9.2}$$

where E denotes the mathematical expectations operator, I_t is the information set on which agents base their expectations and η_{t+k} is a random forecast error, orthogonal to the information set.[5] In the foreign exchange literature the assumption that $\lambda_t = \alpha_0$ implies the absence of a time-varying risk premium, while in the term structure literature it implies the absence of a time-dependent term premium. This joint hypothesis is usually tested using the following regression equation:

$$\Delta s_{t+k} = \alpha_0 + \beta_0 f p_t + u_{t+k}, \tag{9.3}$$

where u_{t+k} is a random error term. The standard expression for the probability limit (Plim) of β_0 in (9.3) is:

$$\beta_0 = \frac{Cov(fp_t, \Delta s_{t+k})}{Var(fp_t)}. \tag{9.4}$$

As we shall see when turning to our empirical results, estimated values of β_0 are often significantly below unity and there are essentially two explanations for this. The first relates to the formation of expectations. The existence of learning processes, 'peso' effects or simply irrational information exploitation could all produce this result. Second, if the risk premium is not in fact constant but, rather, time-varying then this could also produce an estimate of β_0 which is less than 1. Insight into these two sources of bias in β_0 may be obtained by re-expressing (9.4), using the definition of rationality given by (9.2), to obtain the following Plim:

$$\beta_0 = \frac{cov(s^e_{t+k} - s_t, fp_t) + cov(\eta_{t+k}, fp_t)}{Var(fp_t)}. \tag{9.5}$$

The two covariance terms in the numerator of equation (9.5) reflect the two potential reasons why β_0 may differ from unity. This may be seen more clearly by using (9.1) to define the premium term, λ_t, and re-expressing (9.5) as:

$$\beta_0 = 1 - \beta_\lambda + \beta_e, \tag{9.6}$$

where:

$$\beta\lambda = \frac{\text{var}(\lambda_t) + \text{cov}(\lambda_t, s^e_{t+k} - s_t)}{\text{Var}(fp_t)}, \tag{9.7}$$

and:

$$\beta_e = \frac{\text{cov}(\eta_{t+k}, s^e_{t+k} - s_t) + \text{cov}(\eta_{t+k}, fp_t)}{\text{Var}(fp_t)}. \tag{9.8}$$

Expressions (9.7) and (9.8) make clear the advantages of having an independent measure of expectations from survey data; its existence means that both the expected exchange rate change and the λ_t term can be calculated. However, for a variety of reasons, such as the impact synchronization of survey responses and the use of a consensus response (mean or median) which is extracted from only a fraction of market participants, it is unlikely that the measured survey expectations will be identically equal to the 'true' expectation value, $\bar{s}^e_{t+k}$. In common with most researchers, therefore, we assume that the measured expected value is equal to the 'true' value plus a random measurement error:

$$\Delta s^e_{t+k} = \Delta \bar{s}^e_{t+k} + \varphi_{t+k}, \tag{9.9}$$

where φ_{t+k} is the survey forecast or measurement error. As long as the discrepancy between the true and reported forecasts are random, econometric estimates which utilize Δs^e_{t+k} will have valid properties (this is discussed in more detail below). An estimate of β_λ may be recovered as $1 - \beta_\kappa$ from (9.10):

$$\Delta s^e_{t+k} = \alpha_0 + \beta_\kappa fp_t + u_{t+k}, \tag{9.10}$$

and an estimate of β_e may be recovered from equation (9.11):

$$s^e_{t+k} - s_{t+k} = \alpha_1 + \beta_e(f_t - s_t) + \epsilon_{t+k}. \tag{9.11}$$

Although the existence of survey data facilitates the decomposition given by (9.6), the use of such data is not entirely uncontroversial. For example, some economists would argue that the expectations of agents are better reflected in actual market prices, since such prices are the prices at which investors trade. In contrast, the answers that investors give survey pollsters may not be an accurate description of their true expectations. There are (at least) two responses to this. First, some survey outfits, such as Consensus Economics of London, actually publish the names of forecasters alongside the forecast; presumably, for reputational purposes, it is in the interests of the forecaster to supply a forecast which is his or her 'best'. Second, whilst recognizing the argument that survey respondents may not always give their true forecast, we would argue that, at the very least, the survey data still contain some useful information which is worthy of study.

9.2 EXPECTATIONAL ISSUES

9.2.1 Rational Expectations

At the centre of the discussion in the previous section is the assumption of rational expectations. As we noted there, this assumption is often invoked in testing the optimality of the forward rate as a predictor of the future spot rate, and such tests usually show that the forward rate is a biased predictor. The existence of survey data can assist in helping to unravel why the forward rate appears to produce biased forecasts of the future spot rate. Thus, equation (9.11) represents a test of the rationality of the survey data and, in particular, is an error orthogonality test which may be stated more generally as:

$$s_{t+k}^e - s_{t+k} = \Gamma X_t + \omega_{t+k}, \qquad (9.11')$$

where X_t is a $(1 \times k)$ row vector, which is the econometricians' observed portion of the 'true' information set, I_t, available to agents, Γ is a $(k \times 1)$ vector of parameters and ω_{t+k} is an error term. The null hypothesis is that Γ equals zero. If this condition is violated then information available to agents at time t has remained unexploited. In equation (9.11), of course, X_t is simply the forward premium. Following Fama's (1976) taxonomy, this would be regarded as a semi-strong form efficiency test since it exploits publicly available information over and above that reflected simply in past forecast errors (a test conditioning solely on past forecast errors would be classified as a weak-form test). When only a constant is included in the information set the error orthogonality test reduces to a test of the unbiasedness of the forecast. The latter may be tested using the following regression equation:

$$\Delta s_{t+k} = \alpha_u + \beta_u \Delta s_{t+k}^e + u_{t+k}, \qquad (9.12)$$

where the hypothesis of unbiasedness involves testing $\alpha_u = 0$ and $\beta_u = 1$. As we shall see, most researchers who have analysed survey data for asset prices have implemented (9.11') and (9.12).

9.2.2 Expectational Mechanisms

Although testing for the rationality of survey expectations is of interest in terms of explaining the poor predictive properties of forward rates, the kind of expectations process that best describes the evolution of survey expectations is of interest in itself. For example, are financial market expectations best characterized as adaptive, extrapolative or regressive? This may be of interest from a theoretical modelling perspective. Thus, most open economy macro-models, with flexible exchange rates, make some assumption about the formation of expectations.[6] It is also an important empirical issue since the perceived excess asset volatility that many commentators have noted (see, for example, McKinnon, 1976; Shiller, 1990) is often attributed to bandwagon (that is, extrapolative) expectations.

The different potential expectations mechanisms referred to above are captured in the following equation:

$$\Delta s_{t+1}^e = \omega + \gamma(s_t - s_{t-1}) + \vartheta(s_t^e - s_t) + \nu(\bar{s}_t - s_t). \tag{9.13}$$

The benchmark, or null hypothesis, could be taken to be that of static expectations. This would be valid if $\gamma = \nu = \vartheta = 0$. Essentially this hypothesis means that investors believe an asset price follows a random walk (with drift). Although the random walk model has been widely canvassed as the benchmark model for asset prices/returns there is now mounting evidence to suggest that the model is not valid.[7] There are four alternatives to the base-line static expectations proposition.

If a purely extrapolative, or bandwagon, approach describes the evolution of the spot price then $\vartheta = \nu = 0$ in (9.13) and γ is expected to be positive; a current change in the spot price is expected to produce a further positive change in the next period. A negative value of γ would imply that the expected spot rate is described by a distributed lag process and therefore an increase in the current spot rate would produce a less than proportionate increase in the expected spot rate – expectations are stabilizing. If expectations are characterized by adaptive expectations then $\gamma = \nu = 0$ and ϑ should lie between 0 and 1. That is, if the period-t spot rate is above the expected value for t, investors will adapt to this forecast error by increasing their expectation of the spot rate for the next period, but not by all of the current forecast error; again expectations are stabilizing or inelastic. Expectations are formed regressively when $\gamma = \nu = 0$ and ν lies between 0 and 1. That is, a movement of the current spot price above the equilibrium spot price, $\bar{s}_t$, generates the expectation of a return to equilibrium; again this would imply that expectations are stabilizing. A fourth expectational process would perhaps be described by some mix of these processes. This mixed model may be referred to as a hybrid model, or an Extrapolative, Regressive and Adaptive Model with Limited Information – MILERA (see Prat, 1994).

9.2.3   Consistency of Expectations

Often in polling forecasters for their view of the future value of an asset price, a forecasting agency will ask respondents for their expectation at a number of horizons (say, three and six months ahead). The availability of such multi-horizon forecasts facilitates a test of the *consistency* of the survey forecasts. A subjective expectation $_{t+i}s^e_{t+k}$ formed at $t+i$ for period $t+k$ ($k>1$) is said to be consistent if expectations of $_{t+i}s^e_{t+k}$ formed at time t are equal to $_ts^e_{t+k}$ for all k (Pesaran, 1989b). Alternatively, consistency can be thought of in terms of expectations formed on the same date, t. As before, $_ts^e_{t+k}$ is the expected spot price formed in t for $t+k$ ($k>t$) and we define $_ts^e_{t+k+j}$ as the expected spot price formed in period t for $t+k+j$ ($j>k$). These two forecasts will be consistent if in iterating forward the shorter forecast (s^e_{t+k}) to period $t+k+j$ gives the same number as s^e_{t+k+j}. Consistency, although a necessary condition of rationality, is actually a weaker condition than rationality since it imposes only the chain rule of forecasting on to subjectively formed expectations (it does not require the expectations process to be equivalent to the underlying stochastic process driving the actual asset price). The consistency of expectations is in fact a standard feature of many tests of the term structure of interest rates.

9.3   DATA SOURCES AND ECONOMETRIC ISSUES

The survey data sources which have been most widely exploited by researchers are as follows. Money Market Services (MMS) (US) have, since 1983, polled in excess of 30 leading forecasters in the US on their views of the expected US dollar bilateral spot exchange rates of the British pound (BP), German mark (DM), French franc (FF), Japanese yen (JY) and the Swiss franc (SF), one week, one month and three months ahead. Similarly, since 1982 MMS (UK) has polled leading forecasters in continental Europe and in the UK to ascertain their forecasts of the same four bilateral currencies. Both the US- and the UK-based pollsters have also conducted surveys of the spot exchange rate and interests rates three and six months ahead. *The Economist* magazine has conducted six-weekly surveys of a sample of around 30 traders on their expectations of the BP, DM, FF, JY and SF against the US dollar, three, six and twelve months ahead. AMEX, over the period from 1976 to 1985, has surveyed a sample of in excess of 250 financial market participants as to their views of the BP, DM, FF, JY, SF against the US dollar (for horizons three, six and twelve months ahead). Consensus Economics of London offers perhaps the widest range of currency forecasts, including established currencies such as those referred to above, and also those for developing countries such as the Asian tigers. Consensus forecasts have the added advantage that they are conducted in the G7 financial centres simultaneously on the currency values three and twelve months ahead and are available from the period October 1989 onwards; Consensus also provides interest rate expectations in addition to its exchange rate expectations. Other survey data sets will be discussed as we proceed.

Before considering some of the empirical evidence on the relationships considered in this section, we must deal with a methodological problem: the overlapping contracts issue. For example, if in testing (9.3) we use a forward exchange rate premium with a one-month contract and weekly data we would expect *a priori* the error term, u_{t+k}, to be serially correlated. This follows because when more than one observation is recorded during the period to maturity the (forecast) error term will not be independent of past forecast errors, but will instead follow a moving average process of order $k - 1$, for a k period forecast. However, ordinary least squares may still be used to estimate an equation like (9.3), since the coefficients will be consistent even in the presence of moving average errors. The standard errors will not, though, be consistent. Practically all of the researchers referred to in this paper use a version of Hansen's (1982) Generalised Method of Moments (GMM) to correct the standard errors. GMM has the additional advantage that it can be used to correct the standard errors for heteroscedasticity (of unknown form), in addition to serial correlation. The GMM estimator for the sample covariance matrix of the OLS estimate of β_0 is:

$$\hat{\Sigma} = (X'X)^{-1}X'\hat{\Omega}X(X'X)^{-1}, \tag{9.14}$$

where $\hat{\Omega}$ is the variance-covariance matrix of the residuals, and the ijth element of $\hat{\Omega}$ is given by:

$$\hat{\lambda}(i, j) = \hat{u}_i\hat{u}_j \quad \text{for } |i - j| \leq (k - 1) \tag{9.15}$$
$$= 0 \quad \text{otherwise,}$$

where $\hat{\lambda}$ is the estimated autocovariance. A potential problem with estimates of $\hat{\Omega}$ is that it need not be positive definite in small samples. To address this problem, Newey and West (1987) suggest, for example, redefining $\hat{\lambda}(i, j)$ in (9.15) as:

$$\hat{\lambda}(i, j) = \begin{cases} u_i \hat{u}_j \delta(i, j) & \text{if } |i-j| < k \\ 0 & \text{if } |i-j| \geq k \end{cases} \tag{9.15'}$$

where the weights $\delta(i, j)$ are given by:

$$\delta(i, j) = 1 - [|i-j|/(m+1)],$$

and where m is chosen just large enough to guarantee positive definiteness. Newey and West suggest setting $m = n$ while, for example, Frankel and Froot (1987) set $m = 2k$.

Since the form of serial correlation is known *a priori*, an alternative estimator that could be exploited in the kinds of test considered in this paper is that of generalized least squares (GLS). Since GLS can also be used to correct for heteroscedasticity it is perhaps surprising that it has not been more widely used by researchers. Perhaps one reason for this is that GLS requires knowledge of the form of heteroscedasticity before it can be utilized, whereas the GMM estimator does not need this prior knowledge. Practically all of the standard errors reported in this paper are constructed using the GMM/Newey and West estimator.

9.4   THE FOREIGN EXCHANGE MARKET

Without doubt, the largest number of tests exploiting survey data have involved using foreign exchange rate data. In the majority of cases such tests have used the mean or median value of a given survey. Recently, however, it has become increasingly fashionable to use disaggregated data, particularly with respect to analysing the market microstructure properties of the foreign exchange market. In sub-section 9.4.1 we present an overview of the disaggregate results, while in 9.4.2 we discuss the disaggregate results. Before turning to these results, however, it is worth presenting an estimated version of (9.3) to motivate our discussion. The example is from MacDonald and Torrance (1990), and is for the British pound sterling, estimated over the period July 1982–April 1987:

$$\Delta s_{t+k} = -0.012 - 6.825 fp_t. \tag{9.16}$$
$$\phantom{\Delta s_{t+k} = }(3.39) \qquad (3.56)$$

Equation (9.16) nicely underscores the point made earlier: the forward premium is a biased predictor of the exchange rate change. In terms of our example, the β_0 coefficient is not even positive, far less is it close to one. It is important to stress that similar results have been obtained for other currencies and other time periods (see MacDonald, 1990; and Engel, 1996).

9.4.1   Aggregate Results

The literature using aggregate survey data is voluminous and was stimulated by the papers of Frankel and Froot (1987, 1989).

Unbiasedness results
Unbiasedness tests have been conducted by Dominguez (1986), Frankel and Froot (1987), MacDonald and Torrance (1988), MacDonald (1990b), MacDonald and Marsh (1996a), Cavaglia *et al.* (1993a), Chinn and Frankel (1994) and Kim (1997). All these papers, with the exception of Cavaglia *et al.*, concentrate exclusively on US dollar bilaterial exchange rates and consider more than one forecast horizon. The particular survey sources used in these papers, along with the sample periods, and a representative set of results are presented in Table 9.1. These indicate that unbiasedness is very strongly rejected for US dollar bilateral exchange rates. The rejection occurs because the estimated value of β_u is significantly less than unity and this rejection is often reinforced by α_u differing significantly from zero. This picture essentially confirms the findings of researchers who have imposed rational expectations, and it is suggestive that one reason why researchers have found the forward premium to be a biased predictor of the future exchange rate is because of some form of expectational failure.

It is important to note that the results reported in Table 9.1 do not necessarily imply irrational information processing (although, of course, they may). In particular, they could simply be picking up a learning effect, a 'peso effect' or a speculative bubble. It is well known that such phenomena can produce a violation of unbiasedness without necessarily violating rationality (see Obstfeld, 1987, for a discussion of this point). We return to this point in the concluding section.

Error orthogonality results
Further evidence on the expectational failures referred to above may be obtained by estimating an error orthogonality condition of the form (9.11) and recovering estimates of β_e. These results are reported in Table 9.2, where we have limited the information set to include only the forward premium; we impose this limitation to conserve space. These results essentially confirm those in Table 9.1: when the information set is expanded to

Table 9.1: *Foreign exchange unbiasedness results*

$$\Delta s_{t+k} = \alpha_u + \beta_u \Delta s^e_{t+k} + u_{t+k}$$

Author	Survey source	Forecast horizon	Sample period	α	β	$t_\beta u = 1$
Dominguez (1986)						
German mark	MMS (US)	1 month	1/83–10/84	0.014 (0.01)	−0.248 (0.39)	*
Swiss yen				0.012 (0.01)	−0.375 (0.43)	*
Frankel and Froot (1987)						
6 currencies, pooled	*The Economist*	6 months	6/81–12/85	11.70 (3.20)	—	*
MacDonald and Torrance (1998)						
DM/US	MMS (UK)	1 week	2/85–5/86(w)	—	−1.059 (0.36)	*
MacDonald (1990)						
BP/US	MMS (UK)	1 month	7/82–4/87(bw)	—	−0.988 (0.55)	*

Chinn and Frankel (1994)						
British pound	*Currency Digest*	3 months	2/88–2/91	−13.230 (6.88)	−1.802 (0.58)	*
German mark				−9.193 (6.31)	−0.640 (0.43)	*
Cavaglia *et al.* (1993b)						
Belgian franc (dm)	*Cross Rates Bulletin*	3 months	1/86–12/90	0.001 (0.002)	0.054 (0.13)	*
French franc (dm)				0.001 (0.003)	0.871 (0.48)	
Kim (1997)						
Australian dollar	MMS	2 weeks	10/84–2/93	−0.0004 (0.0007)	0.236 (0.098)	*

Notes:
* denotes significance at the 5 per cent level.
w denotes weekly observation.
bw denotes bi weekly observation.

Table 9.2: Foreign exchange error orthogonality results

$$s^e_{t+k} - s_t = \alpha_e + \beta_e(f-s)_t + u_{t+k}$$

Author	Survey source	Forecast horizon	Sample period	α_e	β_e	χ
Dominguez (1986)						
German mark	MMS (US)	3 months	1/83–10/84	0.003 (0.01)	−4.960 (0.39)	128.8*
Swiss franc				0.065 (0.01)	−7.890 (0.43)	69.4*
Frankel and Froot (1989)						
6 currencies, pooled	The Economist	6 months	6/81–12/85 (6w)	n.a.	2.988 (1.59)	1.46
4 currencies, pooled	MMS (US)	3 months	1/83–10/84 (w)	n.a.	6.073 (2.33)	11.93*
MacDonald and Torrance (1990)						
BP/US	MMS (UK)	1 month	7/82–4/87 (bw)	0.013 (0.28)	7.698 (2.14)	18.95*
DM/US	MMS (UK)	1 month	7/82–4/87 (bw)	−0.003 (0.004)	−0.279 (0.02)	388.14*

Chinn and Frankel (1994)						
Pooled (25)	*Currency Digest*	3 months	2/88–2/91 (m)	n.a.	−3.468 (0.73)	*
Pooled (25)		12 months	2/88–2/91 (m)	n.a.	−5.201 (0.72)	*
Cavaglia *et al.* (1993b)	*Cross Rates Bulletin*					
Belgian franc (dm)		3 months	1/86–12/90	−0.002 (0.002)	−0.010 (0.23)	
French franc (dm)				−0.003 (0.003)	0.298 (0.17)	

Notes:
* denotes significance at the 5 per cent level.
w denotes weekly observation.
bw denotes bi-weekly observation.
6w denotes observation available every six weeks.
m denotes monthly.
dm denotes German mark.

include an extra variable, over a constant, the null hypothesis is strongly rejected in all cases. Studies, such as Frankel and Froot (1987) and MacDonald (1990), which extend the information set to include previous forecast errors and further lagged forward premia (from the 'own' and other foreign exchange markets), essentially reinforce this finding. One interesting twist to the above story is, however, provided by Cavaglia *et al.* (1993a) who have access to survey data on DM-based bilaterals. As is evident from the set of their results reported in Table 9.2, the null hypothesis cannot be rejected. Indeed, out of the six DM-based currencies studied there is only one rejection at the three-month horizon and three at the twelve-month. These results perhaps suggest that the ERM, by increasing the predictability of spot rates, also improves the efficiency of foreign exchange markets.

Liu and Maddala (1992) take a somewhat different approach to testing orthogonality. In particular, they define exchange rate expectations as rational if s_{t+1} and s_t^e are cointegrated, the cointegrating factor is one and the errors are a white noise process. It is in this sense that their test may be thought of as an error orthogonality test. In practice what this amounts to is testing the stationarity of the series $s_{t+1} - s_t^e$, using a variety of univariate unit root tests and examining the serial correlation properties of this series. The one-week and one-month ahead MMS (US) expectations for the British pound, German mark, Swiss franc and Japanese yen, all against the US dollar, are used for the period from 24 October 1984 to 19 May 1989 (weekly data). For the one-week forecasts a weekly sampling is used, while for the monthly forecasts a monthly sampling is used. The authors find that for all the one-week forecasts they can reject the null hypothesis of no cointegration and, additionally, they find no evidence of serial correlation. However, for the one-month forecasts, although the null of no cointegration can be rejected for all currencies, there is evidence of serial correlation. Liu and Madadala interpret this result as evidence of irrationality.

Time-varying risk premia
The results in sub-sections 9.4.1 and 9.4.2 suggest that some form of expectational failure is, at least in part, responsible for the kind of result noted in (9.16). Further light may be shed on this issue by estimating equation (9.10) which should indicate the importance of both constant and time-varying risk premiums. A summary of the results is presented in Table 9.3. In terms of the MMS results we note that there is a clear difference between the US- and UK-based results. The US-based results of Frankel and Froot (1989, 1990b) show, at most, that there is a significantly positive constant risk premium, whereas the results of MacDonald and Torrance (1988, 1990) demonstrate that both a constant and a time-varying risk

premium are responsible for the rejection. Other aggregate-based results, such as those reported in Cavaglia *et al.* (1993b), tend to favour the latter interpretation. This evidence, that foreign exchange risk premia may be time-varying, has motivated a number of researchers to explicitly *model* the risk premia using survey data. Before discussing this work we briefly overview comparable work using generated measures of the risk premium.

Studies which seek to model the risk premium using generated risk premia (generated on the basis of assuming rational expectations) generally take as their starting point the first-order, or Euler, condition from a representative agent model (see the summaries of this literature in MacDonald, 1990; and Engel, 1996). This condition shows the risk premium to be a function of the ratio of marginal utility in period t, relative to period $t+1$, and has been empirically implemented in one of three ways. First, a number of authors (see, *inter alia*, Hansen and Hodrick, 1983; and Hansen and Richard, 1984) have used the capital asset pricing model (CAPM) and a latent variable estimator to implement the generated risk premium/Euler condition and some (slight) evidence suggests that risk premia are time-dependent and driven by the variables suggested by the CAPM model.

Second, Mark (1985) has suggested testing the Euler condition directly, using the methods of Hansen and Singleton (1982), but finds little evidence in favour of the generated risk premium model (one of his most striking findings is that the estimated value of the risk aversion parameter is too large to be consistent with the model and is not precisely estimated in a statistical sense).

The third approach, proposed first by Domowitz and Hakkio (1985), involves using autoregressive conditional heteroscedasticity (ARCH) based models to capture the time variability of the risk premium in terms of the conditional variance of past forecast errors. Although Domowitz and Hakkio fail to reject the null hypothesis of no risk premium in their ARCH-based models, other studies which have adopted a multivariate ARCH approach have been able to reject the null (see, for example, Nerlove *et al.*, 1988). The evidence on the existence of time-varying risk premia from generated risk premia studies is at best mixed. However, the failure to find clear evidence of a time-varying risk premium in such studies may be due to the imposition of the rational expectations assumption rather than the non-existence of such premia. Survey data would seem therefore to have an advantage in this regard.

The literature which uses survey data to extract measures of risk premia finds much stronger evidence in favour of the existence of time-varying risk. For example, Cavaglia *et al.* (1993b) demonstrate that, on the basis of a representative agent model, the risk premium should be a stationary, or

Table 9.3: *Foreign exchange risk premium results*

$$\Delta s_{t+k}^e = \alpha_\kappa + \beta_\kappa (f-s)_t + u_{t+k}$$

Author	Survey source	Forecast horizon	Sample period	α_κ	β_κ	$t_\beta\kappa = 1$
Frankel and Froot (1989)						
6 currencies, pooled	The Economist	6 months	6/81–12/85 (6w)	n.a.	1.032 (0.17)	0.19
4 currencies, pooled	MMS (US)	3 months	1/83–10/84 (w)	n.a.	−0.182 (0.42)	−2.75
MacDonald and Torrance (1990)						
BP/US	MMS (UK)	1 month	7/82–4/87 (bw)	0.001 (0.00)	0.873 (0.44)	−0.28
DM/US	MMS (UK)	1 month	7/82–4/87 (bw)	−0.007 (0.001)	−0.026 (0.003)	342
Chinn and Frankel (1994)						
British pound	Currency Digest	3 months	2/88–2/91	−13.230 (6.88)	−1.802 (0.58)	*

German mark					−9.193	0.640	*
					(6.31)	(0.43)	
Cavaglia et al. (1993b)	Cross Rates Bulletin	3 months	1/86–12/90				
Belgian franc (dm)					0.001	0.054	*
					(0.002)	(0.13)	
French franc (dm)					0.001	0.871	
					(0.003)	(0.48)	

Notes:
* denotes significance at the 5 per cent level.
w denotes weekly observation.
bw denotes bi-weekly observation.
6w denotes observation available every six weeks.

I(O), process and should have an AR1 representation. They demonstrate that this is indeed the case for their survey data set. Giorgianni (1996) and MacDonald (1996) have attempted to model, with some success, survey-based risk premia using measures of the conditional variances of fundamentals, such as money supplies and inflation. This topic would seem to offer an exciting avenue for further research.

Expectational mechanisms

Given the strong rejection of 'rationality' noted above, it is clearly of interest to examine alternative hypotheses about expectations formation.[8] Frankel and Froot (1987, 1990a), Cavaglia *et al.* (1993a), MacDonald and Torrance (1988) and Prat and Uctum (1999, 2000) have all tested variants of equation (9.13). In terms of the foreign exchange market, testing for the kind of expectational mechanism which best describes agents' expectations formation takes on a special significance since a key feature of the recent experience with floating rates has been the pronounced volatility of such exchange rates. One explanation that is often advocated for this volatility is that it reflects the behaviour of 'noise traders' who adopt bandwagon forecasting methods; that is, they simply extrapolate last period's change into a future change in the same direction. Survey data should help to shed some light on this issue.

A summary of the extant results are reported in Table 9.4. In summary form, all the equations which feature forecast horizons longer than three months exhibit clear evidence of stabilizing expectations (and given the significance of the explanatory variables a clear rejection of the null of static expectations). However, the three-month pooled results of Frankel and Froot, the results of MacDonald and Torrance (1988) and a further paper by Frankel and Froot (1990b) – in which they examine a range of short MMS expectations (one week, two weeks, one month and three months) for the Japanese yen – all find significant evidence of destabilizing expectations. The work of Cavaglia *et al.* (1993a) and of Prat and Uctum, which focuses on longer horizons, essentially confirms the long-horizon findings of Frankel and Froot (1987), since across maturities and currencies there is again clear evidence that expectations are stabilizing.'

Why the difference between the short and long ends of the forecast horizons? One explanation may lie in the fact that agents who provide forecasts for short periods tend to base their forecasts on chartist or extrapolative methods.

A final point to make with regard to the results reported in this section is that even rejecting bandwagon or extrapolative expectations in favour of the alternative of stabilizing expectations does not necessarily rule out the existence of speculative bubbles that are constantly forming and bursting, since such bubbles would not be captured by the tests noted in Table 9.4.

Consistency results

Froot and Ito (1990) examine the consistency of expectations from four survey sources: *The Economist* (three-, six- and thirteen-month horizons for the BP, DM, FF, JY and SF, over the period June 1981 to August 1987), MMS (US) (one-week and one-month horizons for the BP, DM, JY and SF, over the period April 1984 to April 1987), MMS (UK) (one-week and one-month horizons for the BP, DM, JY and SF, over the period April 1984 to April 1987), JCIF (Tokyo) (one, three and six months for the JY, over the period May 1985 to June 1987). Froot and Ito assume that the 'short' and 'long' forecasts are formed as a linear combination of current and lagged spot rate changes, plus disturbance terms; this is essentially an extrapolative model. The requirement of consistency then imposes restrictions on the parameters and the disturbances across the equations representing the different expectations horizons, much as in a standard VAR analysis.[10] Froot and Ito find that across all the survey data bases and forecast horizons (in all, 20 different time series sets) consistency is strongly rejected and therefore short-term expectations are seen to overreact relative to longer-term expectations in response to a current exchange rate change. This short-term overreaction would seem to be consistent with the findings of extrapolative expectations at short horizons noted in the previous section.

Bénassy and Raymond (1995) test the consistency of expectations for four exchange rates (DM, FF, JY and ST) using three different survey data sets (Banque Nationale de Paris, sample April 1983 to June 1993; *The Economist*, sample June 1981 to January 1989; Consensus Economics, sample January 1991 to September 1993). One novelty of their work is that they use a broader variety of expectational mechanisms to generate the short- and long-run expectations than Froot and Ito (that is, a mix of adaptive, extrapolative and regressive expectations). However, despite allowing for such generality, Bénassy and Raymond still convincingly reject the consistency of expectations.

9.4.2 Disaggregate Results: Do Foreign Exchange Forecasters Have Heterogeneous Expectations?

All the research discussed above exploits aggregate survey data, either mean or median data. The use of aggregate survey data often reflects the practical limitation that the disaggregate data used to generate a mean or median value is simply not made publicly available by the forecast organization. The reluctance of survey agencies to provide the disaggregate data often

Table 9.4: Foreign exchange expectational mechanisms results

$$\Delta s^e_{t+k} = \omega + \gamma(s_t - s_{t-1}) + \vartheta(s^e_t - s_t) + \nu(\bar{s}_t - s_t)$$

Author	Survey source	Forecast horizon	Sample period	γ	ϑ	ν
Frankel and Froot (1987)						
Pooled	*The Economist*	3 months	6/81–12/85	−0.416 (0.021)	0.079 (0.020)	0.039 (0.010)
Pooled	*The Economist*	6 months	6/81–12/85	−0.073 (0.025)	0.051 (0.016)	0.036 (0.010)
Pooled	AMEX	12 months	1/76–8/85	−0.379 (0.079)	0.095 (0.021)	0.079 (0.034)
Pooled	MMS (US)	3 months	1/83–10/84	0.039 (0.01)	−0.027 (0.02)	−0.021 (0.01)
MacDonald and Torrance (1988)						
DM/US	MMS (UK)	1 week	2/85–5/86 (w)	0.079 (0.04)	−0.043 (0.03)	—
DM/US	MMS (UK)	2 weeks		0.117	−0.083	
Cavaglia *et al.* (1993a) FF/US	*Cross Rates Bulletin*	3 months	1/86–12/90	−0.404 (0.069)	0.112 (0.033)	−0.310 (0.004)

FF/US	*Cross Rates Bulletin*	6 months	1/86–12/90	−0.529 (0.088)	0.140 (0.033)	—
FF/US	*Cross Rates Bulletin*	12 months	1/86–12/90	−0.623 (0.149)	0.199 (0.032)	—
Prat and Uctum (2000)						
FF/US	Consensus	3 months	11/89–10/90	−0.098 (0.02)	0.130 (0.04)	0.048 (0.01)
FF/US	Consensus	12 months	11/89–10/90	−0.025 (0.01)	0.017 (0.05)	0.116 (0.03)

Note: w denotes weekly observation.

reflects confidentiality issues. A forecaster would presumably be less likely to provide his or her forecasts to an agency if an academic researcher produced evidence, say, that the forecasts contained a consistent bias. However, recently one or two forecasting agencies have begun to release the disaggregate data underlying their consensus forecasts; the data are usually provided on the basis that the confidentiality of a forecaster is respected. In discussing the different disaggregate results, we use the same section headings utilized for the aggregate results, with the addition of a section on the causes of dissagregate heterogeneity.

Unbiasedness results

Ito (1990) uses a survey data base, collected by the Japanese Centre for International Finance, which consists of the individual responses (44 in total) of a number of financial and non-financial institutions on their expectations of the yen–dollar exchange rate, one, three and six months ahead for the sample May 1985 to June 1987. He groups the survey responses into six industrial classifications: banking, security companies, trading companies, companies in the export industries, insurance companies, and companies in the import industries. He finds that unbiasedness is rejected in a small number of instances for the short horizons, but unanimously rejected for the six-month horizon.

MacDonald (1992) uses a disaggregate survey data base supplied by Consensus Forecasts of London to test the unbiasedness of individual forecasters (sample period October 1989 to March 1991). This survey data base is particularly valuable since it contains disaggregate survey responses for three key currencies (dollar–sterling, dollar–mark, and dollar–yen) conducted simultaneously in seven financial centres. Although these results tend to confirm the aggregate unbiasedness results, in the sense that the vast majority of forecasters do not have unbiased forecasts, there is a significant minority that do produce unbiased forecasts. An interesting aspect of this study is that German forecasters have almost a 100 per cent record in producing unbiased forecasts of the German mark, but do as well as other forecasters for the other currencies. MacDonald and Marsh (1996a), and Chionis (1998) have updated the Consensus unbiasedness results (sample period October 1989 to March 1995) and essentially confirm the findings of MacDonald.

Error orthogonality results

Ito's (1990) error orthogonality tests are conducted using the forward premium, past forecast errors and the past exchange rate change as informational variables. He finds that orthogonality is overwhelmingly rejected across the forecast horizons and across individuals. MacDonald

(1992) finds that the forecasters who produce biased forecasts also failed the error orthogonality test (9.11) when the information set consisted of the fourth lagged survey forecast error (the fourth lag was used to avoid potential misalignments which may have produced spurious correlations). MacDonald and Marsh (1996a) and Chionis (1998) have extended and updated the Consensus results of MacDonald using the forward premium as the informational variable; again the null hypothesis of orthogonality was rejected in the vast majority of cases.

Expectational mechanisms
In MacDonald (1992), a comprehensive examination of the expectations formation mechanisms of all of the respondents to the Consensus survey is undertaken. In estimating (9.13) MacDonald found that the null hypothesis of static expectations could not be rejected in the vast majority of cases; however, a significant minority of forecasters displayed evidence of bandwagon effects.

Bénassy *et al.* (1999) use the Consensus survey data base, of three- and twelve-month expectations, to examine the adaptive, extrapolative, regressive and mixed expectations models. Both fixed effects and random effects panel estimators are used to estimate these models. Clear evidence of heterogeneity amongst forecasters is reported, although the vast majority of them have stabilizing expectations at both forecast horizons.

Other disaggregate topics: heterogeneity, market microstructure and risk
One of the key advantages that disaggregate survey data have over aggregate data is that it facilitates testing for heterogeneous behaviour amongst forecasters. The rational expectations hypothesis, by definition, rules out the existence of such differences between forecasters since the 'true' stochastic process is unique. The results reported in the previous sub-sections on unbiasedness, orthogonality and expectational mechanisms reveal that there are differences between forecasters. However, a number of researchers have focused more directly on this topic using the following method.

Suppose an individual j makes a forecast of the (log) exchange rate at time t which consists of two parts. Part X_t which is based on public information, I_t, and is common to all forecasters, plus an individual, or idiosyncratic effect, g_j. This individual's forecast is then the sum of these two parts, plus an individual random disturbance term, u_{jt}, which could occur as a result of rounding or measurement errors:

$$s_{jt}^e = X_t + g_j + u_{jt}. \tag{9.17}$$

The average forecast at time t is then:

$$s^e_{At} = X_t + g_A + u_{At}. \tag{9.18}$$

Normalizing such that g_A equals zero and subtracting (9.18) from (9.17) we obtain:

$$s^e_{jt} - s^e_{At} = g_j + [u_{jt} - u_{At}]. \tag{9.19}$$

The individual effects, g_j, may then be retrieved from a regression of the difference between an individual and the average forecast on a constant term; a non-zero g_j indicates that an individual's forecasts are biased compared to those of the representative, or average, forecaster. Note that this test tells us nothing about the forecasting *ability* of the individual.

One attractive feature of the above tests is that there is no need to specify the common forecast element, X_t, or the information set, I_t, on which it is based, so long as it can be assumed common to all individuals. However, it is possible to test for idiosyncratic coefficient terms on information in I_t. Suppose that in addition to individual biases (the g_js) each forecaster places different weights on some element of the publicly available information set; for concreteness assume this element to be the forward premium which holds at time t, fp_t. Then:

$$s^e_{jt} = X'_t + g'_j + \beta_j fp_t + u_{jt}, \tag{9.20}$$

where X'_t is the common forecast term based on I_t, less the forward premium, and g'_j is the new individual bias. Specifying the equivalent equation for the average forecast and subtracting as above implies that:

$$s^e_{jt} - s^e_{At} = g'_j + [\beta_j - \beta_A]fp_t + [u_{jt} - u_{At}]. \tag{9.21}$$

This somewhat richer formulation allows us to test for both individual biases ($g'_j \neq 0$) and idiosyncratic effects ($\beta_j - \beta_A \neq 0$).

Ito finds that there are important differences between the industrial classifications (noted above). In particular, he finds that around half of the forecasters have significant individual effects. Additionally, heterogeneity exhibited itself in terms of significant idiosyncracies: in using the exchange rate change in (9.21) instead of fp_t, Ito found that forecasters in the export sector are biased toward yen depreciation and importers are biased toward yen appreciation.

Due to the international nature of their database, MacDonald and Marsh (1996b) are able to push the above tests a little further. In particular, the Consensus data set allows calculation of the above effects with respect to both the overall average and also to the relevant country average.

This, in turn, allows an examination, amongst other aspects, of whether individuals are more inclined towards, say, a dollar depreciation than the overall average of their fellow countrymen. This distinction may be important if the information set is not common to all forecasters, due to time zone or language-induced informational differences: averaging within a country is less likely to result in problems arising from such informational asymmetries. MacDonald and Marsh find very strong evidence of heterogeneity for both the three- and twelve-month horizons. Using the country average or the 'world' average does not change this result, and MacDonald and Marsh infer from this that informational assymetries between nations are small and insignificant. They also find evidence of idiosyncratic effects (using both the forward premium and the exchange rate change).

Having established that forecasters are heterogeneous, MacDonald and Marsh then go on to test whether such differences of opinion translate into different forecast performances using a version of Prentice's reduced rank statistic. Overall they find that differential forecast performance is indicated for all three currencies at both forecast horizons, but is strongest for the twelve-month forecasts and especially for the Japanese yen. However, although there are differences in forecasting performance, MacDonald and Marsh demonstrate that very few forecasters outperform a random walk at short horizons, although a substantial number do so over longer horizons. The final stage in the MacDonald and Marsh strategy involves testing an implication of the market microstructure literature.

The market microstructure literature[11] takes as its starting point the huge volume of foreign exchange market trade which takes place on a day-to-day basis (a recent issue of *The Financial Times* estimates the total volume as $1.2 trillion). It seems impossible to explain this volume using standard open economy models relying on rational expectations, since such a huge volume of trade must presumably rely on a dispersion of beliefs about the future path of exchange rates. The market microstructure literature therefore takes as its starting point that agents are heterogeneous and seeks to build models which capture the interrelationships between information flows, heterogeneity and the implications of the latter for volume and price volatility (see Lyons, 1991, 1993, for a market micro exchange rate model). Using a mean-variance model due to Varian (1989), MacDonald and Marsh (1996b) examine the effect of heterogeneity, as measured by the standard deviation of the Consensus expectations, on foreign exchange turnover, as measured by the daily average dollar value of trade in the relevant IMM futures pit (on the Chicago Mercantile Exchange) measured over a period that covers two weeks prior to the day on which the expectations are surveyed, together with the two subsequent weeks. They find that for the DM and JY the dispersion of expectations is positive and significant at the 5 per cent level, thereby confirming a central tenet of the market microstructure literature.

Chionis and MacDonald (1997b) push the market microstructure tests of MacDonald and Marsh further by exploiting the Consensus disaggregate survey data in a number of ways. In particular, they use Granger causality testing methods to examine the interrelationships between volume, volatility and dispersion (for the bilateral UD dollar rates of the BP, DM and JY spot rates) and report 'strong evidence of heterogeneity causing both volume and volatility'. They also examine the usefulness of the conditional volatility, as measured by a GARCH model, in proxying trading volume and find only limited support for this hypothesis.

A final strand of the literature in this area involves using disaggregate survey data to generate risk premia. Chionis and MacDonald (1997a) exploit a version of the Cash-in-Advance model to derive a model of the risk premium. This model, which contains two groups of investors (sophisticated and noisy), produces an equation which links the risk premium to the conditional variances of fundamentals and idiosyncratic effects. The risk premium equation is implemented using an ARCH-in-mean modelling strategy and significant and sensible estimates of the individual risk premia are reported for the BP, DM and JY (respectively, 75, 62.5 and 80 per cent of the total number of individual equations). One of the key findings of this paper is that the significance of the risk premium essentially vanishes when consensus measures of risk are utilized (irrespective of whether such measures are generated from survey data or from actual data using the rational expectations hypothesis). Since practically all the extant research on the foreign exchange risk premium exploits such consensus measures, this may help to explain why so few researchers have found evidence in favour of time-varying risk premia.

9.5   BOND MARKETS AND THE TERM STRUCTURE OF INTEREST RATES

Research on the term structure of interest rates focuses on explaining the yield gap, or spread; that is, the difference between the yield on a long-term government bond and that on a short-term government bond. Often the long bond has a maturity of ten years, or greater, and the short bond is a three-month Treasury bill rate; however, term structure studies also focus on the shorter end of the market comparing, say, the yield on a six-month bond with that on a three-month bond. Without doubt the model which most researchers base their work on is the expectations hypothesis (EH) of the term structure, which posits that the yield on a long-term bond is the weighted average of the current short rate and all expected future short rates over the horizon of the long rate (see Shiller *et al.*, 1983, for a useful survey of this model). In the purest form of the EH, the observation of a positive yield gap would imply that investors expect future short interest rates to be increasing, while a negative yield gap would imply that they expect falling short-term yields. A less pure form, often taken as the alternative hypothesis to the pure EH, is that investors require a term premium over and above the discounted expected yield to persuade them to hold long-term government debt. The term premium has been variously interpreted as a liquidity premium or an inflation premium.

The extant empirical evidence on the EH model which relies on *actual* interest rate yields, rather than *survey* expectations, strongly indicates that the yield spread has predictive power at both the very short and long ends of the maturity spectrum. However, despite this, when the EH model is formally tested it is usually rejected (see, for example, Campbell, 1995). There are three, essentially equivalent, ways of testing the EH (see Shiller *et al.* 1983): in terms of the relationship between the yield on a long-term interest rate and that on a short-term rate (see Campbell and Shiller, 1987); in terms of holding period returns (Shiller *et al.* 1983); and in terms of the relationship between spot (that is, actual) interest rates and forward interest rates, where the latter are derived from spot rates with differing maturities.

In the context of the EH view of the term structure, the relationships presented in section 9.2, the λ_t term in expression (9.1) is labelled the term premium and in the purest form of the EH model it is zero since this model implies that forward rates are equal to expected future spot rates. As is evident, this interpretation of the term structure model immediately raises the same kinds of issue we addressed when discussing the foreign exchange market.

Thus, if we tested the EH model using (9.3) – that is, we imposed rational expectations to proxy the expected interest rate – a rejection of the model in terms of α_0 and β_0 not being equal to their prior values would be difficult to interpret: it could imply that expectations are in some sense 'irrational' or that term premia are important. As we have indicated, the majority of research does reject the null as represented by (9.3) and a representative result is presented here from MacDonald and Macmillan (1994) where the forward rate is calculated from six- and three-month UK Treasury bill rates for the period October 1989 to October 1992:

$$\Delta s_{t+k} = -0.555 + 0.268 fp_t + u_{t+k}, \qquad (9.22)$$
$$\quad\;\; (0.06) \quad\; (0.05)$$

where standard errors are noted in parenthesis. Predicated on the assumption of rational expectations, this equation indicates that around 30 per cent of the variation in the forward rate is due to variation in expectations and 70 per cent to variation in the term premium. However, as in the foreign exchange market literature, this interpretation is contingent on the existence of rational expectations; the availability of survey data should again prove useful in helping to unravel the source(s) of the rejection. Before considering survey-based tests, however, it is worth mentioning potential problems associated with small-sample bias.

A number of papers (see, for example, Mankiw and Shapiro, 1986; and Bekaert *et al.*, 1997) have indicated that the small-sample properties of the different alternative ways of testing the EH (using actual data, rather than survey data) are likely to be poor, even with relatively large sample sizes. For example, Bekaert *et al.* (1997) show that even with a sample size of 524 monthly observations the slope coefficient in an equation such as (9.22) can be biased. The problem arises because this kind of test essentially represents a transformation of serial correlation coefficients. When a variable exhibits persistence there are well-known downward biases in OLS estimates of autocorrelation coefficients. Since most of the recent literature which exploits survey data to test the EH exploits variants of (9.3), this may be an important reason why estimated values of β_0 differ significantly from unity. Of course, this point may also have implications for the kinds of tests considered in section 9.4.

A representative set of survey-based tests of the EH hypothesis are presented in Table 9.5.[12] The Froot (1989) results are perhaps the most comprehensive in terms of the number of countries and contracts covered. He considers two separate data sets. The first is culled from the *Goldsmith Nagan Bond and Money Market Newsletter*, and consists of three-month, twelve-month, twenty-year and thirty-year US government bonds over the period 1969 to 1986. The second is from Money Market Services (US) and consists of three-month euro-rate expectations for the US, UK, Germany, Japan and Australia.

Irrespective of the country considered, Froot's estimates of β_0 are significantly different from unity, indicating a clear rejection of the pure EH model. The US seems to produce the most dramatic violation, with a point estimate of β which is closer to minus one than plus one. This biasedness finding may be interpreted as a result either of a significant term premium, which is correlated with the spread, or of an expectational failure (in particular, a failure to adjust expectations of future rates rapidly enough). Using survey data to estimate (9.10), Froot finds that the coefficient on the forward premium, β_κ, moves closer to plus one for US short rates (and also for a number of other US term structure equations considered), but that

Table 9.5: *Term structure relationships*

Author	Survey source	Forecast horizon	Sample period	β_0	β_κ	$t_{\beta\kappa} = 1$
Froot (1989)	MMS (US)	3 months	1/83–10/84			
United States				−0.93	0.32	*
				(0.28)	(0.39)	
Germany				0.44	0.26	*
				(0.18)	(0.10)	
Japan				0.51	0.38	
				(0.14)	(0.14)	
Batchelor (1990) DM/US	MMS (UK)	1 week	7/82–5/86 (w)		−1.059	*
					(0.36)	
MacDonald and Macmillan (1994) 25 individuals, pooled (UK)	Consensus	3 months	10/89–10/92	0.27	0.42	*
				(0.13)	(0.03)	
MacDonald and Macmillan (1996) 25 individuals, pooled (US)	Consensus	3 months	10/89–3/95	0.68	0.35	*
				(0.06)	(0.03)	

Notes:
* denotes significance at the 5 per cent level.
w denotes weekly observation.

the point estimates for the other countries move further away from unity. However, interestingly, he finds for long rates that the estimates of β_κ *are* statistically indistinguishable from unity. This implies, counterintuitively, that term premia are important for short rates but not for long rates. Reinforcing this, Froot finds that, on regressing the US survey forecast errors on to the forward pemium, the point estimates of β_e are not significantly different from zero, but at the longer end of the maturity spectrum they are significantly negative, suggesting that long rates are exceptionally volatile: agents would do better to place more weight on the contemporaneous short rate and less weight on the contemporaneous longer rate in forming their expectations. In contrast to the US-based estimates of β_e, Froot finds positive values for other countries. This, therefore, implies that more than 100 per cent of the deviation from the expectations hypothesis in non-US countries is due to the term premium, while in the US a positive proportion is due to expectational errors.

Batchelor (1990) uses Blue Chip Financial Forecasts' monthly mean expectation of the three-month US Treasury bill interest rate for the period October 1982 to March 1987. Equations (9.3) and (9.10) are estimated and the point estimates of β_0 and β_κ are reported in Table 9.5. These indicate that 60 per cent of the variation in the forward premium is due to variation in expected interest rate changes and 40 per cent to variation in the term premium. In Batchelor and Dua (1991) a disaggregate version (for 13 individuals[13]) of the Blue Chip survey data is used to test the rationality of the forecasts, rather than trying to disentangle term structure effects. Interestingly, and in contrast to most of the other research reported in this paper, only one forecaster fails the unbiasedness and orthogonality tests (other variables examined, such as inflation, do not perform so well in these kinds of tests).

MacDonald and Macmillan (1994) utilize the disaggregated data set of 25 forecasters supplied by Consensus Economics of London, for the period October 1989 to October 1992. The panel estimates of β_0 and β_κ from this disaggregate data set are reported in Table 9.5, and indicate that for the UK around 60 per cent of the variation in the forward premium is due to variation in the term premium and 40 per cent due to variation in expected interest rate changes; these results are essentially the opposite of those reported by Batchelor for the US. MacDonald and Macmillan also estimate β_0 and β_κ for each individual forecaster and find that for the vast majority the rejection in an equation like (9.3) is due to both variation in the term premium *and* the expected interest rate change. Interestingly, however, for two forecasters the pure expectations model cannot be rejected (in the sense that the joint hypothesis of $\alpha_\kappa =$ and $\beta_\kappa = 1$ cannot be rejected) and another two seem to attribute all of the variation in the forward premium to changes in the term premium. As in the foreign exchange literature, expectations of interest rates seem to exhibit evidence of heterogeneity.[14]

Kim (1997) tests the unbiasedness of Australian-sourced MMS expectations of short- and long-term interest rates. The sample period runs from 2 August 1985 through to 21 January 1993, and the horizons studied are two and four weeks ahead. For both short and long rates Kim produces a decisive rejection of the unbiasedness hypothesis.

Rather than adopt a regression-based testing method, Kane (1983) uses a number of statistical tests to determine the properties of a variety of survey-based measures of the term premium. The survey data were collected by the author for four dates – January 1969, July 1979, October 1970 and January 1972 – using 170 individuals on each date, and relates to four different maturities (six-month, one-year, two-year and ten-year).[15] The statistical tests conducted are: t-tests of significant differences in respondents' mean term premia; Mann–Whitney tests of differences between the means of two samples of term premia; binomial tests to determine the number of observed premia that are positive; and rank correlation and concordance tests of the influence of interest rates on the level of the term premia. Amongst the author's findings are clear evidence that term premia are non-zero and a failure to reject the maturity ranking predicted by the liquidity preference approach (that is, the term premia rise as the maturity rises). The latter means that for any holding period an investor can generally expect to earn more by placing funds in a long-term instrument than a short-term one. Statistical tests demonstrate that term premia are time-varying and positively related to the level of interest rates.

9.6   STOCK MARKET EXPECTATIONS

The J.A. Livingstone survey has proved a popular source of expectations data on many series, and a number of researchers have used their forecasts of the Standard and Poor's Composite Index. Since 1947, Livingstone has posted a questionnaire in May and November of each year to academic, business and government economists who are asked to give their forecasts of the level of the Index for the end of the forthcoming June and December. Lakonishok (1980) found evidence of bias in these forecasts for the period 1947 to 1974, although he noted that they seemed to be improving towards the end of his data sample. Brown and Maital (1981), using essentially the same data set, were unable to reject the hypothesis that the forecasts were free of bias, despite a negative point estimate of β_u for the six-month horizon (but they did note, however, that the forecasts were not 'fully' rational over the twelve-month horizon).[16] Pearce (1984) strongly rejected the unbiasedness and error orthogonality hypotheses over both forecast horizons and noted that the coefficients were unstable, attributing this to the changing composition of the survey or the erratic movements of the index. Using the data in a disaggregate form still lead to a rejection of unbiasedness and error orthogonality. A major problem in testing the propositions outlined above is the determination of the base date when the forecasts are made and hence an accurate calculation of the expected change in the index. Both Pearce (1984) and Dokko and Edelstein (1989) tried to overcome this by using the expected 'forward' change determined from the six- and twelve-month forecasts. This had no effect on Pearce's conclusions but Dokko and Edelstein, using a more complex method of calculation,[17] found the Livingstone survey predictions to be unbiased.

Prat (1994) examines the Livingstone stock price expectations for the extended period of 1956 to 1989. He finds that the unbiasedness hypothesis is rejected for six- and twelve-month horizons, again due to statistically significant constant terms (the measures of β_u were insignificantly different from zero). Furthermore, tests of the error orthogonality condition, using publicly available information such as short- and long-term interest rates, produced statistically significant rejections of the error orthogonality condition. In terms of expectations formation, Prat finds support for the MILERA, or hybrid, expectations formation model: the expected change of the Livingstone forecasts were a weighted average of the three components reflected in equation (9.13), and all the coefficients suggested stabilizing behaviour (furthermore, the coefficients did not exhibit any instabilities over time).

Abou and Prat (1995) extend the work of Prat by examining the disaggregate responses to the Livingstone Standard and Poors stock price survey data. They find that expectations are biased regardless of whether the consensus, groups of individual forecasters or individual forecasters themselves are examined (indeed, all of the individual forecasters produced biased forecasts). Abou and Prat (1996) find, using the same data set as in their previous study, that both individuals and various groups of individuals use a weighted average of the three basic processes described in (9.13).

One important potential problem with the Livingstone data set is that it is, as we have noted, constructed from a postal questionnaire, with the implication that respondents will in all probability have access to different information sets at the time of their response. This could possibly introduce important biases into the survey expectations. The survey data set used by MacDonald and Marsh (1993) is constructed on a single day by telephone and this therefore reduces the problem of the precise dating of forecasts faced by researchers using the Livingstone survey data. More specifically,

MacDonald and Marsh (1993) use MMS (US) survey expectations on the Dow Jones Industrial Average (cash market) and the Standard and Poor's 500 Index futures contract, traded on the Chicago Mercantile Exchange, for the period November 1987 to October 1991 (the survey data consist of the median response of between 20 and 40 US economists and traders who are questioned in a telephone survey).

Other stock market forecast data sets studied have been qualitative. Fraser and MacDonald (1993) examine the qualitative expectations of the CAC general stock price index, collected from a number of leading French financial institutions by Recherche économique et sociale. Using the methods of Knobl (1974) and Carlson and Parkin (1975) to obtain a quantitative response, Fraser and MacDonald find that the unbiasedness hypothesis is rejected for this data (due to significant α terms), and there are some violations of the orthogonality condition (due to significant lagged forecast errors). Additionally, Fraser and MacDonald were unable to reject the null of static expectations in favour of any of the alternatives described by equation (9.13).

9.7   SUMMARY AND CONCLUSIONS

Biasedness and the violation of simple orthogonality conditions seem to be common findings when survey data are used to analyse the expectations of asset prices. How should such findings be interpreted? In this paper we have been careful to refer to violations of unbiasedness and orthogonality using the general term 'expectational failure'. This encompasses simple irrationality, 'peso' and learning effects and speculative bubbles.[18] In the context of financial expectations, it is worth emphasizing that forecast accuracy is not the only objective of professional analysts: directional forecast ability, for example, is often taken to be as important (if not more so) than unbiasedness. However, despite this, the consistency with which unbiasedness is rejected – for different sample periods, different financial assets and by different researchers – seems to make it hard to avoid the conclusion that it implies some form of irrationality amongst market participants.[19]

The biased nature of expectations seems to be confirmed by those studies which have focused on expectations formation: there is a good deal of evidence from both direct tests of expectations mechanisms and from consistency tests that short-term expectations are excessively volatile and exhibit bandwagon effects. Longer-term expectations, however, seem to be regressive and therefore stabilizing. This finding would seem to be consistent with the noise trader model of de Long *et al.* (1990), where in the short-term asset prices are driven predominantly by noise traders, who use chartist and other non-fundamental methods, but in the longer term are driven by the 'smart money' who base their expectations on fundamentals and, ultimately, correct the overreaction imparted into asset prices by the noise traders (further support for this view is to be found in Frankel and Froot's (1990a) model of chartists and fundamentalists).

Survey data can, however, be used to pursue other aspects of asset price behaviour. It can be informative about the existence of risk premia in asset markets. In this paper we have demonstrated that for both bond and foreign exchange markets the standard result of forward rate biasedness is due, at least in part, to time-varying premia. For the foreign exchange market this finding is, we believe, extremely important since a large literature, predicated on the assumption of rationality, finds little evidence in favour of significant risk premia in currency markets; recent research using survey data has been able to relate survey-based measures of exchange risk premia in a natural way to 'fundamentals'. Similarly for bond markets, the existence of survey data has demonstrated that part of the reason why the expectations model of the term structure fails is because of the importance of significant time-varying term premia and that these term premia vary across countries. A useful topic for future research would be to relate term premia to fundamentals – in a similar manner to recent work in foreign exchange markets – in a bid to unravel what variables are driving term premia.

The final area in which survey data are making important inroads into our understanding of the workings of asset prices is in terms of the issue of heterogeneous expectations. As we have noted, so much of modern macroeconomic theorizing is based on the assumption of a unique expectation: the rational expectation. However, researchers have found the massive trade in assets that takes place on a daily basis hard to reconcile with the assumption of unified expectation. There has of late, therefore, been considerable interest in the market microstructure of financial markets. The market microstructure literature has as its central premise the proposition that agents have heterogeneous expectations either because of idiosyncracies in exploiting a common information set, or because information sets actually differ across individuals. Either way, recent research using disaggregate foreign exchange survey data has demonstrated that foreign exchange market participants do indeed have a diversity of expectations, thereby dealing another blow to rational expectations, and that such expectations bear a significant relationship to important indicators from the market microstructure literature (such as volume and volatility).

In sum, expectations do not appear to be rational, asset markets are risky and the diversity of expectations we observe in asset markets seem to offer support to the market microstructure hypothesis. With the aid of survey data further research of this latter hypothesis seems merited (particularly for bond and stock markets where survey data have been underutilized for this purpose). In the meantime, international macroeconomic models which rely on the paradigms of risk neutrality and simple-minded rationality should, perhaps, be treated with a measure of caution since they may conceal more than they reveal about the real-world behaviour of asset prices.

NOTES

1. The Livingstone inflation expectations series are amongst the best known and most widely researched survey data.
2. To our knowledge this is the first paper to overview the literature on these three markets. Previous surveys of the use of survey data in foreign exchange markets are Tagaki (1991) and Bénassy and Raymond (1994a). Less comprehensive studies are to be found in MacDonald (1990), the update in MacDonald and Taylor (1992), and Frankel and Rose (1995).
3. We drop the $t + k$ superscript in future usage of the forward/futures rate.
4. We use the term forward premium throughout to encompass the premium on both the forward and futures rates; nearly all of the extant survey research in financial markets exploits the forward rate.
5. As we shall see below, in the presence of overlapping data the error term in (9.2) need not be serially uncorrelated.
6. The seminal Dornbusch (1976) overshooting result hinges crucially on the assumption of regressive expectations. Argy and Porter (1972) have illustrated the effect that differing expectational mechanisms can have on the predications derived from the Mundell–Fleming model.
7. See, *inter alia*, MacDonald and Marsh (1996b) for the foreign exchange market, Poterba and Summers (1988) for the stock market and Begg (1978) for the bond market.
8. It is of course true that these other hypotheses need not be inconsistent with rational expectations.
9. Cavaglia *et al.* (1993a) also estimate their model for exchange rates against the German mark and these exhibit similar properties to the US dollar rates.
10. See Pesaran (1989a) for a critique of the approach used by Froot and Ito.
11. See Flood (1991) for a survey of this literature as it relates to the foreign exchange market.
12. One of the earliest tests of the EH using survey data is that of Friedman (1979), who used expectations data constructed from the *Goldsmith-Nagan Bond and Money Market Letter*. As in the tests reported in Table 9.5, Friedman finds clear evidence of a term premium effect. However, all of his regressions feature the *levels* of actual and expected interest rates and therefore may be spurious since the levels of interest rates are likely to be non-stationary.
13. Up to 50 forecasters actually respond to the Blue Chip survey at any one time, but the 19 chosen by Batchelor and Dua are the only forecasters who produced a consistent set of survey responses over the whole sample period.
14. MacDonald and Macmillan (1996) derive a similar set of results for the US.
15. The survey questionnaire used by Kane was similar to that originally devised by Kane and Malkiel (1967). The latter authors examined (without using formal statistical methods) the statistical distributions of 90-day US Treasury bills and 10-year bond rate expectations, for 200 US financial institutions. The survey was conducted on 1 April 1965 and they report a lack of uniformity amongst agents' expectations. This, in turn, implied

that the demands for various maturities of debt are not infinitely elastic at the going rate. They interpret this as evidence in favour of a term premium and evidence against the EH.

16. They report that twelve-month forecast errors were correlated with money supply and wage rate data.
17. This method was based on some fairly strong assumptions and the use of the Capital Asset Pricing Model.
18. Models which exploit a speculative bubble to explain the biasedness finding usually assume the bubble is rational; that is, it is consistent with the underlying model. Of course, such bubbles do not have to be rational.
19. Although it is important to emphasize again that studies which use a consensus measure of expectations may only be tracking the consensus of a small number of professional analysts rather than the 'true' market consensus. Further, as we have noted, issues of small sample bias also cloud the interpretation of the biasedness finding.

REFERENCES

Abou, A. and G. Prat (1995), 'A propos de la rationalit des anticipations boursières: quel niveau d'aggrégation des opinions?', *12èmes Journées de microéconomie appliqué*, June, 1–33.

Abou, A. and G. Prat (1996), 'Formation des anticipations boursières: que nous enseignent les données individuelles?', translated as Chapter 12 of this volume.

Argy, V. and M. Porter (1972), 'The forward exchange market and the effects of domestic and external disturbances under alternative exchange rate regimes', *IMF Staff Papers*, 19, 503–27.

Batchelor, R. (1990), 'On the importance of the term premium', London: City University Business School, mimeo.

Batchelor, R. and P. Dua (1991), 'Blue chip rationality tests', *Journal of Money, Credit and Banking*, 23, 692–705.

Begg, D.K.W. (1978), *The rational expectations revolution*, Oxford: Philip Allen.

Bekaert, G., R.J. Hodrick and D. Marshall (1997), 'On biases in tests of the expectations hypothesis of the term structure', *Journal of Financial Economics*, 44, 309–48.

Bénassy, A. and H. Raymond (1994b), 'L'hétérogenéité des anticipations de d'après les données d'enquêtes: une étude empirique', *Document travail du thema*, Université de Cergy.

Bénassy, A. and H. Raymond (1995), 'La cohérence temporelle des anticipations de change: une étude sur données d'enquêtes', *Document travail du thema*, Université de Cergy.

Bénassy-Quéré, A., S. Larribeau and R. MacDonald (1999), 'Models of exchange rate expectations', Centre for Financial Markets Research, Discussion Paper no. 10.

Brown, B. and S. Maital (1981), 'What do economists know? An empirical study of experts' expectations', *Econometrica*, 49(2), 491–504.

Campbell, J.Y. (1995), 'Some lessons from the yield curve', *Journal of Economic Perspectives*, 9(3), 129–52.

Campbell, J.Y., and R.J. Shiller (1987), 'Cointegration and tests of present value models', *Journal of Political Economy*, 95, 1062–88.

Carlson, J.A. and M. Parkin (1975), 'Inflation expectations', *Economica*, 42, 123–38.

Cavaglia, S., W.F.C. Verschoor and C.C.P. Wolff (1993a), 'Further evidence on exchange rate expectations', *Journal of International Money and Finance*, 78–98.

Cavaglia, S., W.F.C. Verschoor and C.C.P. Wolff (1993b), 'On the biasedness of forward foreign exchange rates: irrationality or risk premia?', *Journal of Business*, 67, 321–43.

Chinn, M. and J. Frankel (1994), 'Patterns in exchange rate forecasts for twenty-five currencies', *Journal of Money, Credit and Banking*, 26, 760–7.

Chionis, D. (1998), *Short-run and Long-run Foreign Exchange Modelling*, Glasgow: University of Strathclyde.

Chionis, D. and R. MacDonald (1997a), 'Aggregate and disaggregate measures of the foreign exchange risk premium', Glasgow: University of Strathclyde, mimeo.

Chionis, D. and R. MacDonald (1997b), 'Some tests of market microstructure hypotheses in the foreign exchange market', *Journal of Multinational Financial Management*, 7, 203–29.

de Long, J., D. Bradford, A. Shleifer, L.H. Summers and R.J. Waldmann (1990), 'Noise trader risk in financial markets', *Journal of Political Economy*, 98, 703–38.

Dokko, Y. and R. Edelstein (1989), 'How well do economists forecast stock market prices? A study of the Livingstone Surveys', *American Economic Review*, 79(4), 865–71.

Dominguez, K. (1986), 'Are foreign exchange forecasts rational? New evidence from survey data', *Economics Letters*, 21, 277–82.

Domowitz, I. and C. Hakkio (1985), 'Conditional variance and the risk premium in the foreign exchange market', *Journal of International Economics*, 19, 47–66.

Dornbusch, R. (1976), 'Expectations and exchange rate dynamics', *Journal of Political Economy*, 84, 1161–76.

Engel, C. (1996), 'The forward discount anomaly and the risk premium: a survey of recent evidence', *Journal of Empirical Finance*, 3, 123–92.

Fama, E.F. (1976), *Foundations of Finance*, New York: Basic Books.

Flood, M. (1991), 'Microstructure theory and the foreign exchange market', *Federal Reserve Bank of St Louis, Quarterly Review*, 52–70.

Frankel, J.A. and K.A. Froot (1987), 'Using survey data to test standard propositions regarding exchange rate expectations', *American Economic Review*, 77, 133–53.

Frankel, J.A. and K.A. Froot (1989), 'Interpreting tests of forward discount bias using survey data on exchange rate expectations', *Quarterly Journal of Economics*, 104, 139–61.

Frankel, J.A. and K.A. Froot (1990a), 'Chartists, fundamentalists, and the demand for dollars', in A.S. Courakis and M.P. Taylor (eds), *Private Behavior and Government Policy in Interdependent Economies*, Oxford: Clarendon Press.

Frankel, J.A. and K.A. Froot, (1990b), 'Exchange rate forecasting techniques, survey data, and implications for the foreign exchange market', Working Paper no. 3470, Cambridge, MA: National Bureau of Economic Research.

Frankel, J.A. and A. Rose (1995), 'A survey of empirical research on nominal exchange rates', in S. Grossman and K. Rogoff (eds), *The Handbook of International Economics*, Amsterdam: North-Holland.

Fraser, P. and R. MacDonald (1993), 'The efficiency of CAC stock price forecasts', *Revue Économie*, 44, 991–1000.

Friedman, B. (1979), 'Interest rate expectations versus forward rates: evidence from an expectations study', *Journal of Finance*, 34(4), 965–73.

Froot, K.A. (1989), 'New hope for the expectations hypothesis of the term structure of interest rates', *Journal of Finance*, 44, 283–305.

Froot, K.A. and T. Ito (1990), 'On the consistency of short-run and long-run exchange rate expectations', *Journal of International Money and Finance*, 8, 487–510.

Giorgianni, L. (1996), 'On expectations and risk premia in foreign exchange markets: evidence from survey data', PhD dissertation, University of Pennsylvania.

Hansen, L.P. (1982), 'Large sample properties of generalized method of moments estimators', *Econometrica*, 50, 1029–54.

Hansen, L.P. and R.J. Hodrick (1983), 'Risk averse speculation in the forward foreign exchange market: an econometric analysis of linear models', in J.A. Frenkel (ed.), *Exchange Rates and International Macroeconomics*, Chicago: University of Chicago Press, for National Bureau of Economic Research.

Hansen, L.P. and S. Richard (1984), 'A general approach for deducting testable restrictions implied by asset pricing models', University of Chicago, mimeo.

Hansen, L.P. and K. Singleton (1982), 'Generalised instrumental variables estimation of nonlinear rational expectations models', *Econometrica*, 50, 1269–86.

Ito, T. (1990), 'Foreign exchange rate expectations: micro survey data', *American Economic Review*, 80, 434–9.

Kane, E.J. (1983), 'Nested tests of alternative term-structure theories', *Review of Economics and Statistics*, 65, 115–23.

Kane, E.J. and B.G. Malkiel (1967), 'The term structure of interest rates: an analysis of interest-rate expectations', *Review of Economics and Statistics*, 49, 343–55.

Kim, S.-J. (1997), 'Testing the rationality of exchange rate and interest rate expectations', *Applied Economics*, 29, 1011–22.

Knobl, A. (1974), 'Price expectation and actual price behaviours in Germany', *International Monetary Fund Staff Papers*, 21, 83–100.

Lakonishok, J. (1980), 'Stock market return expectations: some general properties', *Journal of Finance*, 35(4), 921–31.

Liu, P.C. and G.S. Maddala (1992), 'Rationality of survey data and tests for market efficiency in the foreign exchange market', 11, 366–81.

Lyons, R.D. (1991), 'Private beliefs and informational externalities in the foreign exchange market', mimeo.

Lyons, R.D. (1993), 'Tests of microstructural hypothesis in the foreign exchange market', Working Paper no. 4471, Cambridge, MA: National Bureau of Economic Research.

MacDonald, R. (1990), 'Exchange rate economics', in G. Bird (ed.), *The International Financial Regime*, London: Academic Press.

MacDonald, R. (1990b), 'Are foreign exchange market forecasters rational', Some survey based tests', *Manchester School of Economic and Social Studies*, 58, 229–41.

MacDonald, R. (1992), 'Exchange rate survey data: a disaggregated G-7 perspective', *Manchester School of Economic and Social Studies*, 60, 47–62.

MacDonald, R. (1996), 'The foreign exchange market: is it risky?', Glasgow: University of Strathclyde, mimeo.

MacDonald, R. and P. Macmillan (1994), 'On the expectations view of the term structure, term premia and survey-based expectations', *Economic Journal*, 104, 1070–86.

MacDonald, R. and P. Macmillan (1996), 'Survey based expectations and term premia from a US term structure', University of Strathclyde, mimeo.

MacDonald, R. and I.W. Marsh (1993), 'The efficiency of spot and futures stock indices: a survey based perspective', *Review of Futures Markets*, 12(2), 431–54.

MacDonald, R. and I.W. Marsh (1994), 'Combining exchange rate forecasts: what is the optimal consensus measure?', *Journal of Forecasting*, 13, 313–32.

MacDonald, R. and I.W. Marsh (1996a), 'Hétérogénéité des prévisionnistes: une exploration des anticipations sur le marché des changes', *Economie et prévision*, 125, 109–116.

MacDonald, R. and I.W. Marsh (1996b), 'Foreign exchange market forecasters are heterogeneous: confirmation and consequences', *Journal of International Money and Finance*, September, 15, 665–85.

MacDonald, R. and M. Taylor (1992), 'Exchange rate economics', *International Monetary Fund Staff Papers*, 39, 1–57.

MacDonald, R. and T.C. Torrance (1988), 'On risk, rationality and excessive speculation in the Deutschmark–US dollar exchange market: some evidence using survey data', *Oxford Bulletin of Economics and Statistics*, 50, 544–61.

MacDonald, R. and T.C. Torrance (1990), 'Expectations formation and risk in four foreign exchange markets', *Oxford Economic Papers*, 42, 544–61.

Mankiw, N.G. and M. Shapiro (1986), 'Do we reject too often? Small sample properties of rational expectations models', *Economics Letters*, 20, 139–45.

Mark, N. (1985), 'On time-varying risk premia in the foreign exchange market', *Journal of Monetary Economics*, 16, 3–58.

McKinnon, R. (1976), 'Floating exchange rates 1973–74; the emperor's new clothes', *Carnegie Rochester Series*, 3.

Nerlove, M., F.X. Diebold, H. van Beeck and Y. Cheung (1988), 'A multivariate ARCH model of the foreign exchange market', University of California, mimeo.

Newey, W.K. and K.D. West (1987), 'A simple positive semi-definite, heteroskedastic and autocorrelation consistent covariance matrix', *Econometrica*, 55, 703–8.

Obstfeld, M. (1987), 'Peso effects and speculative bubbles and tests of market efficiency', Working paper no. 2176, Cambridge, MA: National Bureau of Economic Research.

Pearce, D.K. (1984), 'An empirical analysis of expected stock price movements', *Journal of Money, Credit and Banking*, 16(3), 317–27.

Pesaran, H. (1989a), *The Limits to Rational Expectations*, Oxford: Basil Blackwell.

Pesaran, H. (1989b), 'Consistency of short-term and long-term expectations', *Journal of International Money and Finance*, 8, 511–20.

Poterba, J.M. and L.H. Summers (1988), 'Mean reversion in stock prices', *Journal of Financial Economics*, 88, 27–59.

Prat, G. (1994), 'La formation des anticipations boursières', *Economie et prévision*, 112, 101–25.

Prat, G. and R. Uctum (1996), 'La formation des anticipations de change', *Economie et prévision*, 125(4), 117–35.

Prat, G. and R. Uctum (2000), 'The evidence of a mixed expectation generating process in the foreign exchange market', Chapter 11 of this volume.

Shiller, R.S. (1990), *Market Volatility*, MIT Press.

Shiller, R.J., J.Y. Campbell and K. Schoenholtz (1983), 'Forward rates and future policy: interpreting the term structure of interest rates', *Brookings Papers on Economic Activity*, 1, 232–42.
Tagaki, S. (1991), 'Exchange rate expectations: a survey of survey studies', *International Monetary Fund Staff Papers*, 38, 156–83.
Varian, H.R. (1989), 'Differences of opinion in financial markets', in: C.C. Stone (ed.), *Financial Risk: Theory, Evidence and Implications*, Boston, MA: Kluwer Academic.

10. The inconsistency of the exchange rate forecast term structure*

Agnès Bénassy-Quéré and Hélène Raymond†

INTRODUCTION

Expectations are at the core of recent explanations of exchange rate volatility. Various assumptions have been proposed for modelling the forecasts (rational, extrapolative, naive, mimetic expectations and so on) and used in models of exchange rate determination. This line of research helps us to understand the poor out-of-sample performance of popular macro-economic models (Meese and Rogoff, 1983), and it provides new explanations of exchange rate dynamics (Frankel and Froot, 1986). In this context, surveys on exchange rate expectations are precious: they allow us to test for expectations specifications without any joint assumption (like perfect capital mobility and risk neutrality). Of course, these data should be interpreted with caution since they cannot perfectly reflect the behaviour of the market. This is because (a) all panellists are equally weighed in the published market average; (b) some panellists may not reveal their true expectations when the surveyed horizon does not fit their own working horizon, and (c) given the high volatility of exchange rates, unavoidable time discrepancies between the answers matter. Nevertheless, the high number of surveys now partly compensate for these drawbacks.[1]

Survey data on exchange rate expectations have widely been studied.[2] Forecasts are generally biased, and the errors are not orthogonal to the information available at the time of the forecasts. The rational expectations assumption seems to be rejected by survey data. This raises the questions of (a) what is the process followed by the forecasts? and (b) are the various

* A previous French version entitled 'La cohérence temporelle des anticipations de change: une étude sur données d'enquêtes' has been published by the two authors in the French review *Economie et prévision* (special series, no. 123–4, 1996 (2/3), 97–111). But this chapter is somewhat modified with respect to the French version.
† We are grateful to Michel Boutillier, Benoît Mulkay and to the participants in the CEBI seminar for their remarks. All errors and deficiences remain ours.

forecasts consistent one with another? This paper deals with the latter question. More specifically, we study whether forecasts at various horizons are consistent, that is, whether the series of short-run forecasts lead to the same long-run expectations as the long-run forecasts themselves. For instance, we check whether the three-month expectation of the six-month expectation equals the nine-month expectation. Of course, the consistency of the forecast term structure must be studied on the basis of a single set of information for long-run expectations and for the corresponding series of short-run expectations. Given that the surveys do not provide forecasts of the forecasts, it is necessary to rely on models of the forecasts which can be iterated to obtain the required expectations. The consistency of the forecast term structure then means that iterating the short-run forecasting model leads to the same expectation as the direct use of the long-run model. Rational expectations are consistent, but the consistency of the forecast term structure does not imply rationality. It is an internal consistency, which is conditional to the model selected by the forecasters but not to the whole available information. The forecasts at different horizons can be consistent even if the true process of the exchange rate is completely different from the forecasted process and if expectations errors are auto-correlated.

Froot and Ito (1989) were the first to build and apply to exchange rates a test of the consistency of the forecast term structure which was conditional to an extrapolative forecasting model. Ito (1990) also tested for the consistency of the forecast term structure within the extrapolative framework, but on individual data. Bellando (1991) applied the method proposed by Pesaran (1989) to test for consistency in the case of an adaptive model which is compared to an error-correction process *à la* Meiselman (1962) –Mincer (1969). The results of these studies differ according to the surveys, the currencies and the theoretical framework: although expectations generally appear inconsistent, this result is not systematic.

The validity of these tests is conditional on a good modelization of expectations and on the quality of the data. This means that questions (a) and (b) above are related to one another. In this context, it is interesting to use various specifications and various data sets. After presenting the consistency test as developed by Froot and Ito (1989) and Pesaran (1989), we apply the test to three data sets, conditionally to extrapolative, adaptive, regressive and mixed expectation processes successively. These models correspond to the usual typology of the processes in the literature. They also fit the stylized fact of chartist expectations which was evidenced by Allen and Taylor (1989) for short-run horizons. If macroeconomic models do not outperform the random walk in out-of-sample forecasts, then the naive model, which is a special case of the above processes, is the best model for

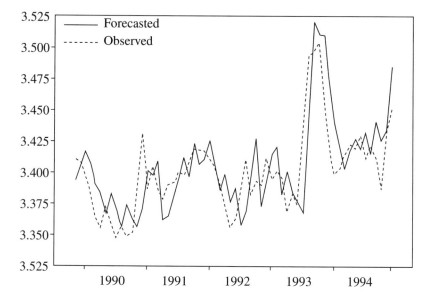

Source: Consensus Forecasts

Figure 10.1: Three-month forecasts and the observed exchange rate at the time of the forecasts: the DM/FF case

exchange rate forecasting. Figure 10.1 shows that, indeed, expectations follow the last exchange rate observed.[3] Finally, fundamentalists who, according to Allen and Taylor (1989), become prominent at long-run horizons, are taken into account in the regressive model where a slow adjustment towards an equilibrium exchange rate is expected.

10.1 TESTING THE CONSISTENCY OF THE FORECAST TERM STRUCTURE

Following Pesaran (1989), the forecast term structure is consistent if the expectation made at time t of the exchange rate that will be expected at time $t+i$ for time $t+j$ ($j>i>0$) equals the forecast made at time t for the exchange rate at time $t+j$. The consistency condition between short-term expectations ($j-i$ horizon) and long-term expectations (j horizon) can be written:

$$S^a_{t,j} = E^*_t(S^a_{t+i,j-i}) \qquad (10.1)$$

with:

$$S^a_{t+i,j-i} = E^*_{t+i}(S_{t+j})$$

where $S^a_{t,j}$ is the expectation at time t of the exchange rate (in logarithm) in $t+j$; that is, the expectation at time t of S_{t+j}, which is the logarithm of the exchange rate observed in $t+j$. $E^*_t(\ )$ is the subjective expectation operator which is conditional to the available information at time t. It is equivalent to the conditional expectancy only if forecasters are rational. Here, forecasters do not necessarily use all the available information: they limit themselves to a specific framework which selects part of the information and does not necessarily minimize forecast errors.

In a general framework of mixed, extrapolative-adaptive-regressive expectations, the forecasting process at the jh horizon can be written:

$$S^a_{t,jh} - S_t = a_{jh} + w_{jh}(S_t - S_{t-h}) + b_{jh}(S_t - S^a_{t-h,h}) + q_{jh}(\overline{S}_t - S_t) \quad (10.2)$$

$\overline{S}_t$ is the long-run, equilibrium exchange rate; j is the number of three-month periods in the forecasting horizon ($j=1, 2, 4$, for three-, six- and twelve-month expectations respectively); jh is the horizon measured as a number of periods. As the periodicity differs across surveys, it is necessary to use a frequency parameter h which equals 1 for a quartely survey (BNP), 2 for a six-week frequency (*The Economist*) and 3 for monthly data (Consensus).

Equation (10.2) encompasses the extrapolative model ($b=q=0$), the adaptive model ($w=q=0$), and the regressive model ($w=b=0$). In the first two cases, the forecasts for all horizons are always assumed to depend on the information about the last three months. This simplification is necessary to derive the consistency conditions.

This model could be rearranged as a constrained error-correction model in the case of cointegration between $S^a_{t,jh}$, S_t, $\overline{S}_t$ (and $S^a_{t,h}$ for $j \neq 1$). However, the samples are too short to test for cointegration. In addition, our presentation allows us to interpret directly the terms as traditional forecasting processes whose combination can result either from individual 'schizophrenia' or from the aggregation of heterogeneous individuals (the data used are market averages).

Before deriving the consistency restrictions, it is necessary to specify the long-run equilibrium expectation. It makes sense to assume that the expected long-run equilibrium exchange rate is independent of the forecast horizon:

$$E^*_t(\overline{S}_{t+jh}) = \overline{S}_t \qquad \text{for } j = 1, 2, 4 \qquad (10.3)$$

The problem is to define the long-run exchange rate $\bar{S}_t$. Following Frankel and Froot (1987a), the two simplest specifications are either a constant or a purchasing parity variable. The latter solution will be chosen here.

According to equation (10.1), the consistency between the three-month and six-month forecasts implies:

$$S_{t,2h}^a = E_t^*(S_{t+h,h}^a) \tag{10.4}$$

Using (10.2) we get:

$$E_t^*(S_{t+h,h}^a) = E_t^*(S_{t+h} + a_h + w_h(S_{t+h} - S_t) + b_h(S_{t+h} - S_{t,h}^a) + q_h(\bar{S}_{t+h} - S_{t+h})) \tag{10.5}$$

and

$$E_t^*(S_{t+h}) = S_t + a_h + w_h(S_t - S_{t-h}) + b_h(S_t - S_{t-h,h}^a) + q_h(\bar{S}_t - S_t) \tag{10.6}$$

From (10.3)–(10.6) comes:

$$S_{t,2h}^a - S_t = (2 + w_h - q_h)a_h + (1 + w_h - q_h)w_h(S_t - S_{t-h})$$
$$+ (1 + w_h - q_h)b_h(S_t - S_{t-h,h}^a) + (2 + w_h - q_h)q_h(\bar{S}_t - S_t) \tag{10.7}$$

Identifying (10.7) to (10.2) for $j = 2$, four consistency restrictions can be derived between three- and six-month expectations:

$$c_1 = a_{2h} - (2 + w_h - q_h)a_h = 0 \tag{10.8a}$$

$$c_2 = w_{2h} - (1 + w_h - q_h)w_h = 0 \tag{10.8b}$$

$$c_3 = b_{2h} - (1 + w_h - q_h)b_h = 0 \tag{10.8c}$$

$$c_4 = q_{2h} - (2 + w_h - q_h)q_h = 0 \tag{10.8d}$$

The four consistency restrictions between six- and twelve-month forecasts are derived in a similar way:

$$c_5 = a_{4h} - (2 + w_{2h} - q_{2h})a_{2h} = 0 \tag{10.9a}$$

$$c_6 = w_{4h} - (1 + w_{2h} - q_{2h})w_{2h} = 0 \tag{10.9b}$$

$$c_7 = b_{4h} - (1 + w_{2h} - q_{2h})b_{2h} = 0 \tag{10.9c}$$

$$c_8 = q_{4h} - (2 + w_{2h} - q_{2h})q_{2h} = 0 \tag{10.9d}$$

Finally, it is easy to derive the restrictions for the three- and twelve-month expectations by substituting (10.8a)–(10.8d) into (10.9a)–(10.9d).

The conditions for the extrapolative model are obtained with $b = q = 0$, those for the adaptative model with $w = q = 0$, and those for the regressive model with $w = b = 0$. The statistic used is:

$$z = c'[g' V(\hat{\beta} - \beta)g]^{-1}c$$

where c is the vector of the constraints, β is the vector of the parameters whose consistency is tested, $\hat{\beta}$ is the vector of the estimated parameters, g is the matrix of the derivatives of the constraints with respect to the parameters. Asymptotically, this statistic follows a χ^2 with degrees of freedom equal to the number of constraints (Greene, 1993).

It is important to notice that tests of the consistency of the forecast term structure are conditional on the use by the forecasters of (a) a time-invariant model for each horizon; and (b) the same method (either extrapolative, adaptative, regressive or mixed) for all horizons. Condition (a) means that the forecasting process does not change over time. In fact, panellists may forecast that they will use a different model in the future. A modification of the model for short-run expectations might even restore some consistency between forecasting methods that differ across horizons.[4] This possibility is not taken into account by the tests which exclude non-linear expected paths. Here, however, the use of various forecasting models allows us to figure out such a situation.

10.2   DATA AND METHODOLOGY

We use data from three different surveys: Banque Nationale de Paris (BNP), *The Economist* and Consensus, whose main features are reported in Table 10.1. The expectations concern DM/USD, yen/USD, Sterling/USD and FF/DM exchange rates. *A priori*, the impact of the European exchange rate mechanism is ambiguous. On the one hand, the relative stability of intra-ERM exchange rates should imply more consistency in the forecasts. But, on the other hand, modifications of the forecasting model before realignments may introduce a spurious inconsistency between the forecasts at different horizons.

Individual data are aggregated into mean or median forecasts (individual expectations are confidential), which may introduce a bias given that (a) expectations are heterogeneous across forecasters (Allen and Taylor, 1989; Ito, 1990; McDonald and Marsh, 1995), and (b) the individual expectations are equally weighted, whatever the corresponding volume of

Table 10.1: The data

	Banque Nationale de Paris	The Economist	Consensus Forecasts
Exchange rates	DM, yen and £/$, DM/FF	DM, yen and £/$, DM/FF	DM, yen and £/$, DM/FF
Horizons	3 and 6 months	3, 6 and 12 months	3 and 12 months
Frequency	3 months	6 weeks	1 month
Periods	83.II–94.IV	June 81–Jan 89 (end of the survey)	Nov 89–Dec 94
Number of observations	47	63	62
Participants	15 experts of international markets	14 international banks	130 agents of which 3/4 are fin. institutions
Available statistics	median, min. and max.	median	mean and dispersion
Collecting method	last month of each quarter	by phone 2 days before publication of the review	by fax, before the first Monday of each month

Notes: The DM/FF are derived from the $/FF and $/DM forecasts in The Economist and Consensus surveys. The exchange rates are quoted in number of yens, Deutschmarks and Sterling pounds per dollar and in number of French francs per Deutschmark.

transactions. This shortcoming is partially offset by the use of three different surveys.

The time samples of the three surveys do not coincide. As their frequencies and collecting methods also differ, comparisons are quite difficult. In fact, there is no overlapping between *The Economist* and Consensus, while the overlapping between BNP and Consensus is narrow. Thus, the regressions are carried out on the whole observation period for each survey, as well as on the April 1983–January 1989 sub-period which is common to BNP (24 observations) and *The Economist* (47 observations).

Observed exchange rates are monthly averages except for Consensus, which provides the observed exchange rate the day before each expectation is collected (first Monday of each month). This differentiated choice is justified by unequal precision in the dating of the three surveys, although the Consensus precision is debatable as far as three-month and twelve-month expectations are concerned.

As highlighted above, survey data suffer from measurement errors. At least for sampling and aggregation problems, they imperfectly reflect the *market expectation*. In addition, individual data themselves can differ from the genuine expectations. However, measurement errors are not prejudicial to regression results as long as these errors have traditional features and do not affect the explanatory variables. Thus, the estimations of the extrapolative and of the regressive models do not suffer from measurement errors, while estimations of the adaptive model should be biased. In the latter case, it is especially difficult to build converging estimators, and heavy assumptions are necessary. Thus, this bias is simply not corrected for in existing studies. As it should affect the various horizons in a similar way, we consider this bias not relevant for consistency tests. Here, estimations for the various horizons were carried out simultaneously using the SUR (Seemingly Unrelated Regressions) method for each survey and each exchange rate.

10.3   CONSISTENCY TESTS CONDITIONAL TO AN EXTRAPOLATIVE MODEL

The extrapolative model is often preferred to other basic expectational mechanisms because it seems to better fit exchange rate survey data.[5] For each horizon *jh*, the extrapolative process links the expected rate variation to the last observed variation:

$$S^a_{t,jh} - S_t = f_{jh} + w_{jh}(S_t - S_{t-h}) \tag{10.10}$$

The consistency restrictions are derived from (10.8)–(10.9) with $b = q = 0$ and $a = f$:

$$f_{2h} = f_h(2 + w_h) \text{ and } w_{2h} = w_h + w_h^2$$

for the consistency between three- and six-month extrapolative expectations;

$$f_{4h} = f_{2h}(2 + w_{2h}) \text{ and } w_{4h} = w_{2h} + w_{2h}^2$$

for the consistency between six- and twelve-month extrapolative expectations (*The Economist*);

$$f_{4h} = f_h(4 + 3w_h + 2w_h^2 + w_h^3) \text{ and } w_{4h} = w_h + w_h^2 + w_h^3 + w_h^4$$

for the consistency between three- and twelve-month extrapolative expectations (Consensus).

Consistency tests are carried out on the constant f, on the parameter w (Appendix A) and on both parameters simultaneously (Table 10.2). The consistency of the forecast term structure is rejected, except in the case of three- and six-month DM/FF forecasts which are systematically consistent.

Table 10.2: *Results of the consistency tests conditional to an extrapolative model*

	BNP		Economist		Consensus
	83.II–94.IV	83.II–89.I	81.II–89.I	83.II–89.I	89.11–94.12
Test on 3–6 months: f, w (χ_2^2)					
$/DM	7.3[a]	5.5[b]	30[a]	34[a]	–
$/yen	11[a]	11[a]	21[a]	28[a]	–
$/£	3.6[b]	3.1[b]	18[a]	15[a]	–
DM/FF	1.4	1.2	4.4	0.8	–
Test on 6–12 or 3–12 months: f, w (χ_2^2)					
$/DM	–	–	57[a]	48[a]	3.19
$/yen	–	–	63[a]	55[a]	12[a]
$/£	–	–	23[a]	18[a]	14[a]
DM/FF	–	–	5.7[b]	0.5	14[a]

Notes:
[a] Rejection of consistency restrictions at 5%.
[b] Rejection of consistency restrictions at 10%.

There is no overreaction of the expectations to the current exchange rate: according to the regression results reported in Appendix A, w is generally negative.[6] It means that the forecasters expect the dollar exchange rates to move back towards their past levels. When interpreting the negative sign of w for the dollar, one must keep in mind the large fluctuations of the dollar during the period under review: it looks as if the market participants had been surprised, first, by the extent of the dollar rise and, afterwards, by its decline. The DM/FF forecasts pooled by *The Economist* show that, on the contrary, forecasters expected the last observed movements in the exchange rate to continue. This can be due to the lack of credibility of the EMS over the regression period.

These results should be considered with some caution as the extrapolative model leaves a large part of the forecasts changes unexplained, especially for the DM/FF and for short-term horizons. Three-month forecasts seem thus to follow a naive strategy, which could reflect the prominence of chartist expectations at this horizon. But these results rely on a restrictive model where forecasts are based on the last observed variation in the exchange rate despite the lack of autocorrelation in exchange rate variations. Other models could be more adequate, especially for short-term forecasts.

10.4   CONSISTENCY TESTS CONDITIONAL TO AN ADAPTIVE MODEL

The adaptive model implies a greater rationality on behalf of the forecasters as they are supposed to take their last forecast errors into account. We assume that expectations are adapted according to the last observed short-term error:

$$S^a_{t,jh} - S_t = l_{jh} + b_{jh}(S_t - S^a_{t-jh,jh}) \tag{10.11}$$

The consistency restrictions are derived from (10.8)–(10.9) with $w = q = 0$ and $a = l$:

$$l_{2h} = 2l_h \text{ and } b_{2h} = b_h$$

for consistency between three- and six-month adaptive forecasts;

$$l_{4h} = 2l_{2h} \text{ and } b_{4h} = b_{2h}$$

for consistency between six- and twelve-month adaptive forecasts (*The Economist*);

$$l_{4h} = 4l_h \text{ and } b_{4h} = b_h$$

for consistency between three- and twelve-month adaptive forecasts (Consensus).

Tests of the consistency of adaptive forecasts at different horizons lead to a systematic rejection of this hypothesis for the yen and Deutschmark against the dollar (Table 10.3 and Appendix B). On the contrary, the consistency of the DM/FF expectations can never be rejected on the BNP data. The results on the two others data sources vary across the period and the horizons under review. In general, consistency can less often be rejected for the DM/FF than for the other exchange rates.

Table 10.3: *Results of the consistency tests conditional to an adaptive model*

	BNP		Economist		Consensus
	83.II–94.IV	83.II–89.I	81.II–89.I	83.II–89.I	89.11–94.12
Test on 3–6 months: f, w (χ_2^2)					
$DM	8.9[a]	5[b]	28[a]	32[a]	
$/yen	11[a]	5[b]	25[a]	30[a]	
$/£	5.3[b]	2.9	14[a]	12[a]	
DM/FF	2.3	1	3.3	13[a]	
Test on 6–12 or 3–12 months: f, w (χ_2^2)					
$DM			40[a]	30[a]	6.3
$/yen			50[a]	34[a]	20[a]
$/£			16[a]	13[a]	5.4[b]
DM/FF			3.7	1.2	8[a]

Notes:
[a] Rejection of consistency restrictions at 5%.
[b] Rejection of consistency restrictions at 10%.

The estimates show that there is no overreaction of the expected rate of the current exchange rate: the b parameter lies between -1 and 0 (Appendix B). The forecasters seem to correct their previous forecasts in the following way: if they have overestimated the dollar over one period, they will revise their previous expectation downwards: $S^a_{t, jh} - S^a_{t-jh, jh} = \ell_{jh} + (1+b)(S_t - S^a_{t-jh, jh})$

Once again, the results should be interpreted with some caution as the adaptive model does not fit the data well, especially the DM/FF forecasts.

As with the extrapolative model, the adaptive model lacks theoretical reference which could anchor the expectations.

10.5   CONSISTENCY TESTS CONDITIONAL TO A REGRESSIVE MODEL

In the regressive model, a slow adjustment to the long-run exchange rate
$\overline{S}_t$ is expected:

$$S^a_{t,jh} - R_t = k_{jh} + q_{jh}(\overline{S}_t - S_t) \qquad (10.12)$$

The expected long-run exchange rate is defined here as the nominal
exchange rate which would have maintained the real exchange rate at its
mean level on the whole period under review:

$$\overline{S}_t = R + P_t - P^*_t$$

where R is the logarithm of the average real exchange rate over the regression period and P_t is the logarithm of the general level of prices (P^*_t in the
foreign country).

Consistency restrictions are derived from (10.8)–(10.9) with $w = b = 0$
and $a = k$:

$$k_{2h} = k_h(2 - q_h) \text{ and } q_{2h} = 2q_h - q^2_h$$

for the consistency between three- and six-month regressive forecasts;

$$k_{4h} = k_{2h}(2 - q_{2h}) \text{ and } q_{4h} = 2q_{2h} - q^2_{2h}$$

for the consistency between six- and twelve-month regressive forecasts (*The
Economist*);

$$k_{4h} = k_h(4 - 6q_h + 4q^2_h - q^3_h) \text{ and } q_{4h} = 4q_h - 6q^2_h + 4q^3_h - w^4_h$$

for the consistency between three- and twelve-month regressive forecasts
(Consensus).

The results of the tests vary considerably across the currencies, the
periods and the surveys under review (Table 10.4 and Appendix C). The
consistency of \$/DM forecasts is often rejected, while the consistency of
DM/FF forecasts cannot be rejected in most cases. But the results differ
across the surveys: consistency is less often rejected on Consensus and BNP

Table 10.4: Results of the consistency tests conditional to a regressive model

	BNP		The Economist		Consensus
	83.II–94.IV	83.II–89.I	81.II–89.I	83.II–89.I	89.11–94.12
Tests on 3–6 months: f, w (χ^2_2)					
$DM	9.9[a]	4	13.8[a]	14.7[a]	
$/yen	3.2	0.7	0.7	6.2[a]	
$/£	2.3	1.4	8.1[a]	10.1[a]	
DM/FF	4	1.9	2.8	0.6	
Tests on 6–12 or 3–12 months: f, w (χ^2_2)					
$DM			41.2[a]	32.4[a]	0.3
$/yen			46[a]	39.5[a]	7.3[a]
$/£			20.2[a]	12[a]	4
DM/FF			6.8[a]	8.3[a]	4

Note: [a] Rejection of consistency restrictions at 5%.

data, while the tests on *The Economist* data are the only ones to reject the consistency of $/£ forecasts.

According to the estimates detailed in Appendix C, regressive expectations are rather stabilizing: the q parameter is rarely both negative and significantly different from zero.

The regression fitness increases with the length of the forecasting horizon: 'fundamentalist' methods seem to be used more often in the long term than in the short term. This result corroborates the conclusions of Allen and Taylor (1989). It is consistent with our previous results which show that forecasters either expect a regression towards the last observed exchange rate (extrapolative model with a negative w parameter), or perpetuate their past error (adaptive model with a b parameter). However, the regression fitness for the regressive model varies across currencies: it is rather good for the dollar against the Deutschmark and the yen while it is bad for the $/£ and DM/FF rates.

10.6 CONSISTENCY TESTS CONDITIONAL TO A 'MIXED MODEL'

Until this point, forecasts were assumed to rely on a single scheme: either extrapolative, adaptive or regressive. But studies of individual forecasts

Lessons from survey data

(Frankel and Froot, 1987b; Allen and Taylor, 1989; Ito, 1990; McDonald & Marsh, 1995) show that heterogeneous forecasting methods are used by survey participants. Subsequently, the average forecast should follow a mixed extrapolative-adaptive-regressive process (Prat and Uctum, 1996) rather than a simple model. Here consistency of the forecast term structure is tested assuming a mixed forecasting model (equation (10.2)).[7]

The results of the consistency tests differ widely across the periods, the currencies and the surveys (Table 10.5 and Appendix D). However, the use

Table 10.5:   Results of the consistency tests conditional to a mixed model

	BNP		The Economist		Consensus
	83.II–94.IV	83.II–89.I	81.II–89.I	83.II–89.I	89.11–94.12
Tests on 3–6 months: f, w	(χ_4^2)				
$DM	7.3	11.1[a]	27[a]	38.6[a]	–
$/yen	9.7[a]	13.7[a]	12.4[a]	31[a]	–
$/£	4.6	2.8	11.2[a]	16.1[a]	–
DM/FF	11[a]	4	26[a]	25[a]	–
Tests on 6–12 or 3–12 months: f, w	(χ_4^2)				
$DM	–	–	53[a]	43.5[a]	9.3[a]
$/yen	–	–	60[a]	53[a]	3
$/£	–	–	19[a]	15.3[a]	5.3
DM/FF	–	–	21[a]	9.7[a]	18[a]

Note: [a] Rejection of consistency restrictions at 5%.

of a mixed model increases the number of consistency rejections for DM/FF. But because the regression fitness is still poor for this exchange rate, these results must be interpreted with some caution. The rejection of the consistency hypothesis for the forecasts of the $/DM is mostly due to the regressive component of the model which is strongly significant at the twelve-month horizon (Appendix D). For the $/£ exchange rate, only *The Economist* forecasts are inconsistent. The rejection of the consistency hypothesis in this case is due to the constant term and to the regressive component. This heterogeneity in the results across the surveys may partly be explained by the poor fit of the mixed model on the $/£ forecasts for BNP and Consensus surveys.

The estimates reported in Appendix D confirm the conclusions obtained with the three basic expectational processes: the longer the forecasting horizon the better the regression fitness of the model. It is especially good for the twelve-month forecasts of the \$/yen and the \$/DM. For the short term (three months), the average forecast seems to follow a naive process, with or without a drift $(S_{t,jh}^a = c + s_t)$, which corresponds to rational expectations according to Meese and Rogoff's (1983) famous result. The three-month forecasting model (naive model) thus differs from the forecasting model used at a twelve-month horizon (mixed model). But the naive model is nested in the mixed model: assuming a general extrapolative-adaptive-regressive model to test consistency is correct *ex post*. The results, however, differ greatly according to the exchange rates: even for long-term horizons, the model fits the DM/FF expectations poorly, which could be due to a 'target zone' effect. There are also some differences across surveys: the comparison between the BNP and *The Economist* surveys on the same sub-period shows that the mixed model explains better *The Economist* series than the BNP series. Lastly, even if the mixed model fits the series better than each of its components separately, the three parameters (w, b, q) are rarely simultaneously significant.

10.7 CONCLUSION

The frequent rejection of the unbiasedness and orthogonality hypotheses on survey data about exchange rate forecasts casts doubts on the rationality of forecasters. This result could be due to errors in the measures of the forecasts or to a 'peso' phenomenon.[8] But the diversity of the regression periods limits the scope of this interpretation. The rejection of the rationality hypothesis could alternatively be explained by inefficient use of the available information. This inefficiency is probably partly due to the high level of 'noise' versus 'signal' on the exchange rate market, but it could also be related to an inconsistency in the forecasts. To clear up this point, four different models were regressed with forecast series coming from three different surveys, and the consistency of the forecast term structure was subsequently tested.

Our regression results match the conclusions of Allen and Taylor (1989): long-term forecasts are more 'fundamentalist' (that is, they refer to a long-term equilibrium exchange rate) than short-term forecasts (naive model). In other words, the shorter the forecasting horizon the less the models are able to explain a significant part of forecast changes.

This diversity in the forecasting models used across horizons may explain the rejection of the hypothesis of a consistent forecast term structure: the iteration of the short-term naive model cannot result in a regression towards a long-term equilibrium exchange rate. However, the rejection of consistency is not systematic: it depends on the exchange rates, the surveys studied and, to a lesser extent, the models tested (extrapolative, adaptive, regressive or mixed). The results of the tests differ across the exchange rates: the consistency is more often rejected for the $/DM and $/yen rates than for the $/£ and especially the DM/FF rate. But the estimated models do not fit the forecasts of the latter exchange rates well (especially the DM/FF forecasts), so the results for these exchange rates should be interpreted with some caution. The three basic models (extrapolative, adaptive, regressive) are nested in the mixed model. This general model provides the best fits for long-term forecasts, but is not superior to the basic processes on three-month forecasts. Despite these varying results, the frequent rejection of the consistency hypothesis strengthens the rejection of the rational expectation hypothesis, of which it is a necessary condition.

Because samples were too short, it was not possible to test for the stability of the estimates. However, the conclusions of the tests do not change when the year 1994 is omitted from the BNP and Consensus series: the rejection of the consistency hypothesis does not seem to depend on the periods under review. However, the use of different forecasting methods across the horizons can be accompanied by changes in forecasting methods over time. This forecasting strategy is not necessarily irrational: forecasters can revise their forecasting models over time in order to make their short-run expectations consistent with their long-term forecasts. More general consistency tests should be devised to take this possibility into account.

APPENDIX A

Table A10.1a: *Detailed consistency tests on $/DM extrapolative forecasts*

	BNP		The Economist		Consensus
	83.II–94.IV	83.II–89.I	81.II–89.I	83.II–89.I	89.11–94.12
f_h	−0.004	−0.02	−0.03	−0.02	0.012
	(−1)	(−3.6)	(−13)	(−11)	(5)
w_h	−0.06	−0.11	−0.015	−0.004	−0.1
	(−1)	(−1.5)	(−0.4)	(−0.1)	(−2.7)
R^2a	0.00	0.04	0.00	0.00	0.09
f_{2h}	0.005	−0.027	−0.05	−0.05	
	(0.7)	(−4.4)	(−21)	(−17)	
w_{2h}	−0.18	−0.28	−0.16	−0.17	
	(−1.75)	(−3.2)	(−4)	(−17)	
R^2a	0.04	0.27	0.2	0.22	
f_{4h}			−0.08	−0.08	0.04
			(−21)	(−17)	(9)
w_{4h}			−0.39	−0.4	−0.17
			(−6)	(−6)	(−2.43)
R^2a			0.36	0.4	0.08
Test on 3–6: f (χ^2_1)	4.2[a]	0.7	0.00	0.5	0.5
w (χ^2_1)	2.3	4.4[b]	30[a]	35[a]	2.5
Test on 6–12 or 3–12: f (χ^2_1)			13[a]	6.4[a]	
w (χ^2_1)			37[a]	36[a]	

Notes:
[a] Rejection of consistency restrictions at 5%.
[b] Rejection of consistency restrictions at 10%.
In brackets: *t* statistic.

229

Table A10.1b: *Detailed consistency tests on $/yen extrapolative forecasts*

	BNP		The Economist		Consensus
	83.II–94.IV	83.II–89.I	81.II–89.I	83.II–89.I	89.11–94.12
f_h	−0.008	−0.02	−0.03	−0.02	0.006
	(−2.6)	(−3.9)	(−13)	(−14)	(3.3)
w_h	−0.08	−0.09	−0.1	−0.03	−0.12
	(−1.6)	(−1.1)	(−3.2)	(−1.4)	(−3.2)
R^2a	0.035	0.01	0.13	0.02	0.22
f_{2h}	−0.008	−0.03	−0.06	−0.05	
	(−1.55)	(−5.4)	(−22)	(−23)	
w_{2h}	−0.26	−0.38	−0.21	−0.18	
	(−3.1)	(−3.7)	(−6)	(−5.8)	
R^2a	0.15	0.34	0.33	0.4	
f_{4h}			−0.09	−0.08	0.02
			(−22)	(−23)	(7.3)
w_{4h}			−0.39	−0.33	−0.24
			(−6.6)	(−6.4)	(−5)
R^2a			0.4	0.45	0.42
Test on 3–6: f (χ^2_1)	2.1	0.1	0.3	3.5[b]	
w (χ^2_1)	7[a]	9.2[a]	21[a]	28[a]	
Test on 6–12 or 3–12: f (χ^2_1)			14[a]	8.8[a]	1
w (χ^2_1)			33[a]	30[a]	12[a]

Notes:
[a] Rejection of consistency restrictions at 5%.
[b] Rejection of consistency restrictions at 10%.
In brackets: t statistic.

Table A10.1c: Detailed consistency tests on $/£ extrapolative forecasts

	BNP		The Economist		Consensus
	83.II–94.IV	83.II–89.I	81.II–89.I	83.II–89.I	89.11–94.12
f_h	0.004	−0.008	−0.006	−0.005	0.02
	(0.7)	(−1)	(−2.8)	(−2.2)	(7.1)
w_h	−0.09	−0.19	−0.11	−0.12	−0.08
	(−1.1)	(−1.7)	(−3.3)	(−3.1)	(−2.7)
R^2a	0.00	0.07	0.14	0.15	0.16
f_{2h}	0.02	−0.006	−0.012	−0.012	
	(2.7)	(−0.8)	(−5)	(−4.1)	
w_{2h}	−0.14	−0.29	−0.2	−0.21	
	(−1.5)	(−2.7)	(−5.2)	(−4.7)	
R^2a	0.03	0.2	0.29	0.3	
f_{4h}			−0.02	−0.02	0.05
			(−5)	(−4.4)	(13)
w_{4h}			−0.35	−0.36	−0.15
			(−5.9)	(−5.3)	(−3.6)
R^2a			0.35	0.36	0.26
Test on 3–6: f (χ^2_1)	2.3	0.9	0.1	0.2	
w (χ^2_1)	1.4	2.5	18[a]	15[a]	
Test on 6–12 or 3–12: f (χ^2_1)			0.8	0.1	6.2[a]
w (χ^2_1)			22[a]	18[a]	7[a]

Notes:
[a] Rejection of consistency restrictions at 5%.
In brackets: t statistic.

Table A10.1d: Detailed consistency tests on DM/FF extrapolative forecasts

	BNP		The Economist		Consensus
	83.II–94.IV	83.II–89.I	81.II–89.I	83.II–89.I	89.11–94.12
f_h	0.002	0.005	0.01	0.009	0.001
	(3.5)	(3.5)	(6.6)	(5.5)	(1.3)
w_h	−0.13	−0.23	0.13	0.1	−0.12
	(−2.4)	(−2)	(1.6)	(1)	(−1.9)
R^2a	0.09	0.11	0.02	0.00	0.05
f_{2h}	0.006	0.01	0.03	0.02	
	(4.8)	(5.1)	(10)	(9.8)	
w_{2h}	−0.2	−0.12	0.29	0.13	
	(−2.1)	(−0.7)	(2.3)	(1)	
R^2a	0.066	0.00	0.06	0.00	
f_{4h}			0.05	0.04	0.002
			(11)	(11)	(1.9)
w_{4h}			0.4	0.1	−0.39
			(2.1)	(0.5)	(−4.3)
R^2a			0.05	0.00	0.26
Test on 3–6: f (χ^2_1)	0.7	0.7	0.3	0.7	
w (χ^2_1)	0.9	0.1	2.7[b]	0.0	
Test on 6–12 or 3–12: f (χ^2_1)			5[a]	0.4	0.5
w (χ^2_1)			2.8[b]	0.0	13[a]

Notes:
[a] Rejection of consistency restrictions at 5%.
[b] Rejection of consistency restrictions at 10%.
In brackets: t statistic.

232

Table A10.2a: Detailed consistency tests on $/DM adaptive forecasts

	BNP		The Economist		Consensus
	83.II–94.IV	83.II–89.I	81.II–89.I	83.II–89.I	89.11–94.12
l_h	−0.004	−0.017	−0.027	−0.024	0.01
	(−1)	(−3.3)	(−12)	(−11)	(4.3)
b_h	−0.1	−0.08	−0.036	−0.015	−0.14
	(−1.97)	(−1.3)	(−1.2)	(−0.5)	(−4.1)
R^2a	0.06	0.02	0.01	0.00	0.21
l_{2h}	0.005	−0.022	−0.05	−0.046	
	(0.8)	(−3.7)	(−20)	(−17)	
b_{2h}	−0.22	−0.24	−0.17	−0.17	
	(−2.7)	(−3.21)	(−4.8)	(−4.4)	
R^2a	0.12	0.28	0.26	0.27	
l_{4h}			−0.07	−0.07	0.04
			(−19)	(−16)	(8.5)
b_{4h}			−0.38	−0.38	−0.24
			(−6.7)	(6.2)	(−3.9)
R^2a			0.41	0.43	0.19
Test on 3–6: l (X^2_2)	4.4ᵃ	1.3	1.9	0.3	
b (X^2_1)	3.9ᵃ	3.9ᵃ	28ᵃ	31ᵃ	
Test on 6–12 or 3–12: l (X^2_1)			24ᵃ	14ᵃ	0.3
b (X^2_1)			23ᵃ	19ᵃ	6ᵃ

Notes:
ᵃ Rejection of consistency restrictions at 5%.
In brackets: t statistic.

Table A10.2b: *Detailed consistency tests on $/yen adaptive forecasts*

	BNP		The Economist		Consensus
	83.II–94.IV	83.II–89.I	81.II–89.I	83.II–89.I	89.11–94.12
l_h	−0.008	−0.018	−0.026	−0.022	0.0001
	(−2.6)	(−3.9)	(−12)	(−15)	(0.04)
b_h	−0.11	−0.09	−0.11	−0.034	−0.17
	(−2.3)	(−1.2)	(−3.7)	(−1.5)	(−4.3)
R^2a	0.08	0.02	0.17	0.02	0.22
l_{2h}	−0.007	−0.027	−0.05	−0.05	
	(−1.3)	(−4.2)	(−22)	(−24)	
b_{2h}	−0.27	−0.3	−0.23	−0.18	
	(−3.5)	(−2.7)	(−7)	(−6.2)	
R^2a	0.19	0.21	0.44	0.43	
l_{4h}			−0.08	−0.07	0.009
			(−22)	(−22)	(2.1)
b_{4h}			−0.41	−0.32	−0.36
			(−8)	(−6.6)	(−5.4)
R^2a			0.51	0.46	0.32
Test on 3–6: l (χ_1^2)	3[b]	0.9	0.2	0.5	
b (χ_1^2)	6[a]	3.6[b]	25[a]	30[a]	
Test on 6–12 or 3–12: l (χ_1^2)			26[a]	20[a]	1.3
b (χ_1^2)			27[a]	12[a]	18[a]

Notes:
[a] Rejection of consistency restrictions at 5%.
[b] Rejection of consistency restrictions at 10%.
In brackets: t statistic.

Table A10.2c: Detailed consistency tests on £/$ adaptive forecasts

	BNP		The Economist		Consensus
	83.II–94.IV	83.II–89.I	81.II–89.I	83.II–89.I	89.11–94.12
l_h	0.003 (0.6)	−0.007 (−0.9)	−0.005 (−2.6)	−0.005 (−2.1)	0.012 (0.4)
b_h	−0.13 (−1.6)	−0.17 (−1.6)	−0.12 (−4.1)	−0.12 (−3.9)	−0.06 (−2.4)
R^2a	0.03	0.05	0.21	0.22	0.07
l_{2h}	0.016 (2.7)	−0.003 (−0.5)	−0.01 (−4.8)	−0.01 (−4.1)	
b_{2h}	−0.23 (−2.4)	−0.29 (−2.8)	−0.19 (−6)	−0.2 (−5.7)	
R^2a	0.096	0.22	0.37	0.39	
l_{4h}			−0.02 (−4.7)	−0.02 (−4.4)	0.04 (14)
b_{4h}			−0.33 (−7)	−0.35 (−6.4)	−0.1 (−2.9)
R^2a			0.43	0.45	0.11
Test on 3–6: l (χ^2_1)	1.9	0.8	0.0	0.0	
b (χ^2_1)	3.2[b]	2.1	14[a]	12[a]	
Test on 6–12 or 3–12: l (χ^2_1)			1	0.2	3.2[b]
b (χ^2_1)			15[a]	12[a]	2.5

Notes:
[a] Rejection of consistency restrictions at 5%.
[b] Rejection of consistency restrictions at 10%.
In brackets: t statistic.

235

Table A10.2d: *Detailed consistency tests on DM/FF adaptive forecasts*

	BNP		The Economist		Consensus
	83.II–94.IV	83.II–89.I	81.II–89.I	83.II–89.I	89.11–94.12
l_h	0.002	0.004	0.014	0.01	0.001
	(3.2)	(3.2)	(8.6)	(6.7)	(1.8)
b_h	−0.14	−0.21	0.09	0.11	−0.13
	(−2.8)	(−2.2)	(0.9)	(1)	(−2.6)
R^2a	0.12	0.13	0.00	0.00	0.09
l_{2h}	0.005	0.01	0.03	0.022	
	(4.6)	(5.7)	(11.9)	(10.8)	
b_{2h}	−0.25	−0.19	−0.03	−0.2	
	(−2.9)	(−1.3)	(−0.2)	(−1.4)	
R^2a	0.13	0.03	0.00	0.02	
l_{4h}			0.05	0.04	0.001
			(13)	(11)	(1.6)
b_{4h}			−0.006	−0.31	−0.3
			(−0.0)	(−1.4)	(−4.2)
R^2a			0.00	0.02	0.22
Test on 3–6: l (χ_1^2)	0.5	0.9	1.6	0.1	
b (χ_1^2)	1.8	0.0	1.3	12[a]	
Test on 6–12 or 3–12: l (χ_1^2)			3.6	0.9	2
b (χ_1^2)			0.0	0.6	6.5[a]

Notes:
[a] Rejection of consistency restrictions at 5%.
In brackets: t statistic.

Table A10.3a: *Detailed consistency tests on £/DM regressive forecasts*

	BNP		The Economist		Consensus
	83.II–94.IV	83.II–89.I	81.II–89.I	83.II–89.I	89.11–94.12
k_h	-0.005	-0.02	-0.03	-0.024	0.012
	(-1)	(-3.4)	(-14)	(-11)	(5.11)
q_h	0.04	-0.02	-0.009	-0.011	-0.12
	(1.8)	(-0.7)	(-0.7)	(-0.9)	(2.8)
R^2a	0.05	0.00	0.00	0.00	0.1
k_{2h}	0.004	-0.026	-0.05	-0.05	
	(0.7)	(-3.7)	(-20)	(-16)	
q_{2h}	0.15	0.05	0.04	0.04	
	(4.9)	(-1.3)	(2.6)	(2.4)	
R^2a	0.32	0.03	0.08	0.09	
k_{4h}			-0.08	-0.08	0.04
			(-22)	(-17.8)	(11)
q_{4h}			0.15	0.15	0.43
			(6.4)	(6.4)	(6.5)
R^2a			0.39	0.45	0.4
Test on 3–6: k (χ_1^2)	4[a]	0.9	0.5	0.1	
q (χ_1^2)	5.7[a]	3.2[b]	13.3[a]	14.6[a]	
Test on 6–12 or 3–12: k (χ_1^2)			31.7[a]	21.9[a]	0.0
q (χ_1^2)			12.2[a]	11.5[a]	0.2

Notes:
[a] Rejection of consistency restrictions at 5%.
[b] Rejection of consistency restrictions at 10%.
In brackets: t statistic.

237

Table A10.3b: *Detailed consistency tests on $/yen regressive forecasts*

	BNP		The Economist		Consensus
	83.II–94.IV	83.II–89.I	81.II–89.I	83.II–89.I	89.11–94.12
k_h	−0.007	−0.017	−0.03	−0.02	0.002
	(−2.65)	(−3.9)	(−12.8)	(−14.5)	(1)
q_h	0.04	0.02	0.02	0.003	0.12
	(3.4)	(0.9)	(2.4)	(0.5)	(0.6)
R^2a	0.18	0.00	0.07	0.00	0.41
k_{2h}	−0.005	−0.03	−0.05	−0.05	
	(−2.65)	(−3.8)	(−21)	(−20)	
q_{2h}	0.1	0.04	0.06	0.03	
	(4.8)	(1.42)	(4.8)	(3.5)	
R^2a	0.31	0.04	0.26	0.18	
k_{4h}			−0.09	−0.07	0.01
			(−23)	(−22.7)	(5.2)
q_{4h}			0.12	0.09	0.3
			(7.3)	(6.5)	(14)
R^2a			0.45	0.46	0.77
Test on 3–6: k (X_1^2)	2.6	0.6	0.04	0.7	
q (X_1^2)	0.5	0.04	0.7	5.9[a]	
Test on 6–12 or 3–12: k (X_1^2)			45[a]	36.1[a]	1
q (X_1^2)			1.3	2.6	6.4[a]

Notes:
[a] Rejection of consistency restrictions at 5%.
In brackets: *t* statistic.

238

Table A10.3c: Detailed consistency tests on $/£ regressive forecasts

	BNP		The Economist		Consensus
	83.II–94.IV	83.II–89.I	81.II–89.I	83.II–89.I	89.11–94.12
k_h	0.003	−0.007	0.02	0.02	0.01
	(0.7)	(−0.9)	(1.41)	(1.3)	(6.6)
q_h	0.07	0.03	−0.03	−0.04	0.01
	(2.1)	(0.5)	(−1.9)	(−1.6)	(0.4)
R^2a	0.07	0.00	0.04	0.03	0.00
k_{2h}	0.015	−0.0053	−0.007	−0.02	
	(2.6)	(−0.7)	(−0.4)	(−0.8)	
q_{2h}	0.1	−0.005	−0.007	0.012	
	(2.8)	(−0.1)	(−0.3)	(0.4)	
R^2a	0.13	0.00	0.00	0.00	
k_{4h}			−0.08	−0.13	0.04
			(−3)	(−3.3)	(15)
q_{4h}			0.07	0.13	0.09
			(2.3)	(2.9)	(3.7)
R^2a			0.07	0.13	0.17
Test on 3–6: k (χ_1^2)	12	0.6	7.7[a]	10.1[a]	
q (χ_1^2)	0.4	0.7	8.1[a]	10[a]	
Test on 6–12 or 3–12: k (χ_1^2)			13.1[a]	10.6[a]	3.7[b]
q (χ_1^2)			16[a]	11.5[a]	1

Notes:
[a] Rejection of consistency restrictions at 5%.
[b] Rejection of consistency restrictions at 10%.
In brackets: t statistic.

Table A10.3d: Detailed consistency tests on DMIFF regressive forecasts

	BNP		The Economist		Consensus
	83.II–94.IV	83.II–89.I	81.II–89.I	83.II–89.I	89.11–94.12
k_h	0.002 (3.1)	0.003 (3)	0.014 (8.9)	0.01 (6.6)	0.001 (1.9)
q_h	-0.02 (-0.83)	-0.07 (-1.3)	0.03 (0.5)	-0.08 (-1.25)	-0.006 (-0.3)
R^2a	0.00	0.02	0.00	0.01	0.00
k_{2h}	0.005 (4.4)	0.01 (5.7)	0.03 (12.5)	0.02 (12)	
q_{2h}	0.05 (0.9)	-0.07 (-0.9)	-0.009 (-0.12)	-0.22 (-2.8)	
R^2a	0.00	0.00	0.00	0.12	
k_{4h}			0.05 (14.4)	0.04 (13.5)	0.002 (2.4)
q_{4h}			0.0008 (0.00)	-0.43 (-3.4)	0.12 (3.4)
R^2a			0.00	0.18	0.14
Test on 3–6: k (X_1^2)	0.6	1.3	2.2	0.4	1.4
q (X_1^2)	3.1[b]	0.3	1	0.3	2.9[b]
Test on 6–12 or 3–12: k (X_1^2)			6[a]	8[a]	
q (X_1^2)			0.05	0.2	

Notes:
[a] Rejection of consistency restrictions at 5%.
[b] Rejection of consistency restrictions at 10%.
In brackets: *t* statistic.

240

APPENDIX D

Table A10.4a: *Detailed consistency tests on $/DM mixed forecasts*

	BNP		The Economist		Consensus
	83.II–94.IV	83.II–89.I	81.II–89.I	83.II–89.I	89.11–94.12
a_h	−0.002	−0.02	−0.015	−0.014	0.005
	(−0.7)	(−3.2)	(−4)	(−3.5)	(2)
w_h	0.37	−0.25	0.43	0.45	0.46
	(2.1)	(−1)	(3.25)	(3)	(4.3)
b_h	−0.38	0.1	−0.42	−0.42	−0.59
	(−2.5)	(0.5)	(−3.52)	(−3.2)	(−5.3)
q_h	0.017	−0.03	−0.009	−0.008	−0.07
	(0.8)	(−1.2)	(−0.8)	(−0.7)	(−1.3)
R^2a	0.13	0.01	0.14	0.13	0.38
a_{2h}	0.005	−0.024	−0.04	−0.04	
	(0.9)	(−3.1)	(−8.7)	(−7.8)	
w_{2h}	0.42	−0.07	0.38	0.36	
	(1.7)	(−0.2)	(2.4)	(1.92)	
b_{2h}	−0.48	−0.17	−0.49	−0.48	
	(−2.2)	(−0.7)	(−3.4)	(−2.8)	
q_{2h}	0.12	0.03	0.03	0.03	
	(3.7)	(0.9)	(2.1)	(2.1)	
R^2a	0.36	0.24	0.33	0.34	

Table A10.4a: (cont.)

		BNP		The Economist		Consensus
		83.II–94.IV	83.II–89.I	81.II–89.I	83.II–89.I	89.11–94.12
a_{4h}				−0.07	−0.06	0.03
				(−11)	(−11.2)	(7.7)
w_{4h}				0.48	0.38	0.71
				(2.4)	(1.75)	(3.9)
b_{4h}				−0.73	−0.65	−0.75
				(−4.1)	(−3.2)	(−4)
q_{4h}				0.13	0.13	0.27
				(7.3)	(7.6)	(3.2)
R^2a				0.68	0.73	0.47
Test on 3–6: a	(χ_1^2)	2.3	1.9	0.2	1.2	
w	(χ_1^2)	0.1	0.2	2	2.6	
b	(χ_1^2)	0.02	0.9	0.6	0.7	
q	(χ_1^2)	3.4[b]	3.8[b]	6.75[a]	7.4[a]	
Test on 6–12 or 3–12: a	(χ_1^2)			26[a]	17.8[a]	0.1
w	(χ_1^2)			0.03	0.16	1.6
b	(χ_1^2)			0.09	0.004	0.9
q	(χ_1^2)			4.4[a]	4.2[a]	2.9[b]

Notes:
[a] Rejection of consistency restrictions at 5%.
[b] Rejection of consistency restrictions at 10%.
In brackets: t statistic.

Table A10.4b: *Detailed consistency tests on $/yen mixed forecasts*

	BNP		The Economist		Consensus
	83.II–94.IV	83.II–89.I	81.II–89.I	83.II–89.I	89.11–94.12
a_h	−0.009	−0.02	−0.02	−0.02	0.001
	(−2.6)	(−3.1)	(−6)	(−7)	(0.7)
w_h	0.08	−0.02	0.1	0.04	0.1
	(0.6)	(−0.1)	(0.9)	(0.4)	(0.7)
b_h	−0.15	−0.06	−0.2	−0.08	−0.17
	(−1)	(−0.3)	(−1.7)	(−0.6)	(−1.2)
q_h	0.03	0.014	0.008	0.0003	0.08
	(2.1)	(0.7)	(0.8)	(0.04)	(3)
R^2a	0.15	0.00	0.16	0.00	0.4
a_{2h}	−0.01	−0.04	−0.05	−0.04	
	(−2.3)	(−5.5)	(−12)	(−12)	
w_{2h}	−0.25	−0.68	0.023	0.07	
	(−1)	(−2.7)	(1.95)	(0.5)	
b_{2h}	0.05	0.34	−0.4	−0.23	
	(0.2)	(1.3)	(−3.5)	(−1.6)	
q_{2h}	0.08	0.02	0.03	0.02	
	(3.5)	(0.9)	(2.8)	(2.6)	
R^2a	0.32	0.34	0.53	0.5	
a_{4h}			−0.08	−0.07	0.01
			(−15)	(−16)	(5.5)

Table A10.4b: (cont.)

	BNP		The Economist		Consensus
	83.II–94.IV	83.II–89.I	81.II–89.I	83.II–89.I	89.11–94.12
w_{4h}			0.22	−0.08	0.05
			(1.43)	(−0.4)	(0.34)
b_{4h}			−0.52	−0.17	−0.14
			(−3.4)	(−1)	(−1)
q_{4h}			0.08	0.07	0.25
			(6)	(6.7)	(9)
R^2a			0.71	0.71	0.79
Test on 3–6: a (x_1^2)	1	0.13	0.8	0.2	
w (x_1^2)	2.5	7[a]	1.3	0.02	
b (x_1^2)	0.9	2.6	3.3[b]	1.1	
q (x_1^2)	0.4	0.02	0.4	3[b]	
Test on 6–12 or 3–12: a (x_1^2)			27[a]	12[a]	0.9
w (x_1^2)			0.15	0.8	0.1
b (x_1^2)			0.04	0.1	0.1
q (x_1^2)			1.35	3.2[b]	0.6

Notes:
[a] Rejection of consistency restrictions at 5%.
[b] Rejection of consistency restrictions at 10%.
In brackets: t statistic.

244

Table A10.4c:: Detailed consistency tests on $/£ mixed forecasts

	BNP		The Economist		Consensus
	83.II–94.IV	83.II–89.I	81.II–89.I	83.II–89.I	89.11–94.12
a_h	0.003	−0.008	0.022	0.04	0.008
	(0.6)	(−1)	(1.8)	(2.7)	(3.5)
w_h	−0.05	0.16	0.32	0.34	0.34
	(−0.3)	(0.7)	(2.5)	(2.4)	(2.9)
b_h	0.14	0.05	−0.39	−0.4	−0.39
	(0.9)	(0.2)	(−3.5)	(−3.6)	(−3.4)
q_h	0.05	−0.004	−0.03	−0.06	−0.009
	(1.6)	(−0.1)	(−2.1)	(−3)	(−0.5)
R^2a	0.04	0.00	0.31	0.41	0.16
a_{2h}	0.015	−0.005	−0.001	0.007	
	(2.4)	(−0.7)	(−0.1)	(0.3)	
w_{2h}	−0.12	0.17	0.31	0.38	
	(−0.7)	(0.9)	(2.1)	(2.2)	
b_{2h}	0.27	0.18	−0.46	−0.5	
	(1.6)	(1)	(−3.5)	(−3.6)	
q_{2h}	0.08	−0.06	−0.009	−0.02	
	(2)	(−1.1)	(−0.5)	(−0.8)	
R^2a	0.14	0.2	0.4	0.44	
a_{4h}			−0.07	−0.09	0.03
			(−3.6)	(−3.1)	(10)

Table A10.4c: (cont.)

	BNP		The Economist		Consensus
	83.II–94.IV	83.II–89.I	81.II–89.I	83.II–89.I	89.11–94.12
w_{4h}			0.56	0.69	0.43
			(2.6)	(2.7)	(2.8)
b_{4h}			−0.8	−0.9	−0.5
			(−4.2)	(−4.1)	(−3.2)
q_{4h}			0.07	0.09	0.07
			(3)	(2.6)	(3)
R^2a			0.52	0.54	0.27
Test on 3–6: a (χ_1^2)	1.9	0.9	6.8[a]	13[a]	
w (χ_1^2)	0.6	0.003	0.6	0.4	
b (χ_1^2)	2.2	0.4	0.2	0.2	
q (χ_1^2)	0.4	0.3	6.7[a]	13[a]	
Test on 6–12 or 3–12: a (χ_1^2)			9[a]	10.3[a]	2.6
w (χ_1^2)			0.7	0.6	0.7
b (χ_1^2)			1.2	0.6	0.6
q (χ_1^2)			11.3[a]	12[a]	5.9[a]

Notes:
[a] Rejection of consistency restrictions at 5%.
In brackets: t statistic.

Table A10.4d: Detailed consistency tests on DM/FF mixed forecasts

	BNP		The Economist		Consensus
	83.II–94.IV	83.II–89.I	81.II–89.I	83.II–89.I	89.11–94.12
a_h	0.002	0.005	0.011	0.01	0.001
	(3.1)	(3.3)	(4.8)	(5)	(2.1)
w_h	0.008	−0.19	0.2	−0.02	−0.2
	(0.1)	(−0.9)	(1.5)	(−0.14)	(−1.6)
b_h	−0.17	−0.08	−0.09	0.12	0.03
	(−1.2)	(−0.4)	(−0.6)	(0.8)	(0.3)
q_h	−0.04	−0.09	0.04	−0.08	−0.03
	(−1.4)	(−1.5)	(0.6)	(−1.1)	(−1.1)
R^2a	0.12	0.14	0.00	0.00	0.11
a_{2h}	0.004	0.009	0.02	0.02	
	(3.6)	(4)	(6)	(7.6)	
w_{2h}	0.4	0.23	0.77	0.25	
	(1.73)	(0.7)	(4.1)	(1.4)	
b_{2h}	−0.61	−0.36	−0.74	−0.38	
	(−2.7)	(−1.3)	(−3.3)	(−2.2)	
q_{2h}	0.07	−0.002	0.07	−0.16	
	(1.4)	(−0.02)	(0.9)	(−1.9)	
R^2a	0.18	0.00	0.18	0.17	
a_{4h}			0.04	0.04	0.002
			(7.5)	(9.3)	(2.2)

Table A10.4d: (cont.)

		BNP		The Economist		Consensus
		83.II–94.IV	83.II–89.I	81.II–89.I	83.II–89.I	89.11–94.12
w_{4h}				0.98	0.04	−0.33
				(3.5)	(0.15)	(−2)
b_{4h}				−0.9	−0.39	−0.03
				(−2.7)	(−1.4)	(0.2)
q_{4h}				0.04	−0.4	0.07
				(0.35)	(−3)	(2.4)
R^2a				0.13	0.19	0.32
Test on 3–6:a	(χ^2_1)	0.1	0.02	2.5	1.4	
w	(χ^2_1)	3.6[b]	1.7	21[a]	6.2[a]	
b	(χ^2_1)	4.3[a]	0.9	21[a]	23.4[a]	
q	(χ^2_1)	6.9[a]	2.3	0.007	0.0	
Test on 6–12 or 3–12:a	(χ^2_1)			12.4[a]	3.7[b]	2.1
w	(χ^2_1)			1.4	1.9	1.6
b	(χ^2_1)			1.4	0.5	1.8
q	(χ^2_1)			1.3	0.05	6.1[a]

Notes:
[a] Rejection of consistency restrictions at 5%.
[b] Rejection of consistency restrictions at 10%.
In brackets: t statistic.

NOTES

1. The tests presented in this paper are based on three different surveys.
2. For a survey of this literature, see Takagi (1991) and Bénassy and Raymond (1997).
3. Whatever the currencies considered, surveyed expectations are close to the last observation. However, the expectations do not perfectly fit the naive model (based on the random walk), although they do not beat the random walk (Bénassy and Raymond, 1996).
4. Allen and Taylor (1989) show that speculators tend to be chartists for short-run horizons but fundamentalists in the long-run.
5. See Bénassy and Raymond (1997).
6. Only the DM/FF forecasts from *The Economist* survey appear destabilizing in the sense of an overreaction to the current exchange rate.
7. Our mixed model differs from the model used by Prat and Uctum (1996) on the definitions of the basic sub-models. They take the twelve-month forecast as the long-term equilibrium exchange rate (in the regressive component), whereas we keep reference to the PPP.
8. That is, expectations of large exchange rate fluctuations which do not happen over the period under study.

REFERENCES

Allen, H. and M. Taylor (1989), 'Charts, noise and fundamentals: a study of the London foreign exchange market', CEPR Discussion Paper no. 41, September and *Economic Journal*, 100 (Conference 1990), 49–59.

Bellando, R. (1991), 'Analyse et enjeux des anticipations de taux de change: une appréciation à partir de données d'enquêtes', thesis, Université d'Orléans.

Bénassy, A. and H. Raymond (1996), 'Les erreurs de prévision de change ont-elles des caractéristiques hétérogènes?', *Economie et prévision*, 125, 137–57.

Bénassy, A. and H. Raymond (1997), 'La formation des anticipations de change d'après les données d'enquêtes: un bilan de la littérature', *Revue d'économie politique*, 107(4), 421–56.

Frankel, J.A. and K. A. Froot (1986), 'The dollar as a speculative bubble: a tale of fundamentalists and chartists', Working Paper no. 1854, Cambridge, MA: National Bureau of Economic Research.

Frankel, J.A. and K.A. Froot (1987a), 'Using survey data to test standard propositions regarding exchange rate expectations', *American Economic Review*, 77(1), 133–153.

Frankel, J.A. and K.A. Froot (1987b), 'Short-term and long-term expectations of the yen/dollar exchange rate: evidence from survey data', *Journal of the Japanese and International Economies*, 1, 249–74.

Froot, K.A. and T. Ito (1989), 'On the consistency of short-run and long-run exchange rate expectations', *Journal of International Money and Finance*, 8(4), 487–510.

Greene, W.H. (1993), *Econometric Analysis*, London: Macmillan.

Ito, T. (1990), 'Foreign exchange rate expectations: micro survey data', *American Economic Review*, 80(3), 434–49.

McDonald, R. and I.W. Marsh (1995), 'Foreign exchange market forecasters are heterogeneous: confirmation and evidence', in *Communication au colloque sur la formation des anticipations économiques*, Paris, Sorbonne, 12 and 13 June.

Meese, R. and K. Rogoff (1983), 'Empirical exchange rate models in the seventies: do they fit out of sample?', *Journal of International Economics*, 14, 3–24.

Meiselman, D. (1962), *The Time Structure of Interest Rates*, Englewood Cliffs, NJ: Prentice-Hall.

Mincer, J. (1969), 'Models of adaptive forecasting', in J. Mincer (ed.), *Economic Forecast and Expectations: Analysis of Forecasting Behavior and Performance*, New York: Colombia University Press for NBER.

Pesaran, H. (1989), 'Consistency of short-term and long-term expectations', *Journal of International Money and Finance*, 8(4), 511–16.

Prat, G. and R. Uctum (1996), 'La formation des anticipations de change: l'hypothèse d'un processus mixte', *Economie et prévision*, 125, 117–36.

Takagi, S. (1991), 'Exchange rate expectations: a survey of survey studies', *IMF Staff Papers*, 33(1), 156–83.

11. The evidence of a mixed expectation generating process in the foreign exchange market

Georges Prat and Remzi Uctum

INTRODUCTION

Exchange rate dynamics are widely contingent upon how exchange rate expectations are formed, whether these expectations are right or wrong. Hence, to understand how exchange rates are determined, it is fundamental to identify which process generates their expectations. One way to sort out the unobservable feature of expectations is to use survey data.

In their survey papers on exchange rate expectations, Takagi (1991), Bénassy and Raymond (1997) and MacDonald (Chapter 9 of this book) show that regardless of the source of the survey data, the type of the data used (consensus versus microdata) and the horizon of expectations, three main lessons arise from the existing literature. First, expectations revealed by survey data do not conform to the rational expectation hypothesis. Second, it is difficult to posit a traditional expectational process which holds for all currencies; in all cases, the importance of the unexplained variance of the expected variable suggests that some important effects are missing in the model. Third, in most cases, these presumed missing effects seem not to be attributed to any kind of omitted macroeconomic variables.[1]

This failure in modelling how expectations are formed may be the result of two hypotheses implicitly admitted in the literature: (a) the same process prevails at any time of the sample period; and (b) this unique process is one of the five previously mentioned processes. This paper attempts to relax this last hypothesis. In fact, some studies using survey data have already dropped assumption (b) for different market prices. Examples of studies on inflationary expectations are Frankel (1976), Severn (1983), de Leeuw and McKelvey (1984) and Curtin (1981), who use respectively a regressive-adaptive process, an extrapolative-regressive process, an extrapolative-adaptive process and an extrapolative-regressive-adaptive process.[2] On

251

stock price expectations, the two studies relaxing assumption (b) are Prat (1994) and Abou and Prat (1997). An example on oil price expectations is provided by Prat and Uctum (1998). These three studies use three-mixed processes. Concerning price expectations in the foreign exchange market, examples are given by Frankel and Froot (1987) who use an adaptive-extrapolative two-mixed process with microdata from Amex surveys (London) and MMS surveys, and Prat and Uctum (1996) who use a three-mixed process with Consensus Forecasts' survey data. All these studies show that mixed processes generally improve our understanding of how expectations are formed with respect to basic processes.

Compared to Prat and Uctum (1996), this paper extends to six (from previously three) the number of currencies taken into account and tests the performance of a new specification of the mixed model (ERAMLI: Extrapolative, Regressive and Adaptive Model with Limited Information). We then examine the stability of the structural parameters of this model with respect to the considered currencies and with respect to the sample period.

Section 11.1 presents the basic processes and the ERAMLI, and section 11.2 provides empirical results on six currencies.

11.1   PRESENTATION OF THE PROCESSES

Generally speaking, a limited information model (LIM) is not compatible with the Muthian rational expectation hypothesis (REH) which involves an unrestricted set of (costless) information. Because the REH is drastically rejected by survey data, we focus here on the various types of LIM which also are grounded on some rationality. Indeed, because information and its treatment are costly, a LIM may represent an *economically* rational behaviour (Feige and Pearce, 1976): agents collect and use information until equality is reached between the marginal disutility of the cost of information and the marginal utility of this information with respect to the expected decrease in the forecast error. This cost-and-advantage approach leads individuals to use a limited set of information, which may be more or less narrow according to each individual.[3] All agents adopt the same rationality but each of them reaches her/his own optimal position.

In the class of LIMs, one can admit in a first approximation that the cost of information is time invariant and the same for all processes. We then can easily admit that a sufficient condition for an agent to maximise his or her utility function is to minimize his or her quadratic forecast error. This is an all the more important condition in the case of an expert since he is motivated to establish his credibility. Under these conditions, suppose that the spot rate is generated by an infinite series of random shocks. Then the adaptive expectational process is known to provide the minimal forecast error variance (Muth, 1960). Suppose now that the spot price is generated by an autoregressive representation with specific constraints on coefficients; then, the error variance is minimized when the forecast is formed using an extrapolative process (Baillie and McMahon, 1992, p. 93). A situation where the optimal process is regressive raises if the spot rate is characterized by a mean-reversion dynamics (Holden *et al.*, 1985, pp. 54–5). We can infer from this that if the spot price has a complex temporal structure based on two or three of these dynamic features, the optimal process in the sense of providing the minimum forecast error variance will be a two-mixed or a three-mixed LIM.

This paper considers the three traditional expectational processes which are the extrapolative process, the regressive process and the adaptive process. It shows that none of them provides a good representation of experts' expectations and explores the relevance of a weighted average of these processes (ERAMLI).

A crucial point to be introduced at this stage is that the choice of a process is based on the *perceived* dynamics and not on the 'true' dynamics. If these perceived dynamics differ according to agents, expectational processes will be characterized by a group-heterogeneity effect.[4] A straightforward consequence at the aggregate level is that the 'consensus' will be represented by a mixed expectational process, the weights depending on the size of each group. Any imperfect perception – due to costly information and cognitive inability – leads agents to choose a wrong expectational process. In this case, agents will interpret any systematic forecast error as a process selection error. This additional information impulses agents to reconsider their perceptions of the spot rate dynamics and therefore the expectational process. If these dynamics remained unchanged over time, then through a learning behaviour expectations would become equivalent to the Muthian rationality. But in the extent that there is no reason for these dynamics to remain unchanged over time, the LIMs are not likely to become rational in the Muthian sense. In any case, the latter will be also tested in our framework. We now present formally the specifications retained. These are the three traditional basic processes and the ERAMLI.

Let $S(t)$ and $\tilde{S}^a(t)$ be respectively the level of the spot exchange rate and its expected value for a given horizon at time t; then, $s(t)$ and $\tilde{s}^a(t)$ are the natural logarithms of $S(t)$ and $\tilde{S}^a(t)$. Let $\tilde{\dot{s}}^a(t) = \tilde{s}^a(t) - s(t)$ be the expected rate of change in the spot exchange rate, formed at time t for a given future horizon.

It may seem surprising that both the naive and the rational expectations hypotheses do not appear among the three basic processes taken into account. The naive process $\tilde{s}^a(t) = s(t) + \epsilon(t)$ is implicitly embodied in the above framework because the endogenous variable is not the expected level $\tilde{s}^a(t)$ but the expected *change* $\tilde{\mathfrak{s}}^a(t) = \tilde{s}^a(t) - s(t)$. This implies that the naive hypothesis is a particular case of the other processes (when all the structural parameters are null). Concerning the absence of the rational expectations hypothesis from our framework, this is not an *a priori* hypothesis but a result based on past empirical outcomes. Previous calculations have indeed shown that the addition of the rational process[5] to any other basic expectational process or to the ERAMLI is statistically insignificant.[6]

A general feature that should be underlined is that survey data only provide a proxy of the true expected value $\tilde{S}^a(t)$. Let $S^a(t)$ denote the consensus (arithmetic average of answers) which stems from the survey (see sub-section 11.2.1). The expected change provided by survey data is then $\tilde{\mathfrak{s}}^a(t) = S^a(t) - S(t)$. We admit that replacing $\tilde{S}^a(t)$ by $S^a(t)$ generates a measurement error which consists of a systematic bias a_k and a white noise $\eta_k(t)$, both being conditional on the prevailing process k.[7] We can formulate this assumption as follows:

$$\tilde{S}^a(t) = S^a(t) \exp[a_k + \eta_k(t)]$$

or $\tilde{s}^a(t) = s^a(t) + a_k + \eta_k(t)$ in logarithmic form. This assumption leads to the introduction of an intercept in each process.[8]

11.1.1 Extrapolative Process

According to this very classical process, the expected value of $S(t)$ depends on the rate of change observed during the n last months:[9]

$$\tilde{\mathfrak{s}}^a(t) = \gamma(s(t) - s(t-3)) + \alpha_1 + \epsilon_1(t) \tag{11.1}$$

where $\epsilon_1(t)$ is the empirical error term, which is a white noise if and only if all agents use this process effectively. Although the theoretical sign of the parameter γ is more likely to be positive, a negative value is conceivable in so far as it can reflect a naive regressive process (sytematic turning tendency). The intercept α_1 stands for the systematic measurement bias, while $\epsilon_1(t)$ captures both the measurement white noise $\eta_1(t)$ and the standard error term of the process.[10]

11.1.2 Adaptive Process

The retained process is formulated as follows:

$$\tilde{\mathfrak{s}}^a(t) = (1-\beta)(s^a(t-1) - s(t)) + \alpha_2 + \epsilon_2(t) \tag{11.2}$$

where $0 \leq \beta \leq 1$ and $\epsilon_2(t)$ is the empirical error term. As in the extrapolative process, $\epsilon_2(t)$ captures both the stochastic component of the measurement error in expectations $s^a(t)$ and $s^a_{(t-1)}$ and the error associated to the theoretical model. The constant term α_2 stands for the measurement bias.

It is worth noting that when the time span of the future horizon of $\tilde{s}^a(t)$ equals one month, and when we consider monthly observations, equation (11.2) becomes the true traditional adaptive model. But when the horizon equals three months with monthly observations (as is the case with our data), equation (11.2) is the expression of the adaptive model *under the assumption of an early reappraisal of expectations*. It is possible in fact, even *very likely* indeed, that individuals will not wait until the three-month horizon is accomplished to reappraise their expectations. When, during the survey procedure, the spot rate at the beginning of the month is known, individuals will probably compare this last one to the exchange rate which they had expected during the last survey, that is, a month before, and not three months previously (as the true adaptive model says).[11] This hypothesis leads to much better results than the hypothesis of a 'pure' adaptive process.

11.1.3 Regressive Process

Let $\tilde{s}(t)$ represent the logarithm of the exchange rate value which is considered as being 'normal' (that is, the 'target'). The retained regressive process is a simple error correction model:[12]

$$\tilde{s}^a(t) = \mu_1(\tilde{s}(t-1) - s^a(t-1)) + \mu_2(\tilde{s}(t) - \tilde{s}(t-1))$$
$$+ s^a(t-1) - s(t)) + \alpha_3 + \epsilon_3(t) \tag{11.3}$$

where $0 \leq \mu_i \leq 1$ $(i = 1,2)$ and $\epsilon_3(t)$ is the empirical error term capturing both the stochastic component of the measurement errors (resulting from $s^a(t)$, $s^a(t-1)$ and $\tilde{s}(t)$) and the error associated with the model. The intercept α_3 may capture biases in the measurement of expectations and the target.[13] On the other hand, and contrary to the standard formulations, there is no reason to consider here that the adaptive process (11.2) is a particular case of the error correction model (11.3).[14]

11.1.4 Extrapolative-regressive-adaptive Mixed Process

Weighting equations (11.1), (11.3) and (11.2), we get the ERAMLI:

$$\tilde{s}^a(t) = d_1\gamma(s(t) - s(t-3)) + d_2\mu_1(\tilde{s}(t-1) - s^a(t-1))$$

$$+ d_2\mu_2(\bar{s}(t) - \bar{s}(t-1)) + [d_2 + d_3(1-\beta)](s^a(t-1) - s(t)) \quad (11.4)$$
$$+ [d_1\alpha_1 + d_2\alpha_3 + d_3\alpha_2] + \epsilon_4(t)$$

with $0 < d_i < 1$, $i = 1,2,3$ and $d_1 + d_2 + d_3 = 1$ and where $\epsilon_4(t)$ is the empirical error term.

As we have noted above, each of the three basic processes systematically calls for an intercept which may capture a measurement bias. In fact, many experiments have shown that suppressing these constants is an exorbitant constraint. For the ERAMLI, the constant term derives from the weighted average of the three basic processes, and thus this composite constant may be significantly different from zero even though the above intercepts are not null. On the other hand, all processes are of order 1 because we found that orders greater than 1 are not empirically significant. However, as mentioned above, the optimal lag embedded in the extrapolative process appears to be three months.[15]

11.2   EVIDENCE OF MIXED EXPECTATIONS

11.2.1   Data from Consensus Forecasts Surveys

At the beginning of each month, Consensus Forecasts (CF) asks about 180 economy and capital market specialists in about 30 countries to estimate future values of a great number of variables, such as the production growth rate, inflation rate, unemployment rate, wage rates, new housing starts, company profits, interest rates and so on, and *exchange rates*. As this survey started in 1989, we now have at our disposal a sufficient amount of data to run reliable econometric tests.

The exchange rates represent different domestic prices of the US dollar. In the last days of each month, CF sends a questionnaire by fax to each of the bodies (scattered throughout the world) who have agreed to participate in this survey, in which they (usually their representatives) are asked their opinions concerning, among other things, the future *numerical* value[16] of exchange rates for *three- and twelve-month horizons*. CF requires a very specific day for the answers (by fax): that is, at the beginning of the following month. This day is as a rule the same for all respondents.[17] Finally, given that the questions concern the *expected levels* of exchange rates, the *expected change rates* can only be determined with respect to the last spot rate which is assumed to be known by the individuals on the day of the answer (reference rate). It is clear, therefore, that any mistake in the choice of the reference rate date implies a mistake in the measurement of the expected change; but because the spot rate values considered in this paper are dated from the day required by CF for their answers, the concentration of the answers on the same day implies that we can retain the same spot rate for all respondents.

Every month the CF newsletter publishes, for each of the two horizons, the simple arithmetic averages of the individual expected values of exchange rates[18] (*consensus* values). These *consensus* values will be used in this paper. From now on, $S(t)$ stands for the observed foreign exchange rate (FF/\$, DM/\$, yen/\$, £/\$, ITL/£, NG/\$) on the day t of the answers and $S^a(t)$ represents the expected value of $S(t)$ at time t for $t + 3$ months. In equation (11.4), the observed rate of change over the three previous months, the expected rate of change $\mathfrak{s}^a(t)$ for the three following months, the adaptive component and the second component of the regressive processes are expressed in per cent per quarter.

11.2.2 Evidence of the Complementarity of the Three Processes

The assumption we are testing for is that the exchange rate expectations are not generated by only one of the three simple processes, but by a *weighted average of these three processes* (ERAMLI). In order to run the calculations, we need an hypothesis about the 'normal' value of the exchange rate; we suppose that the 'normal' value is given by the long-term expectation, that is:

$$\bar{s}(t) = s^a_{LT}(t) \qquad (11.5)$$

where $s^a_{LT}(t)$ represents the twelve-months-ahead expected exchange rate provided by the survey data.[19]

Since we are not looking for the weighting coefficient values of the three processes, we write the ERAMLI (11.4) in the following form that we estimate by OLS:

$$\mathfrak{s}^a(t) = K_1.\text{EXT}(t) + K_2.\text{REG1}(t) + K_3.\text{REG2}(t)$$
$$+ K_u.\text{ADA}(t) + K_0 + \epsilon_4(t) \qquad (11.6)$$

where (all variables are expressed on a quarterly basis):

$\mathfrak{s}^a(t) = s^a(t) - s(t)$
$\text{EXT}(t) = s(t) - s(t-3);$ \hspace{2cm} $K_1 = d_2\gamma$
$\text{REG1}(t) = s^a_{LT}(t-1) - s^a(t-1)$ \hspace{1cm} $K_2 = d_2\mu_1$
$\text{REG2}(t) = 3[s^a_{LT}(t) - s^a_{LT}(t-1)];$ \hspace{1cm} $K_3 = d_2\mu_2$

$$\text{ADA}(t) = \tfrac{3}{2}[s^a(t-1) - s(t)]; \qquad\qquad K_u = d_2 + (1 - d_1 - d_2)(1 - \beta)$$

$$K_0 = d_1\alpha_1 + d_2\alpha_3 + (1 - d_1 - d_2)\alpha_2$$

Table 11.1 gives estimations of the basic processes and of the ERAMLI. Stationary (ADF) test and Ljung–Box serial correlation test have been applied to the residuals of each of the three basic processes and of the ERAMLI (see the two last columns of Table 11.1).[20] When the intercept was not significantly different from zero, it has been dropped in the course of the final estimation. These results call for the following comments.

For the six currencies, $s^a(t)$ and the *extrapolative process*[21] did not appear to be cointegrated. This process is thus to be rejected regarding this test. On the other hand, we found cointegration between $s^a(t)$ and the *adaptive process*, which is a necessary condition to accept the process. Nevertheless, the Ljung–Box test shows (except for the £/$ exchange rate) that the residuals are autocorrelated, which suggests that some factors are omitted.

We estimated the *regressive process* by regressing $s^a(t)$ on its three components $\text{REG1}(t)$, $\text{REG2}(t)$ and $\text{ADA}(t)$. As required by equation (11.3), if this basic process is relevant by itself, we then must find that the coefficient of $\text{ADA}(t)$ is not significantly different from 1. Because this condition is rejected (for the six currencies, the coefficient is near 0.5), we conclude that a *regressive-adaptive* two-mixed process holds. But for two currencies (FF/$ and DM/$) there is autocorrelation of residuals, which again suggests that some factors have been omitted in the regression.

In the case of four currencies (FF/$, DM/$, yen/$ and ITL/$), the *extrapolative-adaptive* two-mixed process either presents time-dependent residuals or is not cointegrated. Hence, this process does not provide a general representation of expectations for all the currencies.

As a result, the ERAMLI appears to be the *only* process which represents a cointegrated vector with no serial correlation in residuals,[22] for each of the six currencies. All the estimated parameter values have the expected signs and are significant at the 5 per cent significance level,[23] and this result shows the complementarity of the three processes.[24] It should be noticed that the ERAMLI involves on both sides not only the spot exchange rate at time t but also an expectational variable (that is, the three-month expected exchange rate on the left-hand side and the twelve-month expected exchange rate on the right-hand side); this raises the question of whether or not there exists some structural necessity behind the ERAMLI. Deriving from the ERAMLI an equivalent equation, we show in the Appendix that empirical results in Table 11.1 are not due to such a necessity. Finally, it is worth noting that there is no way to identify econometrically between the

Table 11.1:   *Exchange rate expectations for the six currencies: estimates*[a] *of the parameters*

EXT	REG1	REG2	ADA	Intercept[d]	$\bar{R}^2$ (SE)	Residuals: ADF[b]	Residuals: Ljung–Box Prob.[c]
FF/\$ (1990.02 to 1997.06) (N = 89)							
−0.120				1.33	0.146	UR2	0.00%
(4.0)				(7.5)	(1.66)	5%	
			0.262	0.82	0.590	NUR0	0.02%
			(11.4)	(6.3)	(1.14)	1%	
0.100			0.341	0.67	0.643	NUR0	1.73%
(3.6)			(11.0)	(5.2)	(1.07)	1%	
	0.090	0.285	0.486	0.21	0.850	NUR1	2.71%
	(2.8)	(11.2)	(19.8)	(2.0)	(0.69)	5%	
0.051	0.134	0.269	0.515		0.857	NUR0	12.22%
(2.8)	(5.2)	(9.8)	(22.1)		(0.68)	1%	
DM/\$ (1990.02 to 1997.06) (N = 89)							
−0.111				1.24	0.133	UR2	0.00%
(3.8)				(7.0)	(1.68)	5%	
			0.236	0.769	0.506	NUR2	0.06%
			(9.7)	(5.5)	(1.26)	10%	
0.083			0.308	0.70	0.573	NUR0	1.25%
(2.9)			(9.5)	(5.0)	(1.18)	1%	
	0.122	0.308	0.508		0.847	NUR1	2.53%
	(4.7)	(12.6)	(20.3)		(0.71)	5%	
0.037	0.126	0.287	0.519		0.854	NUR0	4.09%
(2.1)	(4.9)	(11.0)	(20.7)		(0.69)	1%	
Yen/\$ (1990.02 to 1997.06) (N = 89)							
−0.159				0.37	0.224	UR1	0.00%
(5.1)				(1.8)	(1.85)	5%	
			0.281	0.13	0.671	NUR1	0.00%
			(13.6)	(1.0)	(1.23)	10%	
0.111			0.365		0.721	UR3	14.29%
(3.9)			(12.8)		(1.11)	5%	
	0.098	0.318	0.542		0.893	NUR1	42.53%
	(3.9)	(12.0)	(21.1)		(0.68)	1%	
0.058	0.114	0.287	0.559		0.904	NUR0	45.96%
(3.2)	(4.7)	(10.7)	(22.4)		(0.65)	1%	

Table 11.1: (cont.)

EXT	REG1	REG2	ADA	Intercept[d]	$\bar{R}^2$ (SE)	Residuals: ADF[b]	Ljung–Box Prob.[c]
£/\$ (1990.02 to 1997.06) (N = 89)							
−0.049				1.13	0.039	UR2	5.33%
(2.1)				(7.7)	(1.35)	5%	
			0.159	0.86	0.345	NUR2	7.14%
			(6.7)	(6.8)	(1.11)	10%	
0.078			0.226		0.405	NUR0	23.60%
(3.1)			(7.2)		(1.06)	5%	
	0.111	0.280	0.498		0.763	NUR0	14.69%
	(3.5)	(11.9)	(17.4)		(0.66)	1%	
0.039	0.115	0.264	0.513		0.790	NUR0	45.96%
(2.6)	(3.8)	(11.3)	(19.0)		(0.62)	1%	
ITL/\$ (1990.02 to 1997.06) (N = 89)							
−0.102				1.43	0.132	UR2	0.02%
(3.7)				(7.7)	(1.69)	5%	
			0.219	1.01	0.536	NUR0	0.02%
			(9.9)	(7.3)	(1.23)	1%	
0.071			0.272	0.857	0.566	NUR0	0.17%
(2.6)			(9.2)	(5.9)	(1.19)	5%	
	0.022	0.270	0.490	0.30	0.803	NUR0	2.82%
	(0.5)	(10.4)	(17.0)	(2.3)	(0.80)	1%	
0.049	0.087	0.255	0.523		0.806	NUR0	6.33%
(2.8)	(2.8)	(10.5)	(20.5)		(0.79)	1%	
NG/\$ (1990.02 to 1997.06) (N = 89)							
−0.167				1.70	0.139	UR0	0.01%
(3.8)				(6.4)	(2.45)	5%	
			0.311	0.90	0.520	NUR0	17.91%
			(9.6)	(4.2)	(1.83)	1%	
0.101			0.381		0.542	NUR0	91.78%
(2.2)			(8.6)		(1.79)	1%	
	0.185	0.301	0.499		0.792	NUR0	75.05%
	(4.7)	(9.2)	(17.1)		(1.21)	1%	
0.053	0.180	0.284	0.522		0.798	NUR0	60.62%
(1.9)	(4.7)	(8.5)	(16.6)		(1.18)	1%	

Notes:

[a] The numbers in parentheses are the Student's t values.

[b] ADF: Augmented Dickey–Fuller test with an intercept for basic processes and without intercept for ERAMLI. NURn or URn means No Unit Root or Unit Root for the residuals (with n lags). Percentages indicate the level of significance.

[c] Ljung–Box Prob.: if prob > 5%, the null stating that the residuals are independent is accepted. The Ljung–Box test takes into account one lag.

[d] α_1, α_3, α_2 (basic processes) or K_0 (ERAMLI).

extrapolative-regressive process and the ERAMLI, because they are both represented by the same regression equation. In the following, we will choose to call this process an ERAMLI.[25]

A last – but not least – question is to know to what extent the estimates of the ERAMLI depend on the currencies. One way to answer this question is to know whether or not there exists a given estimated model which is not significantly different from the estimated ERAMLI in the case of each currency, the goal being to put into evidence an invariance of the expectational behaviour on the foreign exchange market irrespective of the currency.[26] The most intuitive such model is the ERAMLI estimated by pooling the six currencies (each of them covering the period from June 1990 to June 1997). We then apply an F-test to compare the ERAMLI estimated for each of the six currencies with the ERAMLI estimated on pooled data (Table 11.2).

Table 11.2: Exchange rate expectations estimated on pooled data (FF/\$, DM/\$, yen/\$, £/\$, ITL/\$, NG/\$), 1990.06 to 1997.06 (N=6×85=510): estimates[a] of the parameters

EXT	REG1	REG2	ADA	Intercept[b]	$\bar{R}^2$ (SE)
−0.115				1.25	0.130
(8.8)				(15.4)	(1.84)
			0.300	0.79	0.528
			(23.9)	(12.5)	(1.35)
0.097			0.325	0.64	0.574
(7.5)			(23.0)	(10.2)	(1.29)
	0.104	0.288	0.502		0.826
	(6.9)	(26.2)	(43.7)		(0.82)
0.052	0.122	0.271	0.529		0.838
(6.4)	(9.2)	(24.7)	(48.4)		(0.79)

Notes:
[a] The numbers in parentheses are the Student's *t* values.
[b] α_1, α_3, α_2 (basic processes) or K_0 (ERAMLI).

The six calculated F-statistics are as follows:

$$F(FF/\$) = 0.095 \quad F(DM/\$) = 0.383 \quad F(YEN/\$) = 0.479$$

$$F(£/\$) = 0.366 \quad F(ITL/\$) = 1.268 \quad F(NG/\$) = 0.833$$

Because all the F values are much smaller than the critical value of F(4.81) at 5 per cent level of significance, that is, 2.48, we conclude that the null hypothesis asserting that the *same* ERAMLI prevails in the case of each of the six currencies is acceptable. As a result, the ERAMLI estimated on the pooled data sample (last line of Table 11.2) may be regarded as the relevant expectational process for any of the six rates of change considered.[27] Figure 11.1 shows that throughout the period from June 1990 to June 1997 and for each currency sample, the fitted values of the expected rate of change according to the reference ERAMLI remain close to the observed values. We observe that for each currency, the main fluctuations are well represented. Taking into account the autoregressive form of the ERAMLI, it is important to note the absence of any systematic lags between the fitted and observed values, which is the sign of a good specification of the ERAMLI.

The acceptance of the same ERAMLI regardless of the currency is in fact not a very surprising result for two reasons: (a) each rate of change is the amount of the domestic currency per US dollar; and (b) the same group of experts is questioned for all currencies. On the other hand, the psycho-sensorial character of the ERAMLI reinforces the fact that structural parameters may be invariant according to the currencies. It is interesting to note that this 'currency invariance' has a straightforward implication on the euro/\$ exchange rate: the ERAMLI obtained on pooled data is likely to represent also the expectational behaviour on the euro/\$.

Of course, these results do not allow us to say anything about whether or not the parameters of the ERAMLI are time-stable. To test time-stability, we implemented two kinds of tests: (a) a Chow-test for each currency, and (b) an F-test for the pooled sample.

The Chow-test is applied to two sub-samples of 44 and 45 observations respectively with October 1993 as the starting point of the second sub-sample. The ERAMLI for each currency is found to be stable at the 5 per cent level of significance only for the yen/\$ and DM/\$ exchange rates, that is, for one-third of the considered currencies.

The F-test is implemented to analyse the time-stability of the parameters of the (unique) ERAMLI estimated over the whole pooled sample. We reorganized the pooled sample by dividing each currency series into five sub-periods of $85/5 = 17$ observations and by stacking together the data from the six currencies for each sub-period. We then obtained a pooling of the overall data with five sub-samples of $6 \times 17 = 102$ observations each. We applied an F-test to compare the ERAMLI esimated over the five sub-samples and the ERAMLI estimated over the whole pooled sample. The five values obtained for F are given in the last column of Table 11.3: the time stability hypothesis is accepted only for the last sub-period February 1996–June 1997, but is rejected for the other four.

These two tests show that it seems difficult to admit that estimates of the ERAMLI are time-invariant although they are likely to be 'currency-invariant'. In fact, the time instability of the parameters of the ERAMLI may *a priori* have two non-exclusive meanings:

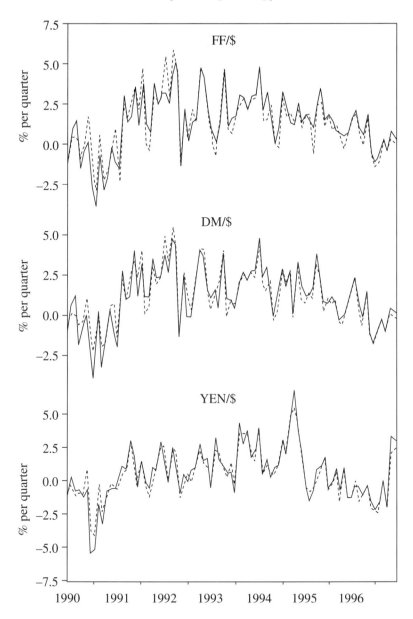

Note: All fitted values of this figure are given by the same ERAMLI (see Table 11.2, last line): $\hat{s}^q(t) = 0.052\ \text{EXT}(t) + 0.122\ \text{REG1}(t) + 0.27\ \text{REG2}\ (t) + 0.529\ \text{ADA}(t)$

Figure 11.1: Expected change of exchange rates: observed and fitted values according to the ERAMLI estimated on pooled data (June 1990–June 1997)

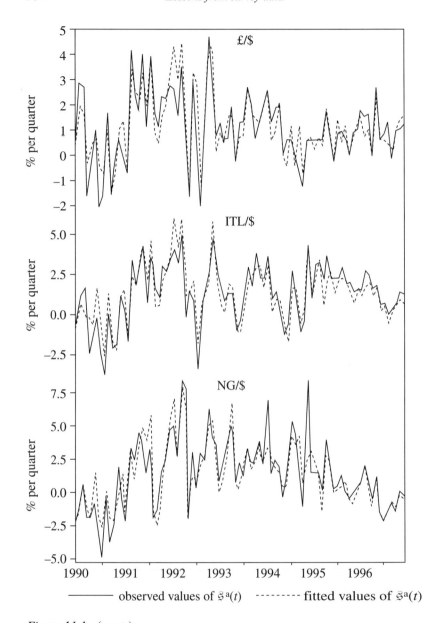

Figure 11.1: (cont.)

1. At any time, the consensus of expectations is formed by an ERAMLI[28] where the composite coefficients are intrinsically and continuously time-varying.
2. At every point in time, the chosen model (basic or mixed) changes over time while the parameters characterizing the relevant process(es) remain unchanged. For example, if in sub-period 1 the extrapolative process is chosen with a higher frequency than in sub-period 2, we would observe – as we do (Table 11.3) – that the OLS parameter

Table 11.3: Exchange rate expectations according to the ERAMLI estimated on pooled data: analysis of the time variability of the parameters (equation (11.6))[a]

EXT	REG1	REG2	ADA	$\bar{R}^2$ (SE)	F[b]
Sub-period 1: 1990.06 to 1991.10 (N=17×6=102)					
0.075	−0.025	0.311	0.582	0.809	5.58
(4.0)	(0.6)	(11.4)	(19.4)	(0.89)	
Sub-period 2: 1991.11 to 1993.03 (N=17×6=102)					
0.036	0.138	0.232	0.452	0.820	3.99
(2.7)	(6.4)	(12.0)	(20.9)	(0.84)	
Sub-period 3: 1993.04 to 1994.08 (N=17×6=102)					
0.025	0.240	0.220	0.470	0.843	6.18
(1.4)	(9.2)	(8.3)	(23.7)	(0.61)	
Sub-period 4: 1994.09 to 1996.01 (N=17×6=102)					
0.004	0.215	0.344	0.545	0.774	6.30
(0.2)	(6.7)	(12.4)	(18.5)	(0.80)	
Sub-period 5: 1996.02 to 1997.06 (N=17×6=102)					
0.078	0.102	0.261	0.554	0.846	1.13
(4.1)	(3.6)	(11.9)	(25.4)	(0.46)	
The whole period: 1990.06 to 1997.06 (N=85×6=510)					
0.052	0.122	0.271	0.529	0.838	
(6.4)	(9.2)	(24.7)	(48.4)	(0.79)	

Notes:
[a] The numbers in parentheses are the Student's *t* values.
[b] The critical value of F (4, 98) for $\alpha = 5\%$ is 2.46. If F is smaller than this critical value, the null hypothesis, stating that the parameters estimated over the sub-period are not significantly different from the parameters estimated over the whole period, is accepted for a 5% level of significance.

associated with this process is larger in the first sub-period than in the second sub-period. If the appearance frequency of this process is not high enough, we would observe that the coefficient of this process is poorly significant, as we indeed find in sub-period 4.

It is clear that any attempt to differentiate between these two hypotheses requires the implementation of specific and more sophisticated econometric methods.

11.3   CONCLUSION

There is an empirical complementarity among adaptive, regressive and extrapolative expectational processes in the foreign exchange market (we call this mixed model an ERAMLI). The empirical performance of such a mixed expectational model explains why expectations revealed by surveys do not confirm the rational expectations hypothesis and why the traditional simple models are not appropriate to describe their formation.

Moreover, this model prevails with the same set of parameters for the six currencies considered, but the estimates exhibit a slight time-instability. We intend to explore the causes of this time-instability in further work.

APPENDIX: ESTIMATING AN EQUIVALENT FORM OF THE ERAMLI

Expression (11.6) of the ERAMLI may be written as follows:

$$
\begin{aligned}
(3k'_3\, s^a_{\mathrm{LT}}(t) - s^a(t)) &= (\tfrac{3}{2} k'_4 - k'_1 - 1)\, s(t) + \mathrm{k}'_1\, s(t-3) \\
&+ (k'_2 - \tfrac{3}{2} k'_4)\, s^a(t-1) + (3k'_3 - k'_2)\, s^a_{\mathrm{LT}}(t-1) - k'_0 + \epsilon'_4(t)
\end{aligned}
\tag{11.6$'$}
$$

where theoretically $k'_i = k_i\ (i = 0, \ldots, 4)$.

In relation (11.6$'$) all expectational variables dated at time t are gathered on the left-hand side while actual and lagged spot variable and lagged expectational variables are gathered on the right-hand side. There is thus no possibility for equation (11.6$'$) to be necessarily validated because of common informations on both sides of the equation. By iterating the values of k'_3 over [0,1] and using pooled data ($N = 510$), the following optimal composite estimates are obtained (as in equation (11.6), the intercept was not significantly different from zero and therefore has been dropped in the course of the final estimation):

$$3 \times 0.27\, s^a_{LT}(t) - s^a(t) = -0.261\, s(t) + 0.0518\, s(t-3)$$
$$(29.0) \qquad (6.6)$$

$$-0.670\, s^a(t-1) + 0.688\, s^a_{LT}(t-1) + u(t)$$
$$(36.7) \qquad (58.1)$$

$$SE = 0.794\% \qquad \overline{R}^2 = 0.9998$$

For the optimal value $k'_3 = 0.27$, these estimates lead to $k'_1 = 0.052$, $k'_2 = 0.12$ and $k'_4 = 0.527$. Because these values remain very close to those obtained in Table 11.2 (that is, $k_1 = 0.052$, $k_2 = 0.122$, $k_3 = 0.271$ and $k_4 = 0.529$), we can conclude that the estimates obtained with the structural form of the ERAMLI cannot be attributed to any statistical necessity.

NOTES

1. As a typical example, the spreads between rates of inflation, rates of interest, change in money supplies and cumulative balance of payments may *a priori* appear as factors determining exchange rate expectations. Nevertheless, empirical studies have generally shown that these variables are poorly significant.
2. For a broader presentation of this literature, see Prat (1988, ch. 2).
3. Such a limit exists for an expert because the larger the information, the more complex and costly becomes the treatment of the information. The expert cannot collect information indefinitely to make his or her decision. This is confirmed by Gennotte and Leland (1990) who asked traders on NYSE market to provide the information their expectations are grounded on, and found that agents base their forecasts on observed stock prices rather than fundamentals. In a LIM applied to the foreign exchange market, expectations are explained only by actual and past values of the spot rate and of the expectations. But this does not necessarily mean that fundamentals are excluded from the set of information. This is because both the target embedded in the regressive process and the spot rate itself may explicitly convey the influence of macroeconomic variables.
4. An illustration of this group-heterogeneity effect is given by the methods used by traders to forecast financial market prices: the 'chartists' are supposed to adopt an extrapolative process while 'fundamentalists' are supposed to adopt a regressive process where the target may or may not include limited information (Frankel and Froot (1986, 1990)).
5. That is the rate of change which occurs during the time span corresponding to the horizon of expectation.
6. If the rational process was significant, this would mean that there exists a group of rational agents but not that agents mix rational and one, two or three of the basic processes based on limited information.
7. To understand the two components of the measurement error we recall the microfoundations of expectations. If an agent is not directly motivated by the outcome of his answer, his responses may convey errors between his true opinion and his effective answer. This is because he will not be motivated enough to get all the relevant information required for an unbiased answer. Of course, when an average of answers is considered, such errors still exist. Furthermore, because we model the expected *rate of change* $\tilde{s}^a(t) = s^a(t) - s(t)$

of the consensus, microfoundations of expectations are respected at the aggregate level only when the consensus $S^a(t)$ is calculated as a *geometric average*. Because the consensus published by Consensus Forecasts is an arithmetic average, this generates a systematic bias embedded in the intercept a_k. An additional interpretation of measurement errors lies classically in the size and the representativity of the sample.

8. In the long run, the exchange rate does not exhibit a significant drift (Figure 11.1 shows that the expected change in exchange rate varies around zero). It is thus not necessary to introduce a specific constant term in the processes to capture this drift.

9. It is possible to assume different coefficient values with n-order lagged extrapolative components:

$$\tilde{s}^a(t) = \gamma_0 + \sum_{i=1}^{n} \gamma_i [s(t-i+1) - s(t-i)] + \epsilon_1(t)$$

Preliminary tests showed that $n = 3$ and that $\gamma_1 = \gamma_2 = \gamma_3$. In this case equation (11.1) holds.

10. The extrapolative process ($k = 1$) should in fact be written as:

$$\tilde{s}^a(t) = \tilde{s}^a(t) - s(t) = \gamma(s(t) - s(t-3)) + \nu_1(t)$$

where $\nu_1(t)$ stands for the standard stochastic term. Introducing the error measurement assumption $\tilde{s}^a(t) = s^a(t) + a_1 + \eta_1(t)$ in the process leads us to find equation (11.1) where $\epsilon_1(t) = \nu_1(t) - \eta_1(t)$ and $\alpha_1 = -a_1$.

11. The true standard adaptive process for expectation $s^a(t)$ with three months time span horizon is (we neglect the error terms and the bias):

$$s^a(t) - s^a(t-3) = \beta'(s(t) - s^a(t-3)) \tag{11.i}$$

The assumption of an early reappraisal of expectations leads to the following relation:

$$s^a(t) - s^a(t-1) = \beta(s(t) - s^a(t-1)) \tag{11.ii}$$

Equation (11.2) is formally equivalent to (11.ii). A fully convincing argument supporting this assumption is grounded on the fact that (11.ii) defines $s^a(t)$ as a weighted average of past *monthly* values of $s(t)$ (the weights decreasing geometrically), while the true adaptive model (11.i) defines $s^a(t)$ as a weighted average of past *quarterly* values of $s(t)$: with our monthly observations, it appears that relation (11.ii) is more appropriate than relation (11.i)!

12. The standard equation of the simple error correction model contains two terms representing an adjustment of the expectation $s^a(t)$ towards its normal value $\bar{s}(t)$ (we neglect the error term and the bias):

$$s^a(t) - s^a(t-1) = \mu_1(\bar{s}(t-1) - s^a(t-1)) + \mu_2(\bar{s}(t) - \bar{s}(t-1))$$

Rearranging terms such that the endogenous variable becomes $\tilde{s}^a(t) = s^a(t) - s(t)$, we obtain equation (11.3).

13. Note that although the ECM (11.3) incorporates a more sophisticated dynamics than the traditional regressive process $\tilde{s}^a(t) = \mu(\bar{s}(t) - s(t))$, they both converge towards the same target $\bar{s}(t)$.

14. In relation (11.3), the expectation $s^a(t)$ converges towards its normal value $\bar{s}(t)$, while in the adaptive model (11.2), $s^a(t)$ converges towards the observed value $s(t)$.

15. See note 9.

16. Among the 12 surveys listed by Bénassy and Raymond (1997), only the survey conducted by the Godwins Institute (London) is based on questions which require a qualitative answer.

17. Historically, we notice that this day may be the 1st, the 2nd, the 3rd, the 4th or the 5th

of a month. The effective horizons, however, always remain strictly equal to three and twelve months. If, for instance, the answers are due on 3 May (which was the case in May 1993) the future values are asked for 3 August 1993 (three months ahead) and for 3 January 1994 (twelve months ahead). Besides, since *the individual answers are confidential* and the consensus is only disclosed to the public during the month following the survey month, it does not seem justified to object that, for reasons which are inherent to speculative games, individuals might not reveal their 'true' opinion.

18. Some experts may not provide a response for a given currency at a given time because they lack information about that currency at that time. Therefore the consensus is not biased either by noise traders or by any loss of information (all the informed agents do respond).

19. We recall that the intercept α_1 may capture a systematic bias when we replace $\bar{s}(t)$ by $s_{LT}^a(t)$. Another important question is to model $s_{LT}^a(t)$. First attempts where the 'normal' value in the regressive process is assumed to be a constant suggest that an ERAMLI still prevails.

20. The expected change of the exchange rate $\bar{s}^a(t)$ represents the observable endogenous variable for all purposes. Preliminary ADF tests have shown that $\bar{s}^a(t)$ is not a stationary variable. It is then all the more relevant to know if $\bar{s}^a(t)$ and a given process are cointegrated.

21. Note that the negative sign found for γ should be interpreted rather as a naive regressive process (where $\bar{s}(t) = s(t-3)$) than as an extrapolative process in the usual sense.

22. The three-month lagged extrapolative process with monthly data may involve serial correlation of residuals due to overlapping data. However, the Ljung–Box test has rejected the serial correlation hypothesis for the ERAMLI (this result holds for all currencies with one exception: for the DM/\$ currency, the threshold of acceptance of the null in the Ljung–Box test is lowered to 4 per cent instead of 5 per cent). In fact, this result is the one we would expect to find when agents refer effectively to a time span of three months in their extrapolative behaviour.

23. We must especially underline that the extrapolative element acts in the ERAMLI with a positive sign, contrary to what is generally obtained with the basic extrapolative process. This result is satisfactory since it conforms to the intuitive idea that the extrapolation should maintain the past direction of the market.

24. There is no problem of estimation resulting from colinearities between exogeneous variables. Indeed, following Johnston (1963), there is significant bias due to colinearity if (a) the R^2 of the regression of each exogenous variable on the others is greater than 0.90; and (b) these R^2 are greater than the R^2 of the structural model. For each of the six currencies, we found that these two conditions do not hold in the case of the ERAMLI.

25. In research in progress, where a 'change-in-process' framework is considered, we are able to identify between the two processes: our first outcomes show some predominance of the ERAMLI with respect to all other processes including the extrapolative-regressive one.

26. An alternative approach would consist in running an F-test for the $C_6^2 = 15$ combinations of two currencies. Nevertheless, this framework does not allow us to identify a unique reference model for all currencies.

27. Because both the unit root test and the serial correlation test involve lagged residuals, none of the ADF and Ljung–Box tests can be implemented on pooled data which involves time-discontinuities.

28. For instance, *each* agent may weigh in his own way the three processes (so that the consensus leads to average weights), or *some* agents may be systematically extrapolative while *others* are regressive and *others* adaptive (here, the weights reflect the percentage of extrapolative, regressive or adaptive agents). Of course, in each case agents may also combine processes. Only an analysis of disaggregated data could possibly sort out the interpretation of the composite coefficients of the ERAMLI.

REFERENCES

Abou, A. and G. Prat (1997), 'Formation des anticipations boursières: "consensus" versus opinions individuelles', *Journal de la Société de Statistique de Paris*, (2), 13–22.

Baillie, R. and P. MacMahon (1992), *The Foreign Exchange Market: Theory and Econometric Evidence*, Cambridge: Cambridge University Press.

Bénassy-Quéré, A. and H. Raymond (1997), 'Les anticipations de change d'après les données d'enquêtes: un bilan de la littérature', *Revue d'économie politique*, 107(4), 422–56.

Curtin, R.T. (1981), 'Determinant of price expectations: evidence from a panel study', Centre for International Research on Economic Tendency Surveys (CIRET) Conference, 30 September, Athens, Greece.

de Leeuw, F. and M.J. McKelvey (1984), 'Price expectations of business firms: bias in the short and long run', *American Economic Review*, 74(1), 99–110.

Feige, E.L. and D.K. Pearce (1976), 'Economically rational expectation: are innovations in the rate of inflation independent of innovations in measures of monetary and fiscal policy?', *Journal of Political Economy*, 84(3), 499–522.

Frankel, J.A. (1976), 'Inflationary expectations and some dynamic aspects of the welfare costs', in M. Parkin and G. Zis (eds), *Inflation in the World Economy*, Manchester: Manchester University Press.

Frankel, J.A. and K.A. Froot (1986), 'Understanding the US Dollar in the eighties: the expectations of chartists and fundamentalists', *Economic Record*, 62, Supplementary Issue, 24–38.

Frankel, J.A. and K.A. Froot (1987), 'Using survey data to test propositions regarding exchange rate expectations', *American Economic Review*, 77(1), 133–53.

Frankel, J.A. and K.A. Froot (1990), 'The rationality of the foreign exchange rate: chartists, fundamentalists, and trading in the foreign exchange market', *American Economic Association Papers and Proceedings*, 80(2), 181–85.

Gennotte, G. and H. Leland (1990), 'Market liquidity, hedging and crashes', *American Economic Review*, 80(5), 999–1021.

Holden, K., D.A. Peel and J.L. Thompson (1985), *Expectations: theory and evidence*, New York: St Martin's Press.

Johnston, J. (1963), *Econometric methods*, Tokyo: McGraw-Hill.

Muth, J.F. (1960), 'Optimal properties of exponentially weighted forecasts', *Journal of the American Statistical Association*, June, 299–306.

Prat, G. (1988), 'Analyse des anticipations d'inflation des ménages, France et Etats-Unis', Paris: Economica.

Prat, G. (1994), 'La formation des anticipations boursières', *Economie et prévision*, 112(1), 101–25.

Prat, G. and R. Uctum (1996), 'La formation des anticipations de change: l'hypothèse d'un processus mixte', *Economie et prévision*, 125, 117–35.

Prat, G. and R. Uctum (1998), 'How are oil price expectations formed? Evidence from survey data', in Colloque 'Dynamique des prix et des marchés de matières premières: analyse et prévision', 5–6 November, Grenoble, France.

Severn, A.K. (1983), 'Formation of inflation expectation in the UK', *European Economic Review*, 20, 349–63.

Takagi, S. (1991), 'Exchange rate expectations: a survey of survey studies, *IMF Staff Papers*, 38(1), 156–83.

12. Modelling stock price expectations: lessons from microdata

Alain Abou and Georges Prat

INTRODUCTION

According to the standard stock valuation model, the price of a stock (or a stock price index) can be written as follows:

$$P(t) = \frac{D(t) + (P^a(t) - P(t))}{i(t)}$$

with:

P: stock price;
D: dividend per share;
P^a: expected value of P;
i: discount rate.

This relation shows that when the expected change of stock price $(P^a(t) - P(t))$ increases, market price $P(t)$ also increases. In this case, for a given value of $i(t)$, if expectations are extrapolative (for example, $P^a(t) - P(t) = \gamma(P(t) - P(t-1))$, then $(P^a(t) - P(t))$ gets up again and so on, which shows that the expectational process has a *destabilizing effect* on stock prices. By contrast, if expectations are regressive (for example $P^a(t) - P(t) = \mu(PN(t) - P(t))$, with $PN(t) = $ 'normal' economic value), the expectational process represents a *stabilizing* strength pushing stock prices towards their 'normal' value. Of course, if expectations are based at the same time on the two previous processes, the whole effect may or may not be destabilizing, depending on the values of the strengths characterizing each of the two components. If expectations are naive (that is, $P^a(t) = P(t)$), the return equals the dividend yield $(D(t)/P(t) = i(t)$, so that $P(t) = D(t)/i(t))$. If expectations are rational (that is, $(P^a(t) - P(t)) = (P(t+1) - P(t)) + \epsilon(t))$, then $[(P(t+1) - P(t))/P(t)] + D(t)/P(t) = i(t) + \epsilon(t)/P(t)$, which shows that, when the deviation of the discount rate from its mean value (i_0) is supposed to be a white noise (that is, $i(t) = i_0 + \varphi(t)$), the stock return follows a motion close to a random walk.

Hence, whatever their nature may be, *expectations govern the actual stock market prices*, so that identifying the process which generates them is crucial. Using survey data to measure stock price expectations, this paper aims to shed some light on the question of the underlying generation process. In his pioneer work published in the first issue of the review *Econometrica* (1932), Alfred Cowles showed that experts' stock price expectations are not more performant than a heads or tails game! After a long span of time characterized by a lack of studies on this field, numerous authors have (since the 1980s) explored the expectational processes for financial asset prices and especially for stock prices.[1]

Two main lessons arise from this literature, whatever the survey data, the level of aggregation (consensus versus microdata), and the horizon of forecasts are. First, the rational expectation hypothesis is strongly rejected. Second, it is difficult to bring to the fore a traditional expectational process which is reliable among the class of limited information models,[2] such as extrapolative, regressive or adaptive processes; in any case, the magnitude of the unexplained variance leads to the conclusion that significant exogenous variables are missing.[3]

Using stock price expectations from the Livingston's panel, we confirmed previously the drastic rejection of the Rational Expectation Hypothesis (REH), this result prevailing whatever the level of aggregation is.[4] Moreover, we also found that none of the traditional extrapolative, regressive and adaptive processes can explain in a valuable manner how stock price forecasts are formed. In this paper, we aim to single out that a *weighted average of these three basic processes* (the so-called ERAMLI: Extrapolative, Regressive and Adaptive Model with Limited Information) gives a valuable representation for these expectations. The economic intuition which is behind the ERAMLI is described by Prat and Uctum in Chapter 11 of this book (pp. 252–3): because information and its treatment are costly, an ERAMLI *may* represent *economically* rational behaviour (Feige and Pearce, 1976).

Section 12.1 presents the data and the specification of the ERAMLI. Section 12.2 reports econometrical results.

12.1   THE DATA AND THE MODEL

12.1.1   Data from Livingston surveys

The expected values of the Standard and Poor's (S&P) 400 industrial stock prices index are given by surveys managed by J. Livingston since 1952. Each

June and December, between 40 and 70 experts (business men, bankers, academics and so on) give their opinion about the future S&P six and twelve months ahead.[5] Denote:

$P(t)$ actual S&P stock price index at month t (average of daily prices for month t); $p(t) = \ln P(t)$;

$^iP^a(t)$ S&P index expected at time t by agent i for time $t+6$ months; $^ip^a(t) = \ln {}^iP^a(t)$;

$^i\bar{P}^a(t)$ S&P index expected at time t by agent i for time $t+12$ months; $^i\bar{p}^a(t) = \ln {}^i\bar{P}^a(t)$;

t date of the survey (June and December);

$\ln$ natural logarithm.

The *rate of change* in S&P expected by expert i for six months ahead equals the ratio of the expected level of S&P to the base index (that is, the index observed at the time of his or her answer). But an individual's base indexes are not directly available because we do not know the day the response is given. Indeed, because questions are asked during the month preceding the month (t) of the survey, it is probable that answers from some experts are dated before (t) or just at the beginning of (t), even if they are sent during month (t). In order to minimize measurement bias for expected rates of change, we considered, for each expert, the base index $^i\bar{P}(t)$ corresponding to a geometric average of the price indexes observed during (t) and $(t-1)$:

$$^i\bar{P}(t) = P^{(1-\alpha i)}{}_{(t)} . P^{\alpha i}(t-1) \text{ with } 0 \le \alpha^i \le 1 \tag{12.1}$$

or:

$$^i\bar{p}(t) = p(t) - \alpha^i . (p(t) - p(t-1)) \tag{12.2}$$

This assumption shows that, like the expected index, the base index is specific to expert i. Equation (12.2) implies that the implicit dating of the base is between 15 May and 15 June (for the June survey) or between 15 November and 15 December (for the December survey). The rate of change in S&P expected by expert i at time t for six months ahead is then given by:

$$^ip^a(t) = {}^ip^a(t) - {}^i\bar{p}^a(t) \tag{12.3}$$

Over the period 1952.12–1989.06 (35 years), the full sample reports the answers of 162 experts, that is, 2108 microdata.[6] It is worth emphasizing that the rate of filling up of the whole $[i \times t]$ matrix is 17 per cent, so it seems rather difficult to apply panel data econometrics which would allow us to treat simultaneously the time and agent dimensions.[7]

12.1.2 The Model

This chapter aims to modelize stock price expectations at the *six-month horizon*. Prat (1994) considered a specification of the ERAMLI for the twelve-month horizon. We subsequently wished to link six-month to twelve-month expectations, and this has led us to a new formulation of the ERAMLI which has also been successfully applied to the foreign exchange market (see Chapter 11).

The basic expectational processes are assumed to be the three traditional extrapolative, regressive and adaptive ones. The omission of both the naive and the rational expectations hypotheses from the basic processes taken into account may be surprising. Concerning the naive process, according to which we have $^ip^a(t) = p(t) + \epsilon^i(t)$, it is in fact implicitly present in the above framework because the endogenous variable is not the expected log-level $^ip^a(t)$ but the expected change $^i\mathfrak{p}^a(t) = {^ip^a(t)} - p(t)$. As a result, this implies that the naive hypothesis is a restriction of the other processes (when all the structural parameters are null). Concerning the rational expectations hypothesis, this is not an *a priori* hypothesis but a lesson from our empirical results. Indeed, first calculations have shown that the adjunction of the rational process[8] to any other basic one, or to the ERAMLI, is not statistically significant. Hence, as a result, we considered the rational expectation hypothesis to be outside our framework.

Extrapolative process
According to this very classical process, the expected value of P depends on the rate of change observed during the previous survey, that is, during the previous six months:

$$^i\text{EXT}(t): \quad ^i\mathfrak{p}^a(t) = \gamma^i.(^i\bar{p}(t) - p(t-6)) + \gamma_0^i + {^i\epsilon^E}(t) \qquad (12.4)$$
$$0 \leq \gamma^i \leq 1$$

If this process is empirically relevant, $^i\epsilon^E(t)$ is a white noise. Although the expected sign of the parameter γ^i is probably positive, a negative value remains admissible in so far as it can reflect a naive regressive process (systematic reversal tendency). The component $\gamma^i(^i\bar{p}(t) - p(t-6))$ refers to the short term while the intercept γ_0^i captures the long-run extrapolative component of $p(t)$.[9]

Regressive process

Let $^ip^n(t)$ represent the logarithm of the value of stocks which is considered to be 'normal'; in order fully to specify the regressive model, we need an hypothesis about the 'normal' value of the stock price. From a theoretical point of view, this 'normal' value may represent some *fundamental level* of stock price or, more simply, some long-term expectation $^i\bar{p}^a(t)$ which appears to be a 'target' for the short-term expectation. In this paper, we assume that:

$$^ip^n(t) = {}^i\bar{p}^a(t) + k_0^i \qquad (12.5)$$

where $^i\bar{p}^a(t)$ represents the twelve months ahead (log) expected stock price provided by the expert i[10] and k_0^i a constant measuring a systematic additive bias (positive or negative) implied by the approximation of the 'normal' value by the long-term expectation.[11]

The specification if a simple Error Correction Model (ECM):[12]

$$^iREG(t): \quad {}^i\mathfrak{p}^a(t) = \mu_1^i({}^i\bar{p}^a(t-6) - {}^ip^a(t-6)) + \mu_2^i({}^i\bar{p}^a(t) - {}^i\bar{p}^a(t-6))$$
$$+ ({}^ip^a(t-6) - {}^i\bar{p}^a(t)) + \mu_0^i + {}^i\epsilon^R(t) \qquad (12.6)$$

$0 \le \mu_1^i; \mu_2^i \le 1; \mu_0^i = \mu_1^i.k_0^i + \gamma_0^i$

As for the extrapolative process, the parameter μ_0^i may be negative or positive because it may capture both a systematic bias in the target ($\mu_1^i.k_0^i$) and the long-term trend component γ_0^i of the rate of change in the target.[13] Under particular conditions, the traditional regressive process[14] appears as a polar case of (12.6).

Adaptive process

This process is formulated as follows:

$$^iADA(t): \quad {}^i\mathfrak{p}^a(t) = (1 - \beta^i).({}^ip^a(t-6) - {}^i\bar{p}(t)) + \beta_0^i + {}^i\epsilon^A(t) \qquad (12.7)$$

$0 \le \beta_0^i \le 1$

The constant term β_0^i captures the long-term *trend* in stock price expectations.[15] Contrary to the general case, here the adaptive process (12.7) does not have to be considered as a particular case of the ECM (12.6), so these two processes are not redundant.[16]

Extrapolative-regressive-adaptive mixed process

Weighting equations (12.4), (12.6) and (12.7), we get the so-called ERAMLI according to which the expected rate of change in stock prices is a weighted average of the three basic processes:[17]

$$^ip^a(t) = a^i.^iEXT(t) + b^i.^iREG(t) + c^i.^iADA(t) \qquad (12.8)$$

with $a^i + b^i + c^i = 1$ and $a^i \geq 0$; $b^i \geq 0$; $c^i \geq 0$.

Relations (12.2)–(12.8) allow us to deduce the following reduced testable specification of the ERAMLI:[18]

$$^ip^{a'}(t) = A^iEXT'(t) + B1^i.^iREG1(t) + B2^i.^iREG2(t) + C^i.^iADA'(t)$$
$$>0 \qquad\qquad >0 \qquad\qquad\quad >0 \qquad\qquad\quad >0$$

$$+ D^i.BASE(t) + CTE^i + \epsilon^i(t) \qquad (12.9)$$
$$<0 \qquad\qquad ?$$

with:

$^ip^{a'}(t)$	$= {}^ip^a(t) - p(t)$
$(A^i)\ EXT'(t)$	$= (a^i.\gamma^i)(p(t) - p(t-6))$
$(B1^i)\ ^iREG1(t)$	$= (b^i.\mu_0^i)(^i\bar{p}^a(t-6) - {}^ip^a(t-6))$
$(B2^i)\ ^iREG2(t)$	$= (b^i.\mu_2^i)(^i\bar{p}^a(t) - {}^i\bar{p}^a(t-6))$
$(C^i)\ ^iADA'(t)$	$= (b^i + c^i(1 - \beta^i))(^ip^a(t-6) - p(t))$
$(D^i)\ BASE(t)$	$= -(\alpha^i(1 + b^i + c^i + a^i.\gamma^i - c^i.\beta^i)(p(t) - p(t-1))$
CTE^i	$= a^i.\gamma_0^i + b^i.\mu_0^i + c^i.\beta_0^i$
$\epsilon^i(t)$	$= a^i.^i\epsilon^E(t) + b^i.^i\epsilon^R(t) + c^i.^i\epsilon^A(t)$

Six marks may be stressed:

1. The composite parameters A^i, $B1^i$, $B2^i$ and C^i are expressed as a combination of structural parameters characterizing the processes and their weights. Because the expected signs of the structural parameters are known, we can see that the expected signs of the composite parameters are all positive. Concerning the coefficient D^i, its expected sign is negative because we have $\alpha^i > 0$ and $(1 + b^i + c^i + a^i.\gamma^i) > c^i.\beta^i$. Finally, the expected sign of the intercept CTE^i remains unknown because k_0^i may take a negative or positive value, although the other components of CTE^i are supposed to be positive (the trend of S&P is increasing).
2. All components are first-order processes because greater orders have been found not to be significant.[19]
3. The three basic processes systematically call for a constant term which can capture long-run deterministic behaviour and a systematic measurement error in determining the 'normal' value in the regressive process, or individual characteristics as a structural degree of optimism.
4. The ERAMLI is a general specification embedding the three tradi-

tional basic processes. Because this allows us to test the significance of each component separately, it seems unnecessary to test the basic processes themselves.

5. The ERAMLI involves on both sides of the equation not only the stock price at time t but also, in an implicit manner, the six-month expected index;[20] this raises the question of whether or not there exists some structural necessity for the ERAMLI to be validated.[21] Deriving from the ERAMLI an equivalent equation, we show in Appendix A that the empirical results presented in Table 12.1 are not implied by such necessities.

6. According to equation (12.9), the endogeneous variable $^ip^{a'}(t) = {^ip^a(t)}$ $- p(t)$ contains the observed log-price $p(t)$, constraining the coefficient of this variable to equal unity. To know if this constraint is acceptable, each estimation of (12.9) has been systematically controlled by a regression where the endogenous variable becomes the expected log-level of the price $^ip^a(t)$, while the observed log-price $p(t)$ is added to the other exogenous variables. This last specification allows us to test the assumption that the coefficient of regression of $p(t)$ equals 1, which is an implicit assumption in (12.9). In fact, we obtained in any case estimates not significantly different from unity, and this result confirms that the ERAMLI is well specified when we consider the expected rate of change $^ip^{a'}(t)$ as the endogenous variable.

12.2 EVIDENCE OF MIXED EXPECTATIONS AT THE NEW YORK STOCK EXCHANGE

The ERAMLI (12.9) has been estimated according to three levels of aggregation:

- *the macro level*: that is, pooling all individual responses in order to determine the average model while taking into account the microeconomic character of these expectations. The important number of observations allows us to analyse the time stability of the model by considering ten periods (see 12.2.1).
- *the group level*: that is, pooling individual expectations according to both the professional affiliation of the respondents and their degree of optimism (see 12.2.2).
- *the agent level*: that is, considering time series expectations for each expert who answered to a significant number of successive surveys (see 12.2.3).

Table 12.1: Stock price expectations according to the ERAMLI: pooling all individuals over ten sub-periods

EXT' (A)	'REG1 (B1)	'REG2 (B2)	'ADA' (C)	BASE (D)	CTE	R̄² (RMSE)	F test (%) PR1[a]	PR2[b]
1952.12–1955.12 (N = 209)								
0.015 (0.2)	0.476 (8.4)	0.633 (17.7)	0.663 (12.0)	−0.350 (2.3)	−0.0046 (0.8)	0.677 (0.043)	8.72	16.99
1956.06–1959.06 (N = 224)								
0.242 (4.2)	0.397 (8.1)	0.480 (12.4)	0.578 (12.5)	−0.700 (2.3)	−0.0066 (1.5)	0.554 (0.047)	0.98	0.21
1959.12–1962.12 (N = 240)								
0.326 (5.9)	0.476 (10.2)	0.459 (14.8)	0.639 (13.6)	−0.354 (3.9)	−0.0029 (0.9)	0.602 (0.048)	0.01	0.01
1963.06–1966.06 (N = 264)								
0.147 (1.9)	0.377 (8.3)	0.396 (10.3)	0.406 (7.9)	−0.311 (2.2)	−0.0083 (1.9)	0.391 (0.042)	0.01	0.01
1966.12–1969.12 (N = 200)								
0.056 (0.8)	0.649 (12.3)	0.505 (14.1)	0.523 (10.1)	−0.201 (1.7)	−0.0084 (2.4)	0.602 (0.041)	0.02	0.02
1970.06–1973.06 (N = 193)								
−0.063 (1.2)	0.639 (11.0)	0.608 (15.9)	0.586 (11.7)	−0.198 (1.9)	−0.0012 (0.3)	0.692 (0.038)	0.15	0.12

Period	A	B1	B2	C	D	CTE		PR1	PR2
1973.12–1977.06 (N = 164)	−0.009	0.509	0.510	0.539	−0.122	−0.0124	0.584	1.06	1.66
	(0.2)	(8.6)	(12.4)	(9.0)	(0.9)	(2.1)	(0.041)		
1977.12–1981.06 (N = 208)	−0.106	0.574	0.704	0.811	−0.367	−0.0197	0.743	0.01	0.01
	(1.6)	(9.9)	(18.5)	(18.4)	(2.5)	(4.0)	(0.049)		
1981.12–1985.06 (N = 209)	0.205	0.524	0.508	0.590	−1.02	−0.0115	0.561	3.05	10.44
	(3.0)	(8.4)	(11.3)	(9.0)	(4.7)	(2.3)	(0.045)		
1985.12–1989.06 (N = 197)	−0.024	0.495	0.559	0.616	0.645	−0.0326	0.602	2.03	8.99
	(0.4)	(9.0)	(15.2)	(12.2)	(2.0)	(4.4)	(0.045)		
1952.12–1989.06 (N = 2108)	0.132	0.490	0.556	0.660	−0.335	−0.0050	0.647		
	(7.7)	(30.0)	(47.1)	(45.0)	(8.6)	(4.4)	(0.047)		

Notes:
Figures in brackets under the estimates are Student's t values.

[a] PR1: Probability for the estimates of A, B1, B2, C, D, CTE over the sub-period to be equal to the values obtained over the whole sample period (at bottom of the table).

[b] PR2: Probability for the estimates of A, B1, B2, C over the sub-period to be equal to the values obtained over the whole sample period (at bottom of the table).

12.2.1   Pooling All Individuals for a Given Period

The underlying assumption is that all experts use the same ERAMLI: we then have to estimate parameters A, B1, B2, C, D and CTE which adjust all individuals (then, the index *i* disappears from parameters). It is worth noting that, in order to appreciate the relevance of the least-squares estimation method, we tested collinearities between exogenous variables and checked the independence and heteroscedasticity of residuals both in the time and agents dimensions: we conclude that the least-squares method may be used with our data with rather weak bias (see Appendix B). Table 12.1 gives least-squares results for the whole sample period 1952.12–1989.06 and for ten sub-periods of about 200 observations each.[22]

Whatever the sample period is, all parameters are significant with the expected sign.[23] Although the extrapolative component cannot be neglected, the regressive and adaptive processes appear to be the dominant ones.[24] Because correlations between the expected variation of stock prices and each of the four components considered separately are close to zero,[25] we see that the explanation of expectations is given by the *structure* of the ERAMLI itself.[26]

The negative value of coefficient D obtained for nine of the ten sub-periods shows that it seems appropriate to take into account both the stock price indexes during the month of the survey and during the former month. The positive sign for parameter D during the last sub-period may indicate that the variable BASE captures both the datation of the base index and a short-term extrapolative component. This sub-period reports the October 1987 crash, so the drastic fall in prices affects expectations in the same direction. On the other hand, the systematic negative value of the intercept CTE may indicate that the long-term expectation is a proxy in excess of the unknown 'normal' value of stocks. However, CTE is not significant for four of the ten sub-periods.

It is worth noting that we have tested *fixed time effects* by including dummies in the regression over the whole sample of pooled microdata (each dummy equalling one for a given survey and zero otherwise). All dummies appeared to be insignificant at the 5 per cent level.[27] Because the extrapolative component also represents a common temporal factor, this component becomes itself non-significant. These results hold whether or not we add dummies representing the experts' professional affiliation.

In order to test if a same model prevails for the ten sub-periods, we used the F statistic to test the equality of the estimated parameters for one given sub-period to those obtained over the whole sample period.[28] Two sets of parameters are considered: (a) the six parameters of the ERAMLI (probability PR1); and (b) the only four structural parameters (probability PR2); coefficients D and CTE remain free because they are assumed to capture bias specific to the sub-period. The values of PR1 and PR2 given in the last two columns of Table 12.1 show that the stability hypothesis is generally rejected except for the first sub-period, if the constraint is related to the six parameters (PR1 > 5%), and for three sub-periods when only the four structural parameters are constrained (PR2 > 5%). As a result, the parameters of the ERAMLI do not appear to remain stable although their values remain within a small range.

Figure 12.1 exhibits for the ten sub-periods the estimated parameters A, B1, B2 and C. First, it appears that the regressive (B1, B2) and adaptive (C) coefficients clearly overcome the extrapolative one (A). Second, B1, B2 and C are each negatively correlated with A: this indicates a substitutability between the stabilizing components (adaptive and regressive) and the destabilizing one (extrapolative) over time.

12.2.2 Pooling Individuals Pertaining to a Same Group over the Whole Sample Period

Two criteria have been considered:

- *the professional affiliation criterion* The Livingston survey distinguishes seven groups of economists according to their professional affiliation: commercial banks, investment banks, universities, non-financial private sector, government, syndicates and others. This criterion may be supposed to be linked with *the degree of nearness to the stock market*; as an example, experts from the banking sector probably have better access to information about the stock market than other groups;
- *the degree of optimism criterion* For a given survey, that is for each value of t (e.g.: June 1970), we clustered expectations into four classes: the first class takes up the 25 per cent upper optimistic opinions about the future value of stock price, while the last and fourth class reports the 25 per cent lower optimistic opinions.[29]

In a first approach, the ERAMLI has been estimated by pooling micro-data according to (a) the seven professional groups; and (b) the four degree of optimism classes. By using the F test in order to compare the estimates across these groups, we found that:

1. concerning the professional criterion, we may admit two homogeneous groups:

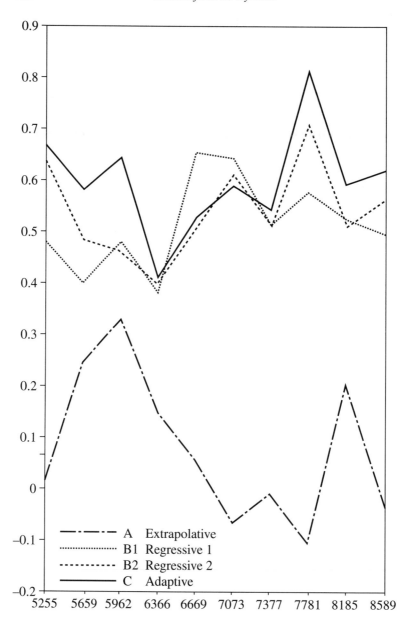

Note: [a] See Table 12.1.

Figure 12.1: Estimated parameters A, B1, B2 and C according to ten sub-periods[a]

(a) a group G1 assumed to be 'near the market': commercial banks, investment banks, universities, and others;

(b) a group G2 assumed to be 'away from the market': non-financial private sector, governments, syndicalists;

2. concerning the degree of optimism criterion, we still may admit two homogeneous classes:

(a) a class of optimists, C1, which represents for each survey expectations above the median value of all answers;

(b) a class of pessimists, C2, which represents for each survey expectations below the median value of all answers.

Given this first round, it is worthwhile to test whether these two criteria are or are not orthogonal. We then define a new partition of the entire sample of 2108 observations over the whole period 52.12–89.06 *across the two above criteria*:

- experts who are both 'near the market' and optimistic (G1, C1);
- experts who are both 'near the market' and pessimistic (G1, C2);
- experts who are both 'away from the market' and optimistic (G2, C1);
- experts who are both 'away from the market' and pessimistic (G2, C2).

Table 12.2 gives estimates of ERAMLI for each of these four samples; we notice that the number of observations always remains large enough to allow robust estimations.[30] Except for the extrapolative component for group (G2, C1), the four components of the ERAMLI are always statistically significant with the expected theoretical sign. The F statistic shows that the two above criteria are discriminative ones: none of the four cross groups uses the same model although they use an ERAMLI specification. We indeed observe significant differences between estimates whose magnitudes often range in a proportion from 1 to 2.

12.2.3 Working with Experts' Individual Time Series

When an expert *i* has answered consecutively N*i* times it is easy to estimate the ERAMLI for this expert if N*i* is large enough. In order to ensure this last condition, we began to select only experts who have answered *at least* to 29 consecutive surveys: we found 21 experts fulfilling this condition (nine academics, five belonging to a commercial bank, three to a private non-financial firm, and only one for each of the four other groups). Ten experts had answered at least 36 consecutive surveys, three more than 50 surveys and one expert had answered 70 surveys!

Table 12.2: Stock price expectations according to the ERAMLI: pooling cross groups according to nearness to market and optimism criteria, 1952.12–1989.06

EXT' (A)	REG1 (B1)	REG2 (B2)	ADA' (C)	BASE (D)	(CTE)	R̄² (RMSE)	F Test (%) PR1[a] / PR1'[c]	PR2[b] / PR2'[d]
G1, C1: Near the market and optimists (N = 672)								
0.130	0.294	0.335	0.449	−0.580	0.034	0.504	0.00	0.00
(4.8)	(11.7)	(16.8)	(17.4)	(9.7)	(15.3)	(0.041)	0.00	0.00
G1, C2: Near the market and pessimists (N = 853)								
0.153	0.426	0.516	0.600	−0.455	−0.024	0.628	0.00	0.00
(6.2)	(18.3)	(29.0)	(27.9)	(7.8)	(14.2)	(0.045)	0.00	0.00
G2, C1: Away from the market and optimists (N = 252)								
0.016	0.528	0.375	0.454	−0.141	0.023	0.586	0.00	0.00
(0.4)	(10.1)	(11.9)	(12.4)	(1.5)	(6.8)	(0.037)	0.00	0.00
G2, C2: Away from the market and pessimists (N = 331)								
0.076	0.570	0.638	0.674	−0.266	−0.018	0.683	0.01	0.01
(2.0)	(14.0)	(20.7)	(19.5)	(3.1)	(8.0)	(0.037)	0.01	0.02

Notes:
Figures in brackets under the estimates are Student's t values.
[a] PR1: Probability for the estimates of A, B1, B2, C, D, CTE obtained for the cross group to equal the values obtained for all experts with the same nearness to market.
[b] PR2: Probability for the estimates of A, B1, B2, C obtained for the cross group to equal the values obtained for all experts with the same nearness to market.
[c] PR1': Probability for the estimates of A, B1, B2, C, D, CTE obtained for the cross group to equal the values obtained for all experts with the same degree of optimism.
[d] PR2': Probability for the estimates of A, B1, B2, C obtained for the cross group to equal the values obtained for all experts with the same degree of optimism.

This first round has shown that the ERAMLI is a relevant approach to model individual expectations in stock prices. For three-quarters of the 21 experts, this model explains more than 70 per cent of the variance of expectations, despite the fact that the extrapolative component is significant for only one-third of experts. Other components are always significant except for academic expert no. 118 whose answers contradict the ERAMLI hypothesis. These first results lead us to conclude that a large majority of experts adopt a mixed expectational behaviour. This implies that the ERAMLI estimated on pooled microdata does mainly exhibit an average behaviour of experts characterized by the simultaneous use of one of the three basic expectational processes.

However, because the 21 experts' time series do not cover the same period (some answered during the 1950s, others during the 1960s, '70s or '80s), this approach is not relevant to analysing the heterogeneity of experts' expectational behaviour viewed through the parameters of the ERAMLI. In order to answer this question, we selected the only 12 experts who participated in at least 24 consecutive surveys over the period 1952.12–1968.06.[31] These 12 time series now cover approximately the same period and this allows us to test if parameters are expert-dependent or not. Table 12.3 gives the results.

The F test compares the estimates for each expert with those obtained by pooling the 12 sub-samples (we notice that the ERAMLI estimated over this last sample is not significantly different from the one obtained over the whole sample (345 observations throughout the period 1952.12–1968.06). Except for expert no. 27, probabilities PR1 and PR2 allow us to accept H0, that is the equality between the ERAMLI for each expert and the one obtained by pooling the 12 sub-samples or all the individuals over the period 1952.12–1968.06. Moreover, these results are more impressive to the extent that these 12 experts relate to different professional groups.

12.3 CONCLUSION

We have given evidence of a complementarity among adaptive, regressive and extrapolative expectational processes for expert forecasts at the NYSE. This result prevails whatever the level of aggregation is: by pooling all individual responses, groups of experts (institutional memberships; degree of optimism), and finally, by considering individual expectations time series. The regressive and adaptive components systematically overcome the extrapolative one. This result shows that expectations represent a stabilizing strength for the stock market and that we are far from the rational expectations hypothesis.

Table 12.3: *Stock price expectations according to the ERAMLI: estimations for the 12 experts who answered at least 24 times over the period 1952.12–1968.06*

i[a]	NOBS[b]	CLAS[c]	FIRS[d] LAST[e]	EXT' (A_i)	'REG1 $(B1_i)$	'REG2 $(B2_i)$	'ADA' (C_i)	BASE (D_i)	('CTE)	$\bar{R}^2$ (RMSE)	F (%) PR1[f]	PR2[g]
14	27	SYND	5506 6806	0.161 (2.1)	0.409 (3.4)	0.561 (13.3)	0.701 (9.9)	−0.295 (3.8)	−0.003 (1.4)	0.959 (0.009)	3.17	24.21
22	30	BCOM	5312 6806	0.239 (1.7)	0.417 (3.5)	0.612 (5.7)	0.887 (6.8)	−0.578 (1.8)	0.015 (1.6)	0.671 (0.041)	2.18	39.12
27	31	NONF	5306 6806	0.050 (0.9)	0.689 (3.6)	0.806 (14.1)	0.804 (11.4)	−0.256 (2.6)	−0.016 (2.8)	0.938 (0.013)	0.77	0.29
28	30	NONF	5312 6806	0.043 (0.4)	0.543 (4.1)	0.645 (10.8)	0.628 (6.4)	−0.060 (0.3)	−0.013 (1.9)	0.851 (0.031)	3.86	63.16
51	29	BCOM	5406 6806	0.143 (1.1)	0.835 (4.4)	0.604 (6.1)	0.699 (5.3)	−0.532 (2.7)	−0.009 (1.6)	0.713 (0.027)	2.56	23.53
58	29	DIVE	5406 6806	0.226 (1.1)	0.811 (4.5)	0.504 (4.2)	0.809 (3.6)	−0.429 (1.5)	0.023 (2.2)	0.485 (0.018)	1.24	11.01
62	28	UNIV	5412 6606	0.135 (1.1)	0.860 (4.0)	0.813 (9.2)	0.942 (7.8)	−0.122 (0.6)	0.035 (2.2)	0.792 (0.028)	2.42	12.10
64	32	BINV	5212 6806	0.220 (2.3)	0.441 (4.1)	0.530 (9.9)	0.626 (7.6)	−0.597 (4.7)	−0.012 (2.8)	0.839 (0.020)	5.83	69.69
70	24	BINV	5512 6706	0.257 (1.3)	0.925 (4.1)	0.725 (6.1)	0.868 (4.9)	−0.585 (1.5)	−0.030 (3.0)	0.617 (0.041)	2.80	20.33
72	27	BCOM	5506 6806	0.086 (0.4)	0.398 (1.6)	0.568 (3.5)	0.584 (2.6)	−0.985 (2.1)	−0.006 (0.2)	0.472 (0.064)	7.49	98.69

			NOBS	A	B1	B2	C	D	CTE	PR1	PR2
75	32	UNIV	5212	0.272 (1.6)	0.605 (5.2)	0.701 (3.7)	−0.200 (0.8)	−0.020 (2.5)	0.522 (0.038)	2.74	59.76
			6806	0.253 (1.3)							
101	25	UNIV	5606	0.142 (0.8)	0.350 (2.0)	0.461 (2.2)	0.149 (0.4)	0.006 (0.5)	0.044 (0.047)	6.83	78.97
			6806	0.266 (1.2)							
Pooling the 12 experts (N=345)				0.178 (4.3)	0.465 (12.0)	0.575 (22.5)	0.685 (20.4)	−0.418 (5.8)	−0.005 (2.1)	0.698 0.037	
Pooling all individuals (52.12/68.06) (N=1054)				0.227 (8.0)	0.462 (20.0)	0.507 (30.5)	0.628 (29.4)	−0.429 (8.2)	−0.003 (2.1)	0.614 0.047	

Notes:

Figures in brackets under the estimates are student's t values.

[a] i expert's number in the survey

[b] NOBS: number of observations

[c] CLAS: professional affiliation

[d] FIRS: year and month of the first observation

[e] LAST: year and month of the last observation

[f] PR1: Probability for the estimates of A, B1, B2, C, D, CTE of expert i to equal the values obtained over the 12-expert sample (N=345).

[g] PR2: Probability for the estimates of A, B1, B2, C of expert i to equal the values obtained over the 12-expert sample (N=345).

Another main result is that parameters of the ERAMLI appeared to be more time and group dependent than related to specific individual characteristics. A significant part of the heterogeneity of stock price expectations rests upon the fact that agents weigh the three basic processes according to their nearness to the market and their degree of optimism. These results show that, at a given time, the source of heterogeneity is more basically grounded on parameter variability across groups than on the type of expectational process, and this may be considered as a rather weak form of heterogeneity.

However, the econometric validation of the ERAMLI for an expert over any sample period does not necessarily mean that this process is used at every point of time: the weights of the relevant elements of this model may reflect either the fact that this agent always weighs the three basic processes, or the fact that he uses only one process at a given time and another process at another time, so that the ERAMLI appears to be significant over any sample period. This question defines a new field of research.

APPENDIX A: ESTIMATING AN EQUIVALENT EQUATION OF THE ERAMLI

By pooling all individuals over the whole period, expression (12.9) of the ERAMLI is equivalent to the following (because the underlying assumption is that all experts use the same ERAMLI, the index i disappears from the parameters):

$$
\begin{aligned}
B2'.^i\bar{p}^a(t) - ^ip^a(t) = &(C' - A' - 1).p(t) + A'.p(t-6) \\
&+ (B1' - C').^ip^a(t-6) + (B2' - B1').^i\bar{p}^a(t-6) \quad (12.9') \\
&- D'.BASE - CTE + \epsilon'(t)
\end{aligned}
$$

In relation (12.9'), all expectational variables which are dated at time t are gathered on the left-hand side while actual and lagged spot variable and lagged expectational variables are gathered on the right-hand side. There is thus no possibility for equation (12.9') to be necessarily validated by reason of common information on both sides of the equation. By applying an iterative procedure on B2' over [0, 1] and using pooled data (N = 2108), the following optimal estimates are obtained:

$$
\begin{aligned}
0.559^i\bar{p}^a(t) - ^ip^a(t) = &-0.4396.p(t) + 0.1141.p(t-6) + \\
&(109.3) \qquad (8.4)
\end{aligned}
$$

$$-0.1936.^{i}p^{a}(t-6) + 0.0780.^{i}\bar{p}^{a}(t-6)$$
$$\quad (9.2) \qquad\qquad (4.9) \qquad\qquad (12.9'')$$

$$-0.2778.\text{BASE} - 0.0090 + u'(t)$$
$$\quad (8.7) \qquad\qquad (1.1)$$

RMSE $= 0.0470$; $\bar{R}^2 = 0.9698$

For the optimal value B2$' = 0.56$, these estimates lead to A$' = 0.114$, B1$' = 0.481$, C$' = 0.674$, D$' = 0.278$, CSTE$' = 0.0090$ and RMSE$' = 0.0470$. These values remain close to those obtained in Table 12.1 (which are A $= 0.131$ (*0.017*), B1 $= 0.490$ (*0.016*), B2 $= 0.556$ (*0.012*), C $= 0.660$ (*0.015*), D $= -0.336$ (*0.039*), CTE $= -0.0050$ (*0.0011*) and RMSE $= 0.04713$; standard errors of estimates are in parentheses).

These results are confirmed with the individual time-series corresponding to expectations of expert no. 28, who responded 70 times consecutively. Hence, because we can recombine the structural form of the ERAMLI (12.9) with the estimates from equation (12.9$'$), we can conclude that the estimates obtained directly using the structural form (Table 12.1) cannot be attributed to any statistical necessity.

APPENDIX B: TESTING THE RELEVANCE OF THE LEAST-SQUARES METHOD APPLIED TO OUR DATA

In order to appreciate the relevance of the least-squares estimation method used, we tested collinearities between exogenous variables and checked the independence and heteroscedasticity of residuals.

Concerning *collinearities*, we observed that the multiple determination coefficients between each exogenous variable and the four others are much less than 0.90 and always inferior to the R^2 of the ERAMLI; according to Johnston (1985), this allows us to conclude that there is no significant bias resulting from collinearities. This result is confirmed by other statistics: partial coefficients of correlation between exogenous variables are always less than 0.48 and the minimum eigenvalue is greater than zero, which confirms that there is no statistical problem in computing the estimates.

Concerning the independence of residuals, we looked at individual and time dimensions of the data. We first considered the *hypothesis of independence between residuals obtained for different experts*, which is implicit to the least squares method. Because the component EXT$'(t)$ represents a common factor, such a dependence *a priori* exists; moreover, other common information probably underlies the long-term (12-month) expectations which intervene in the two regressive components. Then, the question is to know if this dependence is high enough to induce serious econometric problems. To address this question, we selected 12 individual time series, each corresponding to a specific expert *over the same period (1952.12–1968.06)*. We computed coefficients of correlation between the 66 pairs of residuals of the ERAMLI applied to each of the 12 sub-samples. All coefficients average 0.20, only 12 per cent of them appearing to be significantly different from zero at the 5 per cent level. Thus, we can conclude that the hypothesis of independence may be accepted in a first approximation. Concerning the *serial correlation of residuals*, a test has been implemented with the Durbin–Watson statistic. The DW has been applied to each of 21 individual time series, each corresponding to one expert who answered at least 29 times. All the DW statistics were found to be inside the bracket (1.9–2.2), which shows that there is no serious problem due to serial correlation.

We finally checked simultaneously the transversal (experts) and horizontal (time) *heteroscedasticities*. First, Table 12.1 shows that, *on average*, there is no serious problem regarding heteroscedasticities (the ten RMSE values remain quite close from one sub-period to another). Second, using a pooling of the above 12 individual time series *over the period 1952.12–1968.06*, we computed the normalized residuals (residual (i,t)/pooled standard error): we found that only seven values out of the 345 observations are out of the range of significance at the 5 per cent level $[-1.96; 1.96]$. This confirms that there is no serious problem of heteroscedasticity.

As a whole, these numerous statistical tests allow us to consider that the least-squares estimation method is relevant to our data. Moreover, it is interesting to note that the distribution of residuals of the ERAMLI applied to the whole sample follows a Normal law, and this is a condition for the statistical tests to hold.

NOTES

1. See especially Abou and Prat (1997a, 1997b), Dokko and Edelstein (1989), MacDonald and Marsh (1992), Mpacko-Priso (1996), Pearce (1984) and Prat (1994). See also references at the end of this paper and those given by MacDonald (Chapter 9 of this book).
2. According to this class of models, the expected variable depends on its past values and on the actual and past values of the observed variable. No other explicit economic variables figure in the model.
3. See especially Abou and Prat (1997b). Prat and Uctum (see Chapter 11 of this book) recall that these difficulties seem to have a more general character: they also hold for exchange rate expectations and for inflationary expectations.
4. Abou and Prat (1997a) give detailed support for this result.
5. About 99 per cent of answers give forecasts for the two horizons.

6. The 2 per cent of answers leading to the largest prediction error (in absolute value) have been removed from the sample.

7. Although there exist recent methods which allow incomplete panels to be treated (for example, see Matyas and Sevestre, 1992), we consider that our matrix is not fulfilled enough seriously to envisage applying such a method. Moreover, these methods are perhaps not fully operative enough to be implemented by researchers who are not specialists in the econometrics of panel data.

8. That is, the rate of change which occurs during the horizon time span.

9. In fact, this process may be expressed as follows:

$$ {}^i\mathrm{p}^a(t) = \gamma^i \left[\Delta p(t) - \overline{\Delta}\, p\right] + \overline{\Delta}\, p = \gamma^i\, \Delta p(t) + \gamma_0^i \qquad \Delta p(t) = p(t) - p(t-6) $$

where $\gamma_0^i = (1 - \gamma^i)\, \overline{\Delta} p$ and $\overline{\Delta} p$ stands for the long-run rate of change in $P(t)$.

10. Recall that Prat (1994) has shown that an ERAMLI leads to valuable outcomes in explaining the 12-month stock price expectations using consensus data.

11. Note that when a white noise is added to the left-hand side of equation (12.5), the estimation of the ERAMLI remains unchanged because this stochastic measurement error is captured by the error term ${}^i\epsilon^R(t)$ of equation (12.6).

12. The standard equation of the simple ECM takes into account two terms representing an adjustment of the expectation ${}^i p^a(t)$ towards its normal value ${}^i \bar{p}^a(t)$:

$$ {}^i p^a(t) - {}^i p^a(t-1) = \mu_1^i({}^i \bar{p}^a(t-1) - {}^i p^a(t-1)) + \mu_2^i({}^i \bar{p}^a(t) - {}^i \bar{p}^a(t-1)) + \mu_0^i $$

Rearranging terms in order that the endogenous variable becomes ${}^i p^a(t) = {}^i p^a(t) - p(t)$, we obtain equation (12.6).

13. See note 6. Indeed, the long-term trends of $p(t)$ and of ${}^i \bar{p}^a(t)$ are confounded.

14. Note that although the ECM (12.6) incorporates a more sophisticated dynamics than the simple traditional regressive process, they both converge towards the same target.

15. The standard adaptive process for a six-month span horizon for ${}^i p^a(t)$ is:

$$ {}^i p^a(t) - {}^i p^a(t-6) = \beta(p(t) - {}^i p^a(t-6)) + \beta_0^i + {}^i \epsilon^A(t) $$

where $\epsilon(t)$ is a white noise. This last equation leads to (12.7).

16. Indeed, according to (12.6), the expectation ${}^i p^a(t)$ tends to its 'normal' value ${}^i \bar{p}^a(t)$, while according to the adaptive model (12.7), ${}^i p^a(t)$ converges towards the observed value $p(t)$.

17. In fact, the weighting coefficients a^i, b^i and c^i which are implicitly embedded in the parameters of the three processes can *a priori* have two non-exclusive meanings:

- 'the representative agent' formulates his expectation by combining the three basic processes according to subjective proportions (that is, the agent chooses the ERAMLI at any time);
- the weight of each basic process in the ERAMLI depends on its frequency over the estimation period.

18. The sign ' attached to some components figures the substitution of $P(t)$ (observable) to the individual basis ${}^i \overline{P}(t)$ (unobservable) in this component, according to relation (12.2).

19. A consequence is that we cannot discriminate between the *extrapolative-regressive* process and the ERAMLI.

20. Indeed, we have the identity:

$$ {}^i \bar{p}^a(t) = {}^i p^a(t) + ({}^i \bar{p}^a(t) - {}^i p^a(t)) $$

which means that the 12-month expected (log) index equals the six-month expected (log) index plus the forward expected rate (that is, the rate expected at time t for the time-span $(t+6; t+12)$).

21. Another way to consider this question is to point out that the following identity holds:

$$\text{REG2}(t) = {}^i\mathfrak{p}^{a'}(t) - \text{ADA}'(t) - \text{REG1}(t) + ({}^i\bar{p}^a(t) - {}^ip^a(t))$$

Because, in the ERAMLI, ${}^i\mathfrak{p}^{a'}(t)$ is explained by REG2(t), and because REG2(t) includes implicitly ${}^i\mathfrak{p}^{a'}(t)$, one can think that REG2(t) will be necessarily significant, this necessity leading automatically to the (positive) significance of ADA'(t) and REG1(t) in order to compensate the (negative) influence of the variables on REG2(t). Of course, it is worth underlining that this reasoning ignores the fact that, in the above identity, the endogenous variable ${}^i\mathfrak{p}^{a'}(t)$ appears only because we introduce artificially the forward expected rate $({}^i\bar{p}^a(t) - {}^ip^a(t))$, which is not a relevant variable of the ERAMLI. The equivalent equation estimated in Appendix A puts an end to this discussion.
22. Because each sub-period contains a significant number of experts belonging to various groups, the drifts on parameters may be attributed mainly to a *time* effect rather than to a *group* factor.
23. It is worth noting that the extrapolative element acts with a positive sign, contrary to what is generally obtained with the basic extrapolative process. This result is highly satisfactory since it seems to conform more to what one might expect from this process.
24. The relative weakness of the extrapolative term may be related to various causes: (a) a real behavioural effect; (b) a specification error for this component; (c) this term is common to all experts, contrary to other components (index *i* is omitted from EXT'(t) because we model micro expectations for a macro variable).
25. Correlations (r²) between PT6' and the exogenous variables are the following for the 1952.12–1989.06 period:

$$({}^i\text{PT6}', \text{EXT}') = 0.01; ({}^i\text{PT6}', {}^i\text{REG1}) = 0.07; ({}^i\text{PT6}', {}^i\text{REG2}) = 0.03;$$
$${}^i\text{PT6}', {}^i\text{ADA}') = 0.09; ({}^i\text{PT6}', \text{BASE}) = 0.03.$$

26. R² for the ERAMLI are greater than those generally obtained with microdata. An explanation is that the target of the regressive process (for example, the long-term expectations) captures in a valuable manner perceptions and expectations about fundamentals, without compelling us to state what these fundamentals are. Appendix B to this paper shows that this does not imply any statistical necessity.
27. Except the dummy corresponding to the 1973 oil shock.
28. To avoid the implicit hypothesis of independence of the sub-samples, we also implemented a *Student t-value test*. To do so, we added dummies traducing two kinds of fixed effects: (a) a period effect (dummy = 1 if period X and O otherwise); and (b) an affiliation effect (dummy = 1 if the expert belongs to the profession Z and O otherwise). Then, a *unique* estimation is made to calculate the values of the six parameters of the ERAMLI for each of the ten periods, which allows us to test if equality between the values of parameters may be assumed to remain stable over time. Although some dummies were insignificant, the test still rejected the stability of the parameters of the ERAMLI over the ten sub-periods (even when we only consider the four structural parameters).
29. Because the pooling approach does not involve groups of *experts* (as was the case for the professional affiliation criterion) but a class of *individuals* in the statistical sense, any expert *i* may rank among the optimistic at time *t* and among the pessimistic at time *t + n*. Hence, the degree of optimism criterion aims to discover if experts use the same ERAMLI whether they are optimistic or pessimistic. A previous statistical analysis has shown that only a few experts always belong to one of the four classes.
30. We checked that the time distribution of observations for each cross group is quite uniform. Thus, there is no period bias in the estimates in Table 12.2.
31. Over the period 1968.12–1989.06, it has not been possible to select a number of experts large enough to ensure valuable comparisons.

REFERENCES

Abou, A. and G. Prat (1997a), 'A propos de la rationalité des anticipations boursières: quel niveau d'agrégation des opinions?', *Revue d'économie politique*, (5), 647–69.

Abou, A. and G. Prat (1997b), 'Formation des anticipations boursières: "consensus" versus opinions individuelles', *Journal de la Société de Statistique de Paris*, (2), 13–22.

Cowles, A. (1932), 'Can stock market forecasters forecast?', *Econometrica*, 1, 309–24.

Dokko, Y. and R.H. Edelstein (1989), 'How well do economists forecast stock market prices? A study of the Livingston surveys', *American Economic Review*, 79(4), 865–71.

Feige, E.L. and D.K. Pearce (1976), 'Economically rational expectation: are innovations in the rate of inflation independent of innovations in measures of monetary and fiscal policy?', *Journal of Political Economy*, 84(3), 499–522.

Johnston, J. (1985), *Méthodes économétriques*, vol. 1, Paris: Economica.

Lakonishok, J. (1980), 'Stock market return expectations: some general properties', *Journal of Finance*, 35(4), 921–31.

MacDonald, R. and I.W. Marsh (1992), 'The efficiency of spot and futures stock indexes: a survey based perspective', Department of Economics and Management, University of Dundee.

Matyas, P. and P. Sevestre (1992), *The Econometrics of Panel Data: Handbook of theory and applications*, Amsterdam: Kluwer.

Mpacko-Priso, A. (1996), 'Anticiper rationellement les cours boursiers: une épreuve hors de portée?', *Economie appliquée*, 49(2), 35–78.

Pearce, D.K. (1984), 'An empirical analysis of expected stock price movements', *Journal of Money, Credit and Banking*, 16 (3), 317–27.

Prat, G. (1994), 'La formation des anticipations boursières', *Economie et prévision*, 112(1), 101–25.

Index

Abel, A.B. 164
Abou, A. 6, 9, 10, 15, 204, 252
adaptive expectation 29
adaptive model 6, 133, 146, 214
    consistency tests 222–4, 233–6
adaptive process 10, 254–5
aggregate results 181–91
Akerlof, G. 25
Allen, B. 29
Allen, H. 214, 215, 218, 225, 226, 227
American Statistical Association
    (ASA) 158
AMEX 179
    surveys 252
anticipation function 6
ARCH models 157, 169
    and risk premia 187
Arrow, K. 5, 29
ASA-NBER surveys 10, 13, 157,
    158–60
asset price expectations 1–2
asymptotics, of a stochastic trend
    111–12
Aumann, R.J. 26, 35, 49
'auto-validation' 5
Azariadis, C. 5, 27, 63
Azuma's inequality 120, 122

Bachelier, L. 46
backward martingale convergence
    theorem 122–3
Baillie, R. 252
bandwagon approach 9, 177, 190
Banerjee, A.V. 82
Banque Nationale de Paris 191
Batchelor, R. 3, 8, 10, 13, 131, 157, 202
Bayesian rationality 34
Bekaert, G. 200
Bellando, R. 214
Bénassy-Quéré, A. 9, 14, 191, 195, 251
Berry 104

Besancenot, D. 4, 8, 10, 12
Bikhchandani, S. 82
Binmore, K. 34
Blanchard, O.J. 98
Blue Chip Financial Forecasts 202
Bollerslev, T. 169
bond markets 198–203
Borel, E. 35–7, 39–44, 45, 49
Brennan, M. 64
Brown, B.W. 162, 203
Broze, L. 2
Bucklew, J.A. 112

Cagan hypothesis 133
Cagan, P. 22
Campbell, J.Y. 199
capital asset pricing model (CAPM)
    187
card games 45
Carlson, J.A. 131, 205
Case, K.E. 81
Cash-in-Advance model 198
Cass, D. 63
Cavaglia, S. 181, 186, 187, 190
centipede game 48
central limit theorem 102–4, 116
Chan, K.C. 92, 109
chance 45, 46
Chebyshev's inequality 100, 103
Chernoff's bound 100–102, 104
Chicago Mercantile Exchange 197,
    205
Chinn, M. 181
Chionis, D. 194, 195, 198
Cicero 21
collective expectations 7
common knowledge 12, 26, 52, 75
conditional volatility 198
confirmed expectations 11, 32
    economic theory 27–8
    game theory 28–9

295